SHELLEY

SHELLEY

A Life Story

by

EDMUND BLUNDEN

'He lives by a law which is not visible to vulgar eyes; he enters into the world of spirits; he compares the greatest things; sets eternity against time; and chooses rather to be for ever great in the presence of God when he dies, than to have the greatest share of worldly pleasure whilst he lives.'
WILLIAM LAW'S "SERIOUS CALL"

READERS UNION · COLLINS

Inscribed
TO MY CLAIRE

This volume was published in 1948 in complete conformity with the authorized economy standards. First published in 1946 by Collins, it is set in 11 point Baskerville and has been reprinted at Collins Clear-type Press, Glasgow. It is one of the books produced by Readers Union Ltd., of 38 William IV Street, Charing Cross, London, and of Letchworth, Hertfordshire, for sale to its members only. Membership of RU may be made at all bookshops and particulars are obtainable at the above addresses

CONTENTS

PREFACE

ABOUT eighty years ago it occurred to Sir George Grove, whose labours on the lives of the musicians make all of us his debtors, that he was the man to write a life of Shelley, and he instantly began making lists of surviving persons who had known the poet and others whom he should consult. The project, to our loss, was soon given up. The Dean of St. Paul's, H. H. Milman, was prompt to discourage it, partly on the ground that he had known Shelley at Eton and Oxford. But times change. In the absence of Dean Milman many persons have appeared as Shelley's biographers, and some have required two volumes apiece for their works. Among these have been, first, Edward Dowden in 1886, and in this century Walter Peck in America and lately in America again Newman I. White. With these should be gladly remembered Roger Ingpen, whose " Shelley in England " was crammed into one weighty volume.

In their publications individual qualities arise with which I do not pretend to compete ; information is collected which I do not necessarily employ ; and many Shelleyans, myself included, will read and consult them in future. But I have not had Shelleyans in my mind during the composition of the pages following more prominently than the general reader, to whom I have hoped to give the clearest narrative I could of a most adventurous and many-sided life, unified by a deepening faith in the artist's duty and power in human advancement. To express this in another term, I confess that if I were asked to name an example of the supreme capacity called genius, few names would present themselves sooner than that of Shelley ; and the Promethean fire of his existence as well as of his writings lures us through the most prosaic accounts or analytical criticisms of him. But no informed narrative of his experiences could well be altogether prosaic. He will never be mentioned even by his adversaries without a difference.

A narrator of Shelley's course, however, is beset with many persistent difficulties. Sometimes information is superabundant, sometimes it is quite lacking, and very often it is unreliable. This it can be even where it looks not only entertaining but authoritative. Medwin, Trelawny, even Peacock among the most deliberate of Shelley's early biographers need to be watched with some nicety, and Hogg must be read with the proviso that he

fancied himself as a novelist in the old school of comic extravagance. The topic is familiar to Shelleyans and wants no expansion
in this place. Moreover the industry of forgers of documents
marketed as Shelley's is about to reach its centenary. I have
simply kept clear of some papers on which I felt a doubt ; and
this was as well, for while my work went on a group of American
investigators were equally doubtful and exceedingly busy. Their
findings are shortly to be published under the title " The Shelley
Legend," and will expose a much larger mischief done by the
forgers to the poet's accepted biography than many of us suspected. Elsewhere I have done my best to sift the original from
the distorted ; to discern where Hogg is enclosing the truth,
Peacock editing it, Medwin almost remembering it and so on.
Some problems may never be settled, and the narrator can only
say that they exist. Who can tell what passed between Shelley and
Harriet before they separated and while their separation was
uncertain ? Or identify the lady of the electric poison in " Epipsychidion " ? Or even explain the queer letter from Shelley to
Ollier his publisher about a secret and urgent payment to an
unnamed visitor ?

Few perhaps who look into Shelley's life would not wish to
solve the problem of Harriet and her final tribulations. It is my
belief that her descendants possess the evidences which would
even now illuminate this shadowed theme. I have not attempted
to induce them to disclose what may have been preserved by
Eliza Westbrook, the elder sister who became a wealthy old lady
in Somerset, for I did not set out to write a life of Harriet Shelley
but of an English poet. Yet all that has been imparted concerning Harriet awakens an intense admiration for her and a
desire, which does not diminish our love of Shelley, to honour
her memory. What might she not have been with some slight
change of time and circumstance—a woman of deepest gener-
osities, unforced abilities ? I am not among those who think
that the twentieth century with its eroded soil, 100,000 lb. bombs
and cameras that cannot lie is the flower of all time, but I should
like to have seen Harriet as a twentieth-century woman.

Other mysteries of the mind tantalise every observer of Shelley
himself and his relationships, yet many such must belong to every
embodiment of the creative spirit. In one respect he presents no
difficulty to the commonest insight ; in the confluence of many
strengths within that small head. To pass any considerable time
in his company, through what is known of him now, is to be
persuaded that in intellectual or in active life there was little
which was not at his command. Many-sided, he chose poetry for

his special conquest. Had he lived beyond his thirtieth year, he might have turned his attention to other masteries. But, if his creed holds, the chronicle of Shelley is to be continued by another hand.

For help of many kinds, I have the pleasure of thanking many friends, and in particular : Sylva Norman (the accurate authority on most aspects of the subject) ; H. Clifford Smith, Esq., who shared with me his unequalled knowledge of University College, Oxford, in Shelley's time and lent me papers once belonging to his grandfather Sir William Smith, editor of *The Quarterly Review;* Mr. M. Buxton Forman, Capt. Rupert Hart-Davis, Mrs. Siegfried Sassoon, Miss Rudston Brown, the late S. E. Winbolt, Mr. K. T. Parker, Mr. John Greenlaw, Mr. E. J. Finch, Professor Newman White, Mr. Philip Tomlinson, Mr. Theodore G. Ehrsam, Mr. J. H. Preston (the Curator of Keats House), the Rev. C. A. Chastel de Boinville and Lady Mander, who all answered my inquiries or lent me books with great readiness. I do not add what would be a voluminous list of works consulted ; it would make perhaps, in normal circumstances of paper supply, an addition interesting to many. The heaviest disadvantage of writing such a work in war-time has been the inaccessibility of the special Shelley collections, the contents of which however have been previously explored and published by many writers ; it is likely that nothing of transforming significance has escaped notice in other years so far as those collections go.

E. B.

I

THE SHELLEYS

SHELLEY : to English ears the music of the name seems to have been destined long ago for a poet's possession. It has become associated almost entirely with one unforgettable being of lyrical genius. The eye of an occasional law student may brighten at the words, " the rule in Shelley's case," which does not turn out to be a case involving the poet. In the history of English society, painting, calligraphy, ornithology, the name makes transient appearances. But in the ordinary course of mention and allusion " Shelley " brings to mind no other person than the master-singer who is the subject of so many books and conversations. What Percy Bysshe Shelley was, what he did and suffered, and the writings which he has left us are indeed the means of a fame sufficient for any one lineage, and we easily forget the rest.

Genius, time and reputation have done their work ; and it has been often felt or concluded that Shelley, as if by some inexplicable chance or caprice of nature, sprang in his single greatness out of a family which apart from him continued through the centuries without distinction, energy or noble error. Undoubtedly the way in which Shelley lived and the nature of his vision of gods and men would have perplexed all or almost all his ancestors, just as the new style in which he wrote English poetry would have astonished such of them as had some acquaintance with its standard examples. On closer view he appears not utterly isolated from all those others. Here and there some touch of them survives in him to make us aware that the poet was of their breed, and to limit if not to overcome the supposition that except for him there is little colour in the annals of the Shelleys. To what extent the scientist of heredity is able to see him deriving from them is a question beyond my range, yet characteristics of theirs, unless we yield all to coincidence, make it desirable to approach him through some of the Shelleys before him. A glance at the fragmentary records is justified moreover because Shelley himself was perfectly well aware, in no spirit of vanity, that he belonged to an ancient house ; because he grew up amidst its relics and in responsibility to the local world which it had shaped ; because indeed but for its stored-up power and fortune he could not have led the life that he did. Even his endeavours in the cause of the less fortunate part of society, his contributions to an overthrow of the old order, inevitably rested upon that order and had the mark of the aristocrat, much as we find with Tolstoi.

The story therefore opens much earlier than the French Revolution which was dislodging aristocratic heritage at the time of Shelley's birth. When the pedigree of Shelley was first made public from the books of the College of Arms—in 1880—it was shown beginning in the paternal line with Henry Shelley of Worminghurst in Sussex, who died in 1623. The stretch of time from Henry to Percy Bysshe Shelley was already an extensive period of family pride and south-country recognition ; but a commentator on the pedigree observed, concerning the accompanying shield of twenty-one quarterings, that " the simplicity of some of the arms bespeaks the high antiquity of several of the families with whom the Shelleys intermarried." Fuller inquiry has traced the family of the poet, although it is a younger branch, to an ambassador to Spain in 1205, Sir Thomas. Those who may wish for more have the tradition that the Shelleys came over with the Conqueror.

It is from the fifteenth century that some matters preliminary to the life of the poet can be collected with tolerable certainty. One among his ancestors particularly stirs romantic curiosity. John Shelley, M.P. for Rye in 1415 and other years married Beatrix Hawkwood, whose mother Donnina was the daughter of Bernabo Visconti, Duke of Milan. Curiosity has to be content with her name. We seem to foreknow the poet more clearly when among these distant generations instances of unflinching support of a cause come into view. For his part in an endeavour to set up King Richard II, Sir Thomas Shelley, great-uncle of John already mentioned, was sent to the scaffold. The episode incidentally shows that between the family of Shelley and the Dukes of Norfolk a connection existed—the same which is seen in the nineteenth century, and in the biography of the poet. It emerges conspicuously in the execution of one of the Dukes and one of the Shelleys for a conspiracy against Queen Elizabeth in favour of Mary Queen of Scots. This violent ending in public was not to be paralleled in the fate of the poet, however obviously it would have been his in the earlier day ; but we hear of one odd parallel, not quite so tragic, in the conduct and the treatment of Thomas Shelley, a Fellow of New College, Oxford. Refusing to attend divine service, he was " removed " in 1567.

Other ghosts of the Shelley line arise from what was once the busy English scene, and they are not the least of those who played their parts in its chronicle drama. To note only two or three of them, one as judge of the Common Pleas bore to Cardinal Wolsey the demand of King Henry VIII for the surrender of York Place ; his son Richard became English Grand Prior in Spain ; one of the Sir Johns was killed at the taking of the Island of Rhodes ; Edward Shelley of Worminghurst was Master of the Household to Henry VIII, Edward VI and Queen Mary—a surprising continuity ; but the most Shelleyan man of them all in our sense was that young Captain who served at Boulogne in 1545 under the command of the poet Henry Howard, Earl of Surrey. He was deprived by his death in the field of the promotion immediately intended for him. " I dare promise," the Earl had just written, " more of that man, his truth and honesty, than of any man that 1 know alive."

Passing from the sixteenth century and the age of Elizabeth, the Shelleys no longer produced such representatives in chivalry and state affairs ; even their posture during the clash of Cavalier and Roundhead is undefined and undescribed. They lived in hall and place as country gentlemen, satisfied with their small kingdoms which indeed were enough to manage if managed well —safe properties in Sussex. Some of the line were barristers. In 1733 Edward, son of Timothy Shelley of Thakeham, was Treasurer of the Middle Temple in London. He was not the only one of those Shelleys to receive part of his education at the University of Oxford ; and their number included one or two members of parliament. They did not neglect to acquire houses and lands. One of these additions was Fen Place, in the parish of Worth, brought by the marriage of John Shelley (1666-1739) to Hellen, daughter of Robert Bysshe ; but the union also brought into memorable relation with their name that which the poet was to bear. In literary history it has another if microscopic existence, since at the beginning of the eighteenth century Edward Bysshe, Gent. published *The Art of English Poetry*, a handbook which went through several impressions, useful to all but poets born, and not discoverable in the long catalogue of works studied by Shelley.

It has been mentioned that this brief retrospect is chiefly concerned with a younger branch of the Shelley family. During the period the elder branch, the Shelleys of Michelgrove, with their baronetcy of 1611, had made the greater figure in the world. If that was to be altered, it was for the Shelleys of Worminghurst and Fen Place to bring forth a new champion, a man of imaginative and executive abilities. Timothy (1701-1771), the third son of John and Hellen Shelley, may have shown signs of power ; he did not stay in Sussex, but went to North America, where there were Shelleys already. He is described as " a Merchant." He married Joanna Plum of Newark, New Jersey ; their three sons

were John, Bysshe and Piercy. The second of these, who is sometimes referred to as Shelley's American grandfather, was born in
New Jersey in 1731. He proved to be the most remarkable of
the eighteenth-century Shelleys, and claims a more extensive
place than his predecessors in this narrative.

The father of this Bysshe returned to England on his inheriting
Fen Place, which his son John inherited from him, and is buried
at Warnham. Piercy may have passed on his name to the poet,
but is not more than a shadow. Bysshe was a boy when he left
America for Sussex, so that the old story of his having been a
quack doctor in America has to be given up. Bysshe was a boy
of such promise, or such pleasing looks and manners, that his
grandparents quickly made a favourite of him. From his grandfather he received a legacy of £2000 and some valuables, from
his grandmother money, land and personal treasures ; and she
gave her executor instructions to ensure that he was well educated.

This was a useful start, but Bysshe Shelley was formed for the
building of a big fortune. His first marriage, in June, 1752, was
an important step towards his ultimate wealth. The young bride
was the daughter of the Rev. Theobald Michell, D.D. of Horsham
and of Wadham College, Oxford—a country rector of considerable means who had died in 1737. He possessed some property
of value at East Grinstead. Mary Catherine Michell was brought
up by guardians, from whose care the attractive Bysshe took her
as soon as possible to the wedding at Keith's Chapel in Mayfair.
Of the Michell family and its ancient dignity it may be enough
to note that it possessed chapels both in Warnham Church and
in Horsham Church ; and there had been earlier matches
between Shelleys and Michells. By Mary Catherine Bysshe
had two sons and one daughter. After her death in 1760, it is
possible that Bysshe married again, and that the poor lady
selected did not last long ; for there is a story that he had three
wives in all. In 1769 he certainly married another. This may
have been a love-match but was in any case a practical move,
since the new wife was Elizabeth Jane Sidney Perry, to whom the
historic and delightful Manor of Penshurst might have come.
There were numerous children of this marriage, and in 1793 one
of the sons, John Shelley, by sign manual as his mother's heir
assumed the name and arms of Sidney. As John Shelley-Sidney
he was made a baronet in 1818. These circumstances make it
look improbable that Penshurst would have come to Bysshe's
heirs through the first marriage. Yet one of them at a later date
took pleasure in fancying that it might, and everybody would
acknowledge the poetic and patriotic fitness had Penshurst's

memories of Philip and of Algernon Sidney, of Ben Jonson and Edmund Waller become still richer by the company of that one. The Sidney heiress died in 1781, and it was the assertion of the poet—speaking, it is true, in a burst of violence—that her husband treated her and his other wives very badly.

Timothy, Bysshe's son by his first marriage, now comes more prominently into the story. In the year 1774, aged twenty-one, he went up to Oxford as an undergraduate and for some reason chose to give his father's residence on the form of admission as Red Lion Square, London. Timothy was something of an elderly undergraduate. Besides the education of Oxford, he made the Grand Tour of Europe, that regular gentlemanly study of foreign society which some writers on him mention as though in his case it was an absurdity. In 1778 he took the degree of B.A., in 1781 that of M.A., and between those dates he became a student of Lincoln's Inn ; if anything can be deduced, it is that he was a steady, punctilious young man. His respect for and gratitude to University College were betokened by his gift of a beautiful silver candlestick, which the Fellows happily forgot to eject in the later year when they ejected his son. Extant portraits of Timothy Shelley by Romney and of Bysshe Shelley by Beechey invite us to read the men in a manner which the handful of information and misinformation in print does not stimulate.

In one thing these portraits agree, if it is right to gather from them that father and son possessed a quality which they did not bring to perfection in the conditions of their lives. Otherwise the contrast between the two is striking. Bysshe, with his beautiful top hat in his hand, has been described as looking like an eminent envoy, and the spectator might well suppose the picture to be that of a man who had done great things. And yet there is more in it than this. The handsome creature gives the impression that behind the mask, behind the impeccable clothes he is sitting back and, like Chaucer's Troilus, laughing and laughing at this world ; unmistakably a dangerous man to fall out with, but one who so long as he was called master—and there is no question that authority looks through those eyes—could be greatly generous to those whom he regarded as the fools of time.

Timothy with the more fixed countenance, the exquisitely moulded lips, is clearly not his father's rival in spiritual stature. No sign of the comic genius lightens his cautious face. Yet the easy displeasure or disagreement which the lips betray does not prevent us from seeing in his eyes a way of studying his problems with firm principle and some patience. If we may believe what has been only casually recorded, Bysshe and his son were not on good terms. Such a dissonance would hardly be surprising. The ardour of the father, his love of the game of life, his lurking humour would scarcely imply a constant joy over the solemnity of Timothy. For all that it is Timothy who takes the trouble to illustrate his father's humour in an anecdote : it was towards the end of Bysshe's long life, and in the office of a lawyer. A document lay there waiting to be signed. The lawyer remarked that any pen would do. " Oh ! ho ! " said the poet's grandfather, " and with great gravity produced Mrs. Clarke's leg that is sold in Ivory as a Toy at Worthing." Mrs. Clarke, a merry mistress, was much in the news just then in consequence of a famous lawsuit.

Political business occupied much of the time of Bysshe and Timothy Shelley alike. Where they stood in such matters is best put in a few words by Leigh Hunt : " The family connexions of Shelley belonged to a small party in the House of Commons, itself belonging to another party. They were Whig Aristocrats ; a distinction that, within a late period "—he was writing in 1828— " has been handsomely merged by some of the bearers of it into the splendour of a more prevailing universality." Again, Hunt groups them among the genuine country gentlemen like Coke of Norfolk. These Shelleys were much in the company and the confidence of Charles Howard, Duke of Norfolk, their neighbour in Sussex. He " uniformly supported the popular cause " and was a fighter for parliamentary reform ; if it was alleged that he himself was as deeply committed to the traffic in boroughs as any nobleman of the age, what of it ? His answer to the charge was that he was ready to give up all his influence in this matter of elections as soon as a better system was established.

For almost half a century Horsham had been a pocket borough, and Lord Irwin had lately captured the votes. Our " independent Senator " the Duke, the friend of the Prince Regent and of Charles James Fox, succeeding to his father's title and seat in the House of Lords in 1786, promptly moved upon this little political stronghold. His method was to pack juries so as to drive Lady Irwin from the Court Baron and the Court Leet. By defying act of parliament he managed a temporary victory, and in this way enabled his young friend Timothy Shelley to be M.P. for Horsham from 1790 to 1792. On petition Lady Irwin gained the day and Timothy lost the seat. His attendance at debates is quietly commemorated in one of the many vivid stage directions for *The Dynasts* by Thomas Hardy.

If Timothy Shelley needed any consolation for his exclusion from those momentous debates on the unrest of Europe, he could surely find it now that he had settled with his bride Elizabeth at

Field Place, Warnham. Almost a century had passed since this estate had come into the Shelley property, through a marriage with one of the Michells. Elizabeth was no stranger to the place. She was one of the Pilfolds who had been at Warnham for many generations, though her father had an estate at Effingham in Surrey ; her mother was Bethia White, also of a Horsham family. Elizabeth was baptized at Horsham in February, 1763, and married to Timothy at West Grinstead a few miles distant in October, 1791. In a stately sort of way she was a beauty, wrote good letters, had some taste in literature, and knew the country and the countryman's recreations well. Long after the events which these pages tell afresh had come and gone, this lady was remembered in Horsham for her benevolence, which was not of the severe kind : for example, when Mayday brought into action two competing sets of Jacks-in-the-Green, she " used to patronise them handsomely by giving them plenty to eat and drink, and a good round sum of money. She one year gave one party a new set of dresses, fitting them out in a very gay manner."

But, to return to the year 1791, it is to be explained how the young couple could occupy Field Place. Until 1790 it had been the residence of Bysshe's elder brother John, who built the neat stables and is supposed to have planted what was called the American Garden, but of whom there is not much else to say ; he died without issue, and Bysshe became the owner. Bysshe however thought he needed not to live at Field Place, since he was rebuilding a magnificent mansion for himself, or perhaps for a dream self, at Goring on the coast of the English Channel. Field Place accordingly became the home of Timothy and Elizabeth, and the date of their marriage may well have waited upon that by which the house became part of Bysshe's property. Here on August 4th, 1792, Elizabeth gave birth to a son who received the names Percy Bysshe. Though the first of these names was not entirely new in the family it was infrequent, and if it was given in honour of the child's great-uncle it may also have come from vague medievalism and the desire to connect the Shelley tradition with the famous Percys who had formerly owned the Petworth estates.

The arrival of the little boy gave great pleasure to his grandfather, who began to treat him with something of the fond indulgence which he had known himself from his grandparents. How old Bysshe would have laughed to read what the most eminent of the child's biographers has written of him in his later life : " still toiling at the punishment assigned to the avaricious, rolling before him to the grave a golden weight which perpetually

increased." The same writer promptly contradicts himself by
noticing that Bysshe grown old lived in great simplicity and in a
" cottage house "—Arun House near Horsham Church. It is a
charming Georgian dwelling, with a long garden descending
under tall trees to the mill stream, and certainly the old gentleman
protected by an old man-servant of similar opinions would nowadays be praised for his good sense in choosing to live there at the
town end with a minimum of fuss. But perhaps he intended later
on to startle the world. He was getting rid of about £80,000 of
" the golden weight " in the adventures of building his Folly
overlooking the Southern sea. The design was doomed never to
be completed, but Castle Goring is still there in its significant
duality, being in fact " a pair of buildings joined in the centre,
having two distinct styles of architecture, which were also carried
out in the interior decorations." The south-west front was
Palladian, the north-east modern Gothic in imitation of part of
Arundel Castle, as also in compliment to the Duke of Norfolk
with his yet vaster recreations of antique tower and battlement.
Bysshe did not follow the Duke in having himself portrayed in a
painted window as Solomon.

The poet Shelley as a youth and in his most voluble stage
dismissed his grandfather's memory with no ceremony whatever :
" I always regarded him as a curse upon society." Perhaps it was
with such things in mind as the use of immense wealth for purposes
like the building of Castle Goring that Shelley wrote so cuttingly.
Viewed as a Sussex character, who happened to pick up riches as
easily as a carp grows fat, Bysshe Shelley was not as bad as all
that. Nor was he every way unusual except in the scale of his
operations. It was not because his notions could bring him any
new luxury that he put them into action, but as they made
history and stamped an impress on his part of the world. " I can,
and I will." It did not concern him to exert this power over
people who were not in competition with him, and so he naturally
made his call every day at the Swan Inn in Horsham and had his
talk with the friendly workaday townsfolk there. For this he has
been abused. In our time it is probable that he may even be
commended. When the aristocrat, the artisan, the tradesman
and the peasant were terms all bearing a dignity, though the era
of this understanding was ebbing away, Bysshe Shelley was not
acting in a way that was not well understood. The Duke of
Norfolk himself, " the Lord of Horsham," as often as he visited
the town, was looked for at the Anchor Inn, and would have
been disappointed if he had not met his town crier ablaze with
gold and silver on the premises. It was therefore no freak in

Bysshe to sit with his homely friends of the shop, the office and the farm, exchanging old times or political futures while the landlord of the Swan smiled on the scene. At this inn, it may be noted, his grandson occasionally entertained a visitor.

In the year 1806, when Bysshe Shelley was seventy-five, he was made a baronet. The honour might not have been conferred but for the brief appearance of the Grenville Ministry, which restored the Duke of Norfolk to favour and saw him nominated to the Lord Lieutenancy of Sussex. Sir Bysshe now took an interest in the earliest literary amusements of his grandson at Field Place, and lived long enough to have a say in other matters of a less playful kind concerning him ; and there is not much else to fill the picture of his closing years. An obsession kept him busy ; he was afraid he might not have enough ready money in the house. In course of time his executors found the banknotes which he had hidden here and there, amounting to above £12,000. It would be a pity to conclude that this was the man ; this was the decline of a once remarkable man, who with some slight change of constitution might have given the name Shelley a greatness in another sphere of action. Sir Bysshe died in 1815, and Timothy, now M.P. for Shoreham, succeeded to the title.

Since Horsham and its affairs have been occasionally mentioned in these notices of one of its families, and as this small town was that to which as a child Shelley came very often, it may be well to sketch though briefly the town that he knew. Not that its appearance has altogether changed. There in the clay country of the Weald, with the sandstone ridges north of it and the South Downs between it and the sea, it keeps its narrow streets, some of its ancient trees and houses and names, its thirteenth-century church with the lovely shingled spire sheltering memorials of Michells and Shelleys, and the vault still claimed by a small inscription as Sir Timothy's. Park and farm come close to its life, and you do not have to travel far beyond its boundaries to find " heath, and pines, and brooks running swiftly in deep, narrow little valleys." But much in the way of living which flourished in smaller communities of the reign of George III is quite gone. The shops which the Shelleys patronised were low-pitched rooms with low windows and small panes, displaying very little to buy because their owners were craftsmen working principally on orders. From hats to harness people could get what they required in Horsham, for Horsham made " a number of things." The fact and the evidence of hard work were seldom varied, but when they were, it was by festivals like Mayday, the July Fair, Bonfire Day, Gooding Day, and each of these had its own glorifications. To the July Fair which lasted almost a week folk came in from the country by hundreds and thousands, and " bough houses " for their refreshment crowded the roadways. At Christmas—and this was within living memory until the first world war—Sir Timothy Shelley used to distribute great quantities of beef. His son would have helped in the arrangements.

Here or at Warnham Village we should have many a day heard the bells, beautifully rung. The Horsham society of ringers has a long history, and in Shelley's time liked to ring complete peals of 5040 changes. At the Swan Inn, or any other, Sir Bysshe could reward the singing of the Sussex labourer. Many of the old fellows had a host of songs in their memory, and some had a talent for making up more. In Horsham Shelley could now and then see yoked oxen pulling their broad-tyred wagons ; he could catch the Oxford coach which called daily at the King's Head. Horsham had its printer, its stationer, its lawyers, among them the family of Medwin, cousins to the Shelleys ; the name and the firm survive in the town to this day. Perhaps the last of the partners to remember Shelley and dispense good stories of him was Pilfold Medwin who died in the eighties aged 96. To touch in one or two more traits of the Horsham of Shelley : an occasional public execution drew large crowds ; an occasional wife-sale produced lots of fun and little money ; and night funerals with torchlight processions were not discontinued until Shelley beneath a distant sky had undergone a more fiery funeral.

II

FIELD PLACE

TWO MILES out of Horsham to the north-west, not far from the
county boundary, the river Arun and the Roman road called
Stane Street, stood and still stands Field Place. In the summer
season at least it is a house of enchantment, such as Walter de la
Mare might create in a poem. Like others round about it has a
mighty roof of Horsham stone, and a line of chimneys like towers.
It " is very rambling, with long passages and odd corners, turn-
ings and recesses, floors on different levels "—a long low house
in which the work of several periods is combined. It stands in a
park which like most in the district has long been shaded with
great trees, and it has its own little brook and lake. Before
Shelley knew this home, its masters had laid out fine gardens
and orchards, as well as " the American garden," described fifty
years ago as " a long strip of green, softly turfy and sweetly
shaded, with circles and crescents of rhododendrons ; here and
there ornamental pines of many kinds, cedars, beeches, birches,
and a fruit tree—plum or apple—set among them, weeping
ashes, dropping branch-tops to earth and making tents of greenery
where one might sit hid, unseen yet seeing." The description is
not amiss to-day. Not far off is the farm pond, but it would
rather be Warnham Great Pond which called Shelley. In one
of his lyrics we have a scene of hard winter with a great silence
and stillness only stirred by the millwheel's sound ; as a child he
knew that sound from the watermills at Warnham and Broad-
bridge. From the garden he could see the line of the South
Downs and in another direction the seemingly mountainous
region round Hindhead. The whole estate was such as might
fill his days with pleasant adventures. Charming or wild, secret
or sunlit, these glades and groves and gills had. much to give
to a sensitive child, and yield him imagery for his later concepts.
Birds, butterflies and moths abounded in this part of Sussex,
though the appearance of a golden eagle over Horsham in
Shelley's boyhood was irregular. The reckless bird was soon shot
and made a paragraph in the newspapers ; it is tempting and
harmless to think that the metaphysical eagles in Shelley's verse
are of Field Place origin.

The children of Timothy and Elizabeth Shelley in this beautiful Place forty miles from London were seven in number —Percy Bysshe, Elizabeth, Mary, Hellen who died in infancy, another Hellen, Margaret and John. The last of these was born in 1806. The two of them whose memories of their early life and their extraordinary brother have been preserved were Hellen and Margaret, who both lived unmarried into old age. Some letters of Hellen to her nephew's wife are the main source, and a clear and sweet one, for our knowledge of Shelley's childhood. His beauty at that time was conspicuous and his nature enchanting ; yet his father who really loved him, but whose views on life and position required early action, was strong on the plan of educating him thoroughly. At the age of six Shelley trotted away every day to learn Latin from the curate at Warnham, a Welshman named Evan Edwards. This discipline was not all. To one who in after years hinted that the poet's erratic course must have begun through inordinate liberties allowed him in childhood, Timothy Shelley replied : " I can assure you that I never gave him Liberties, that from six years of age he has never been kept *one day* from School when he ought to be there, and in his Holydays I read the Classics and other Books with him in the full hopes of making him a good and gentlemanly Scholar." An exceedingly good scholar Shelley became. The plain foundations laid by Mr. Edwards served. But it was the gentlemanly scholar whom Timothy Shelley really wanted to see. He was preparing his son not as a translator of Plato or a complete author but for the public and social life where well-graced oratory, elegance of expression ready for all occasions, and a reference to ancient example and wisdom in the affairs of kingdoms and estates were the contemporary requirement. The elder Pitt could overawe the House with a single Latin quotation.

Moreover the father was anticipating the time when his boy would follow in his steps not only as a politician and a man of the time, but also as a landowner and a practical agriculturist— in short a capable Sussex squire. Timothy's wife was in full agreement ; she knew a great deal about horses, not so much about Homer. So for a time we see the boy who was to write " Prometheus Unbound " shaping as a recruit in rural employments. " He would ride through the Sussex lanes and roads with Lucas, his father's steward," meeting all too many people who were out of work and finding poverty, as the Sussex stoics said, though no sin, precious inconvenient. Lucas was touched to see how eager Shelley was during these rounds to help the unlucky ones ; " he would give lavishly, and if he had no money with him would borrow of me." This part of Sussex was well known for its success in pig-rearing, and unromantic as it may sound Shelley got to know something about that. Without the know-ledge his satirical poem of years later, " Swellfoot the Tyrant," would never have had the strength and gusto which entertain its readers. One word in it, " ruta-baga," meaning the Swedish turnip, takes us back at once to Shelley on the farm, and his father's farm most likely ; when he was a boy this ruta-baga was only beginning to be tried by progressive husbandmen, and his father was widely esteemed as one of that kind.

Shelley enjoyed his tours of the estate and familiarity with what was going on, and the anecdotes of him at this period are the proof of it. He was proud of qualifying as " Sussex." When he was still very young he went to see a Colonel Sergison who chanced to be visiting his lawyer in Horsham, and in the local dialect he asked for a job as gamekeeper's boy. The colonel was taken in and kindly said he should have it ; " and then, of course, there was an explosion of laughter." Another innocent piece of counterfeiting, " a morning's event," may be taken as his sister Hellen gives it. " As we were sitting in the little breakfast-room our eyes were attracted by a countryman passing the window with a truss of hay on a prong over his shoulders ; the intruder was wondered at and called after, when it was discovered that Bysshe had put himself in costume to take some hay to a young lady at Horsham, who was advised to use hay-tea for chilblains." This must have been when Shelley was fourteen or so. He was a great favourite with the servants at Field Place, and with the outdoor workers. His father failed to notice him beguiling one or two of them into the harness-room for games of cards, when his constant partner was the rather nervous coachman with his repeated question " Be I to play trumps, Mr. Bysshe ? " A later joke of Shelley's, with an element of serious meaning in it, may close these notes on Shelley and agriculture : when he signed the register at Edinburgh on his first marriage, he set down his occupation as " Farmer, Sussex."

Hellen's reminiscences of Shelley in the part of eldest brother are brief, but they are enough to convey the affection, the thought-fulness and the fancy which he bestowed on the younger ones. He would take them for walks, such as the locally famous one to Strood Park, and make little adventures for them, like getting them across the ha-ha. At home on the lawn under the fir-trees he found time to play and romp with them, and though he was apt to be violent at other times his gentleness then was unfailing. But what gave greatest or best remembered delight all round was his art of telling wonder-stories and making the surroundings of Field Place the abode of fantastic creatures.

His performance started with the house itself, which was full of inspiration for his purpose. Upstairs under the roof there were a big garret and a closed room only to be entered by a trap-door in the garret floor. " This unknown land was made the fancied habitation of an Alchemist, old and grey, with a long beard. Books and a lamp, with all the attributes of a picturesque fancy, were poured into our listening ears. We were to go and see him ' some day ' ; but we were content to wait, and a cave was to be dug in the orchard for the better accommodation of this Cornelius Agrippa. Another favourite theme was the Great Tortoise that lived in Warnham Pond ; and any unwonted noise was accounted for by the presence of this great beast, which was made into the fanciful proportions most adapted to excite awe and wonder." The Pond, alas, is shrinking steadily from its old extent, suited to such Tortoises.

The preternatural historian also supplied a Great Old Snake who picked up a living about the garden. Shelley must have heard people talk of the local dragon of St. Leonard's Forest, that lovely woodland with its water-lily pools and lilies of the valley which he knew well and which in part would one day be his ; probably his monsters were relatives of that one. Unlike many dragons this one can be dated ; he is the subject of a pamphlet of August, 1614, when he was alive and well in the Forest " to the great Annoyance and divers Slaughters both of Men and Cattell, by his strong and violent Poyson." Sometimes Shelley and his listeners were all " translated " : " we dressed ourselves in strange costumes to personate spirits or fiends, and Bysshe would take a fire-shovel and fill it with some inflammable liquid and carry it flaming into the kitchen and to the back door ; but discovery of this dangerous amusement soon put a stop to many repetitions."

In these fable-weavings something of the desire to be an author is seen, and it can be otherwise traced in Shelley from tender years. We know next to nothing of his father's library, but Timothy had his regular London bookseller, by name Clio Rickman, a friend of the " impious " Tom Paine ; now and then he subscribed to some new publication, including Clio Rickman's poems. We have seen how Timothy lost no time in bringing his son towards classical literature, and Hellen describes how the boy was requested " to repeat long Latin quotations, probably from some drama ; for he would act " as he recited. The English writer with whom we first find Shelley pleased is one who had a

lasting effect on his poetical style. Still a child, he read Gray's
Ode on a Favourite Cat drowned in a tub of goldfishes, and, as
his mother often recalled, he recited it entire after the one reading.
The first English composition by him is also about a cat, and " a
cat in distress." The text comes to an end before we are told
what the trouble was ; but the most interesting thing in these
colloquial stanzas is that the little boy who writes turns his mind
away from cats to human kind and their burdens:

> You'd not easily guess
> All the modes of distress
> Which torture the tenants of earth ;
> And the various evils
> Which, like so many devils,
> Attend the poor souls from their birth.

Before very long it had occurred to Shelley as to many another
juvenile poet that it would be a great thing to have some of
his own works in print, and his grandfather was taken with this
innocent vanity enough to pay for some printing at Horsham.
In those days the bill could not be large. The results have
disappeared, and so has that play which Shelley and Hellen
made up together and solemnly sent up to London to be considered by Charles Mathews.

So we see this boy already trying to take a share in the
activities of the grown man ; and this early endeavour was at
once the blessing and the curse of his station in life. He rushed
forth in Utopia and collided with the world ; and the spectacle
of his precocious improvisings, however comical it can be, surely
attracts us to him. Unaware as yet of the cross-currents and
rapids which complicate all our days, he was swift with a passion
for getting something done and exercising the power of goodness
armed with imagination—and wealth. The episode that follows
is undated, but even if it belongs to the period when he had
passed beyond childhood it none the less reveals how early he
felt the impulse to work for the betterment of society. " He had
a wish to educate some child, and often talked seriously of
purchasing a little girl for that purpose : a tumbler, who came
to the back door to display her wonderful feats, attracted him,
and he thought she would be a good subject for the purpose, but
all these wild fancies came to naught He would take his pony
and ride about the beautiful lanes and fields surrounding the
house, and would *talk* of his intention, but he did not consider
that board and lodging would be indispensable." Had someone
protested to him that his design was the mere dream of a boy,

no doubt he would have referred to such senior example as Thomas Day, the popular author of " Sandford and Merton," who had been greatly discussed. Day had selected two foundling girls, named them Lucretia and Sabrina, and attempted to shape their minds and manners to his liking.

Probably it was at a later date, but still early in his life, when Shelley caused some stir in Horsham circles by unconventional behaviour at a dance—by an action of no importance in itself, but signifying a generous courage. The dance was one at which the young gentleman from Field Place was expected to lead forth one of the ladies of rank and fashion who had assembled. Besides those, sitting rather lonely though not unobserved, was a girl who had been seduced—and everybody knew it. That was enough for Shelley. He made his way to this unlucky and un-pitied girl, and handed her forth in his sweetest style.

This incident must at all events have been much later than the time of his going away to boarding-school, which was when he was ten years old. What he looked like then is known from a miniature ; the name of the artist, the Duc de Montpensier, suggests that some occasion at the Duke of Norfolk's house led to its being painted. The Duc, one of the Bourbons, was addressed in verse by Thomas Moore during that year 1802 and praised for his interpretation of spiritual gifts. Moore's poem however does not refer to a portrait of Shelley, but one of the Lady Adelaide Forbes at Donington Park.

These are the pencil's grandest theme,
Divinest of the powers divine
That light the Muse's flowery dream,
And these, oh Prince ! are richly thine.

If the Duke had been informed by an angel that the slender little boy in the frilled collar sitting to him in sleepy Sussex was to be the most ardent idealist in the length of English poetry, he could not have made his drawing a prettier announcement of the news. The face is strong. We are looking at one who has been brought up in the air of riches and responsibility and the confidence that wishes can be fulfilled ; but he is radiant with fine sympathy too. The boy seems saying, " I see what should be done, and it will delight me to do it."

The private school to which Shelley was now sent bore the name of Sion House Academy, and its buildings more or less remain in a state of decline at Isleworth. Shelley's cousin Thomas Medwin preceded him as one of the fifty or sixty pupils. In later life the drifting Medwin came under the observation of W. M.

Thackeray as a bore of singular dreariness, and was awarded the name of Captain Sumph. It is a pity that Thackeray was not there in Shelley's day to describe Sion House Academy, though it was a well-respected school of its type. The neighbourhood was not notably good for a poet's education ; the chief poetical allusion to it occurs in the last stanza of Thomson's " Castle of Indolence," thus :

> Even so through Brentford town, a town of mud,
> An herd of bristly swine is pricked along.

Still, the academy had a garden. The master, Dr. Greenlaw, was a Scot ; which assures us that the subjects taught—Latin, Greek, French, writing, arithmetic, geography, the elements of astronomy —would be taught accurately.

The trouble at Sion House Academy was the old convention that boys must behave like man-eaters to newcomers and unusual boys. No easier target could have appeared than the boy from Field Place, beautiful and rhapsodical. The attack astonished him, and drove him to two perilous lines of defence : scorn and solitude. Although even in boys' schools there are intervals in the sport of provocation and ragging, and the victim is not always the same, it is hard to deny that Medwin is right in painting Shelley's experiences at Brentford in dark colour. The tale of persecution is confirmed by a schoolfellow named John Rennie— the first engineer to be knighted since Sir Hugh Myddleton who provided Elizabethan London with a water supply. Like the swine in Thomson's simile, Shelley was certainly goaded during his passage through Brentford.

But the place meant something to him which was not so remote from his carefree life at Field Place as the common run of the schooldays was. It had a circulating library, where he found the thrillers of the period—tales of terror, sixpennies long before the Penguins, fantasies, ghoul-mongerings in plenty. We may much prefer the child's own old Alchemist and Tortoise to these manufactured articles ; but it was the season for vampires, castle-spectres and headless horsemen, and Shelley was one of the many who were fascinated. This lasted long with him, and he did not get over it until he himself had concocted some works which should have been more gigantically lurid and sold in larger quantities, than all the rest—if he could have secured such results. A deeper note, however, continues from the ecstasy of Shelley moving among the tales of the supernatural. It is sounded by himself in one of his earliest poems of full sway, the " Hymn to Intellectual Beauty."

> While yet a boy I sought for ghosts, and sped
> Through many a listening chamber, cave and ruin,
> And starlight wood, with fearful steps pursuing
> Hopes of high talk with the departed dead.
> I called on poisonous names with which our youth is fed :
> I was not heard—I saw them not—
> When musing deeply on the lot
> Of life, at that sweet time when winds are wooing
> All vital things that wake to bring
> News of birds and blossoming,—
> Sudden, thy shadow fell on me ;
> I shrieked, and clasped my hands in ecstasy !

The lines almost unveil Shelley reading for the first time and in his own sense Thomson's wish to " hold high converse with the mighty dead," and Dr. Greenlaw's boys passing round the magic sixpennies. But they show how before long all the demon apparatus began to look shabby and poor for him in contrast with the magic of the natural world.

It may be that the portrait of Shelley's grandfather is that of a sort of mystic, who trusted in the discovery of truths less by system than by sudden light through the clouds. If so, the quality descended to Shelley, resolute thinker as he was. " While I was thus musing, the fire kindled." The wonder is however that moments of vision, bringing decisions of importance, happened to him at so early a stage. The discernment of the true sublime, the " awful Loveliness " so different from witches and other night-fears, was one. Another was a view of his own character and purpose, the choice of a battle against despotism within himself and without. He presents it freshly as it happened to him in the dedication of " The Revolt of Islam," and although an intimate friend who heard much from Shelley later touching his school-day trials refers it to Shelley's later school, the details argue that Shelley suddenly saw this destiny at Sion House Academy. The verses have been quoted very often, but, standing as one of the great charters of his career, they can never be set aside :

> Thoughts of great deeds were mine, dear Friend, when first
> The clouds which wrap this world from youth did pass.
> I do remember well the hour which burst
> My spirit's sleep : a fresh May-dawn it was,
> When I walked forth upon the glittering grass,
> And wept, I knew not why ; until there rose
> From the near schoolroom voices that, alas !

Were but one echo from a world of woes—
The harsh and grating strife of tyrants and of foes.

And then I clasped my hands and looked around
  —But none was near to mock my streaming eyes,
Which poured their warm drops on the sunny ground—
  So without shame I spake : ' I will be wise,
And just, and free, and mild, if in me lies
Such power, for I grow weary to behold
  The selfish and the strong still tyrannise
Without reproach or check.' I then controlled
My tears, my heart grew calm, and I was meek and bold.

And from that hour did I with earnest thought
  Heap knowledge from forbidden mines of lore,
Yet nothing that my tyrants knew or taught
  I cared to learn, but from that secret store
Wrought linkéd armour for my soul, before
It might walk forth to war among mankind.

One of Shelley's lifelong habits was noticed while he was at this preparatory school. He had a way of drawing little pictures in his exercise books, and so have many children ; but his way was different. There was some ability and delicacy in his sketches, and possibly he had profited by earlier instruction. His ambition in this direction was inconsiderable. The cedars and pines which he pencilled amid his Latin verses for Dr. Greenlaw at Brentford were the confession of his feelings ; they were the images of return to Field Place. Sometimes in later days (for the subject may as well be traced out here) he would elaborate a drawing, and when he did so he passed beyond the polite accomplishment which then decorated many a journal of travel. He would stand at inn doors while his friends stayed within, and find his materials and his subjects. " There is a spirit in the leaves," and the best of his trees are fluctuant and graceful. Besides trees he enjoyed sketching the wide waters and the sailing boat upon them. Like Catullus, this poetic man knew that a boat would say some glorious things if men knew how to hear, and he saw her in her element not as a mechanical construction but as a natural creature like rock and tree. He did not disdain to draw a paddle-boat. As he became more of a sailor at home and abroad his portraits of ships grew finer ; but something was due to first experiences and the boat that his father kept by Warnham Mill.

It is inconceivable that his habit of profuse letter-writing did not begin early, but few of his boyish letters survive. These express his home pleasures and not the ardours above his years which other evidences call his. In childhood as in manhood he was bound to be different from others, but these letters show him respecting the ordinary manners and rules of good society, including the art of shooting flying. Shelley has been so commonly depicted as going about in rags and tatters that it is well to hear what his sister says about it. On the walk to Strood Park, " our shoes were sadly soiled, and the little one of the party was sadly tired and required carrying ; but she was careful to hold her feet so that [Bysshe's] trousers should not be damaged. . . . And subsequently, Bysshe ordered clothes according to his own fancy at Eton, and the beautifully fitted silk pantaloons, as he stood as almost all men and boys do with their coat tails near the fire, excited my silent though excessive admiration."

The trousers and pantaloons are not immortal ; but taken with others the detail suggests that Shelley, even if he resolved at the age of twelve or so to live in a state of war against despots, was quite prepared to direct his campaign from orderly Field Place, and without eccentricities that only get in the way of the eccentricity which moves mountains. So far, then, his father might trust that his plans for training his successor were going on nicely ; in Sussex and in London Percy Bysshe Shelley would be very much like himself, though he might add the author to the country gentleman and the senator favouring reform. Timothy himself was once again a member of parliament, this time for Shoreham, a seat which he held from 1802 to 1818. The old loyalty to the Duke of Norfolk was concerned in this, and after such generations of family friendship and alliance it was to be expected ; but Timothy deserves some credit for not having wavered. No great while before the Duke had presided at a meeting at the Crown and Anchor tavern, Arundel Street, and he had given the old Whig toast to celebrate the return of Charles James Fox for the city of Westminster, " Our Sovereign, the Majesty of the People." This health, just then, offended King George III, and the Duke was deprived of certain offices.

So things stood ; the Duke was little the worse off, and his dutiful Timothy Shelley had no reason to fear much coming trouble. The time for his son to leave the school at Brentford was approaching, and the next part of his education would be England's best. The boy's promise would steadily become manly readiness. Shelley himself in 1804 may have had hesitations about the beauty of the prospect opening upon him, a new exile from his home and the country round, another school and a far greater school to find or fight his way in. Yet at the same time he like others must have been highly excited and quickened with sense of adventure in the knowledge that he was going to Eton. He wrote his name in the headmaster's entrance book on July 29th, 1804.

Towards the close of his life, far away from his old home, Shelley had some daydreams and he tried to catch them in rhyme. He saw the white mist on Midsummer night, the devils and spectres and angels and fairies of childhood flocking where the owl and bat and nightingale were grown drowsy ; he heard the gnats and the bees and drones of that country. Then he saw a schoolboy lying near a pond in a copse, with the golden bloom of the broom near by and the pine cones falling. Over the onion bed the motes were playing ; and when the schoolboy closed his eyes he saw the fire-tailed stars of the night of his brain speeding about like the birds over the farm pond. This perhaps, in the seeming reality of the experience, was Shelley's last visit to Field Place.

III

ETON

"WHATEVER may be the success in after life, whatever gratification or ambition may be realised, whatever triumphs may be achieved, no one is ever again so great a man as when he was a sixth form boy at Eton "—so wrote a Prime Minister of England ; and at Field Place in 1804 something of this enthusiasm must have been felt during the preparations for Shelley's departure to the great school. Its antiquity and the beauty of its setting were familiar to his family in the Ode of Thomas Gray ; what other school had inspired such a classic ? To this royal foundation, only strengthened by the passage of three centuries and more, and seeming as perpetual as Windsor Castle and the " silver-winding " Thames its neighbours, a boy who loved books, ideas and nature might well be consigned. This great day might be the beginning of great years.

Moreover those who loved Shelley would see nothing but good in what they had heard of the spirit of Eton discipline. Apart from the details of the teaching and the calendar the prevailing idea was that very good one Liberty, or in the handsome prose of a young observer at the time, " that hatred of immoderate restriction which generous talents naturally entertain." Encouragement, thoughtful direction, and the competition of advancing minds were regarded as more fruitful than harsh punishments. The personal resolution and good sense of the boys were valued. Comparatively little in the way of set tasks was officially demanded of them, but much was silently expected. Remembering a few names of those educated under this system, in the era which produced Shelley—such names as Canning, Wellesley, Wellington, Charles James Fox and Grey— we may say that the governing body knew its business. Another way of appreciating the kind of education given at Eton would be to glance at the periodicals brought out there. School magazines very seldom claim any other rank than school magazines ; but *The Microcosm*, a Periodical Work, by Gregory Griffin, of the College of Eton—in fact, by George Canning, J. H. Frere and others in 1787—took its place in the voluminous tradition of *The Spectator* and *The Rambler* as a standard collection of essays. *The Etonian*, a magazine issued by the same Windsor publishers in

32

1820 and 1821, gained a more than local circulation, and remains a striking production by a band of young authors lavish in wit, learning and literary zeal.

One of the writers in *The Etonian* attempted to express the belief that Eton had the secret of training without repressing personality. " Our system," he declared, " may be compared to the hand of the jeweller who was employed in setting the breastplate of the High Priest with precious stones, which merely rounded off the rough prominences, and gave a polish to the gems, so as to reduce the separate parts to harmonize with the whole, without destroying the individual beauty of each ; and the same constitutes the partial metamorphosis of character which takes place at Eton." The sentiment and perhaps its decoration agree with the persuasions of Timothy Shelley, his wife and his small daughters when Bysshe, or " Bit " as they called him, went off by the Windsor coach in 1804. He was no doubt well provided with trunks " duly crammed with the handyworks of affection ; portfolios and blotting-books to put his manuscripts in, ornaments for his mantle-piece, and a neat little needle-book, properly furnished with all its paraphernalia."

Cheered on his way by the philosophic familiarity of the coach-man, Shelley would end his journey outside the Christopher Inn, Eton, the sign of which he was later on to carry off. He then found himself in a whirlwind of 500 boys, and had to discover without delay what the different classifications meant—Oppidan and Colleger, Sixth Form and Fourth, Dandy and Bargee. The full establishment into which he was venturing consisted of a provost, vice-provost, under master, assistants, seventy scholars, seven lay-clerks, ten choristers, and over 400 Oppidans, besides school officers and a staff of servants. The scholars, whose provision was due to statutes dated 1440 and 1444, were distinguished by wearing black gowns and had their headquarters in Long Chamber, reckoned a chamber of horrors ; the Oppidans, whose education and maintenance were at the expense of their relatives, were boarded elsewhere.

Shelley was boarded at first in a low white house in charge of Mr. Hexter, who being a major in the Militia (for the period had its apprehensions of an invasion) was nicknamed Hector. He was the Eton writing-master, a now defunct character who taught other subjects besides calligraphy. The boys enjoyed asking him in class, " Major, will you mend my pen ? " Besides this patriotic master, Shelley came under the care of a " Dame," about whom he may have been as surprised as others ; assuming that they would meet a housekeeper of a commonplace kind, they were received by a lady, dressed very fashionably, in her own elegant room. The impressions of Lord Berners ninety years after Shelley would agree in this with his. In Hexter's house only three lower boys lodged, and acted as fags or factotums for their seniors. Shelley was fag to Henry Matthews, who died a judge in Ceylon in 1828, having made a name with *The Diary of an Invalid* ; but it was too early for literary talks between these two boys. For some time Shelley was the close companion of another fag named Andrew Amos, the son of a Russia merchant ; " Shelley and I used to amuse ourselves in composing plays, and acting them before the other lower boy, who constituted our sole audience." These boys came a little too soon for the unofficial school theatre which was to flourish awhile until the authorities decided that some regular work would have to begin again.

During the greater part of Shelley's time at Eton the head-master was Dr. Goodall, who had no passion for altering things, nor can he be counted among the boy's ogres. " Indeed his countenance was illuminated with an almost perpetual smile. It seemed an odd caprice of fortune by which such a jovial spirit was invested with the solemn dignity of a schoolmaster. He was exceedingly rich in anecdote, and an incomparable teller of a story. Yet was he not deficient in the higher and graver accomplishments." In 1809 Goodall was succeeded by his assistant John Keate, a much smaller man in outward appearance, but different in other ways too ; for Keate made it his business to uphold authority even if he had to flog 80 boys in a day (a total achieved in 1832). Since Shelley came under the instruction of Keate, another poet, some description of the master is due, and the best of several good ones is from the enchanting quill of A. W. Kinglake in *Eothen*. The author entered Eton about ten years after Shelley left.

When he was in Cairo, Kinglake says, he wished to test the powers of a magician, whose art it was to get his attendant boy to " see " on the palm of his hand the likeness of any absent person named by a customer. Kinglake says, " I named Keate. . . . He was little more (if more at all) than five feet in height, and was not very great in girth, but within this space was concentrated the pluck of ten battalions. He had a really noble voice, and this he could modulate with great skill, but he had also the power of quacking like an angry duck, and he almost always adopted this mode of communication in order to inspire respect . . . ; he had such a complete command over his temper —I mean, over his *good* temper, that he scarcely ever allowed it to appear. . . . His red, shaggy eyebrows were so prominent, that he habitually used them as arms and hands for the purpose of pointing out any object towards which he wished to direct attention ; the rest of his features were equally striking in their way, and were all and all his own ; he wore a fancy dress, partly resembling the costume of Napoleon, and partly that of a widow-woman. I could not have named anybody more decidedly differing in appearance from the rest of the human race.

' Whom do you name ? '—' I name John Keate.'

—' Now, what do you see ? ' said the wizard to the boy.— ' I see,' answered the boy, ' I see a fair girl with golden hair, blue eyes, pallid face, rosy lips.' "

Shelley, who seems to have appeared to that boy instead of Keate, saw nothing in Keate except a watchful classical master, but Keate saw something in him. Shelley's Latin prose was apt to include metrical sentences, which got there without his intending them, and the master applied to him the line of Ovid :

Et quod tentabam dicere versus erat.
[And what I tried to say fell into verse.]

Another master with whom Shelley was well acquainted was his tutor Mr. Bethell ; for as he was promoted from the upper fourth form to the sixth he left Hexter's house and had his room over Bethell's study. Bethell (" Vox et Praeterea Nihil ") was regarded as the dullest of men and weakest of Latinists, although he contributes to " Musae Etonenses," but he was gentlemanly, just and quietly courageous—the " modest but stedfast vindicator " of the rights of the scholars by the original statutes. He is the unlucky figure in the story, which has been worked into several versions, of Shelley and his electrifying machine : how Shelley was entertaining some friends with this new wonder and charged the door-handle with the current, and Mr. Bethell hurrying up to stop the noise of the party, and not catching the point of Shelley's warning call, laid his hand on the door-handle. But a similar story is told of Eton a few years later, the door-handle victim on that occasion being the poet W. M. Praed.

These trifles have at least the merit of calling attention to a part of Shelley's intellectual gift and striving in an immature stage. It was nothing astonishing that a wealthy boy should possess an electrical machine and amuse his companions with it ; but Shelley's enthusiasm was for " the general principles of electricity as laid down by Dr. Franklin." He was aware not only of the display but of the secret force behind it. What with others was a fashion in playthings was a deeper pursuit with him, and he is described as "daring and bold" in his electrical experiments; yet they occupied only one corner of the scientific side of his mind.

It is said that Shelley bought his machine as others did theirs from the assistant of a lecturer who had become a well-known figure at Eton and other great schools. Though the education given was first and last classical, this ingenious lecturer in natural philosophy had received real encouragement. Adam Walker, a north-country character, self-taught, had made a number of mechanical contrivances, from revolving lights to musical instruments; but his most profitable work was the lecture on the marvels of nature and of science. Large audiences were assured him at Eton. Shelley was present when Walker's prediction that he would soon be coming down from town not by horses but by steam provoked an uproar from three hundred incredulous boys; among them we may suppose Shelley was silent. His friend Amos did not like the look of things, and thought that old Walker's lectures were an unfortunate occurrence for Shelley, "as they supplied him with the means of producing interesting and dazzling results requiring very little application of mind, and as they increased his aversion to the studies of the school." Another school contemporary, less disturbed about the danger to those prescribed studies, remembered that "Astronomy, like electricity, seized upon his imagination. His jubilee was night. His spirit bounded on the shadow of darkness, and flew to the countless worlds beyond it."

As has been seen, Shelley as a youngster shared the common lot of being a fag. Among the episodes of his school life which did not make his position much happier, much is written of his raising a rebellion against the system. An earlier rebellion had not yet been forgotten by some of the masters. His conspiracy "for a time made the custom pause, at least as far as his own person was concerned." He "complained to the masters, and they would not listen to him;—he at last, with the ambition of a proper genius, succeeded for the first time perhaps since the foundation of the school in organising a whole party against the system; and he was *expelled*." If the sentence was pronounced, it was remitted. The subject has been viewed more tragically than is necessary, because of Shelley's valiant refusal to see it except as a sample of tyranny. An admirer of his, John Moultrie the poet, who went to Eton in 1811, sums up the fagging that he knew. It was hard, he says, on summer evenings when the Thames was all alive with skiffs, to have to fetch and throw in cricket balls for the big hitters, or to bowl them the stuff

they enjoyed hitting ; hard to be at once valet, footman, house-
maid, cook, shoeblack ; hard while one was hungry to spread
an enormous meal for some despot still in bed ; and yet this
moralist finds a virtue in it all. Weaker ones who, unlike Shelley,
learned self-restraint and obedience, met with forbearance and
kindness ; they could take their troubles and their exercises to
their faggers. Moultrie moreover describes fagging as no arbitrary
imposition, but an arrangement accepted as doing good to
everybody in the end. It is quite possible that arguments like
these infuriated the easily vexed Shelley more than any menial
task which as a fag he had to perform.

The author just consulted speaks on another troublesome
topic. He asserts that he arrived at Eton in a defiant mood, ready
to give blow for blow, but found little need of his heroic attitude ;
it was a school of degree and order, where right triumphed over
might, and giving black eyes and bloody noses was not the way
to win respect. Enough exists nevertheless of painful reminiscence
about the physical savagery which was to haunt Shelley's thoughts
of Eton though not to comprise them. He was spurred on, probably when he was a new boy, to single combat ; and being one
" apart from the whole school " in " a wild and marked
peculiarity " which he did not bother to disguise he had worse
ordeals than those. Herd instinct, which also caused the miseries
of a little boy named Hornby, though later on he was the author
of a poem called " Childhood," drove against " mad Shelley,"
leaving this picture on the mind of one W. H. Merle forty years
on : " The Shelley ! Shelley ! Shelley ! which was thundered
in the cloisters was but too often accompanied by practical jokes
—such as knocking his books from under his arm, seizing them
as he stooped to recover them, pulling and tearing his clothes,
or pointing with the finger, as one Neapolitan maddens another.
The result was . . . a paroxysm of anger which made his eyes
flash like a tiger's, his cheeks grow pale as death, his limbs quiver,
and his hair stand on end."

Yet another poet whose ways were queer underwent similar
persecutions at Eton. William Sidney Walker was there before
Shelley departed. His offences included slovenly clothes, poor
sight and satirical speaking. When he was set upon Walker
would run for safety into a master's room, which made matters
worse. His troubles however did not prevent him from looking
back to Eton as a Goshen, " bright with spiritual sunshine " ;
and his letters from school in 1810 and later are cheerful enough ;
his report is simply, " Eton being properly a small world, has its
fashions, amusements, parties, politics, etc. like the great one ;

there is a literary debating society, and other clubs ; and the
newspapers are in incessant circulation."

To Merle's account of a Shelley-baiting may be added a
passage which must have been derived in substance from Shelley's
conversation. In Mary Shelley's novel " Lodore," published in
1835, the character named in the title is vaguely representative
of Lord Byron, but the novelist bestows him upon Eton, and the
afflictions which he endures there are Shelleyan. Another boy
in the story called Derham appears to share these, and the whole
can be regarded as touching Shelley himself. " Lodore's schoolfellows soon discovered his weakness—it became a by-word
among them, and was the object of such practical jokes as seemed
to the self-idolizing boy at once frightful and disgusting. He had
no resource. Did he lay his length under some favourite tree to
dream of home and independence, his tormentors were at hand
with some new invention to rouse and molest him. . . . He poured
forth vehement invective, and hootings were the answer. He
had one other resource, and that in the end proved successful :—
a pitched battle or two elevated him in the eyes of his fellows, and
as they began to respect him, so he grew in better humour with
them and with himself. His good-nature procured him friends,
and the sun once more shone unclouded upon him."

Meanwhile Lodore's friend Derham, " whose slender frame,
fair effeminate countenance, and gentle habits, rendered him
ridiculous to his fellows," fared badly. " The boy was unlike
the rest ; he had wild fancies and strange inexplicable ideas. He
said he was a mystery to himself—he was at once wise and foolish.
The mere aspect of a grammar inspired him with horror, and a
kind of delirious stupidity seized him in the classes ; and yet he
could discourse with eloquence, and pored with unceasing delight
over books of the abstrusest philosophy. He seemed incapable of
feeling the motives and impulses of other boys : when they jeered
him, he would answer gravely with some story of a ghastly spectre,
and tell wild legends of weird beings who roamed through the
dark fields by night, or sat wailing by the banks of streams : was
he struck, he smiled and turned away ; he would not fag ; he
never refused to learn, but could not ; he was the scoff, and butt,
and victim of the whole school."

Mary Shelley gives her two characters peace and even
popularity among the boys at last ; presumably the story of
Shelley in the wars at Eton took a similar course. Even the years
at Mr. Hexter's house had not been unbroken wretchedness. His
companion Amos, whom he nicknamed Apurist (or Non-
Fireworshipper) for lack of interest in Walker's marvels of science,

and with whom in consequence he ceased to go for walks or on the river, could write in 1848, " I think I hear, as if it were yesterday, Shelley singing with the buoyant cheerfulness in which he often indulged, as he might be running nimbly up and down stairs, the Witches' songs in *Macbeth*. I fancy I still hearken to his

> Double, double, toil and trouble,
> Fire burn and cauldron bubble."

The humorous touch was not wanting to Shelley then or later, though intensity of emotion or belief so often overwhelmed it. It is noticeable that his delight in *Macbeth* characterised even his boyhood.

A boy so well accustomed to the society of nature as Shelley, so familiar with park and forest, could not be wholly unhappy in a school which allowed plenty of leisure for exploring its lovely vicinity. Windsor Park was one of his haunts, with its many giant oaks in their prime and pollards in their sturdy grotesqueness, its mingling tints of holly and wild cherry, its heronry, its straying herd of deer. His walks were sometimes shared by a boy named Halliday, who never in a long life lost the " sunny time " or the vision of Shelley's love of nature and " the sparkling poetry of his mind " which "shone out of his speaking eye, when he was dwelling on anything good or great." The two made the usual visits to Burnham Beeches, Stoke Poges and the country churchyard associated with Gray's Elegy, " of which Shelley was very fond." His familiarity with all Gray's poems was indeed part of of his life in Gray's old school, and among the scanty relics of his Latin compositions we have his version in sapphics of the epitaph which concludes the Elegy. Perhaps nothing short of a large-scale map of the country round Eton would complete the list of Shelley's rambles. He could not always go far, but like most Etonians took pleasure in fields and riversides close by and in the Terrace at Windsor Castle, where George III would talk heartily with any boy who happened to meet him. The Terrace was " in bounds," the ways to it were all " out of bounds," but the boys got there without much difficulty.

Beneath, the prospect of many fertile counties with shining farms and villages and woods made one of Shelley's best memories. A detail in Mary Shelley's " Last Man " takes us away from the Terrace to glance at him in a more beloved solitude. It was " a little wood not far distant from Salt Hill. A bubbling spring prattles over stones on one side, and a plantation of a few elms and beeches hardly deserve and yet continue the name of wood.

. . . His happiest hours were spent here. . . . He sat on the rough hewn steps that led to the spring, now reading a favourite book, now musing, with speculation beyond his years, on the still unravelled skein of morals or metaphysics." The scene is now a public garden, with quite Shelleyan weeping-willows.

However trade and traffic have altered Salt Hill on the road from Slough to Maidenhead, it is one of the names that speak of Shelley, and of happy Shelley : we see him there not only as the young hermit but as a schoolboy taking his part in the schoolboy's great occasions. The coming of the railways put an end to the procession known as the Montem which he enjoyed in its glory. Maria Edgeworth wrote a sprightly little play about it. On Whit Tuesday every third year the Montem blazed into life, its object being to beat up a subscription called Salt given to the school captain on his entrance at the university. Before a multitude of admirers, largely persons of rank and fashion, the boys marched through Slough to Salt Hill, then supposed to be a Saxon Barrow ; and on the summit the ensign for the year unfurled the grand standard. The " military " grades, ceremonies, titles belonging to the Montem need not be discussed now, but the dressing up may be noticed since it suited Shelley's fancy. The following dialogue in Maria Edgeworth's play occurs at the Windmill Inn, Salt Hill :

" *Landlady.* Well, this, to be sure, will be the best dressed Montem that ever was seen at Eton : and you Lon'on gentlemen have the most fashionable notions : and this is the most elegantest fancy cap—

" *Mr. Finsbury.* Why, as you observe, Ma'm, that is the most elegant fancy cap of them all. That is Mr. Hector Hogmorton's fancy cap, M'am ;—and here, Ma'm, is Mr. Saul's rich satin bag, covered with gold net. He is college salt-bearer, I understand, and has a prodigious superb white and gold dress. But, in my humble opinion, Ma'm, the marshal's white, and purple, and orange fancy dress, trimmed with silver, will bear the bell ; though, indeed, I shouldn't say that ; for the colonel's and lieutenant's, and ensigns', are beautiful in the extreme. And to be sure nothing can be better imagined than Mr. Marlborough's lilac and silver, with a Roman cap. And it must be allowed, that nothing in nature can have a better effect than Mr. Drake's flesh-colour and blue, with this Spanish hat, Ma'm, you see."

By comparison Shelley's plumage in 1805 seems quite dull— blue jacket, white trousers, silk stockings, pumps, and in the hand a wand ; but in 1808 with the rank of corporal and his own retinue he no doubt became more gorgeous. Montem was not one of the traditions which he proposed to abolish, nor was he the only poet present. He saw the appalling bard—a brick-layer in his other manifestation—who drove his donkeycart to Montems for fifty years, and did a brisk trade with rhymes of the day.

It is time to turn from Shelley's leisure hours to the routine of classwork at Eton as he went through it. He arrived there with sound training in the classics, and he was to depart with a command of them. It was the time in which Porson had won a new distinction for Eton scholarship. Shelley did not aspire to the scholarship of Porson, but he qualified himself to appreciate it. He won his prizes ; reached the sixth form ; and in July, 1810, at the election festival, pronounced his oration—Cicero's speech against Catiline. Of his own accord he translated some books—Hogg says half of the thirty-seven—of Pliny's Natural History, though his work has not been published.

The process of making him fluent in Greek and Latin translation and composition was not sinister. The boys only went into school four times a day and were not there more than three-quarters of an hour at a time. Moreover each week had its different programme, and a Saint's Day or an Anniversary or something of the sort was accepted as a reason for deferring exercises. The only ones which were not permitted to lapse were verses, on which the understanding was that only slackers would be content to produce the quantity actually set. By degrees a boy was trusted to compose upon ideas of his own rather than to translate given passages. Shelley was an opponent of the rage for Latin verse-writing though he could do it. As for reading and construing the ancient authors, he attended his tutor and received his help before performing in class, where he was accord-ingly expected to come thoroughly prepared. In other subjects Shelley received little instruction. Early on he would " learn " geography chiefly by tracing maps on paper over glass, and some arithmetic was practised. The drawing-master was William Evans. Upon the whole not much in the curriculum turned Shelley's tastes and inquiries from the classical texts which thus established themselves firmly beneath a great part of what he was to write in his own tongue.

No library of current reading existed in the school, though Williams's bookshop in the town and Knight's at Windsor were convenient. Novels and romances found their way about. A few years after Shelley's time the younger boys still favoured " a pack of horrible stories of ghosts and enchanted knights, which one sees in innumerable quantities displaying their fairy frontispieces in the shop windows." The reporter adds, " Perhaps too there is a deeper interest in those performances than you would be likely to guess, for some of the Authors may be found at no very great distance, who, actuated no doubt by a very laudable desire of appearing in print, have chosen to try their youthful talents in this romantic style of writing. These things are termed here indiscriminately *Pamphlets*, and every one that comes from the prolific London press, with the words ' By an Etonian ' on the title-page, possesses a natural charm, and is sought for with the utmost avidity by the devourers of this kind of literature."

This local information comes very near the history of Shelley, whose preoccupation with the nonsense of magic and mystery has been seen already. It suggests that in putting together and publishing a romance called *Zastrozzi* he was at once enjoying his Gothic luxuries and seeking distinction among his schoolfellows. He was busy on *Zastrozzi* in May, 1809, and it was brought out by Wilkie and Robinson of Paternoster Row a year later. Meanwhile Shelley had commanded his father's protégé Edward Graham to " pouch the reviewers—£10 will be sufficient, I should suppose." He said that it was " of consequence in fiction to establish your name as high as you can in the literary lists ; " he was being very much the man of the world. If the story is right, he received £40 from his Scottish publisher, and regaled eight Etonians out of this windfall.

Later readers of *Zastrozzi* have not surprisingly detected many marks of imitation in it. In 1806 a more competent spinner of wild tales, Charlotte Dacre, had published *Zofloya, or the Moor*, and her book was much in Shelley's mind as he worked up his own. Where it failed him, others of the class would prompt him with a " horrid " notion or name. Verezzi, for example, came from Mrs. Ann Radcliffe's " Mysteries of Udolpho," the acknowledged masterpiece of the Horrid Novels. An authority on these things, Edith Birkhead, says of Shelley's results : " The incidents are those which happen every day in the realm of terror. The villain, the hero, the melancholy heroine, and her artful rival, develop no new traits, but act strictly in accordance with tradition. They never infringe the rigid code of manners and morals laid down for them by previous generations. The scenery is invariably appropriate as a setting to the incidents, and even the weather may be relied on to act in a thoroughly conventional manner. The characters are remarkable for their violent emotions and their marvellously expressive eyes." It is evident that Shelley, practical in his fashion, meant to provide just what the appetites

of his readers, at Eton in the first place, would find as luscious
as usual.

Still *Zastrozzi* had another aim ; it was one of the activities
by which Shelley, as often as he had the chance, kept the family
at Field Place from being prosaic. His return for the holidays
may have been steady enough, and hitherto he was a dutiful
son even if " the stately bondage of his mother " chafed a little.
No fanciful flight has to be excused if we think of him riding
round the estate with the agent, looking at improvements, com-
plimenting tenants, noting the flourishing appearance of the
wheat, the winter turnips, the sheep and oxen. Such occupations,
hunting and shooting parties would not long satisfy Shelley, who
preferred unconventional diversion. Occasionally he played one
of his pranks in disguise, as when he called on his cousin Harriet
Grove at no less a house than the Duke of Norfolk's, pretending
to be a beggar. But the game of authorship pleased him most,
and he drew Harriet and his sisters into it. *Zastrozzi* was not the
only instance. He persuaded Elizabeth to take a hand in an
absurd farrago called " Original Poetry by Victor and Cazire,"
of which he had an absurd number of copies printed at Horsham
and published at Worthing. A poem by Monk Lewis had somehow got in and at length the book was suppressed. Elizabeth's
contribution was a rhyming letter to Harriet Grove, which by
its manner shows that Anstey's *Bath Guide* was not on the index
at Field Place. It contains one sentiment which strikes deeper
than she guessed ; speaking about men, she observes :

> For they're all alike, take them one with another,
> Begging pardon—with the exception of my brother.

Shelley's Original Poetry was resonant with echoes from Gray,
Chatterton, Scott and so on, and exclamation marks of his own.
" Ghasta or the Avenging Demon ! ! ! " comes to a typical
conclusion :

> Thunder shakes th' expansive sky,
> Shakes the bosom of the heath,
> ' Mortal ! Mortal ! thou must die '—
> The warrior sank convulsed in death.

It was not only in exalted moments that Shelley gave horror
his allegiance. Even an invitation to Field Place was of the same
colouring : " The avenue is composed of vegetable substances
moulded in the form of trees called by the multitude elm trees.
Stalk along the road towards them and mind and keep yourself
concealed as my mother brings a blood-stained stiletto which she

purposes to make you bathe in the lifeblood of your enemy. Never mind the Death-demons and skeletons dripping with the putrefaction of the grave, that occasionally may blast your straining eyeballs. Persevere even though Hell and destruction should yawn beneath your feet."

When he was getting *Zastrozzi* published Shelley was already naming his price for a new romance, and this was probably *St. Irvyne ; or, The Rosicrucian.* He had left Eton when it appeared, and it then bore on the title page the words " By a Gentleman of the University of Oxford " ; yet it is a further exhibition of his schoolboy and family-circle industry, and properly accompanies *Zastrozzi*. It betrays the time spent in perusing *Zofloya*, and William Godwin's *St. Leon.* By way of commemorating the centenary of Shelley's death Andrew Lang read *St. Irvyne* and wrote an ironical notice of it. With some justice he says that Shelley's style here " is more like that of a Baboo than an Englishman . . ." " ' Red thunder-clouds, borne on the wing of the midnight whirlwind, floated, at fits, athwart the crimson-coloured orbit of the moon,' Shelley begins, and you feel at once that this is to be no tame record of middle-class life." To Lang the book " proves that Shelley at Oxford was a donkey, and also demonstrates that we can never tell how a young wild ass may turn out." But the comment misses the main point. Shelley was attempting a hit in the favourite style. He was not wrong in noticing that there was a big audience for the kind of thing, and the dream of the book's " selling mechanically to the circulating libraries " had some sense in it.

At Windsor Shelley became friendly with one who in real life appeared more romantic than any invention ; certainly Dr. James Lind, one of the King's physicians, and a Fellow of the Royal Society, was a strange personage. Many years earlier he has gone out to China as a surgeon, and to Iceland on a scientific expedition with Sir Joseph Banks. He was an astronomer. He had his own printing press and made hieroglyphs for use with it. Antiquities and pictures graced his house, and his trellised and crowded garden is said to have helped in the imagining of a poem called " The Sensitive Plant." Even now that he was past seventy Dr. Lind was innocently delighted with " tricks, conundrums and queer things." A tall, thin, white-haired man, he understood the boy with the deep blue eyes who revealed to him school problems and great intentions. In practical affairs Lind knew how to assist Shelley, who " never mentioned his name without love and veneration."

This kind, unusual physician was to become a figure in Shelley's first poems of wide scope—poems which after the passing of years were still in some degree tales of wonder. If it is ever necessary now to correct the story that Lind and Shelley joined in a sort of commination service against George III, the pages of Edward Dowden contain the facts ; but Lind stands clear of such imputations in Shelley's portrait of him :

> with hair of silver white,
> And lips where heavenly smiles would hang and blend
> With his wise words ; and eyes whose arrowy light
> Shone like the reflex of a thousand minds . . .
> Yet calm and gentle and majestical.

The delightful association of Lind and Shelley helps us to approach the old question whether Shelley's life at Eton was unhappy and disastrous. On that his friend Peacock comments, " Shelley often spoke to me of Eton, and of the persecutions he had endured from the elder boys, with feelings of abhorrence which I never heard him express in an equal degree in relation to any other subject, except when he spoke of Lord Chancellor Eldon. He told me that he had been provoked into striking a penknife through the hand of one of his young tyrants, and pinning it to the desk, and that this was the cause of his leaving Eton prematurely ; but his imagination often presented past events to him as they might have been, not as they were. Such a circumstance must have been remembered by others if it had actually occurred." Leigh Hunt believed that Shelley " was taken from Eton before the regular period for leaving school," but not on account of the penknife incident : " his unconventional spirit, penetrating, sincere, and demanding the justice of things, was found to be inconvenient."

Possibly there is no final answer except that Shelley at Eton had some misery and some serenity, and that his last known allusion to his school speaks of the serenity. His worst days were seemingly the earliest. He provoked enemies, he also attracted friends ; and, the custom being to present friends on leaving with finely bound books, it is significant that he was able to take to Oxford an array of these. Another general custom was kept by boys leaving Eton : they composed verses of gratitude to the school and these were read aloud at a social gathering. There is no such copy of verses in Shelley's juvenilia ; but they may have been written. A small point arises out of one more leaving custom. Boys would then cut their names on one of the panels in Upper School. The name Shelley appears there twice, as if signifying a double portion of regard for the place. But in his time Eton boasted a man who would cut the name for you on payment of half a crown, and who perhaps gave Shelley value for a five shilling piece.

After the owner departed the name did not depend for remembrance among the boys on its being carved in the wood-work. It carried too many good stories, or bad. Evidence is wanting that it was Shelley who during a rat hunt caught one animal of incredible age and size and a most spectral whiteness, and identified him as the ghost of the Founder. A story with early authority is that of Shelley blowing up a dotterel tree, or a forest of trees of all kinds, by means of a burning glass and some gunpowder. This was solemnly published in the *Quarterly Review* by a nephew of the poet Coleridge, as exhibiting Shelley's destructive malice. While the majority who heard such anecdotes took it that Shelley was a freak, a few knew that he was a writer of genius, and though their enthusiasm was tempered with regret and reprobation for his private life they were proud that Eton had once again bred one of the English poets.

Tales of Shelley at school do not point to his being yet the indignant observer of politics, the tireless supporter of public benefits. No sign remains of his taking an interest in a project of his father's. Timothy at the beginning of 1810 was busy with his bill then " passing through the House of Commons, for reviving the ancient Roman road, leading to Arundel, Bognor, and Chichester, from near Dorking." That is, the Stane Street, which ran hard by Field Place. " This great public improvement, effected by the spirit and exertions of some gentlemen in Surrey and Sussex, will shorten the distance to Bognor and Arundel seven miles, and to Chichester two miles, besides passing through a level and fine part of the country."

During the years 1809 and 1810 Shelley was not thinking more of his school friendships, studies and dilemmas than of his cousin Harriet Grove. It was felt in the family that he might marry this fresh and pretty girl, to whom (in the words of her brother) he " was at that time more attached than I can express." He chose a pink dress for her in 1809 ; he confided his literary ideas to her, though the volume by *Victor and Cazire* when he sent it in March, 1810, was doubtfully received. They were sometimes together when the Grove family came to stay at Field Place, sometimes at Ferne in Wiltshire, the home of the Groves ; and one especially happy month was passed in London while both families were guests of one of the Groves in Lincoln's Inn Fields. " Bysshe was full of life and spirits, and very well pleased with his successful devotion to " Harriet. Why then did nothing come of such hopes ?

The reason seems to be that they were both very young, and had yet to find themselves ; or that Harriet was of a disposition too quiet and careful to be wholly or long pleased with Shelley's incorrect bursts of intellectual passion. Her diary, brief and un-coloured, reflects that divergency ; and Charles Grove mentions that after the holiday in London, when Shelley and Harriet had resumed their constant correspondence, " she became uneasy at the tone of his letters on speculative subjects, at first consulting my mother, and subsequently my father also on the subject." Those talks were the beginning of the end, for the judgment of the squire of Ferne was that he did not think the marriage would be for his daughter's happiness. We may wonder if Thomas Grove had ever been much in favour of Shelley as a son-in-law. Mr. Grove was the man who bought Peter Beckford's pack of fox-hounds, and to whom, probably, the sporting classic entitled *Thoughts on Hunting* was addressed.

The disappointment at Field Place was considerable, and Shelley naturally felt it worst. It sounds like the age of Sensibility indeed, and almost a quotation from a novel of the period, to hear that Elizabeth Shelley would watch her brother narrowly in his state of dejection, and accompany him anxiously in his walks with his dog and gun. Whether Shelley's life would have been less bewildering, or his poetry less glorious, had he married his cousin Harriet, is a mystery ; at least his dejection, which belonged to the last months of 1810, passed from him or was much modified by his activities at Oxford. No poem of his mature years turns or perhaps even touches on the possibility that Harriet Grove might have been his wife, unless she is among the veiled ladies in his " Epipsychidion." In November, 1811, she married William Helyar of Coker Court, Somerset, and she lived until December, 1867.

IV

OXFORD

"SHELLEY," his cousin writes, "was sent to *University College* because his father had been at that college, and *Sir Philip Sidney* a benefactor of it." In April, 1810, Sir John Shelley-Sidney nominated him for the Leicester Exhibition which explains the last part of the statement, and on April 10th Shelley went to the College to enter his name. The appearance of the college had undergone changes since his father's days and was more like what we now see. The chapel and the hall especially " had undergone a considerable alteration under the directing taste of Dr. Griffith, the Master, by the lengthening of the windows, the addition of buttresses, battlements and pinnacles, and the changing of the former clumsy centre into an elegant Gothic bow window and pediment." The dream of the past which in one form made Shelley fabricate *Zastrozzi* was present in another to steadier minds,—was curiously redecorating the face even of Oxford.

Entrance was not a troublesome ritual. Shelley had first to find his new tutor ; the tutor, no doubt with a preliminary polite allusion to Etonian attainments, inquired about his reading and requested him to translate at sight some lines from Homer and Virgil. Then he brought the candidate into the presence of the master, who having in turn gone through the business with Homer and Virgil, caused him to write and sign the declaration on admission in a folio register, a few pages further on from an example by Timothy Shelley. "Lubens subscribo " ; the person who sought admission gladly accepted the statutes, and the XXXIX Articles of the Church of England. If Shelley was like most young men who have signed or will sign such forms he hardly realised what might depend upon it. The repetition of the rite before the Vice-Chancellor did not teach him. The subscription was something for which Oxford had fought obstinately for ages ; not many years later it inspired Tom Moore to write a witty little " Scene from a Play, acted at Oxford, called ' Matriculation.' " Next Shelley received his tutor's directions for reading and other hints, and went back to Eton to spend his last summer half.

University College in 1810 was a society of about 200 members but a much smaller number in residence, a dozen being Fellows.

If it had a distinguishing aim among the other colleges, that has not been identified ; its leaders were content to go on in the old ways, apart from the architecture. James Griffith, D.D., the Master from 1808, was a friendly man, as his colleagues observed when they presented him with a set of silver plate in 1806. The portrait of him now hanging in the hall shows his sensibility and courtesy. He was an amateur architect and a water-colourist who could fill his sketchbooks with good topographical drawings ; he practised also what sounds almost a black art, namely, burning pictures in wood with a poker. The results—since such things have not been seen lately—were finer than might be imagined, and needed a good craftsmanship. The altar-piece in the chapel, a copy of Carlo Dolci's " Salvator Mundi," was a specimen of the Master's dexterity and munificence.

But another personality besides the kindly Griffith was power-ful in the college—George Rowley the Dean. He is named as one of the two tutors concerned with Shelley. The Rev. Mr. Rowley was not greatly inclined to searing pictures in wood, or even watching Griffith with his implements in the room where it was done. He was more turbulent, and sometimes looked for trouble. One question is said to have been agitating the College just then. It is difficult to-day to feel that the senior common room and the undergraduates were at odds because Lord Grenville had been lately elected Chancellor of the University, but the assertion is made by one of those undergraduates, who would persuade us that such political prejudices were a disadvantage to Shelley's college life.

The competitors for the Chancellorship, which had been a welcome topic to the political journalists, had been thus characterised by their enemies : Lord Eldon a *novus homo*, Lord Grenville a Papist, and the Duke of Beaufort a fox-hunter. If Eldon, a University College scion, became Chancellor it might follow that blessings in the form mostly of church preferments would flow towards that College. Grenville however gained the day. " By his family and his connexions, as well as by disposition, Shelley was attached to the successful side ; and although it was manifest that he was a youth of an admirable temper, of rare talents and unwearied industry, and likely therefore to shed a lustre upon his college and the university itself, yet, as he was eminently delighted at that wherewith his superiors were offended, he was regarded from the beginning with a jealous eye." Political rancour in the early nineteenth century was bitter enough, and it may have been so within the walls of a college ; Shelley does not refer to it in reviewing his Oxford terms.

He came into residence at the " bell-chiming and cloistered "
place at the beginning of Michaelmas term, 1810. He had so far
no reason to be in a mood of discontent,—

> The Chapel, voted a terrific bore,
> The Dons, headpieces for the College door,—

but must have been really pleased with his prospects. His father
made the journey with him to see him comfortably settled, and
Timothy, poor man, was feeling uncommonly cheerful. Calling
on the son of his old boarding-house-keeper, Mr. Shelley found
that another son whom he had known was now in business as a
bookseller ; he marched off with Bysshe to the shop and ordered
him to buy his books and stationery there. The handsome shop
was almost opposite University College. To Henry Slatter and his
partner he said, " My son here has a literary turn ; he is already
an author, and do pray indulge him in his printing freaks." The
spirit of irony could not have been more gratified than with this
unsuspicious recommendation, as will duly appear. Slatter and
Munday were printers and publishers as well as booksellers. In
1803 they had published the second edition of a noble poem
called " Gebir," by Walter Savage Landor. It is probable that
they drew young Shelley's attention to it, since at Oxford he
was always reciting favourite passages from it.

Two months before Shelley a boy from Durham Grammar
School had signed the admission register at University College,
and he may have spent the summer of 1810 in residence. His
name was Thomas Jefferson Hogg. The family was well-to-do,
thanks to Hogg's grandfather who made a fortune as agent to
the Dean and Chapter of Durham Cathedral. The boy was
reserved and whimsical, perplexing his mother sometimes by his
assumed manner ; he was a close student and grammarian.
Beneath his quiet appearance an ambition to amaze the world
was waiting, and chance brought Shelley into his company
almost the first time Shelley dined in hall. The conversation had
led to an alliance of independent wits, based on their feeling
that the rest of the world was rather dense and ought to be
enlightened. In after years Hogg was to compile and write an
unfinished biography of Shelley which has been incautiously used
by his successors, unaware of his extraordinary egotism. The best
of it is the earliest written part describing Shelley at Oxford, but
even that must be understood as partly due to Hogg's notion that
he was a humorous genius entitled to a very free use of literal
truth, as well as a calm and senior mind capable of viewing a
young erratic Shelley with educational patience.

The first impressions of Shelley in Hogg's narrative show that the hobby of scientific experiments, and perhaps the same old electrical machine, had come up to Oxford with the boy. Shelley's rooms in the south-west corner of the principal quadrangle were soon inspected by his new acquaintance, who found them newly painted, papered and furnished but far from tidy. " Books, boots, papers, shoes, philosophical instruments, clothes, pistols, linen, crockery, ammunition, and phials innumerable, with money, stockings, prints, crucibles, bags and boxes, were scattered on the floor and in every place. . . . An electrical machine, an air-pump, the galvanic trough, a solar microscope, and large glass jars and receivers, were conspicuous amidst the mass of matter." These were not all, but Hogg's scrutiny was soon interrupted by business ; he had to turn the handle of the electrical machine in order that Shelley might be electrified, and he must have worked hard, for he declares that Shelley's " long, wild locks bristled and stood on end." For all this Shelley's own interest in scientific recreations did not continue undiminished at Oxford. His literary inventions superseded the others ; and then he found no encouragement as a scientist from the classical Hogg or the spirit of the place. Lectures and demonstrations were indeed given but, according to Hogg, after speeding to hear an old gentleman on mineralogy, Shelley came back determined never to go again.

Outside lecture rooms Shelley at Oxford was almost madly industrious. " No student ever read more assiduously. He was to be found, book in hand, at all hours ; reading in season and out of season ; at table, in bed, and especially during a walk ; not only in the quiet country, and in retired paths ; not only at Oxford, in the public walks, and High Street, but in the most crowded thoroughfares of London." How far this reading followed the requirements of the college is not clear, but Hogg says that Shelley wrote the prescribed words " once a week—a Latin translation of a paper in the *Spectator*." Thomas de Quincey, who was at Oxford a year or two before, had the impression that his tutor and he only exchanged three sentences during his entire stay. Hogg implies that this non-communication was usual. We are told of Shelley's visits to his tutor, but they did not succeed well ; he came under reproof and his wickedly perfect politeness aggravated the tutor. Whether Mr. Rowley or Mr. Davison told him to read Plato or not, besides Xenophon, some Greek plays and some Shakespeare, Shelley read those at the time.

But reading did not fill up his hours. He lost hardly a moment in ensuring that the bookseller patronised by his father indulged

him in his printing freaks, and freakish in truth his first Oxford
publication was. He had hardly been at the University a month
when he sent out " Posthumous Fragments of Margaret Nicholson.
Being Poems found amongst the Papers of that noted Female
who attempted the Life of the King in 1786. Edited by John
Fitzvictor." Who else would have thought of this ridiculous
imposture, or troubled to work it out ? Even Shelley had to be
kept at it by the printer's man, and would answer the call with
stanzas written while the messenger waited. Yet Hogg claims to
have suggested the title and to have shared in the versifying.
Some lascivious lines which were cut out from the copy sent to
Shelley's mother were ascribed to " a friend's mistress." Timothy
Shelley was not let into the secret of the authorship of any of it.
Hogg would have it that the book was mere burlesque, deliberate
" essence of nonsense," but Shelley can scarcely get away with
that. The air-beating romantic, not the jester wrote these efforts
in sentiment and sublimity. " St. Irvyne " of which something
has been said came out next ; then a vanished tract called an
" Essay on Love " ; and then Hogg and he collaborated in a
novel called *Leonora*. Messrs. Slatter and Munday found it full
of dangerous opinions, and it was taken to Mr. King the printer
at Abingdon.

The Christmas vacation of 1810 caused Shelley some pain.
Harriet Grove, Timothy Shelley, Mrs. Shelley and others showed
disapproval of his arguments on the nature of things and the
existence of a deity, and he returned to college all the more intent
on this subject. It was not one which his most liberal friends
would like to see him treating with his natural excitement in a
stronghold of orthodoxy, where to suggest that a bishop might
be fallible was liable to be termed blasphemy. " Oxford,"
Robert Southey wrote, " is a school for divinity, and for nothing
else." Shelley overlooked such disadvantages or went ahead all
the more flamingly in defiance of them. His theological rebellion
was not his only interest : he had discovered logic, attending the
lectures of one of the Fellows—Matthew Rolleston, a prize-poet
also—and saw it as an exciting aid to his work for a brave new
world. He was watching the news of the political front with keen
eyes. And as fast as he could use a pen, he was trying to catch
young Oxford with his authorship. His father essayed to direct
this enthusiasm by urging him to compete for a poetry prize,
and supplied him with information on the subject proposed
which a learned Sussex parson had been employed to gather.

In all his own plans Shelley essayed to create round himself
the sensation of importance and urgency, and he had a method.

Even at school, if his cousin Medwin does not mistake, he had begun baiting a prelate with letters on dogma. He did not much care who his distinguished victims were, so long as he could lure them into letter-writing on his views. Having seen a quarto poetry-book by a precocious child who afterwards became Mrs. Hemans he sent her some of his startling epistles, until her mamma intervened. A set of verses now lost equipped the first move on Walter Scott, whose reply was regarded at Field Place as a great honour. Scott commended the idylls in the style of Gesner, but gave admonitions. " I must warn you against suffering yourself to suppose that the power of enjoying natural beauty, and poetical description, is necessarily connected with that of producing poetry. . . . I would also caution you against an enthusiasm which, while it argues an excellent disposition and a feeling heart, requires to be watched and restrained, tho' not repressed." These and other kindly precepts were appropriate enough for Shelley, but since they recur almost *verbatim* in a letter from Scott to another young poet in 1811 they were in all likelihood Scott's standard defence in such emergencies.

On March 2nd, 1811, Shelley tried to open a correspondence with a busy man who was later to become very much his friend, the editor of the reformist newspaper *The Examiner*. A government prosecution of the proprietors for an attack on military flogging had been unsuccessful, and Shelley perceived his opportunity. His tactics were quite neat : " Sir,—Permit me, although a stranger, to offer my sincerest congratulations on the occasion of that triumph so highly to be prized by men of liberality ; permit me also to submit to your consideration, as one of the most fearless enlighteners of the public mind at the present time, a scheme . . ."

One week later according to an *Oxford Herald* advertisement Shelley published " A Poetical Essay on the Existing State of Things." He meant the profits for a friend of liberty, Peter Finnerty, who had offended authority by attempting to write a critical history of the Walcheren expedition, and was now in Lincoln gaol for a " libellous " Letter to Lord Castlereagh. Probably this Irish journalist's imprisonment was not alleviated by any profits from the poem, though Shelley sent money to his fund ; for no copy of it has come to light. On the evidence of a motto from Southey on the title-page advertised, it would have been a story of want and hunger. Dowden surmised that it was an early form of part of " Queen Mab." Its motto however hints a connection with the Wordsworthian narrative of a mother and her son broken in battle which is represented by a few stanzas in Shelley's works, headed " A Tale of Society as It Is : From Facts. 1811."

> And now cold charity's unwelcome dole
> Was insufficient to support the pair ;
> And they would perish rather than would bear
> The law's stern slavery, and the insolent stare
> With which law loves to rend the poor man's soul—
> The bitter scorn, the spirit-sinking noise
> Of heartless mirth which women, men, and boys
> Wake in this scene of legal misery.

Shelley's lines were not yet such as to certify the rise of a new poet, but they were better than any of his verses since the " Verses on a Cat."

However, as he saw the world in the first months of 1811 from his window not far from the Chapel of University College, those things were subordinate. The big thing was to get people to reconsider the question of God. " Oxford formed the advanced squadron of the English Church ; and by way of a *coup d'essai*, though in itself a bagatelle, what if he should begin with con- verting Oxford ? " During the Christmas vacation he had probably delivered at his printers in Worthing the manuscript of a short specimen of logic, called " The Necessity of Atheism." The printing-house was mainly managed by a clever girl named Philadelphia Phillips who liked Shelley and taught him something of the trade ; so in spite of the ominous title the work was printed. With Hogg's help Shelley had prepared what both thought an unanswerable argument against the accepted notion of God, or at least one which should stir up some powerful reasoner for it. " The senses are the source of all knowledge to the mind." This was the postulate. Dowden's comment is as good as any : " If Shelley's postulate—one common to many thinkers of the eighteenth century—be admitted as true, a logical mind will find it difficult to avoid arriving at Shelley's conclusion."

The writer's name did not appear on the pamphlet. With a glorious parcel of copies from Worthing, while speedy publication was being advertised, Shelley became blissfully busy that February. He had his apprehensions, but they melted into light as he dispatched copy after copy with covering letters signed Jeremiah Stukely or Charles Peyton. These copies went to all university officers, professors and heads of houses in Oxford ; probably to many of their counterparts at Cambridge ; to every bishop in the kingdom, and to others as Shelley decided. But why should these great ones be the only mortals with access to

" The Necessity of Atheism " ? The obvious and handy answer was Messrs. Slatter and Munday's shop-window ; true, these men had shown themselves reluctant to be converted when Shelley obliged them with his logic in person. A bold stroke was wanted,—and it was made easier because Shelley was so familiar a figure to the booksellers' men. Early one morning Shelley entered the shop, strewed the windows and counters with the pamphlets and told the assistant to sell them at sixpence each. This in a manner constituted publication, and lasted twenty minutes. Then entered the Rev. John Walker of New College, who " was attracted by the novelty of the title, to examine the contents." In horror he called for the booksellers, gave them a sermon, and supervised the burning of the copies in the back shop.

Slatter and Munday sent for the author, and he came. They had the assistance of Councillor Clifford, a barrister who had become something of a hero a year or two earlier for leading public opposition to new prices for seats in the London theatres ; but no appeals softened Shelley, not threats even. He was " quite unconcerned," and pointed out that his pamphlet was already in the hands of the Vice-Chancellor and on the breakfast tables of all heads of houses. All that the firm could do was to warn the Worthing printers that they might be prosecuted, and advise the destruction of all copies, the manuscript and everything pertaining to " The Necessity of Atheism."

There perhaps the episode might have ended, but it did not. It was Shelley's belief that the Rev. Edward Copleston of Oriel College, an astute man who could be unorthodox himself, and had had the pamphlet, took the trouble to place the authorship and to inform the University College common-room. De Quincey gives another account of the growing storm ; according to him, the circulation of the pamphlet was an irregularity so conspicuous that the heads of houses met specially to consider it. They knew pretty well who the author was, for it was common knowledge by March 10th. At their meeting, out of forbearance for one so young, they resolved to take no notice of the pamphlet. But then, if De Quincey can be believed, Shelley's all-round bombardment with the copies and letters appealing for reason obliged them to meet again. Very understandably they assembled with irritation and agreed on " certain formalities." As one of their number Dr. Griffith bore their decision to University College, and something had to be done.

The Master must have been sadly bothered by all this. He had heard queer charges against Shelley already ; somebody, either Shelley or the devil, had been posting godless propositions on the door of the chapel. Yet he was not the man to condemn a youth for ever because of such follies. But again these were much talked about, and Shelley's peculiar literary productions too, in other colleges as well as at home. Whatever the Master might do to balance these considerations for himself, he was bound to call a meeting of the seven or eight Fellows in reach, and bring the offender before them.

This meeting took place on the morning of March 25th, 1811. When Shelley came in, he was shown the pamphlet and some notes with it in a hand suspiciously like his. The Master asked him if he could or would deny that the pamphlet was by him. Shelley was stubbornly silent on the point. Any hope that the matter might fall by his disowning the thing, a convenient un-truth, was soon lost. Even Dr. Griffith grew out of temper and Shelley was sent from the room. Sentence on him was being drafted when a manly action by the usual companion of Shelley disturbed the Fellows. " T. J. Hogg immediately appeared, voluntarily on his part, to state that if Shelley had anything to do with it, he (Hogg) was equally implicated, and desired his share of the penalty whatever was inflicted." This development pre-sented no difficulty to such as George Rowley, who perhaps had looked out of the window to see Hogg and Shelley walking up and down the centre of the quadrangle as if proud of their anticipated fate ; " all men are vain, but all hate vanity." The official account which has here been used defines that fate : " Towards the afternoon a large paper bearing the college seal, and signed by the Master and Dean, was affixed to the hall door, declaring that the two offenders were publicly expelled from the college *for contumacy in refusing to answer certain questions put to them.*"

Even if we assume that the Dean and others knew a great deal about Shelley and Hogg, this was a violent revenge for contumacy. Even if those two had scented trouble, they must have been distinctly battered. Shelley had been talking to Hogg about the regrettable shortness of an Oxford career, a few years merely, and now he was being flung out after only a few months. In his wildest moments he had followed a reasonable hope, namely that in the headquarters of debate his wish to see religion logically analysed would find fair and candid disputants. Oxford had not taken the pamphlet in the right way at all. And then there were so many things to clear up, including the now dusty frictional electrical machine—work for days even with a muscular scout and the sympathy of the college porter. For in spite of his atheism, his worrying round with printing and printer's devils, his dining so seldom with the rest in hall, his unusual clothes and their misadventures, " all acknowledged him to have been very good-humoured and of a kind disposition." He was still Shelley from Field Place in the county of Sussex, and something in that made it easier for the sporting types round him to talk to him than to the sardonic intellectual Hogg.

It was made known to the two that they could if they wished take a day or two over their departure ; but they booked places for a London coach of the next morning. Shelley scampered about Oxford to arrange his affairs there and say his good-byes. Although his friend Hogg asserts that the sentence of expulsion threw Shelley into a painful agitation, he did not betray that to others not so intimate. He appeared indeed to meet the misfortune with cool resolution, and declared his intention of emigrating to America. At Wadham College a poet and divine named Charles Strong, who had been helped by Shelley to get subscriptions for the poetry book of one Janetta Phillips, was not grateful. He said that he hoped never again to set eyes on the atheist. Shelley had happier memories of Wadham than this. A Horsham friend had entertained him there one evening with Thomas Barnes, the future editor of *The Times*. In all things Barnes was a hard man to please ; he loved poetry and poets but he chose them strictly. Long afterwards in his editorial overwork he recalled how graceful, delightful and hopeful Shelley had seemed to him that evening at Oxford.

The business which Shelley got through on March 25th, 1811, was various. He joined his booksellers Slatter and Munday in a contract which they might have been expected to avoid ; with him they signed a bond for £800 respecting the copyright of a mass of manuscript about Sweden. It was the work of Mr. Bird, whose real name was John Brown ; he had a pathetic tale to tell of the oppression he had endured in the Navy and his forced resignation. He had already derived £150 from Shelley. This generous youth, now making himself responsible for £800 more, had not money in his pockets for his immediate wants, and Hogg was no better provided ; a visit to one of the Slatters produced the loan of £20. A call at the tailors with pantaloons for repair was soon over. Since he came to college Shelley, as the extant tailor's bill shows, had treated himself well in fine raiment. A Superfine Blue Coat Velvet Collar and Gilt Buttons, another of an Olive colour, figured or striped Marcella waistcoats, One Pair Patent Silk Braces are typical items. The total effect had not pleased every observer in University College, where a newcomer would be regarded as one scarcely entitled to golden opinions and gilt buttons together.

Much is contained in Hogg's recollections of the habits of his friend at Oxford, and it is notable that neither authorship nor winter kept Shelley from his country excursions. It is not easy to map them now. The walk to Shotover Hill with its greensward at the top, its outlook on wide country, its woods and thickets, as well loved by undergraduates then as now, was certainly a favourite ; and on the way Shelley lingered at a pond in a disused quarry which offered his companion no attraction " apart from a certain wildness and barrenness." But scenes like that had for Shelley a mysterious presence, and we have his description of " an adventure " which may be ascribed to the neighbourhood of Headington Quarry. " I was walking with a friend, engaged in earnest and interesting conversation. We suddenly turned the corner of a lane, and the view, which its high banks and hedges had concealed, presented itself. The view consisted of a windmill, standing in one among many plashy meadows, enclosed with stone walls ; the irregular and broken ground, between the wall and the road on which we stood ; a long low hill behind the windmill, and a grey covering of uniform cloud spread over the evening sky. It was that season when the last leaf had just fallen from the scant and stunted ash. The scene surely was a common scene ; the season and the hour little calculated to kindle lawless thought ; it was a tame uninteresting assemblage of objects, such as would drive the imagination for refuge in serious and sober talk to the evening fireside, and the dessert of winter fruits and wine. The effect which it produced on me was not such as could have been expected. I suddenly remembered to have seen that exact scene in some dream of long "—but at this point, though he was writing five years afterwards, Shelley was so strongly affected that he had to drop the pen and escape from the subject. Besides Shotover the towing-path of the Isis and Bagley Wood hold his memory, though he and his companion were not apt to study the precise places through which they talked along. Over their expeditions Shelley threw the haze of his romantic fiction, playing the game of enchanter's country.

This fancy however did not reduce the country character in Shelley to nothing. Hogg was struck by it : " it was his delight to strike boldly into the fields, to cross the country daringly on foot, as is usual with sportsmen in shooting ; to perform, as it were, a pedestrian steeplechase. He was strong, light and active, and in all respects well suited for such exploits." On occasion Shelley, who was a good shot, took out his pair of duelling pistols.

So armed, he gave rise to more than ordinary curiosity in college ; the sight " formed a very remarkable contrast with his mild aspect and pacific habits."

Those who desire to recall Shelley in the country round Oxford must do so without any gracious word from him on its beauties ; he wrote no " Thyrsis," no " Scholar Gipsy." It is through Hogg's local sketches with their element of burlesque that we try to realise him in and about the city ; and the devotee crossing Magdalen Bridge will now and then remember one of Hogg's best and perhaps truest stories. There the young amateur in philosophy and theology will still seem to be grasping the baby in the arms of the young mother passing by, and enquiring " in a piercing voice, and with a wistful look, ' Will your baby tell us anything about pre-existence, madam ? ' " But it is at University College that the clearest memories abide, all passion spent, and history accepted with simplicity. The conflict of traditions and tempers which came to a bitter decision on March 25th, 1811, will be discussed more strenuously in other settings than mine. Wherever it is reviewed, few will judge that Shelley was not extremely unlucky in running into such trouble at so early a stage in an undergraduate's life.

Had he proceeded beyond his poor six months at Oxford, surely Shelley would have discovered more to please him, alike in the architecture and gardens, the books and music, the intellectual companies and the personal intimacies. His delight in the river at Eton would have been continued in summer explorations here among the streams which John Keats was soon to know, " more in number than your eyelashes." Friendships other than Hogg's were promised ; as it was, he was visited by many Etonians ; moreover he attracted by his sincerity and eagerness. Nobody without some charm could have drawn subscriptions to Janetta Phillips's poetry book from older members of University College (other than Hogg). And then, what a talkers' paradise Oxford always was ! If the writings of Shelley so far were chiefly imitative, in borrowed plumes, in his talk he was directly expressing his ideas ; he exulted in talking. He wanted to converse and dispute with the best minds in Oxford, but opportunities were as yet rare.

When Slatter and Munday failed to " reclaim the waywardness of his imagination " by *their* talk, they thought they could still do it by bringing a better reasoner—a Mr. Hobbes who though he published a long poem called " The Widower " was a philosopher like his namesake. Shelley quite readily entered into the oral argument ; it was only when Hobbes sent a long document refuting the points of " The Necessity of Atheism " that he declined to go on, announcing anew that he wished to address the bishops, any or all. Even that pamphlet was a means to an end, for the notes tucked into it challenged the learned recipients to argue the non-existence of God at any convenient time in the schools. Coleridge himself cannot have been more inclined to dialogue or monologue than young Shelley, whose ardour made his Oxford contemporaries aware of him even if they pretended that he dined on arsenic and aqua-fortis ; a slight sign that he was beginning to be a local celebrity is noted by De Quincey, who saw in London a little Indian-ink sketch of Shelley in cap and gown. A queer echo of all this comes from Oxford ten years later, when the poet T. L. Beddoes reported that Shelley Harris, a foolish creature, was going round in ecstasy over Byron's writings. This enthusiast was a grandson of Sir Bysshe by his second marriage.

The morning coach from Oxford to London on March 26th, 1811, duly conveyed Shelley and Hogg. Having arrived, Shelley called on his cousins the Groves in Lincoln's Inn Fields and Thomas Medwin in the Temple. The hunt for lodgings came to an end at No. 15 Poland Street, which can still be seen a few steps out of Oxford Street. The choice as Hogg says was Shelley's, since the name of the street " reminded him of Thaddeus of Warsaw, and of freedom." Their plan was on the face of it simple : to continue the partnership of minds which but for that trouble over the tract on religious assumptions would have ripened steadily at Oxford. The only other literary association of Poland Street is that Dr. Burney had lived there, but nowadays it is difficult to see any reason for his doing so unless it were Shelley's reason.

V

ENGLAND, WALES, SCOTLAND, IRELAND

LONDON as Shelley found it in 1811 was a wartime capital, haunted by one obstinate bogeyman. On the day of the expulsion from Oxford George Cruikshank published a cartoon of Elliston the manager of the Surrey Theatre in the character of " Sylvester Daggerwood " singing the song of " Bonaparte." The audience was represented as contemptuous, but fascinated by this study of Napoleon. Poor crazy creature, and French moreover, he remained at the top of the European bill ; his measure of seizing the continental ports and harassing those he did not seize might prove a serious problem for Londoners. For the time his control of the Continent was growing. Yet the year 1811 in London was not one of the most astonishing or agitating of those many war years, and Shelley might be almost as much interested in Lucien Bonaparte as in the dynast. Lucien, who had literary and scholarly tastes, and was writing an epic on Charlemagne, had recently gone to live at Ludlow in Shropshire, and Shelley (so his father heard) had opened a correspondence with him ; we may easily guess the topic.

At Field Place the results of that topic expressed in a reckless way had produced immediate pain and perplexity. Timothy Shelley was not an ungenerous father, and his discipline of his son had been modified by the feeling that the son had genius, so far as he knew what that was. He leaned towards freedom's side and thought himself an opponent of prerogative ; yet he was too long acquainted with the world to countenance an indiscretion like this. We may know him through his telling Shelley that he would not complain of a love affair but was not going to have an unconventional marriage. The present crisis was even more serious, endangering not only his son's career but the family name and character. Denying the necessity of the Monarchy was just conceivable and in the event of an English revolution would be respectable ; but the Deity of the Church of England had survived Gibbon's " solemn sneer " in Timothy's time, would scarcely become obsolete, and was very powerful.

Several remedies for Shelley's disorder occurred to Timothy. The earliest thought was to detach him from the monopolising

T. J. Hogg, who was suspected of hardening what was only a loose capricious heresy. For this purpose, remembering his own travels and taking the advice of that older traveller Sir Bysshe, Timothy offered Shelley a voyage to the Greek Islands. Napoleon might be threatening Britain's sea power, but that was not considered, and if example were needed the brilliant Lord Byron was somewhere out that way. "Travelling," Timothy reflected, " would of course dispel the gloomy ideas which he has too long fix'd on objects, tending to produce Temporary Insanity, it would have rais'd his depress'd spirits to a proper height of vivacity, and by placing him constantly in the presence of real dignity, bring him naturally to reflect on his *own*. Such a scheme I am confident would effect what no abstract reasoning can produce, dissipate all despairing doubts, tranquilise his perturb'd imagination ' et se sibi reddet amicum.' " But as Shelley refused to be parted from Hogg the Greek voyage was given up.

A similar refusal overthrew the request that Shelley would go home to Field Place to place himself in " the care and society " and obey the instructions of a gentleman to be appointed. The letter of April 5th, 1811 containing this plan was in a grim enough tone ; if it was rejected the father would " withdraw himself " from the son and leave him to the consequences of wickedness and audacity. By April 15th, this firmness backed up by Sir Bysshe had taken the form " No terms but unconditional submission can be admitted now." The happy touch, good sense or good luck had been wanting, for in spite of angry allusions to his father Shelley was as yet unwilling to be exiled from Field Place as well as his university. " I am convinced," his elder cousin John Grove informed Timothy, " that there is nothing he wishes more than to be on terms with you and all his family, but he has got into his head ideas which he will not be prevailed on to relinquish till he is convinced of their being wrong ; he is however very willing to be put right." Shelley's uncle Robert Parker also attempted to mend matters, and sent word, " He's a very acute reasoner and seems to be very fond of it."

At some earlier time or times Timothy had tried to lead his son into the sphere of political life and character by taking him to the House of Commons and pointing out what civil gentlemen the members all were ; and this introductory effort, quite reasonable in a family which played its part in active politics, was supplemented by several conversations between the Eton boy and the Duke of Norfolk. The Duke, compacted of fine perceptions and generous humanities together with a cynical acceptance of life as it is, was frank with Shelley. The sum of his advice was,

" You are young and able, English politics are a close preserve, go in immediately. Your rivals will be mostly stupid or lazy. It would be different if you ventured into the church, or the law, or literature." Now once again Timothy saw a possible solution in a talk with the Duke, who invited him to bring his son to dinner at Norfolk House. What happened is described by Charles Grove (sitting down to gather fragments of the long ago in his Wiltshire rectory). The proposal actually made was that Shelley should be brought in as member of parliament for Horsham. " I recollect the indignation Bysshe expressed after that dinner at what he considered an effort made to shackle his mind, and introduce him into life as a mere follower of the Duke. His father was puzzled what to do when that plan failed."

So the dispute went on, maintained largely by Shelley's subordinating everything to his wish to be proved right or wrong in a piece of reasoning. He was less likely to find merit in anything his father might say on that because he regarded him as in fact another sceptic who had not the courage to avow himself. Timothy was less likely to try reasoning as one scheme after another intended for Shelley's ultimate benefit was rejected :

> And to be wroth with one we love
> Doth work like madness in the brain.

More to embroil these antagonists, it happened that Timothy caused his solicitor William Whitton to send messages which had the effect of petrol on a bonfire. Who was Whitton to address Percy Bysshe Shelley so ? Within this commotion of the spring of 1811 a comparative lull was produced by the Duke of Norfolk and Shelley's uncle Captain Pilfold, who had fought under Nelson and was not desperately alarmed by pamphlets on atheism. Thanks to these friends Shelley was promised £200 a year, with freedom to live where and with what acquaintance he pleased, although the allowance depended on the leniency of his father.

This then was the early result, after Oxford, of Shelley's campaign against common notions of God. His difficulties, though he was too confident and aerial to be long bowed down by them, might appear even to him as difficulties ; but his campaign was not broken off. It was in fact urging his life into a fresh complication, which brings to mind the ancient proverb :

> The seeds of foulest sorrows be
> The fairest things there are to see.

The consequence of his anti-God letters to his Harriet Grove has been seen already ; but another Harriet was to be his, and indeed he had seen and spoken with her before he left Oxford. Their first meeting gave them no indication of the years before them.

Harriet Westbrook, whose clear and elegant beauty was not less than that of Harriet Grove, was at the school of Mrs. Fenning, Church House, Clapham, where Shelley's sisters were being taught. Not much is known of her family. They had, I think, been long established in the City. Her father, John Westbrook, vintner, made a fortune as proprietor of a coffee-house in Mount Street, near the Park, and lived close by ; he also had a house in Wales, and was a sociable man. Harriet was able to dress well and to prepare herself for a comfortable married life— with a clergyman, she sometimes fancied. One of the Shelley girls asked Shelley to take Harriet a present during the Christmas holidays ; and presently Harriet enabled him to communicate with his sister Elizabeth whom he was much concerned to convert to unorthodoxy. When he included Harriet herself in his mission, the girl was troubled : " You may conceive with what horror I first heard that Percy was an atheist ; at least so it was given out at Clapham. At first I did not comprehend the meaning of the word ; therefore when it was explained I was truly petrified. I wondered how he could live a moment professing such principles, and solemnly declared that he should never change mine. I little thought of the rectitude of these principles, and when I wrote to him I used to try to shake them—making sure he was in the wrong, and that myself was in the right. Yet I would listen to none of *his* arguments, so afraid I was that he should shake my belief."

This young lady was shepherded by a sister fourteen years older, black-haired Eliza, who took the friendship of Shelley to be a good thing and one extending the social round. His first impressions of Eliza were " a clever girl, though rather affected." Eliza thought for a moment or two of being in love with Shelley. Subsequent events may suggest that she actually was. For Harriet he appears to have had no feelings beyond liking, and the thought that here was a recruit perhaps for his campaign. His conversations with her were noticed to her disadvantage at school, and returning there from Easter holidays she was tormented. She was styled " an abandoned wretch," and Hellen Shelley alone stuck to her.

Through the spring of 1811 Shelley's mind could not rest from his theological enterprise, and he excluded much because of it. An instance is his estimate of a man who was then the most versatile of the Reformists. In the last weeks at University College

Shelley was seen addressing to Leigh Hunt a letter about a union of intelligent liberals, and he now had the opportunity to meet the man. About the beginning of May he called on a publisher in St. Paul's Churchyard, Rowland Hunter, with a manuscript poem. Hunter declined it but told him to show it to his relative Leigh Hunt, who on hearing of the matter sent Shelley an invitation. Now at this time Hunt was a young man of very many enthusiasms, writing, talking, politics, the classics, the fine arts, the theatre, music, law and lawgivers ; but from several visits Shelley only gave Hogg a report on Hunt's religious opinions. Hunt was, he said, a deist and some of his friends called him an atheist ; Mrs. Hunt, a most sensible woman, was rather a deist too. The editor of *The Examiner* remembered Shelley at nineteen as " a youth not come to his full growth ; very gentlemanly, earnestly gazing at every object that interested him, and quoting the Greek dramatists," or in another's paraphrase, " breathing the classic thoughts of college, ardent with aspirations for the emancipation of man from intellectual slavery, and endowed by Nature with an aspect truly ' angelic.' "

Still, London that summer was a spectacle which Shelley did not altogether ignore, and the exhibition of an earthly potentate brought his thoughts down from the celestial. The frolicsome Prince of Wales, who had been sworn in as Regent in February, did not let the commercial distress all round spoil the series of rejoicings. One famous fête was given at Carlton House on June 19th. The Regent was throned on crimson velvet in a vast conservatory ; among the table decorations were a fountain and canal with goldfishes in it, not to mention gudgeon which arrived unofficially and in the heat looked " fit for dishing up." Next day people were thronging to see these marvels, the Regent having kindly ordered that they should remain a day or two ; and Shelley was ready with a printed satire which he threw into the carriages. Few lines survive :

> By the mossy brink,
> With me the Prince shall sit and think,
> Shall muse in visioned Regency
> Rapt in bright dreams of dawning Royalty.

They suggest that the whole was a parody on Thomas Gray's " Ode on the Spring " with its comparison of sportive insects and human life.

This was not Shelley's only contribution to the play of witticisms on the Regent's gay parade or his person, for in 1812 he got out another broadside in which with careless freedom he

not only imitated an already famous ballad by Coleridge and
Southey but adopted its title. Another young poet, Byron, was
doing much the same a little later, but made it " The Devil's
Drive." Shelley's " Devil's Walk " was not equal to the original,
though the description of the prince was " beastly like."

> For he is fat,—his waistcoat gay
> When strained upon a levee day
>   Scarce meets across his princely paunch ;
> And pantaloons are like half-moons
>   Upon each brawny haunch.

At a later date Shelley preferred a quotation from the Book of
Job, chapter 15 : " Because he covereth his face with his fatness,
and maketh collops of fat on his flanks." The broadside was
risky ; but the government had plenty to do in suppressing more
notorious assailants without chasing the maker of these evanescent
verses.

Life was still defying his plans like theirs. After all the
partnership at No. 15 Poland Street did not endure. Hogg stayed
in London long enough to dine at Miller's Hotel " over Westminster Bridge " with Shelley and his father, and believed he
left a gentlemanly impression on Timothy, although his picture
of a port-coloured old noodle suggests that he should not have
cared in the least about that. Perhaps Hogg had lost more than
Shelley by the Oxford disaster, for he had had hopes of a Fellowship. He was now to prepare for a legal career and went away
to the office of a conveyancer at York, where he passed his days
quietly enough. This could not be said of Shelley, darting hither
and thither, intense, fantastic and lacking occupation. The
nearest he came to finding it was when he attended Abernethy's
anatomical lectures at St. Bartholomew's Hospital ; he had of
course his writing, but that was not yet quite real. His turmoil
remains in the letters which he scrawled, driven on in charge of
an idea, in chase of one, by the spirit of the age as well as his own
dreaming egotism.

In June, 1811, thanks to his maternal uncle in the navy he was
able to date some of these bubbling letters from Field Place ; but
his uncle bears no responsibility for a serio-comic series which
chanced to begin through visits to him at Cuckfield. One of the
two Pilfold girls was being taught by Miss Elizabeth Hitchener,
the schoolmistress at Hurstpierpoint. She was nearly thirty years
old but looked much younger, voluble, tall, thin, dark-com-
plexioned, with black eyes and black hair. Her father had been
one of the innumerable Sussex smugglers and kept an inn, but

she had made her own world, and was in her degree one of the phenomena of the revolutionary age. This made her seek the acquaintance of William Godwin. " I see a being," Shelley wrote to Miss Hitchener, " whose aim like mine is virtue," and soon afterwards " Your Christianity does not interfere with virtue : and why ? Because it is not Christianity ! " Interspersed with much about reason and nature and established religion some details of Shelley's movements went to this lady ; at the end of June he was going to Wales. " My excursion will be on foot, for the purpose of better remarking the manners and dispositions of the peasantry."

This new study might not be expected to keep Shelley walking long, but his destination in Wales promised to please and refresh his mind in a fond delay. He was invited to Mr. Thomas Grove's estate Cwm Elan, which had been celebrated in a delightful topographical poem by a tranquil clergyman, honoured by Wordsworth and Coleridge. Bowles prefixed to his poem a note which shows why Shelley might have found a true refuge : " Coombe-Ellen (in Welch Cwm Elan) is situated among the most romantic mountains of Radnorshire, about five miles from Rhayd'r.—Mr. Grove purchased ten thousand acres and upwards, which he has greatly improved, by draining and watering, and he resides there with his family some of the summer months. As a place, it is well worth the attention of the Poet, the Painter, and the practical Agriculturist." As for its proprietor, the dedication speaks : " To Thomas Grove, Esq., of Fern, in Wiltshire. Dear Sir, these Lines, written at your Summer Residence in Radnorshire, during a visit there, I beg to inscribe to you, as a testimony of esteem for an upright Magistrate, a humane, sincere and sensible Man. Oct. 17, 1798."

How enchanting all might prove, even if the prose or philanthropic part of the improvements were left to Mr. Grove or his son Thomas in succession to him ! Here glens, ravines, rocks and woods, torrents and pools, peasantry and peeping cultivation might charm dullness itself. But in his first letter from Cwm Elan Shelley did not write of those ; in the second he was struck by his own apathy. " I am now with people who, strange to say, never *think* : I have however much more of my own society than theirs. Nature is here marked with the most impressive characters of lordliness and grandeur. Once I was tremulously alive to tones and scenes : the habit of analysing feelings, I fear, does not agree with this. It is spontaneous ; and when it becomes subject to consideration, ceases to exist." Nevertheless Shelley observed, " This valley is covered with trees : so are partly the mountains that surround it," and, "I am not wholly uninfluenced by its tragic in my lonely walks. But I long for a thunderstorm."

It was not merely the question "What can be worse than the present aristocratical system?" which deprived Shelley of the bright tints of the trees on the crags, the music of the waters below, the romance and the fruitfulness of Cwm Elan. A problem in life was becoming his chief concern and obscuring the rest. Harriet Westbrook, pretty child and honest as pretty, had been in a state of wretchedness that summer, and she confided in him in letters which are not extant but which aroused his sense of responsibility. It was he who had disturbed her life by imparting the truth about received religion; he would be to blame if after the summer holidays she returned again into " a little hell of her own." Besides, she had been beautifully attentive when he was ill. In passing a word more is due to Harriet's situation. She had been brought up among the Methodists. Her father was a strict parent and allowed her and her sister but limited society. Hardly any mention is made of her mother, formerly a Miss Elliot,—the " Anne, wife of John Westbrook, esq., of Chapel-street, Grosvenor-square," named in the list of deaths on July 19th, 1819. There was much to make Harriet seek for someone like Shelley.

Feeling that his next decision might be far-reaching, Shelley in Wales made an attempt to know himself, and in spite of Hogg's interpretations he did not think that he was in love with Harriet. Still, it was growing clear that she was in love with him, and the discovery increased the appeal to his chivalry. August, 1811, arrived, and he decided at least to leave Cwm Elan for London, sending his cousin Charles Grove a letter on " what he termed his summons to link his fate with another," with one of his Eton applications of lines from *Macbeth* :

> Hear it not, Percy, for it is a knell
> That summons thee to heaven or to hell.

He found Harriet looking ill, but in a few days she was better; then when he went into Sussex she wrote of more troubles and coercions, and he returned to London. Whatever he had said against marriage, it now offered a way of rescuing Harriet, and when he proposed it she agreed. He told himself that he would have the high task of " moulding a really noble soul into all that can make its nobleness useful and lovely " ; what Harriet's plans were she did not then write, but they surely were summed in the joy of living with a being so bright as Shelley. What else in all the world was there to do?

Since Harriet's age was sixteen (and Shelley's nineteen)

marriage was not the simplest thing to achieve, but with the help of Charles Grove the method was settled. They would be married in Scotland. One morning late in August Shelley and his cousin had breakfast in a coffee-house in Mount Street with a hackney-coach waiting, and Harriet succeeded in joining them without delay. They drove to the city, left in the northern mail coach that evening, sent a note asking Hogg to lend them £10 on their way through York, arrived in Edinburgh. Then Shelley made it as certain as he could that Harriet should not be sent back to Miss Fenning's school. The marriage, which was not even a correct " Scottish marriage," was entered in the register, "August 28, 1811. Percy Bysshe Shelley, farmer, Sussex, and Miss Harriet Westbrook, daughter of Mr. John Westbrook, London." If Shelley thought of his poet Thomas Gray just then, perhaps the words were " Fair laughed the morn."

And then though cash was short they had all Edinburgh for their honeymoon. Their lodgings in George's Street were in a district of modern planning, much admired ; but they could wander in the Old Town with its extraordinary combination of buildings great and small, shapely and uncouth, ancient and modern. Beyond the city nature had supplied daring scenery and man had added a golf course. Shelley did not feel these things so much as the sins of society. Writing to Miss Hitchener several weeks later he said, " My uncle is a most generous fellow. Had he not assisted us, we should still have been chained to the filth and *commerce* of Edinburgh. Vile as aristocracy is, commerce—purse-proud ignorance and illiterateness—is more contemptible." Since Captain Pilfold does not take much more part in the story, he deserves a little more notice before we leave him. Considerably younger than Shelley's mother, he first went to sea as a midshipman in 1788, and in 1805 during the absence of his captain on a court-martial he commanded the *Ajax* in the victory of Trafalgar. On the next Christmas Day he was made post-captain and presented with a gold medal, and in 1808 his name was in the first list of Companions of the Bath. Duties at Plymouth occupied his later years, and he died at Stonehouse on July 12th, 1835.

Letters are often written in the expected mood of the recipient, and this must be allowed for in those written by Shelley to Miss Hitchener. Hogg, visiting his friend in the long vacation, did not find him in such glooms. In the handsome front parlour of a handsome house Shelley looked just as he used to look at Oxford. Hogg was given a room upstairs and altogether found one of the few lodgings which he did not condemn ; even the wine was good.

He did however lose a hat here and he says that " in those days a hat was a hat, costing thirty-five shillings at least." The friends resumed their outings together, even went to church without much benefit, and particularly enjoyed the comet of 1811. It was considered the baleful star of Napoleon, though in France it was believed to improve the vintage ; Shelley and Hogg contemplated it with some emotion in the clear night-sky over Princes Street. The poet knew something of ancient and modern astronomy.

Other studies occupied the mornings, and Shelley had the assistance of a good library ; he translated one of Buffon's works while Harriet translated a new moral tale, *Claire d'Albé*, by Madame Cottin. At tea-time, and there was lots of tea, Harriet might read one of her favourite novels aloud. Hogg was not in the least fond of these but he was taken with the reader. " If it was agreeable to listen to her, it was not less agreeable to look at her ; she was always pretty, always bright, always blooming ; smart, usually plain in her neatness ; without a spot, without a wrinkle, not a hair out of its place. The ladies said of her that she always looked as if she had just that moment stepped out of a glass-case, and so indeed she did." Harriet is not mentioned in a letter written by Charles Kirkpatrick Sharpe, who knew Shelley at Oxford, to introduce the poet and his friend Mr. Hutchinson to Mrs. Balfour. Hutchinson, it may be, was the *nom-de-guerre* of Hogg ; and both visitors were described as dancing eternal quadrilles.

While Shelley and Harriet were thus quietly employed in the Scottish capital, the master of Field Place informed himself on what had happened and he saw nothing idyllic in it. To his mind it looked criminal, and on September 8th he wrote to Mr. John Hogg that his son had withdrawn himself from his protection and set off for Scotland with a young female. The disobedient boy should experience his firmness, and the only communication would be through the lawyer Whitton. After some weeks of this new feud Shelley reported to Miss Hitchener : " That mistaken man, my father, has refused us money, and commanded that our names should never be mentioned. I had thought that this blind resentment had long been banished to the regions of Dullness, comedies and farces ; or was used merely to augment the difficulties and consequently the attachment of the hero and heroine of a modern novel. I have written frequently to this thoughtless man, and am now determined to visit him, in order to try the force of truth ; though I must confess I consider it nearly as hyperbolical as ' music rending the knotted oak.' Some philosophers have ascribed indefiniteness to the powers of intellect, but I question whether it would ever make an inkstand capable of free agency. Is this too severe ? "

This improper description of a parent as an inkstand was written on October 16th, 1811, at York, to which place Shelley had persuaded Harriet to come with him and Hogg the brother of his soul ; with Hogg they must live. But in a day or two Shelley was in Sussex at his uncle's, trying to raise money for personal and still more for benevolent uses. Benevolence stopped short of his father, who was exciting him to a terrible wildness : " I shall take the first opportunity of seeing you ; if *you* will not hear my name *I* will pronounce it. Think not I am an insect whom injuries destroy . . . had I money enough I would meet you in London and hollow in your ears Bysshe, Bysshe, Bysshe . . . aye, Bysshe till you're deaf." Exclamations like these made the intrusive Whitton classify Shelley as " a mad viper," and at Field Place it was feared that he was actually a little mad. On October 25th Timothy wrote, " Had he stay'd in Sussex I would have sworn in Especial Constables around me. He frightened his mother and sister exceedingly, and now if they hear a Dog bark they run up stairs." Even the services of the Duke of Norfolk, who patiently offered them again, seemed ineffectual : " But, your Grace, you cannot do it." The attorney was left in charge of affairs.

Still while he was in his own county Shelley did more than declare he would come and live there. He called on his grand-father who thought that he behaved very well, and he talked with others who might advise him ; but no improvement in his practical affairs appeared. In disappointment he did not trouble to call on his father's lawyer while passing through London. He gathered something of what was gossiped about him in Sussex. " What ! " said the old lady who had educated Miss Hitchener, " a Shelley an Atheist ! " Her astonishment would be shared by others. Popular fancy invented a sort of Jekyll and Hyde nature for Shelley—an Atheistical Clergyman, laden with pack-ages of horrid heresy in print and manuscript, and looking through the windows of Warnham Church in a most treasonable manner.

These legendary tales were an affliction to which Shelley was by now accustomed and which his untamed intellectual pride could at moments enjoy. When he was at York with Harriet again, something quite different befell him, something which cut through his gallant and abstract systems at his primitive self. He had talked with Hogg about what he called " the Godwinian plan " of physical love, declaring that he did not believe in any monopoly of it. He had told Miss Hitchener that Hogg and he considered their property as common. If marriage made Harriet the property of Shelley, Hogg in his absence had made a determined attempt to be co-operative. The story came out when Shelley rejoined Harriet and found her quite altered in her manner towards the friend in whose protection Shelley had explicitly left her.

Writing to Miss Hitchener Shelley put the case as any other man would : Hogg had " attempted to *seduce my wife*." He had done so against all principles of fair play, using all his sophistry to catch an innocent, whose heroic resistance saved her. Shelley felt thus, but in tackling Hogg he tried to be true to his impersonal theories. He quarrelled with the vice, the " great and terrible mistake " rather than with the man. But Harriet was not so theoretical ; she desired to be taken away from Hogg's neighbourhood. She had had her doubts at Edinburgh, she had been addressed by Hogg in a seductive mood before Shelley went south, she had endured his full depravity since—and they had better go. They departed in November without telling Hogg, and a correspondence followed—it has only lately been printed correctly. Shelley insisted that he was unalterably Hogg's friend but that they must remain apart. Harriet was his first consideration : "the very sight of your letters casts her into gloom." Hogg might pretend to have repented—but if he came to stay with them, Shelley was convinced, " you would be driven to this last consummation of your love for Harriet . . . I do not know that absence will *certainly* cure love ; but this I know, that presence will terribly augment the poison."

Perhaps in her husband's absence Harriet had been impelled to send for her sister, and Hogg's hatred for Eliza Westbrook originated then. At any rate she was with the Shelleys when the question where they should go was considered. The answer was Keswick, and Shelley wrote from there to Miss Hitchener on November 8th, 1811, " Harriet and her sister liked this part of the country ; and I was at the moment of our sudden departure indifferent to all places." In removing his home, if home it might yet be called, to Chestnut Cottage, Keswick—it is on the Penrith road—Shelley entered a region to which he could not remain indifferent long ; and two aspects which pleased him are described by himself. " The scenery here is awfully beautiful. Our window commands a view of two lakes, and the giant mountains which confine them. But the object most interesting to my feelings is Southey's habitation. He is now on a journey :

when he returns I shall call on him." As for the natural beauties, Shelley was growing more capable of enjoying them than he had been even of noticing them in the Wye valley ; but he still lacked skill in painting them in words. " I have taken a long *solitary* ramble to-day. These gigantic mountains piled on each other, these water-falls, these million-shaped clouds tinted by the varying colours of innumerable rainbows hanging between yourself and a lake as smooth and dark as a plain of polished jet— oh, these are sights attunable to the contemplation ! " He still fancied that the imported quasi-philosophical attitude was more impressive than the thing itself.

His approach to Robert Southey was that of the young idealist coming to a contemporary whose poems had captivated him by their novelty and fancy, and whose name had been associated with dreams of heroic liberty. Of Southey at Oxford it had been said, " His turn of mind was serious, his affections ardent, and he became a republican." With Coleridge he had created public interest in a plan for a communist colony in America. His heroes had been Wat Tyler and Joan of Arc. Shelley was confident that in meeting Southey he would meet " a *really* great man," and shortly before Christmas, 1811, they were talking together in the house of friendly William Calvert. The conversation was lengthy and " our differences were the subject." Southey found the experience a little odd. " Here is a man who acts upon me as my own ghost would do. He is just what I was in 1794. . . . I tell him that all the difference between us is that he is nineteen and I am thirty-seven." He looked on the atheism, expulsion, metaphysics and method of saving Harriet from school as chiefly amusing ; would not be scared even by a presentation copy of St. *Irvyne* ; chose no harsher title for Shelley than Pantheist.

Southey moreover did his young friends some good turns as a neighbour, and even got their rent reduced. But young artists who meet older ones after idealising them through parts of their works are prone to disappointment and even resentment. Southey's oriental inventions seemed distant from him now, and his discretion had eclipsed his political valour. In fact he was not a genius though he took very great pains. Less than a month after seeing his great man at last Shelley was writing, " He has lost my good opinion. No private virtues can compensate for public language like [his] . . . Southey's conversation has lost its charm, except it be the charm of horror at so hateful a prostitution of talents." A mistake on Southey's part (the characteristic of his later writings) was in some measure the cause of dissension ; and it was the wagging of a finger at Shelley with " Ah ! when you are as old as I am you will think with me."

Perhaps Shelley would have been luckier if he had met other literary men in the Lake District. But De Quincey naturally did not hear in time that he was there. Coleridge was away in London giving an original course of lectures on Shakespeare and Milton. Wordsworth was at home, but though Shelley anticipated a meeting none occurred. He was compelled in his search for intellectual sympathy, as he retreated from Southey's dogmatism, to use his old means, the post. James Montgomery, editor of the *Sheffield Iris*, who had been imprisoned formerly for his liberal opinions, did not respond ; but Shelley had another choice. The ideas of William Godwin had already influenced his own ; and Southey presumably, once a student of Godwin, mentioned that the philosopher was still living. On January 3rd, 1812, as one who has been put in touch with the miraculous, Shelley turned from many difficulties to the composition of one of his queer " first letters."

" . . . The dearest interests of mankind imperiously demand that a certain etiquette of fashion should no longer keep ' man at a distance from man,' and impose its flimsy barriers between the free communication of intellect. The name of Godwin has been accustomed to excite in me feelings of reverence and admiration. I have been accustomed to consider him as a luminary too dazzling for the darkness which surrounds him, and from the earliest period of my knowledge of his principles I have ardently desired to share in the footing of intimacy that intellect which I have delighted to contemplate in its emanations. Considering then these feelings, you will not be surprised at the inconceivable emotion with which I learned your existence and your dwelling. I had enrolled your name on the list of the honourable dead. I had felt that the glory of your being had passed from this earth of ours. It is not so. You still live, and I firmly believe are still planning the welfare of human kind."

This was empurpled prose, yet it might not have been read with unalloyed pleasure by the subject. Godwin was alive enough at a much later date to be enrolled for Hazlitt's far-seeing " Spirit of the Age."

His treatise on " Political Justice " and his sombre novels had given him a stature in the world of thought to which his character in private life did not correspond. His marriage with Mary Wollstonecraft, the beautiful fighter for the Rights of Women, and her death in childbed, had made him a tragic and a romantic symbol. Few men had been better hated, few had seemed so

likely to beget a revolution. Yet at the beginning of 1812 Godwin
was not at his highest point. The clever authors of " Horace in
London " about this time played upon the torpid condition of
his fame and works :

> No longer cry the sprites unblest,
> " Awake ! Arise ! stand forth confest ! "
> For fallen, fallen is thy crest,
> My Godwin !
> Thy muse for meretricious feats
> Does quarto penance now in sheets,
> Or cloathing parcels roams the streets,
> My Godwin !

In his reply to Shelley's praises Godwin complained that Shelley
had kept himself out of sight, whereon an autobiographical letter
was quickly in the post. " I am the son of a man of fortune in
Sussex. The habits of my father and myself never coincided.
Passive obedience was inculcated and enforced in my childhood."
Shelley went on to tell Godwin what he was one day to wish
he had reserved, " I am heir by entail to an estate of £6000
per annum."

In that long outpouring of January 10th, 1812, a visionary
excitement may have affected some details ; at least it was
incorrect that " My father has ever regarded me as a blot, a
defilement of his honour." No other source gives us the malignity
of Timothy thus : " He wished to induce me by poverty to
accept of some commission in a distant regiment, and in the
interim of my absence to prosecute the [' Necessity of Atheism '],
that a process of outlawry might make the estate, on his death,
devolve to my younger brother." It is not otherwise recorded
that Shelley after reading " Political Justice " and becoming an
avowed Godwinian at Eton was twice expelled but recalled at
Timothy's request. We heard of a single expulsion, but not on
this account. Doubtless these assertions had their rise in some
real occurrences or proposals, but imagination shaped them.

Meanwhile things had been actually happening in Shelley's
quarrel with Timothy, partly because he had asked the Duke of
Norfolk to intervene : " to convince my father of the severity of
his conduct ; to persuade him that my offence is not of the
heinous nature that he considers it ; to induce him to allow me
a sufficient income to live with tolerable comfort." The Duke,
whose portrait by Gainsborough is enough to make one love him
with all his faults, was very willing to try ; and he invited Shelley
to bring Harriet and Eliza for a holiday at Greystoke, his castle

twenty miles from Keswick. They spent the first week of December, 1811, there. As republican to republican Shelley wrote to Miss Hitchener that he was " fatigued with aristocratical insipidity," but he liked the Duke and the reception given them all. In spite of Hogg's sneers at Eliza she was a success at Greystoke. The Duke gave Shelley his suggestions for future action in a pleasant way, and upon returning to Keswick Shelley wrote to his father in terms very different from his recent outcries. He asked that his allowance might be continued, spoke of his regret for family differences and desire for reconciliation, but in candour could not promise to conceal his opinions in political and religious matters. The answer was peaceful enough, the allowance was restored, and about the same time Mr. Westbrook was moved to give Harriet £200 a year.

Looking at Shelley's life at Keswick one wonders what time correspondence left him for mountains or meals. The communications with Miss Hitchener were extensive enough— confessions of a child of the period, akin in their flights to the prophetic books of Blake and the journals of Haydon. " Writing is slow, soulless, incommunicative. I long to talk with you ; my soul is bursting. Ideas, millions of ideas, are crowding into it : it pants for communication with you." Occasionally Shelley's humour invaded this rhapsodical ether. " *Do not think I am going to insinuate Christianity*, though I think it is as likely a thing as that you should. I annihilate God ; you destroy the Devil ; and then we make a heaven entirely to our own mind. It must be owned that we are tolerably independent." But high seriousness prevailed, and questions of difficulty like personal survival after death. Shelley was in truth practising his powers of thought and word on Miss Hitchener with a view to teaching the world before long. A new psychological honesty, a new reading of good and evil—these were Shelley's forthcoming gift to the age. " Well, dearest friend, adieu. Changes happen, friends fall around us : what once *was* great sinks into the imbecility of human grandeur. Empires shall fade, kings shall be peasants, and peasants kings : but never will *we* cease to regard each other, because we will never cease to deserve it."

His energy was not to be fully used in his hurried letter-writing, his fight for an income and an understanding with Timothy, the defence of his wife and his principles from Hogg's insinuation. At Keswick he worked on proposed books, and wrote 150 pages of moralisation, besides 200 pages of " a Tale in which I design to exhibit the cause of the failure of the French Revolution, and the state of morals and opinions in France during the latter years of its monarchy. Some of the leading passions of the human mind will of course have a place in its fabric." It will be a pity if this historical novel, " Herbert Cauvin," never comes to light. But it did not turn Shelley's mind from the present and from a plan of action which perhaps became clearer to him as he disputed with Southey.

It was the considerable plan of going over to Ireland (" we are very near Port Patrick ") and persuading the Irish nation into a creed of " love and charity with all men." The moment was not one of unparalleled crisis in Ireland, but during the year 1811 the Irish Catholics had shown great uneasiness over the civil rights withheld from them, and it was one of the first defects observed by Shelley in Southey that he approved of the withholding. Harriet was afraid that Shelley's measures for hastening Catholic Emancipation would land him in gaol, but he did not falter ; he would prepare " An Address to the Irish People " to be printed and distributed in Dublin. For this and the expenses of the tour he must conjure up funds, though he fancied that a collection of his poems published in Dublin would make money.

Before the adventure began Southey " regretted " it ; the Calverts, except Mrs. Calvert, agreed with him ; but Shelley clamoured for Miss Hitchener to join the party. " I am perfectly confident of the impossibility of failure. Let your pure spirit animate our proceedings. Oh, that you were with us ! . . . Happiness and hope attend my dearest friend until we meet at the post office, Dublin ! " But Miss Hitchener had her duties in Captain Pilfold's schoolroom, and some doubts which even touched Shelley ; " My heart rebels against the dismal suggestions of possible evil." Still, " everybody is not killed that goes to Dublin." Supplies of money were raised and at the beginning of February, 1812, the Irish tour opened. It had been a sad farewell to the Calverts and a polite one to Southey, the fallen star. Harriet and Eliza were unlucky in making their first voyage on the Irish Sea which drove their ship north, but after twenty-eight hours she arrived somewhere, and they went on by land to Dublin. There they found lodgings over the shop of Mr. Dunn a draper at 7 Sackville Street. An even more mystical composition than usual streamed off to Miss Hitchener. " The ocean rolls between us. O thou ocean, whose multitudinous billows ever lash Erin's green isle, on whose shores this venturous arm would plant the flag of liberty, roll on ! And with each wave whose echoings die, amid the melancholy silentness shall die a moment too— one of those moments which part my friend and me ! "

VI

IRELAND, WALES AND LONDON

FOR A MOMENT on St. Valentine's Day, 1812, Shelley's Irish plans were in danger. News from Spanish America arrived : revolution in Mexico ! Shelley however contented himself with an anthem to the Brothers who had lifted Freedom's bloodless banners there, and set the echoes of Mount Cotopaxi ringing— no small feat at such a distance. He then looked about for a printer with his " Address to the Irish People," which he had already composed. That was characteristic, but so was the fact that his next move was begun. The address would be " instantly followed by another, with downright proposals for bettering the condition of humankind. I—even I, weak, young, poor as I am—will attempt to organise them, the society of peace and love." Within a fortnight some 400 copies of the first pamphlet had been scattered through Dublin, including 60 public-houses.

The style was practical enough and showed a side of Shelley not always recognised. The matter recalls Dr. Watts's poem beginning " Let dogs delight to bark and bite." Altogether it was a lay sermon preliminary to a detailed political scheme. A millennium was coming ; " Catholic Emancipation, and the restoration of the liberties and happiness of Ireland, so far as they are compatible with the English Constitution " were coming. Wisdom and virtue on the part of the Irish people were essential to their arrival. " Do your work regularly and quickly : when you have done, think, read, and talk ; do not spend your money in idleness and drinking, which so far from doing good to your cause, will do it harm. If you have anything to spare from your wife and children, let it do some good to other people, and put them in a way of getting wisdom and virtue, as the pleasure that will come from these good acts will be much better than the headache that comes from a drinking bout. And never quarrel between each other ; be all of one mind as nearly as you can ; do these things, and I promise you liberty and happiness. But if, on the contrary of these things, you neglect to improve yourselves, continue to use the word heretic, and demand from others the toleration which you are unwilling to give, your friends and the friends of liberty will have reason to lament the death-blow of their hopes."

The moralist did not imagine that these and similar adjurations could be usefully given to all and sundry. He selected his readers : " I stand at the balcony of our window and watch till I see a man *who looks likely* : I throw a book to him." What the signs were on which this depended Shelley does not explain, nor did the Ancient Mariner, wandering from land to land for his converts, but according to Harriet her husband looked very grave as he chose his Irishmen. She was " ready to die of laughter," yet she was thoroughly on the side of her Shelley and the Cause. It was he who first began to waver, not surprisingly, since he saw that he was very young, almost too young to reform the affairs of Britain and Ireland. Harm was done by a wag who put it about that he was only fifteen years old. But Godwin whose counsel he had desired also said, " Your defects do, and always have arisen from this source, that you are still very young, and that in certain essential respects you do not sufficiently perceive that you are so."

Trying to keep his spirits up, he told Miss Hitchener that both parties in Dublin hated him, but neither party took interest enough in him to justify the verb. On the last day of February he at least aroused some symptoms of reaction by making a speech. The friends of Catholic Emancipation assembled in Fishamble Street Theatre mainly to hear Daniel O'Connell, strong and artful. After his address a vote of thanks was given to " the distinguished Protestants who had this day honoured us with their presence," and at the moment Shelley was Protestant enough to respond. His expressions on the sufferings of Ireland went down well, but he pressed on to his great idea that *all* religious opinions should be tolerated and he urged this with some fervour. His hearers had their own views and hissed him ; in later years he remembered those hisses as Lamb did those which damned " Mr. H——." It is observable that in April, 1812, Byron made a speech—very nearly his only one—in the House of Lords, on the subject of Catholic Emancipation.

The objective remaining was the overthrow of the union (1801) of Britain and Ireland. A pamphlet was soon in hand, " Proposals for an Association of the Philanthropists who convinced of the inadequacy of the moral and political state of Ireland to produce benefits which are nevertheless attainable are willing to unite to accomplish its regeneration." A copy reached Godwin in London by March 4th, but it did not gladden him. His disciple had been inattentive, and should have seen that the principle of " Political Justice " was the opposite of association. Bloodshed, bonfire and war, he surmised, would be the outcome

of designs like Shelley's in a country like Ireland. Shelley was
a little disappointed that Godwin was wrong in this forecast.
The Dublin association was to have sown others in Wales and
England, all tending to quiet revolution, but after a fortnight he
admitted that the parent plant was not growing. " Prejudices
are so violent, in contradiction to my principles, that more hate
me as a freethinker than love me as a votary of freedom." At
last Shelley informed Godwin that he withdrew his publications
and would in future labour not for a swift change in society but
" an effect which will take place ages after I have mouldered in
the dust."

Several other details of Shelley's first visit to Dublin are
known, some bringing out the fantasy of it and some showing
his practical ability. Trying to secure support from eminent men
in Dublin, he took a letter of introduction from Godwin to J. P.
Curran, Master of the Rolls. The name was now more brilliant
than the man, who displayed a taste rather for droll stories than
for crusading. It was one more illusion gone. Shelley was happier
with Curran's sleek follower Jack Lawless, an attorney, through
whom he tried to obtain control of a newspaper. Lawless was
busy on a history of Ireland, which later on he published ; Shelley
busied himself over the manuscript and the financing of the work.
Other Dublin acquaintances were of the happy but hard-up
school, and even he said, " *None* will do." The best friend made
in Dublin by Shelley and Harriet was Catherine Nugent, one of
those women whose reward is in heaven. She was, at forty,
working in a furrier's shop ; when Shelley asked if she was married
she replied that her country was her only love, and she had proved
it during the Rebellion by making the round of the prisons. She
at any rate would be moved by Shelley's talk and writings, which
soon included a fine " Declaration of Rights " printed as a
broadsheet. A supply went to Miss Hitchener because Sussex
farmers liked to have something to stick on their walls. The
opening words were in good agricultural style, " Government has
no rights " ; and the government, on inspecting Shelley's parcel,
acquiesced and did nothing.

Harriet still feared that the Habeas Corpus act might be
suspended, and as the glory of the Irish adventure faded they
prepared to go, but where ? Some time before, Shelley had
wished his relative Mr. Medwin to find him a house in Sussex.
" Let it be in some picturesque retired place—St. Leonard's
Forest for instance. Let it not be nearer to London than Horsham." People in that Forest still know Shelley Plain and Shelley
Farm but the names do not commemorate his getting his wish.

He wrote to Miss Hitchener, " We will live with you at Hurst " ; but that on reflection was seen to have its dangers. Wales would be best, and Miss Hitchener and her new American pupils could come : " resign your school and live with us for ever." The Shelley party embarking at Dublin on April 4th, 1812, included a manservant, Daniel Hill or Healy. They were vegetarians now but the voyage made them try a meat course ; from Holyhead they went through North Wales looking for a house, and had no luck. A temporary home was made at Nantgwylt, an old farmhouse with 200 acres of meadow near Thomas Grove's domain. In the familiar surroundings Shelley wrote a poem called " The, Retrospect : Cwm Elan, 1812 " ; certainly he was happier and writing better verse than in 1811.

> Ye jagged peaks, that frown sublime,
> Mocking the blunted scythe of Time,
> Whence I would watch its lustre pale
> Steal from the moon o'er yonder vale :
>
> Thou rock whose bosom black and vast
> Bared to the stream's unceasing flow
> Ever its giant shade doth cast
> On the tumultuous surge below :
>
> Woods, to whose depth retires to die
> The wounded echo's melody,
> And whither this lone spirit bent
> The footstep of a wild intent—

He invoked them all to witness his recovery from former despair, —apparently thoughts of suicide,—" so bright a change."

The Shelleys were delighted with Nantgwylt, and the hope of occupying it permanently did not soon decline, but its owner was hard to please. They were then housed by the Groves, just when they had looked forward to having Godwin's children to stay. Mrs. Grove was much pleased with Harriet, who was in bright spirits in spite of the uncertainties. Sometimes she and Shelley talked of going to Italy for his health, and passports were applied for ; but they did not get so far. A promise of a house took them to Chepstow, but the house was not half built ; going on to Ilfracombe they were made to pause at Lynmouth by the beauty of the place, and the discovery of a cottage to let. It had roses on the walls, a thatched roof, a sea view, a screen of mountains, a delivery of letters twice a week, and a carrier to Barnstaple for all requirements. Now one of the chief problems was to send Daniel Hill back to Dublin, for he was doing no good.

Shelley's " printing freaks " however provided Daniel with occupation. On May 25th, 1812, a bookseller named Eaton, one of the publishers of Tom Paine, stood in the pillory for his trouble. Lord Ellenborough said that he had never seen a more wicked, blasphemous or libellous publication. The punishment included 18 months imprisonment. The newspaper reports enraged Shelley, who soon wrote and sent to the Barnstaple printer a " Letter to Lord Ellenborough." " If the law ' de heretico comburendo ' has not been formally repealed, I conceive that, from the promise held out by your lordship's zeal, we need not despair of beholding the flames of persecution rekindled in Smithfield." The distribution of this " Letter " and the " Declaration of Rights " was ingenious, being done partly in dark green bottles which Shelley launched in the Bristol Channel, partly in balloons ; and it is allowable that in war-time Devonshire these methods were bound to attract some curiosity. Daniel, going round with his share of pamphlets to give out, was apprehended by the policeman and gaoled ; and the Home Secretary was provided with the contents of a bottle and a box fished out of the water. It was decided that Shelley should be kept under secret observation.

Unfortunate Shelley ! With this pretty cottage at Lynmouth, this Valley of the Rocks almost at the door, Miss Hitchener come at last, poetry flourishing, still the frown of government spoiled all. Harriet passed some of her time in hating Lord Castlereagh, and believed that if she met him she would tear him to pieces. How different he was from that perfect creature Lord Stanhope ! the disciple of Rousseau and Voltaire, so plain in his dress and so courteous in his manners as he walked near Chapel Street. The cloud settled on their refuge, and once again, they must depart. The decision might have been less of a secret. William Godwin had been invited to Lynmouth, and that September he decided to go. By land and water he reached the Valley of the Rocks, only to report to his second wife, " The Shelleys are gone ! have been gone these three weeks." They had, and once more were in Wales. It was not only in search of the picturesque that they went there, for Shelley was not Dr. Syntax, but on another mission ;   to help in a piece of work which had been often noticed in the press as a specimen of the power and progress of the Georgian era.

William Alexander Madocks, Esq., Fellow of All Souls College, Oxford, M.P. for Boston, was a man with " ideas "—harbour, highway, plantation schemes in Wales, for which he obtained several acts of parliament. At Tremadoc on Cardigan Bay he bought an estate in 1798, reclaimed 2000 acres of swamp and undertook to reclaim much more by building a mile of embankment with a road along its crest. The newspapers announced the completion in 1811. The hero then had to defend himself from paying tithes on the land reclaimed. He enjoyed these trials. Madocks was also building a small grey town " on a quadrangular plan, with a lofty column in the centre " and a woollen manufactory ; in course of time he put up a church with a lofty spire at Port Madoc. There every Sunday divine service was held in the English language, and in no other church for twenty miles. Misfortunes nevertheless visited Madocks, and on February 15th, 1812, gale and tide greatly damaged his embankment. Shelley would read of this and of the energetic measures, 400 men, 200 horses, 67 carts, for filling the breach. Here was a pioneer, here was a labour worthy of his prompt subvention. Harriet, Eliza and " Portia " or Bessy Hitchener were haled away to Tremadoc.

The improvements included villas for friends of Madocks, " uniting the high pleasures of a select society to the rural quiet and agricultural comforts of the country." On a rock overlooking the town amid thriving woods, and equipped with a neat entrance lodge, now stood the modern mansion Tan yr Allt. It was vacant. In went the Shelleys. Without delay Shelley became a kind of amateur manager for Madocks, whose work, he observed, was in need of funds. Putting down his name for a subscription of £100, he got the agent John Williams to travel the county with him collecting ; and then took his ladies to London in the same cause. Somehow the enthusiasm of the press was not shared by people who in a more enlightened republic would have hastened to subscribe. The darkness was even deeper over Shelley's own county. " They are a parcel of cold, selfish and calculating animals, who seem to have no other aim or business on earth but to eat, drink and sleep."

Yet October and November, 1812, were interesting months to Shelley because Harriet and he saw much of William Godwin at home. Harriet as usual was ready to love all the new acquaintances. She sat at first contemplating Godwin and thinking he looked like Socrates. Mrs. Godwin of the green spectacles, formerly Mrs. Clairmont, was a woman of great magnanimity and independence. Fanny Imlay was very plain, but then, how sensible ; her mother, whose portrait hung in the study, must have been very lovely. " There is another daughter of hers, who is now in Scotland." Harriet noted that the Godwins were sometimes very much pressed for ready money, and that Godwin had given up everything for the sake of Shelley's society. Through

William Godwin, junior, on Guy Fawkes night, Shelley met a man of originality, perhaps the king of the vegetarians ; the child took him to see the fireworks arranged by John Frank Newton, author of " The Return to Nature " recommending vegetable diet. In fact the master vegetarian was Dr. William Lambe, to whom he dedicated the book. Newton, formerly of Christ Church, Oxford, intended to write three more books on the theme.

At this period too Shelley, having lived through his misery over Hogg, met that friend anew ; not that he admitted him to all sides of his life or to Godwin's company. Tremadoc was no secret, and Hogg saw it prosaically—a scheme which might yield the promoter £8000 a year. To that end he was happy to see Madocks working, but did not perceive that the gentry of Sussex were under any obligation. Shelley enjoyed the sarcasm. This friendship was patched up ; another was ending. On the way back to Tan yr Allt Harriet wrote from Stratford to Catherine Nugent, rejoicing that Miss Hitchener had left them (on November 8th). Poor thing, the " Brown Demon " was just a village school-mistress who had been given a transient halo by a youth of genius —and had recognised his genius. She regarded herself chiefly as a means for the development of his mind, though Harriet read her as intending to seduce Shelley. Realising that her influence on him had ceased and that her presence was unwanted, she was in a painful situation. It was hard to return where she was suspected of having followed Shelley as a mistress. Shelley's uproar against her in letters to Hogg is not Shelley at his best. Harriet says that a promise of £100 per annum was needed to get Miss Hitchener away, but her representative after her death, H. Holste, claimed £100 from Shelley's estate as the sum lent by her to Shelley in June, 1812. She died at nearly the date of Shelley's death ; in the interval she had published one or two things, including a poem on " The Weald of Sussex," resumed teaching with success, apparently married an Austrian officer with no such success, and continued to honour her man of genius.

Without her then the Shelleys returned to the engineering at Tremadoc. The sequel is not hard to guess. Harriet's gazette in January, 1813, punished Madocks severely, speaking of his folly and extravagance and dangerousness to the townspeople. " We have been the means of saving the bank from utter destruction." The embankment as it now caught her glance looked " as if a puff of wind from the mountains would send it to oblivion like its founder's name." It stood there drearily signifying to her all that kept Shelley from her so long, and for what ? He " was in the office from morning to night, using every means in his power to show his interest." Shelley at a desk among files, elevations, maps and ledgers is an unusual yet authentic picture. In February, 1813, he was still at it, but his words to Hogg were expressive : " I have been teased to death for the last fortnight . . . I allude to the embankment affairs, in which I thoughtlessly engaged ; for when I come home to Harriet I am the happiest of the happy."

There he could work on literary designs, though nothing in the imaginative part of his life seemed strengthened, much was disturbed by his drudgery at the embankment. His financial worries were not over. Even political ideals were sometimes a cause of unsettled hours, when Godwin of all people had advised him to join the Tories. Yet the attacks on liberty of which he read in his newspapers spurred him on. The patriotism of improvements had faded from his view, but other themes came to stir his generous imagination.

Famous among these was the trial of John and Leigh Hunt as proprietor and editor of *The Examiner* for an offence very much to Shelley's liking—publishing satire on the Prince Regent. If any journalists had determined to expose the follies of the Court, these were the men, and their lives had been burdened already by costly actions brought against them by the ministry ; this time they were convicted of libel and sentenced. Their battle was one of many between the press, as the observer corps of the public, and the ruling class. Their judge was the Lord Chief Justice Ellenborough, a grim opponent enough in the battle ; and as has been seen Shelley was prepared to give Ellenborough a piece of his mind. On this occasion however Shelley wrote no pamphlet, being concerned rather to assist Leigh Hunt in paying the fine of £500 which was part of his sentence ; he sent the prisoner " a princely offer." By what costly devices he would have added £500 and more to his charitable list we can only wonder, but for once he was spared the troubles which his charming and tireless desire to serve liberty would have brought him. Hunt in *The Examiner* declined a subscription, alluding in particular to one splendid offer which was surely that of Shelley, on the ground that he could not take " payment for performing his duty."

Since the peaceful retreat at Nantgwylt was not to be had, in time the pull of London and its politics and culture would have brought Shelley and Harriet back, but a very strange incident changed their life. On the night of February 26th, 1813, as Harriet reports it, a night of roaring wind and rain, an attempt was made to murder Shelley in his house. Shelley had suspected that some trouble was coming and had loaded his pistols, " expecting to have occasion for them " ; and it came when he went downstairs to investigate a noise in one of the parlours. He was shot at, he fired back and the intruder ran out ; but Shelley stayed downstairs till four in the morning when he was shot at again by a man at the window. He snatched an old sword and struck at the assailant. Harriet came down and saw a bullet-hole in Shelley's flannel gown and another in the window curtain. Controversy has been busy round this story since that moment and the only people who decided to leave it alone then were the police of the Tremadoc district. A man named Leeson who disliked Shelley soon gave an explanation : the affair was an invention by this stranger to impose on the shopkeepers, that he might leave the country without paying his bills. This was clever, and was believed. The other theories are that Dan Hill knew more about the disturbance than he pretended ; that Shelley's imagination provided the whole thing ; that the intruder was a farmer who had taken it into his head that Shelley had been shooting his sheep. And indeed it appears that he had in mercy shot one of two left out dying on the mountain.

The Tan yr Allt mystery is unsolved. The farmer long credited with the part of the avenger of his flock is discovered to have been three years of age when the shooting was begun, whoever began it. To him this point about age caused no hesitation, for long afterwards he would give a popular performance of the night's work, and a most forbidding ruffian he looked in this part. So we might proceed long enough ; but the central fact is that Harriet did not suffer from heated imagination, then that Eliza even when she had broken with Shelley often told the story as true, next that in Wales at that date certain characters flourished, conjurers and spell-binders, who were capable of playing such melodramatic pranks upon ill-omened " foreigners."

Whatever Shelley heard and saw that night forced him to fear that the apparition, whom he understood to be substantial flesh and blood, with gun, was still bent on doing violence to Harriet and Eliza. The next day therefore he removed with them to the house of the friendly Solicitor-General of the county seven miles away—an amazingly quick removal, and how the household affairs were settled is another mystery ; but clearly the boy of twenty had for once been tried too far. Not easily overthrown by the surprises of life, he was temporarily in defeat. A cure for his nervousness was sought in an unpolitical return to Ireland and a holiday at Killarney.

It was March and the beginning of the Irish spring, and they found a cottage on an island, but little is known of the Shelleys at Killarney, no anecdote " arising from the conflicting and marvellous stories of waiters, ostlers, fiddlers, buglemen, boatmen and guides." If it was Ross Island which provided the cottage, there the arbutus was seen in its perfection clothing rock and cliff ; that beautiful sight stayed with Shelley all his life. But the month was not out before he was uprooted again, on hearing that Hogg had travelled to Dublin to see him. Hastening to Dublin with Harriet while Eliza remained, and finding that Hogg had gone, Shelley agreed not to return to Killarney, and the address at Dublin shows that they were having to save every penny ; so it was farewell to Ireland. At least he took home some good stories of the character of the Irish, to judge by one recollected by Leigh Hunt : " A friend of ours, who was travelling among them, used to have this proposition put to him by the postilion whenever he approached a turnpike—' Plase your honour, will I drive at the pike ? ' The pike hung loosely across the road. Luckily the rider happened to be of as lawless a turn for justice as the driver, so the answer was always a cordial one—' Oh yes, drive at the pike.' The pike made way accordingly ; and in a minute or two the gate people were heard and seen, screaming in vain after the illegal charioteers."

Nothing further is known of Shelley's collaboration with the improver of Tremadoc, nor has that busy man's comment on it been preserved, except that he told Medwin how admirable a being Shelley was. Shelley's help was more valuable to him than Hogg supposed, for the vast gains calculated by Hogg did not accrue. As a politician, Madocks never attracted more attention than he had done in 1809 in denouncing Castlereagh, unbeloved by Shelley. As a speculator, he declined, and at last retired to Paris, dying there in 1828 aged fifty-four.

Throughout these toilsome times Shelley was building something in his own way which was to survive in something like glory, and letters from him in Ireland in 1812 and 1813 revealed his constancy to this object. He had made the acquaintance in London of a bookseller named Thomas Hookham, junior, of 15 Old Bond Street—a young man of ability and sympathy with a shop that was a meeting-place for " advanced " people. Before going to Killarney Shelley sent to Hookham the manuscript of the ambitious work to which he had so long devoted his powers. " I send you my poem . . . In spite of its various errors I am determined to give it to the world. . . . If you do not dread the arm of the law, or any exasperation of public opinion against yourself, I wish that it should be printed and published immediately. The notes are preparing, and shall be forwarded before the completion of the printing of the poem. I have many other poems which shall also be sent. The notes will be long, philosophical, and anti-Christian. This will be unnoticed in a note. Do not let the title-page be printed before the body of the poem. I have a motto to introduce from Shakespeare, and a preface. I shall expect no success. Let only 250 copies be printed—a small neat quarto, on fine paper, and so as to catch the aristocratic. They will not read it, but their sons and daughters may."

VII

"QUEEN MAB"

DURING the two years which had passed with so many windings since Shelley printed "The Necessity of Atheism" he had published nothing or next to nothing proclaiming him to be at least as much of a poet as a political and theological inquirer. This was the outward appearance only. It has been seen that a notion of getting a volume of verse published led to his first visits to the editor of *The Examiner*, who did not lose his constant reader by his "unusual mode of advising him not to print" his juvenilia ; the voice was the voice of experience. Hunt's advice "still more unusually" was taken, and cheerfully and thoughtfully taken. Shelley continued to practise his art and enlarge his portfolio of poems however his nomadic life and his experiments in practical reforms disturbed that work. By the spring of 1813 his manuscript collection was extensive, but to this day it has remained mainly unpublished. Comment therefore must be limited ; but to judge from the examples which have been printed and Edward Dowden's polite descriptions of other pieces the Shelley of English poetry had not yet arisen.

The problem which had been occupying him with growing distinctness was the discovering of poetical subjects closer to the heart of man than the cloud-stuff of his boyhood. He was not past fabricating wild romances. One is described as " very crude and ghastly-grotesque," a poem in six-line stanzas called " Zeinab and Kathema "—a tragedy of love. Topics made familiar to him in reading " Political Justice " were becoming more important than the demon world. " Zeinab and Kathema " even and a war poem called " Henry and Louisa " contained criticism of life ; the latter exposed lust of glory and conquest, the former the cruelty of sensualism and the injustice of laws indifferently applied. Shelley addressed some poems to Harriet, which have acquired a pathos from the later story of these two,

> Harriet ! let death all mortal ties dissolve,
> But ours shall not be mortal ;

and he expressed as the product of the devotion to one human being the creed by which he saw the whole world of man irradiated :

> The sense of love,
> The thirst for action, and the impassioned thought
> Prolong my being ; if I wake no more,
> My life more actual living will contain
> Than some grey veteran's of the world's cold school,
> Whose listless hours unprofitably roll
> By one enthusiast feeling unredeemed,
> Virtue and Love ! unbending Fortitude,
> Freedom, Devotedness and Purity,
> That life my Spirit consecrates to you.

What he here says of measuring man's time not by years but by " enthusiast feeling " recurs throughout his life.

Still uncertain over the nature of occasions proper for his poetry, Shelley was unformed in the manner of their utterance. He was involuntarily a copyist, and even at that he was restricted, since he had not read widely among the poets of England. The usual run of eighteenth-century men, much reprinted in popular forms, had come his way, besides contemporaries who had pro- voked discussion and said new things. Observers of the imitative tone and sentiment may trace in the address to Harriet the effect of reading Wordsworth's " Tintern Abbey." Sonnets to the Barnstaple balloons and bottles stuffed with " knowledge " have something of Coleridge's early rhetorical show, of Southey's moral murmuring, presented in similar fourteen-liners :

> Vessels of heavenly medicine ! may the breeze
> Auspicious waft your dark green forms to shore ;
> Safe may ye stem the wide surrounding roar
> Of the wild whirlwinds and the raging seas ;
> And oh ! if Liberty e'er deigned to stoop
> From yonder lowly throne her crownless brow . . .

The mechanical anapaests of " On Robert Emmet's Grave " may have seemed appropriate because Tom Moore, the new pride of Erin's poetry, was lavish with the metre ; or Shelley found it in " Hours of Idleness," by young Lord Byron :

> No trump tells thy virtues—the grave where they rest
> With thy dust shall remain unpolluted by fame,
> Till thy foes, by the world and by fortune caressed,
> Shall pass like a mist from the light of thy name.

In brief, had these versifications been from any other pen nothing would ever have been said for, against or about them since 1813 nor would the author have been aggrieved. From the whole

volume containing some 2600 lines he himself in the end selected
only two poems for publication, that " On Death," which did
not appear without revision, and " Falsehood and Vice "—in the
manner of Coleridge's " Fire, Famine and Slaughter."

In this manuscript miscellany therefore, so far as we have
samples of it, little more appears than the proof that Shelley was
already a regular, painstaking student of poetry ; but that
diligence is not a negligible characteristic in any poet. With
Shelley it is almost the story of his life, for all through his indirec-
tions this direction holds. In addition these preliminary verses,
though they lack race, felicities, colour and contrast and would
be thrown aside by most readers with little regret, portray in thin
sepia the generous and combatant young reformist who wrote
them. But while he was assembling these in their group Shelley
had at his elbow a second volume within which he was more
ambitiously and masterfully arranging the long poem which he
dispatched to his friend Hookham from Dublin.

In one way, as he then predicted, it was to have " no success,"
and Hookham refrained from disagreeing to the extent of declining
to publish it ; in another way it had a great, curious and lasting
success—that of the prohibited and subversive idea. " Queen
Mab " was not one of the compositions which make defenders of
public morals blush, it may be, while they issue police instructions,
but it was a document such as the authorities in Shelley's age did
not mean to see circulated, and fugitive publishers liked to print
without permission. The day would come when it was viewed as
the English counterpart of " Die Räuber " of Schiller and
Goethe's " Werthers Leiden " because it warred against the
rottenness of existing things ; when the Chartists, unappeased
by the Reform Bill, carried it with them as their gospel in one
of the many cheap re-impressions. " Queen Mab " went through
a number of these—and how should it not, if we feel that pre-
eminently among boyish poems it represents the vision, the hope,
the ideal world of young unselfishness ?

Its author being Shelley, the poem is in several aspects quite
unlike those by other great spirits, though it yields comparisons
and connections enough. The title first of all is eccentric. In the
end Shelley did not dignify his title-page with a motto from
Shakespeare, which would merely have emphasised the remarkable difference between Shakespeare's Queen Mab and his.
Shelley's Queen of Spells is of another lineage from the dream-
bringer

> whose chariot is an empty hazel-nut,
> Made by the joiner squirrel or old grub.

Instead,

> Behold the chariot of the Fairy Queen !
> Celestial coursers paw the unyielding air ;
> Their filmy pennons at her word they furl,
> And stop obedient to the reins of light.

To have applied the name of Shakespeare's creation to such an angel is odd, but to have given this angel the function of a kind of tutor or lecturer in several subjects is not less so. Mab is what one of Shelley's modern disciples might call the Intelligent Woman's Guide. That the lectures were delivered to an audience of one, no more, and that one a disembodied spirit, is strange again ; but all these points lay in the natural track of young Shelley.

In part the fantastical air and mixed method of " Queen Mab " may be attributed to Shelley's having drawn into one plan the substance of more than one, and with this theory the repeated statement that he was eighteen when he wrote it must be borne in mind. It may have been at Eton that he began the narrative part, at the time when he was especially aflame with tales of wonder ; " Queen Mab " at the outset looks like one of these. We are to visit at least the borderland of the supernatural.

> How wonderful is Death,
> Death and his brother Sleep !

The beautiful, the peerless Ianthe is not dead but sleeping ; but to her sleeping, with more than Aeolian music and more than rainbow light, comes the Queen of Spells, at whose bidding the soul of Ianthe leaves her body,—

> 'twas a sight
> Of wonder to behold the body and soul.
> The self-same lineaments, the same
> Marks of identity were there :
> Yet oh, how different !

In this design of the occult Shelley seems to be working from an inimitable drawing by Blake, of the parting soul lingering above the dead body, published in 1808 among the illustrations to that approved devotional poem " The Grave " by Robert Blair. In passages of " Queen Mab " concerned with graves and church-yards the older poet's voice may be recognised.

The soul temporarily disembodied, with most delicate and solemn poetry, is taken into Mab's celestial car ; " the magic

car moves on," as though an earlier Jules Verne had arranged
its travel through the upper air into the

> immense concave,
> Radiant with million constellations, tinged
> With shades of infinite colour,
> And semicircled with a belt
> Flashing incessant meteors.

But the young poet's genius for unearthly beauty is shown even
more in the description of Mab's palace, or Hall of Spells, from
the floors of flashing light to the vast and azure dome, an illusion
which he forms from his delight in sunsets over the sea. And
here his listeners might be contented to have been conveyed into
such a paradise, but they have been warned ; for already Shelley
has brought in a speech or two by Queen Mab in a less lyrical
metre forecasting the didactic intention of the marvellous journey.
The metrical change is not completed at once, but when the
lectures really begin—perhaps Ianthe could have heard them
nearer home—the blank verse in which so many eighteenth-
century essays and homilies had been written becomes almost
continuous. The lyrical measure of the wonderful recedes.

Suddenly, while Queen Mab is instructing the Spirit in the
kind of truth which had occasioned Shelley's expulsion from
Oxford, a fragment of another work is hooked into the poem—
a specimen of Shelley's mind shaping out the tremendous, the
mediæval sublime. It is a dramatic monologue by the phantom
Ahasuerus in answer to the question " Is there a God ? " For
this Shelley owed something to a tub of old books in Lincoln's
Inn Fields, where he had picked up a periodical containing a
recent German version of the legend of the Wandering Jew. He
had made use of it with his own interpretation in some poems
included in the volume which I have discussed, and now he
conjured Ahasuerus with bold surprise into his big poem,

> Mocking my powerless Tyrant's horrible curse
> With stubborn and unalterable will
> Even as a giant oak, which Heaven's fierce flame
> Had scathed in the wilderness, to stand
> A monument of fadeless ruin there.

The apparition's task is to declare that there is a God of the most
malicious nature and that his followers exhibit inexhaustible
savagery and treachery, but Shelley shows artistic mastery in
dissolving this shade and leaving him among the rumours of
the past :

> Ahasuerus fled
> Fast as the shapes of mingled shade and mist
> That lurk in the glens of a twilight grove
> Flee from the morning beam :
> The matter of which dreams are made
> Not more endowed with actual life
> Than this phantasmal portraiture
> Of wandering human thought.

Later on, when the Fairy exhorts Ianthe to be fearless, Shelley interpolates some lines to a primrose by way of simile ; they hardly fit their corner but their grace makes them welcome.

If then " Queen Mab " was to some extent a mosaic from several parts of Shelley's own work, it may be inquired what works by others stimulated or equipped his mind for the whole undertaking. Seldom has a boy poet taken a theme of such magnitude or discoursed on it so passionately and so resourcefully. but he was not without his predecessors in argument and form. After the lapse of more than a century we shall not know all that Shelley read with the delighted sense, " That is true, that is mine." Yet some certainties remain. At the time when the dream passages of " Queen Mab " were written the fabulous inventions of Southey had a great hold on the poet. Southey's Arabian tale of " Thalaba " begins :

> How beautiful is night !
> A dewy freshness fills the silent air ;
> No mist obscures, nor cloud, nor speck, nor stain,
> Breaks the serene of heaven ;
> In full-orb'd glory yonder Moon divine
> Rolls through the dark blue depths.

Charmed with that opening Shelley is happy to remind his readers of it in a variation. His magic car moves on like Thalaba's little boat ; but Southey's fancy also gave a magic car drawn by " no steeds of mortal race," and another of these wonderful vehicles was running in " The Curse of Kehama " which Southey published in 1810. Even local touches of ornament or the graphic stroke mark Shelley enjoying Southey's arabesque :

> Yon sterile spot
> Where now the wandering Arab's tent
> Flaps in the desert-blast

is from Southey's poetical wilderness.

This indeed is almost entirely a matter concerned with the

wilder passages of " Queen Mab." Shelley did not derive from
Southey, whose long poems sink for lack of philosophy and
symbolism, the substance and zeal of the work as a whole.
Curiously enough, much of what seemed to him and his readers
modern was " old-fashioned." Authors honourably mentioned
and quoted at Field Place and many another country house had
left compositions which in some ways led him to his own. The
reader of Thomson's " Seasons," Young's " Night Thoughts,"
Pope's " Essay on Man," Cowper's " Task," even the old
Cambridge prize poems on the attributes of the Supreme Being
(particularly the series by Christopher Smart) finds Shelley
noticing opinion and phrase there, and naturally ; since these
and others like them were the " Everyman's Library " of that
day. Usually in blank verse and with the aid of some scientific
or as it was then called " philosophical " information the
eighteenth-century writer loved to contemplate, classify and reason
upon the world God made, the condition in which man existed,
what he should hope for and strive for. It had been possible, as
with Thomson's " Seasons," to dismiss silently the scriptural story
of creation and the relevance of Christian doctrine and attain
immense popularity. Behind these poets in his calm grandeur
stood ancient Lucretius, of whom Dryden had observed, " He
could have been everywhere as poetical as he is in his descriptions,
and in the moral part of his philosophy, if he had not aimed
more to instruct in his System of Nature than to delight. But he
was bent upon making Memmius a materialist, and teaching him
to defy an invisible power : in short, he was so much an atheist
that he forgot sometimes to be a poet." If he did so, the defect
was not liable to lose him favour or lessen his example in the
working brain of young Shelley.

In these applauded authors Shelley found encouragement to
proceed with a philosophical poem, not encouragement alone but
hints and supplies of subject matter too, and now and then turns
of expression, devices of style and metrical incision which became
part of his own habit. When we hear him in " Queen Mab "
declaring that through the solar system there is

> wide diffused
> A spirit of activity and life

which

> active, steadfast, and eternal, still
> Guides the fierce whirlwind, in the tempest roars,
> Cheers in the day, breathes in the balmy groves,
> Strengthens in health, and poisons in disease,

we also hear Harriet quoting parallels from her Thomson and
Pope. When he exclaims

> How bold the flight of Passion's wandering wing,
> How swift the step of Reason's firmer tread,
> How calm and sweet the victories of life,
> How terrorless the triumph of the grave !

we are almost persuaded that at school at Brentford or at home
with Timothy he has been made to memorise such of Dr. Young's
thoughts on life, death and eternity as this,

> How counterpois'd man's origin from dust !
> How counterpois'd, to dust his sad return !
> How voided his vast distance from the skies !
> How near he presses on the seraph's wing !

With all these inducements to the writing of " Queen Mab "
others worked, the new outlook or detail of which gave them
brilliance to a youthful contemporary. In the early poems of
S. T. Coleridge the blend of divinity, science, nature-worship,
romance, social and political aspiration was conspicuous : there
they were, " Religious Musings," " The Destiny of Nations,"
" Fears in Solitude," poetic hold-alls bulging with the intellectual
commodities of the time. There Shelley could even find the
epitome of his own damnation of

> Statesmen bloodstained and priests idolatrous
> By dark lies maddening the blind multitude,

notwithstanding Coleridge's hankering for old-style piety ; he
could dwell on sketches of systems of nature or the exposure of
war and war-mongering, with vision of

> Whatever makes this mortal spirit feel
> The joy and greatness of its future being.

Like Coleridge though later Shelley dipped into the poetical
publications of Charles Darwin's encyclopædic grandfather,
Erasmus Darwin, M.D., who supplemented his glazed and painted
verse with a mass of zoological, astronomical and statistical prose
notes. In accordance with the fashion Shelley's own poem was
provided with a cargo of notes.

Those notes do not illustrate the poets as his schoolmasters
so much as the prose works consulted by him, and they are among
the many proofs of Shelley's great intellectual endowment. Here

he is in youth, choosing his key-passages from Ecclesiastes, La-
place, Gibbon, Newton, Bacon, Spinosa, Hume, Cuvier, and other
masters of knowledge and thought ; and at his need he gathers
his evidences from the newest publications like Dr. Lambe's
" Reports on Cancer " and Trotter on the Nervous Temperament.
In the eyes of many Shelleyans one work appears of such power
over him as to turn all the rest into mere casual contribution.
The notes do not in fact elevate Godwin's " Political Justice " to
this height, but we know from other sources how Shelley believed
in it and other writings " of this admirable author." The details
of Godwin's planning for a better world, though Shelley did not
overlook them, were of less moment to his reconstructive spirit
than the main theme, which might almost be given in one word
beloved by Shelley in his aspiring years,—Virtue. A summary
of Godwin's book by a contemporary is of more service in connection with the making of " Queen Mab " than a history of
Godwin's criticisms original or modified on marriage and property : " Virtue consists in producing the happiness of society,
and is the individual interest and the general perfection of man :
he is a being governed by intellectual motives : to inform his
mind on every subject, to the utmost extent of human perfection,
would be to give him motives irresistibly inclining him to virtue,
as defined above : political freedom is an essential means to the
cultivation of his mind in the greatest degree ; and political
freedom and knowledge, necessarily the cause and effect of each
other, would carry him on indefinitely in improvement of mind
and happiness of condition : by the unrestrained cultivation of
knowledge, and universal political freedom, it is possible to make
every individual happy, and happy in a higher degree than the
most fortunate is at present."

This majestic gale bore Shelley on his course with his imagined
Mab amid prospects of human growth and glory. He read also the
essays entitled "The Enquirer" and the novels, "Caleb Williams "
and " St. Leon " in which Godwin portrayed social problems
in different ways. These writings all helped him to see his
subject in its wide range and with the light of hope and promise
glittering over its distances. At the same time " Queen Mab "
is a poem, and it is not to Godwin or Voltaire or Pliny or Rousseau
that we must look for its " studio " so much as the poets whose
music and imagery made ideas even more memorable to Shelley.
He was by nature more conscious of them, and his pleasure in
giving new turns to their conceptions is manifest. Thus he takes
the passage from Gray's " Elegy " on mute inglorious Miltons
buried in country churchyards, and continues it :

S.   D

How many a Newton, to whose passive ken
Those mighty spheres that gem infinity
Were only specks of tinsel, fixed in Heaven
To light the midnights of his native town !

What the Queen of Faery taught, according to her young poet, may be summed up thus : Kings are unnatural, mischievous and uneconomic. Priests and statesmen share with them the dreadful responsibility for war. The wealth of nations is the poison of the human soul. The idea of commerce blasts human life and its native beauty. The only commerce which can yield a different result is that of good words and works. Religion, by which Shelley implies sects and cults rather than the spiritual life, is the real Devil and begetter of devils numberless. A spirit indeed guides the world and its drama, by name Necessity, but man must not shape it in his own image. It has not human sense, it has not human mind. Error has distorted, vice has ensanguined man's past ; but reason and virtue assure him of a serene future.

When and how ? From a partnership of man and Nature, when the globe has swung into another position—an event not altogether remote, since " the poles are becoming every year more and more perpendicular to the ecliptic." This tilt will presently alter and perfect the existence of all. The ice-regions round the poles will be rich and happy land and water ; the deserts will

teem with countless rills and shady woods,
Cornfields and pastures and white cottages.

In the ocean solitudes bright garden-isles will beckon. And one change in especial will regenerate all that lives : man will abandon flesh diet. Man having ceased to devour other creatures except fruit and vegetables will grow free of his diseases, evil passions and vain creeds, becoming " an equal amidst equals " in the dawn of happiness and science, the paradise of peace. Cathedrals and bastilles will fall into ruins, and those ruins will vanish : health will bless all life's stages. Love will be true and kind, woman and man will be on equal terms, prostitution and " prostitution's venomed bane " will be obsolete. All this, Shelley grants, is not to come during " the present " but by " the gradual paths of an aspiring change."

We may smile at the boy of eighteen, or even twenty, offering these fruits of meditation to the world, but they surely distinguish him among marvellous boys. He could not fear to offer them.

Shelley at twenty was certain that he had a mission, and must act ; " that he should materially benefit his fellow-creatures by his actions . . . that his written thoughts would tend to disseminate opinions which he believed conducive to the happiness of the human race." Like Blake and Cobbett he dreamed dreams and saw visions ; but he did not mean to be considered as one whose proper place was the castle of indolence. On this account he undertook the labour of his prose notes, bringing his poetical philosophy into the area of the practical, writing with a sharpness of comment and power of argument beyond his years.

One of the notes extends to the length of an essay and was separately published with the title " A Vindication of Natural Diet." Much like Milton in " Paradise Lost," Shelley connected the original happiness of man and the way to regain it with vegetarianism. He had read much on the question, and in several languages ; he thought that he might put the matter on a scientific footing. " Man resembles no carnivorous animal. There is no exception, unless man be one, to the rule of herbi-vorous animals having cellulated colons." It was all new and exciting. Shelley employed his friend J. F. Newton as an instance of the blessings to be derived from the faith ; did anybody fear that parenthood would be weakened by the vegetable diet ? then look at Newton. His " children are the most beautiful and healthy creatures it is possible to conceive ; the girls are perfect models for a sculptor ; their dispositions are also the most gentle and conciliating ; the judicious treatment which they experience in other points may be a correlative cause of this." The Newtons in fact were among those who are now pleasantly caricatured by James Thurber, but Shelley was not a practical Nudist. We see him, in passing, at his own table, and perhaps wishing for the kitchen garden of his father : " The pleasure of taste to be derived from a dinner of potatoes, beans, peas, turnips, lettuces, with a dessert of apples, gooseberries, strawberries, currants, raspberries, and in winter, oranges, apples, and pears, is far greater than is supposed."

Thus in verse and prose Shelley in 1813 drew a daring portrait of his mind and experience and added mottoes from Voltaire, Lucretius and Archimedes : " Give me a place to stand on and I will move the universe." Before the conclusion he knew that, as times were, he could not publish this book in the usual way. Since he began to write it, through years of strife, homelessness, love and disenchantment, he had proved himself an artist ; much had gone on the clouds or was going, but this had remained, this shaping and harmonising quality. And now that he ended the work, he almost felt like beginning again. Already he was conscious of changes in himself. By way of compromise he proposed to rewrite " Queen Mab " as " The Daemon of the World," a piece of work which is not more of an improvement than such contrivances usually are ; meanwhile, since Hookham was not offering to be the publisher, or sponsor, he would (with his own hands) print this 1813 manuscript and communicate it to those who would read philosophically.

This he did, and the copies bear the words " Printed by P. B. Shelley, 23, Chapel Street, Grosvenor Square. 1813." What Mr. Westbrook felt about that would be worth hearing. Prudence was beginning to show in Shelley's printing freaks, but nothing could prevent this one from being one of the conspicuous actions of his life. His poem with views did not remain a private affair ; it was talked about, hunted for, bought at high prices, and for a good many people became the first or the only thing brought to mind by the mention of Shelley. In the same way Coleridge, long after he had produced the " Ancient Mariner," was commonly considered the author of Lines to a Young Jackass. It is not so much our deeds that travel with us from afar as somebody's anecdotes and impressions of one or two of them.

When Shelley was abroad eight years later a piratical publisher who even in his own line of business was " a scaly fellow " put out an edition of " Queen Mab." The author sent to *The Examiner* a letter disclaiming it. " I have not seen this production for several years. I doubt not but that it is perfectly worthless in point of literary composition ; and that, in all that concerns moral and political speculation as well as in the subtler discrimina- tions of metaphysical and religious doctrine, it is still more crude and immature. I am a devoted enemy to religious, political and domestic oppression ; and I regret this publication, not so much from literary vanity as because I fear it is better fitted to injure than to serve the sacred cause of freedom. I have directed my solicitor to apply to Chancery for an injunction to restrain the sale." . . . By 1823 four or five editions were on sale, and though Shelley's protest had received some attention the heresies of his youth had more. The Satanic School was very welcome to many righteous persons, as they in turn were to Charles Dickens.

One instance will indicate what risks Shelley had run when in the hope of doing the future a service he circulated his poem privately. An enormous review headed " Licentious Productions in High Life " appeared in October, 1822, in the quarterly *Investigator* edited by the Rev. William Bengo Collyer, D.D., LL.D., F.A.S., the Rev. Thomas Raffles, LL.D. (of Liverpool) and James Baldwin Brown, Esq., LL.D. Some of the licentious productions were by Lord Byron, but one, " Queen Mab," was reckoned the winner : " Compared with this, Don Juan is a moral poem, and Cain a homily." The reviewer complained that his blood had curdled while he read the poetry of " Queen Mab," and it was not much uncurdled when he tried the Notes. His distress may now have ended, but the review has the interest of reporting the gossip about Shelley which had gone on since 1810. " Of the authors, one was expelled from the University for printing, for private circulation, these atheistical blasphemies, and the other withdrew, to save himself from the disgrace (for he evidently did not consider it a triumph) of sharing the same fate." Even the last days of Harriet were brutally summarized. Shelley was dead when the review appeared, and the religious reviewer was happy to spread that news.

If we knew the list of those to whom Shelley gave a copy of " Queen Mab " in 1813—Medwin remarks that he " presented it to most of the literary characters of the day "—we should have the map of his hopes at that date in intellectual England. Leigh Hunt's copy, with notes not always in agreement, was probably given then. No doubt exists about Lord Byron's copy, which reached him deprived of the author's accompanying letter while he was bringing out his Turkish Tales. Byron showed it to a literary amateur named William Sotheby " as a poem of great power and imagination," specifying the beauty of the opening lines. In course of time gossips ascribed to Byron the authorship of the notes, which he cautiously disclaimed in 1822 : " No one knows better than their real author that his opinions and mine differ materially upon the metaphysical portion of the work ; though in common with all who are not blinded by baseness and bigotry, I highly admire the poetry of that and his other publications." The scheme of " Queen Mab " had meanwhile sunk into Byron's mind, for his mystery-play entitled *Cain*, 1822, has an episode similar to that of the Fairy and the sleeper's Spirit. Lucifer takes Cain off for a flight through the abyss of space, to demonstrate

the history
Of past, of present and of future worlds.

Part of the exhibition is referred by Byron in his preface to Cuvier's speculations on the pre-Adamite world ; and Cuvier was one of the naturalists cited in Shelley's notes on behalf of the vegetable diet.

The immaturity of " Queen Mab " needs no mark of exclamation, but the boldness of Shelley's system of nature is sometimes expressed so calmly that it may be pointed out. He had not the least belief in the then conventional chronology of the world, and refers to civilisation in Mexico ten thousand years before without apology. His solar microscope convinced him

> that those viewless beings
> Whose mansion is the smallest particle
> Of the impassive atmosphere
> Think, feel and live like man.

He rejected the usual distinction between animate and inanimate.

> The block
> That for uncounted ages has remained
> The moveless pillar of a mountain's weight
> Is active, living spirit.

One strong tenet makes him write in a manner anticipating that of George Meredith and Thomas Hardy when they came to contemplate the riddle of Shelley's contemporary Napoleon. Those great poets might have been thinking, in their considerations of that tremendous man, of what the young Shelley long before wrote upon all our stir and struggle. Necessity was the real dynast.

> All seems unlinked contingency and chance,

yet

> No atom of this turbulence fulfils
> A vague and unnecessitated task
> Or acts but as it must and ought to act.
> Even the minutest molecule of light,
> That in an April sunbeam's fleeting glow
> Fulfils its destined though invisible work,
> The universal Spirit guides ; nor less
> When merciless ambition or mad zeal
> Has led two hosts of dupes to battle-field,
> That, blind, they there may dig each other's graves,
> And call the sad work glory, does it rule
> All passions : not a thought, a will, an act,
> No working of the tyrant's moody mind

passes

> Unrecognised or unforeseen by thee,
> Soul of the Universe !

VIII

MUTABILITY

PERPETUAL motion seems to have been the nature of Shelley's
early domestic life. Returning in April, 1813, from Ireland,
he and Harriet went hither and thither, to be found now in
Mr. Westbrook's house in Chapel Street, now in Cooke's Hotel
near John Murray's office, soon in Half Moon Street, then at
Bracknell in the country near Windsor, in town again in Pimlico
—we need not track Shelley's separate journeyings. In Half Moon
Street they lodged long enough to make friends with the mother
of George Richmond, painter of so many literary lions. She
was to remember how when Shelley came to see her he would lie
down on the hearth-rug with his back to the fire, like a dog, and
after he had become really warm would impart his latest
difficulties.

Harriet reported them in letters to Catherine Nugent. It was
not easy to write in the " scene of confusion " at Cooke's Hotel,
but Catherine was kept informed of the negotiations with Shelley's
father, dropped that June while Shelley declined to write to
Oxford " and declare his return to Christianity." At one moment
it had looked as though Harriet would be writing next from Field
Place. In that prospect she was disappointed, and other matters
depressed her. " What think you of Bonaparte ? To most of the
Irish he is a great favourite : I only wish we had peace. So long
a war as this has been is indeed too dreadful to continue much
longer. . . . We have not seen much of Godwin, for his wife is
so dreadfully disagreeable that I could not bear the idea of
seeing her. Mr. S. has done that away tho' by telling G. that I
could not bear the society of his darling wife." In any case
Shelley must have found hours with Godwin drag heavily, for the
philosopher as Hazlitt describes him had not a word usually to
throw at a dog. Some relief was brought to Harriet by the
departure of the amiable but useless Daniel to Dublin, even if he
did spread stories there of his ill usage by the Shelleys, and much
more by the return of Eliza.

At the end of June Harriet managed to have her first baby
without disaster ; and within a month the little family were
living " merely for convenience " at High Elms House, Bracknell.
Like the girl whose spirit was schooled by Queen Mab, the baby

was called [Eliza] Ianthe, the pretty name found in the poems of
Landor and the dedication of " Childe Harold "—which may be
simple coincidence. Violet Shelley would have meant the same,
and no doubt her parents had their reason for the flower association. " She is so fair," Harriet wrote on October 11th from
Lowood Inn near Windermere, " with such sweet blue eyes, that
the more I see of her the more beautiful she looks."

For Shelley this period was marked not only by the printing
and distribution of " Queen Mab " (he seems to have sent some
copies to America) but by new friendships. Through Hookham,
to whose shop so many clever men came, he had become
acquainted with one who though he was Shelley's senior by seven
years was at about the same stage of a poetical career. Nature
had not framed Thomas Love Peacock for the completion of it,
but as yet his enchanting satirical novels were not foreseen even
by himself, and he was attempting to be solemn and majestic in
long poems, " Palmyra," " The Genius of the Thames," " The
Philosophy of Melancholy." The second of these went into a
second edition, and a copy sent to Shelley by Hookham drew
praise for originality and learning. Like " Queen Mab " it
included prose notes to comfort readers who might not be satisfied
with the verse ; yet the verse was plentiful enough in what the
phase of solitude and sensibility often required, as in its beginning :

> The moonlight rests, with solemn smile,
> On sylvan shore and willowy isle :
> While Thames beneath the imaged beam
> Rolls on his deep and silent stream.
> The wasting wind of autumn sighs :
> The oak's discoloured foliage flies :
> The grove, in deeper shadow cast,
> Waves darkly in the eddying blast.
> All hail, ye breezes loud and drear,
> That peal the death-song of the year !
> Your rustling pinions waft around
> A voice that breathes no mortal sound,
> And in mysterious accents sings
> The flight of time, the change of things.

When Shelley met the author he did not find him so bardic
as all that ; friendship did not blaze up, but each saw something
in the other. During Shelley's residence at Bracknell Peacock
paid a visit and, within his limits, began " observing " Shelley,
leaving details on record which outlive weightier information.

For example Shelley was exceedingly fond of his new daughter and paced the room with her in his arms, singing on three notes (not very true in their intervals) the mysterious song " Yáhmani, Yáhmani, Yáhmani." This lyric did not please Peacock, a judge of music, " but, what was more important, it pleased the child, and lulled it when it was fretful."

There at Bracknell Peacock found Shelley " surrounded by a numerous society, all in a great measure of his own opinions in relation to religion and politics, and the larger portion of them in relation to vegetable diet." It was the coterie of which a glimpse was given in the notes to " Queen Mab," centred in the London house of J. F. Newton—in Chester Street, Grosvenor Square. Newton had succeeded Dr. Lind in catching Shelley's interest with paradox and recondite studies. It was in the nature of things that, twenty years before, Newton had joined with James Boswell and others in signing a declaration of belief in the ridiculous " Shakespeare manuscripts " concocted by W. H. Ireland. His later field of manœuvre was not only vegetarianism, for from that he saw a road to a mystical region marked by the signs of the Zodiac, in one or another of its forms. Even the sign of the Four Horse-Shoes Inn, Bracknell was thus zodiacal. Newton's publications were slight but eccentric ; one with the imprint of Hookham was entitled " Three Enigmas." In becoming a companion of Newton Shelley was on the way towards that circle of symbols and spectral emanations presided over by William Blake ; what would have happened if these two had met is one of eternity's secrets.

A sister of Mrs. Newton, not so inclined to zodiacal teaching, made a greater impression on him still. Harriet de Boinville possessed experience, intellect and beauty—an unusual beauty, her hair having gone silvery white round a young rosy face. It made Shelley speak of her as Maimuna, the sorceress in his favourite poem "Thalaba " by Southey, spinning the magic thread to take the hero prisoner :

> The pine boughs were cheerfully blazing,
> And her face was bright with the flame :
> Her face was as a Damsel's face,
> And yet her hair was grey.

But it was not only the mind and beauty of this lady which charmed Shelley ; it was the story of her adventures as well, and those will excuse a short digression.

Harriet Collins, as she was before marriage, was the eldest daughter of John Collins of Berners Street, who had large estates at St. Vincent's ; he sympathised much with political exiles from revolutionary France and many of them came to his home. An especially welcome guest was Jean Baptiste Chastel de Boinville (born in 1756)—an aide-de-camp of Lafayette and a friend of André Chénier the poet. Harriet, who in a miniature is wearing the wide red sash which signified republicanism, became deeply interested in this widower, and promised to marry him if he resigned his commission ; he did. Mr. Collins refused to approve, and the lovers hastened to Gretna Green in defiance of him ; but before long he relented, and their first child, Cornelia Pauline Eugenia, was born in his house on February 23rd, 1795. Many trying and dangerous events followed, many journeys to and from France ; at last M. de Boinville was *directeur des vivres* under Napoleon, endured the Retreat from Moscow, but died in the hospital at Wilna as a prisoner of war on February 7th, 1813. Besides Cornelia, he left a son named John Collins Alfred Chastel de Boinville, born in 1797 ; and this son in 1817 married Harriet, daughter of the vegetarian Dr. Lambe.

Cornelia de Boinville grew up as one of the loveliest of girls, with a look of eternal tenderness, trust and well-wishing ; her portrait shows her at about the age of seventeen, her brown ringlets falling over her faultless forehead, her blue eyes and delicate lips announcing perfect womanly sincerity and devotion. It was at this time that she married Thomas Turner, a young attorney with a house at Binfield ; yet she continued to live a large part of the year with her mother and to enjoy the same intellectual and political companionships. At Bracknell they entertained a number of mild revolutionaries and enjoyed their discussions, which Shelley shared. Hogg pointed out to him the low origin of some of the party, but Shelley did not quite follow. The easy interval which he now found after the labour of " Queen Mab " did him good, and for once he was not in a vast hurry to enter on some new scheme. He could not of course exist for many weeks without a project, but this time it was no more arduous than reading Petrarch in his Italian under Cornelia's tuition. All this made amends for the discovery that Godwin's house was not the most gracious in the world.

The background of dispute with Field Place was not much altered in the summer of 1813. Once again that patient man the Duke of Norfolk, who must have had a special sympathy with Shelley, did his best. He would have been happy to see all these dartings from place to place ended ; and Shelley had not been back from Killarney long when the Duke called on him at Cooke's Hotel and renewed the quest for a peace between him and his father. Shelley listened to his advice and wrote home in tones of self-criticism, " If I could convince you of the change that has taken place in some of the most unfavourable traits in my character, and of my willingness to make any concession that may be judged best for the interest of my family, I flatter myself that there would be little further need of his Grace's interference. I hope the time is approaching when we shall consider each other as father and son with more confidence than ever. . . ." The promise of this died away. As has been mentioned, Timothy Shelley wanted a concession which his son could not make, though the latter still tried to keep in touch : " I repeat . . . that I am willing to concede anything that is reasonable, anything that does not involve a compromise of that self-esteem without which life would be a burthen and disgrace."

Shelley's twenty-first birthday was approaching. It was a date on which his father pondered anxiously in its significance to the Shelley property, but it meant something besides that. " His mother," Harriet wrote on June 22nd, 1813, " wishes to see him, and has a great affection for him." It is difficult to be sure, but the sequel seems to have been that she invited him to Field Place at the end of July, when Timothy and the three youngest children were away ; although the coming of age was not celebrated like Lord Byron's with a roasted ox and a ball, it had its points. A young officer named Kennedy leaves a descrip-tion apparently of this occasion which Hogg has mutilated, but which retains some spirit. So that Shelley's visit might remain a secret—but it did not—he was given Kennedy's scarlet uniform to walk out in, and became Captain Jones. The cap had to be stuffed, so small was Jones's skull, if the peak was not to rest on his nose. In this uniform Jones was soon at home and enjoying the joke.

Shelley made a friend for life in young Kennedy by this one meeting. " I fancy I see him now as he sat by the window, and hear his voice, the tones of which impressed me with his sincerity and simplicity. His resemblance to his sister Elizabeth was as striking as if they had been twins. His eyes were most expressive ; his complexion beautifully fair, his features exquisitely fine ; his hair was dark, and no peculiar attention to its arrangement was manifest. . . . There was an earnestness in his manner and such perfect gentleness of breeding and freedom from everything artificial as charmed every one." The servants, especially the old butler Laker whom Shelley had once set on fire with his chemical experiments, had told Captain Kennedy that he would find this. Among other things Kennedy noticed that Shelley liked music

chiefly as it brought associations, and several times played on
the piano an air which (they told him) Harriet Grove used to play.

A month or so later Shelley and his father met in a friendly
temper in London while the lawyers went into the questions of
inheritance. Immediate want still harassed Shelley ; old Sir
Bysshe had decided not to help him over that. On September
10th Harriet mentioned " a letter from Mr. Shelley's sister, who
says that her father is doing all in his power to prevent his being
arrested." To get ready money he gave post-obit bonds, which
yielded a fraction of their final price. Again and again he used
this wretched method ; even for buying books he could find no
better. The formula appears in a letter dated December 23rd,
1814 : for classical and other books he would give a bond in the
proportion of £250 for £100 worth, the security being the
reversion of estates worth £7500 a year, his father's age 63 and
his grandfather's 85.

These jugglings with money matters wasted his time and
thought too ; but nothing stopped his search for poetry. At this
date he was still content with contemporary models ; he was even
something of a sonnetteer, like Southey, Coleridge, Lloyd, Lamb
and others. Harriet's eighteenth birthday was honoured with a
sonnet, clearly expressing a sense of her warm love ; and
another piece resembling one by Coleridge on mother and child
was written to Ianthe one month old,

> Dearest when most thy tender traits express
> The image of thy mother's loveliness.

These little poems are not without grace, but it is as biographical
evidence that they hold us. They speak of a tender and assured
devotion. And yet Peacock judged that Shelley during the
months at High Elms was not inwardly at ease. " The child had
a wet-nurse, whom he did not like, and was much looked after
by his wife's sister, whom he intensely disliked." Did Harriet
know that ? But how could she rearrange her life ?

Sometimes Shelley's fantasies made him look like a figure in
Burton's " Anatomy of Melancholy." In 1813 the chimera was
elephantiasis. He thought he had incurred this disease by
travelling in the coach opposite an old lady with very fat legs,
and compelled all his friends to consider the possibility. Peacock
claims to have routed the phantom by quoting Lucretius, who
confined elephantiasis to Egypt. It is possible that Shelley played
up to Peacock's dry wit, and gave him opportunities. About
Shelley's pleasure in reading the novels of Charles Brockden
Brown, the American romancer, Peacock records that " the first

of these novels was ' Wieland.' Wieland's father passed much of his time alone in a summer-house, where he died of spontaneous combustion." Seeking a home in the country, Shelley " always examined if he could find such a summer-house." However Shelley had other reasons for requiring a summer-house. If he brought in Charles Brockden Brown it is unlikely that he was wholly serious, but humorists like Peacock and Hogg are not the likeliest detectors of humour in other men.

The search for a home went on. " When we get our dear Nantgwylt," wrote Harriet on October 11th, 1813—when ! She dated the letter from Lowood Inn near Windermere, though " we do not wish any one to know where we are." The family party included Peacock, who was about to publish a ballad called " Sir Proteus " blowing up the bards of simplicity, spectres and miraculous voyages " beneath the waning moon "—but Shelley was not alarmed. They had gone north in the carriage built for Harriet by Charters of Bond Street, and are seen on their way lingering at Warwick and at Matlock, where Shelley observed not only the scenery but an emporium of " natural history." How he hated it !

The Lakes did not solve the housing problem, and on they drove to lodgings in Edinburgh, still trying to keep their where-abouts quiet. Edinburgh brought Shelley a disciple of uncommon intensity, a Brazilian medical student named Baptista, who recognised in " Queen Mab " the means of reanimating the world. But Shelley's world was one of rapid losses and deaths, and Baptista soon afterwards died. From Edinburgh Shelley went up to town and undertook the indescribable task of financing William Godwin, being himself so much in need of finances that he was seen " forlornly wandering up and down Paternoster-row, and offering to translate from any of the various languages of which he was master." Harriet bore all practical discomforts quietly. She appreciated a tolerant spirit in Edinburgh people. " A little more than two years has passed since I made my first visit here to be united to Mr. Shelley. To me thay have been the happiest and the longest years of my life. The rapid succession of events since that time makes the two years appear immeasurably long. . . . Tho' my age is but eighteen, yet I feel as if I was much older."

Little more of true happiness was awaiting Harriet, who would have been astonished beyond expression to hear that the next house found by Shelley would be the last to lodge them together in any sense of the word " home." It was a furnished house at Windsor, which Shelley might have been expected to avoid if his schooldays had been a series of miseries ; but the banks of the Thames had a charm for him. He and his wife, with Eliza and Ianthe, were at Windsor by the end of 1813. Here presumably he worked on a small prose work, developed from the notes to " Queen Mab," called " A Refutation of Deism." He took it to a firm of printers near his old lodgings in Poland Street, and had it brought out anonymously and in an expensive way " with a view of excluding the multitude from the abuse of a mode of reasoning liable to misconstruction on account of its novelty." Irony, which is admitted to be a dangerous figure, was no great novelty ; but the book attracted no attention.

Very little is known of the intimate life at Windsor which was to end in a crisis in the spring of 1814. It almost seems as though the huge fog of December and the fierce and long frost which followed entered into their souls. There are no printed letters from Shelley to any correspondents during these dark months. Both Shelley and Harriet seem to have been restless and grim in London ; Shelley was the guest of Mrs. Boinville at Bracknell at the close of February and past March 16th. On that day he wrote to Hogg of his reluctance to give up " all that philosophy and friendship combine," " the delightful tranquillity of this happy home," and, it may be felt, the society of Cornelia in particular—but he perceived that he was living as in some dream which would fade in " the cold clear light of morning." An urgent necessity called him away. In order to be on firm ground in what concerned the Shelley estates and the rights of his children, or for other reasons, he now had to go through a ceremony of marriage with Harriet in the Church of England. It had been one of Eliza's great grievances that her sister's wedding in Edinburgh had been such a poor affair, and she may have realised that its legality was most uncertain. The clergyman who gave the licence was in fact tried and sentenced for his activities in 1817. On March 20th Shelley was in London to obtain a real licence, on the 24th he and Harriet were remarried at St. George's, Hanover Square, with John Westbrook as one of the witnesses.

In the middle of April Harriet left Windsor for London with Eliza, who was going to live at Southampton, and Shelley once again repaired to the friendly house at Bracknell. It may be that he had formed too high expectations of the friendship there. The famous " Stanzas—April 1814 " may be interpreted as variously as readers see them ; they could be regarded as a poem intended for a romantic novel, in the manner of that period. But they are most likely a song of experience. " Away ! " . . .

Pause not ! The time is past ! Every voice cries, Away !
  Tempt not with one last tear thy friend's ungentle mood :
Thy lover's eye, so glazed and cold, dares not entreat thy stay ;
  Duty and dereliction guide thee back to solitude.

Away, away ! to thy sad and silent home ;
  Pour bitter tears on its desolated hearth ;
Watch the dim shades as like ghosts they go and come,
  And complicate strange webs of melancholy mirth.

I deduce that Shelley had returned to Bracknell in excitement, to say that at last he had got Eliza out of the house, but that even then she had taken Harriet ; to pour out his troubles and despondings ; and to propose that he should make his home with them at Bracknell and rejoin Harriet no more. Mrs. Boinville had been delighted to offer Shelley rest and society, her daughter had been affectionate and unreserved, but both of them saw his proposal as perilous and wild. Shelley therefore took his way back to an empty house at Windsor.

A few days more brought another dream. He made up his mind to walk to Horsham, and as he went a mastering visionary mood exalted him. He felt certain that the woman who should be his faultless companion was not far away from him. Nevertheless early in May he was with Harriet at Cooke's Hotel and he made an appeal to her in a poem which can be taken as a simple statement. In it he says that his one grief is, his having been alone in knowing the blessings of Harriet's loving look and gentle words. Others who would like to live in her sunshine are doomed to fall beneath her scorn. He therefore, her chosen, admits " too late " that he deserves her hate. But he pleads against *her* hating at all ; the world hates, but she is by nature kind and gentle. If she tries to cure him by hating, it is fatal, and it is unlike her. He ends with a call for pity if not love.

The conversations of which this poem is the epitome may have arisen from Harriet's alarm at Shelley's romantic feelings for Cornelia Turner, and from her own rejection of some would-be lover ; they ended uncertainly, but even when the woman of Shelley's visions had come into his existence (in May or June) he did not know how to proceed. He appealed to Peacock to come up from the country to him, and his friend found him in the sharpest agitation. " Between his old feelings towards Harriet, *from whom he was not then separated*, and his new passion for Mary, he showed in his looks, in his gestures, in his speech, the state of a mind ' suffering, like a little kingdom, the nature of an insurrection.' "

Here the story is transferred once more to the house of William Godwin, where Shelley came on June 18th. His appearance was welcome ; Godwin was to receive a sum of £3000 before he went. Shelley, kept in town to suit the convenience of Godwin's creditors, declined the offer of a room but put up at an inn in Fleet Street. Mary, Godwin's daughter, was now home from Scotland, and seeing her Shelley felt that his dream on the way to Horsham had come true, " a dream from heaven." For her part she then first knew love. It was not surprising that the daughter of Mary Wollstonecraft, hitherto the prisoner of a drastic educational plan, flung herself with glory at the young man who embodied what her mother had wished life to be. Mary was of the type once known as " sweetly pretty," but had what the type mostly lacks—an intellect. Godwin shall continue, and we may make our reservations : " The first week of Shelley's visit passed in perfect innocence ; he was every day impatient to be spared to go to Wales, to secure a retreat he had fixed on, where he might reside with his wife and child, shut out from the rest of the world. . . . On Sunday, June 26, he accompanied Mary, and her sister, Jane Clairmont, to the tomb of Mary's mother . . . ; and there, it seems, the impious idea occurred to him of seducing her, playing the traitor to me, and deserting his wife. On Wednesday, the 6th of July, the transaction of the loan was completed ; and on the evening of that very day he had the madness to disclose his plans to me, and to ask my consent. I expostulated with him with all the energy of which I was master, and with so much effect that for the moment he promised to give up his licentious love, and return to virtue."

By this time Harriet was living in Bath, and had had frequent letters from her husband ; but on July 7th she wrote to Hook-ham with an enclosure for Shelley—" I would not trouble you, but it is now four days since I have heard of him, which to me is an age. Will you write by return of post, and tell me what has become of him, as I always fancy something dreadful has happened if I do not hear from him." Harriet soon had a request from Shelley to come to town. They even visited Godwin together. Shelley had a hope that she would look sympathetically upon his new love. When they met, she drew from him the history which Godwin knew imperfectly. She at any rate blamed Mary; she gathered that Shelley had " thought of me and my sufferings, and begged her to get the better of a passion as degrading to him as herself." Mary had an idea : " Why could we not all live together ? I as his sister, she as his wife ? He had the folly to believe this possible." The meeting produced no plain result

except that Harriet was ill for a fortnight. " He begged me to
live. The doctors gave me over. They said 'twas impossible. I
saw his despair, the agony of my beloved sister, and owing to the
great strength of my constitution I lived ; and here I am, waiting
to bring another infant into this woeful world."

And there were Shelley and Mary, in love and in dilemma.
They seemed unlikely to receive " delight with liberty " either
from Harriet or from Godwin and his wife. When Harriet
recovered she also desired Peacock to see her, and what she told
him showed that she did not accept a separation from Shelley or
believe in the new love. Her comment disproves the notion that
Harriet was unintelligent. " If you have described her correctly,"
said Peacock, " what could he see in her ? " " Nothing but that
her name was Mary, and not only Mary, but Mary Wollstonecraft." The impulse to escape came upon Shelley and his love,
and it happened that the history of Europe now took a turn which
gave them an extremely alluring opportunity. It is well presented
by a contemporary annalist :

> 1814. March 31: The ALLIED ARMIES, with the Emperors of
> Russia and Austria, together with the king of Prussia at their
> head, enter Paris—dethrone Bonaparte—liberate the Pope—
> proclaim the restoration of the Bourbons, in unison with the
> French people—avow civil and religious freedom—and an-
> nounce peace and harmony to the whole world. June 20:
> PEACE proclaimed at London with its usual formalities amidst
> the acclamations of an immense multitude.

The British tourist was soon speeding over the Channel. " Where
is the family," one of Shelley's disapprovers inquired in 1814,
" that has not sent out its traveller, or travellers, to the capital of
France ? Minute oral accounts of its wonders have been rendered
at every tea-table. . . . Where is the newspaper, weekly or daily,
that has not to boast of its special series of articles on Paris ? "

The excitement was shared by Shelley, by Mary and by Jane
Clairmont—and we may suspect that had the last named been
excluded from the plan Shelley made, that plan would have
failed. What Miss Godwin wanted Miss Clairmont also wanted,
adventure above all. We know that her mother was a designing
woman, who had gathered Godwin in with extraordinary ease ;
and Jane was her mother's daughter but had inherited an air of
lazy beauty from some more distant source. She was more of
a child of the warm south than Shelley had yet come upon.
Quick in conversation, adroit in the common round, she well knew
the advantage that she had in her physical vitality and invitation.

In the early hours of July 28th the two girls slipped out of the house in Skinner Street and met Shelley with a post-chaise waiting at the corner of Hatton Garden a few hundred yards away. By four that afternoon they were at Dover, and were carried in a small boat through a night of gusts and sheet lightning to Calais.

The girls had hardly left the house before the alarm was raised. "Five in the morning," wrote Godwin in his neat diary, "M. J. for Dover." Mrs. Godwin did not stop there but traced her daughter Jane in Calais ; there was a long discussion, but the end of it was that Jane chose to continue her travels. Plodding back over the cobbles to the Dover packet Mrs. Godwin must have known that the gods were against her when she met Shelley, who was calmly taking Mary for a walk into the hayfields. The tourists were soon in Paris complaining that the Tuileries gardens were uninteresting, but "we returned," says Mary, "and were too happy to sleep." A little later Shelley sold his watch and chain, and did still better by visiting M. Tavernier, an agent. In the history of asses it is written that part of the cash obtained was spent on one to carry Mary and a portmanteau to Lucerne, but the animal gave up. A mule was then appointed. After four days walking—120 miles—Shelley posted from Troyes a letter inviting Harriet to Switzerland where he would find her a sweet retreat among the mountains ; but she should bring "the two deeds which Tahourdin has to prepare for you, as also a copy of the settlement." Probably the settlement had been drafted in March. Shelley was in fact more certain that a formal separation was agreed upon than Harriet was. His letter did not reach her in time for any action, even had she been persuaded by his idyll.

Scenery and weather as they travelled on were glorious, but Shelley sprained his ankle and at Neuchatel money was badly needed. Shelley presented himself at the bank and brought back a large canvas bag full of silver. But money was still the difficulty. Having taken unfurnished rooms at Brunnen on Lake Lucerne for six months, two days later he marched out with his ladies to begin the journey back to England—partly perhaps because he thought they were being spied upon. The public *diligence par eau* conveyed them down the river Reuss, then they descended the Rhine, and from Bonn they went by road to Rotterdam. There Shelley had to persuade a sea-captain that, though he was not in funds just then, he would be, and on arriving at Gravesend the captain still had doubts. Shelley went to Hookham for money but, not finding him in, applied to Harriet who produced £20 ; so, on September 13th, all were home again—that is, looking for lodgings.

During the tour Shelley had begun a prose romance called "The Assassins," not in allusion to some set of murderers but "an unostentatious community of good and happy men" long ago who left behind the persecutors in Jerusalem and settled in solitudes of Lebanon. Among eternal snows they pitched their tents in the fruitful valley of Bethzatanai, and of all the Happy Valleys feigned in prose or verse none is more blissful than this which Shelley dreamed aloud while Mary wrote down his words on a chilly rainy day at Brunnen. Responsive to the spirit of nature the Assassins made a republic of full benevolence and tranquillity. The tale was unfinished, but that matters little, for the valley scene is the true story; it is Shelley's rendering of the joy which Mary Godwin had brought to life in him. "The very winds breathed health and renovation, and the joyousness of youthful courage. Fountains of crystalline water played perpetually among the aromatic flowers, and mingled a freshness with their odour. The pine boughs became instruments of exquisite contrivance, among which every varying breeze waked music of new and more delightful melody." Here in symbol was the love-triumph of the tour. As a travel experience, it was described in a journal, concise and good, kept sometimes by Mary and sometimes by Shelley and published by Hookham in 1816. Nature's grandeurs and surprises do not occupy it all, for they passed through places shattered and blackened by recent war. Though the hotel proprietress in Paris had warned them against going that way, where "les dames seraient certainement enlevées" by disbanded soldiers, no incidents of the kind happened. Indeed the only act of violence in the journal was committed by Shelley, a thin John Bull, who found some foreigners occupying their seats on the water-diligence and, disliking their rudeness, "knocked one of the foremost down." No retaliation followed, but the seats were not given up.

No mystery surrounds the union of Shelley and Mary, but how that of Shelley and Harriet fell away is past finding out. Some points in the argument will appear later in these pages; for the moment let me try to discern what Shelley or Harriet made of their situation in the autumn of 1814. Originally Shelley had married his pleading schoolgirl in a spirit of chivalry, and almost of educational experiment; but since then he had written many things which would affirm that love had come as well. If he still felt like educating Harriet, it was no longer so simple, for her character was maturing, and as she said she was now older than her years. What had she become? Of her beauty and style all speak delightedly; and Peacock adds a tribute to her

womanhood. " Her manners were good ; and her whole aspect
and demeanour such manifest emanations of pure and truthful
nature, that to be once in her company was to know her
thoroughly. She was fond of her husband, and accommodated
herself in every way to his tastes. If they mixed in society, she
adorned it ; if they lived in retirement, she was satisfied ; if they
travelled, she enjoyed the change of scene."

When Shelley tried to unfold his mind to Peacock, who was
infinitely surprised at the change since the trip to Edinburgh, he
described Harriet as " a noble animal " but not a partner of his
life, because she could not feel poetry or understand philosophy.
When he wrote to Hogg, at last disclosing to him that he had
found Mary, Shelley dwelt on another cause, using terms of acute
and repellent force ; the world of monstrous romance hangs over
his early correspondence with Hogg. He pictured his married
life as the living bound to the dead, according to the metaphor
found in his verses,

> Chain one who lives, and breathes this boundless air,
> To the corruption of a closéd grave ?

In short he had failed in sexual passion for Harriet, but had been
unwilling to let her realise it all at once, and so had had to act
a part and live a lie. Perhaps it was of himself that he wrote in
a note to " Queen Mab " : " Persons of delicacy and virtue,
unhappily united to one whom they find it impossible to love,
spend the loveliest season of their life in unproductive efforts to
appear otherwise than they are, for the sake of the feelings of
their partner or the welfare of their mutual offspring."

It may be that Harriet had noticed this and other reflections
on the evils of marriage, and at last heard something from Shelley
himself, without any longer " understanding the philosophy "
which he had once supposed he taught her. Later on he was to
say officially that " incurable dissensions " disunited them. They
quarrelled, it is held, about the endless presence of Eliza ; about
Harriet's liking smart shops and luxuries ; about Cornelia
Turner ; and some hints of Shelley's might mean that Harriet
was over concerned with his future wealth. I believe that their
main difference is summed in the name Godwin, whose extraction
of large sums from Shelley with constantly painful effects on
Shelley's life and circumstances might make any wife miserable
and draw well-meant protests from her. Doubts about love and
marriage and faithfulness to one beloved might also be traced to
the philosopher. Harriet's account of her troubles written to
Catherine Nugent on November 20th, 1814, begins, " Your fears

are verified. Mr. Shelley has become profligate and sensual, owing entirely to Godwin's 'Political Justice.' The very great evil that book has done is not to be told. The false doctrines therein contained have poisoned many a young and virtuous mind." But to Shelley they were still gospel truth. Virtue rested on them. Godwin was the true prophet.

Before the year was out Shelley, gathering poetical strength, had a moment of detachment in which he seemed to see a greater force than anything in " Political Justice," or in his own treatment of human affairs, urging him on a course beyond foretelling. This force and its appearances he called Mutability, but many poets in the past including Edmund Spenser had hymned that name. Shelley nevertheless brought his originality to it. The Mutability of Spenser was a goddess " all unworthy of the heaven's rule," who was to be supplanted by steadfast Eternity. In Shelley's beautiful little poem she is herself Eternity. " We are as clouds that veil the midnight moon," or Aeolian harps with never a repetition of mood or modulation ; yet however we find vicissitude,

> It is the same ! For, be it joy or sorrow,
> The path of its departure still is free :
> Man's yesterday may ne'er be like his morrow ;
> Nought may endure but Mutability.

IX

"ALASTOR"

OUT OF the sunshine of travels in France, Switzerland, Germany and Holland Shelley might often tell himself that he returned to a place of shades and darkness. In London if anywhere the wealth of mental action was within his reach, but months must pass before he could enjoy a little of it. Nothing could have been less propitious to immediate advance in his poetry and thought than the legal and financial hagglings which he had to endure now. Some ability for the law, and early practice in questions of estate and property, might carry him through these dry and hoarse occasions better than most poets, but it would require considerably more cunning and experience than his to supply any early release from his complications.

Demands from Godwin, from creditors and agents (Peacock being one), the necessities of Harriet, Mary, Jane or as she became known Claire Clairmont, not to mention his own, must be met by the sums he could scrape together from lenders in exchange for parts of the estate which he would inherit. Shelley did not enjoy any more than the next man the pleasure which is imagined in " Hudibras " :

> Doubtless the pleasure is as great
> In being cheated as to cheat.

But he had little chance of evading it. The sort of thing which he was obliged to accept was not confined to the following instance : " Shelley goes to Pike's [a solicitor], to the insurance offices, and the lawyers' ; an agreement entered into for £3000 for £1000." Even the Shelley estates would hardly stand up to such onslaughts if they went on long. Timothy Shelley was unlikely to let them do so, but he must have been in a fresh state of bewilderment over the latest news of his son's private life.

For some weeks Shelley kept closely in touch with Harriet, who with only her £200 a year was little to blame if some previous expenses on her behalf, such as the bill for the carriage so hopefully bought, were pressing upon him. Her difficulty was to live without unhappiness in her father's house and to submit to Shelley's philosophy. He had explained to her that " our connection was not one of passion and impulse. Friendship was its basis." He continued to press for her agreement on that and what followed from it, writing on September 15th that she ought to look on Mary with kindness : " My attachment to Mary neither could nor ought to have been overcome. . . . We met with passion, she has resigned all for me." On the 26th he wrote with indignation, protesting against " unworthy and contemptible proceedings," chiefly what he supposed to be arrangements with lawyers hostile to him. " I was an idiot to expect greatness or generosity from you, that when an occasion of the sublimest virtue occurred you would fail to play a part of mean and despicable selfishness." On October 3rd he observed, " I have done you injury, but surely most innocently and unintentionally, in having commenced any connection with you." In reply Harriet was " very civil," or " good-humoured " ; but at length she wrote in extreme dejection, for which Shelley blamed her sister then on a visit elsewhere. Shelley was asking Harriet after this to find him some money, and save him from prison. Something she was reported to have said at Hookham's towards the end of October was taken to mean that she plotted to expose and ruin Godwin. She had been told by Shelley that Godwin had not favoured the affair with Mary, but it would not be strange if she regarded him, his former theory of virtue and financial enslavement of Shelley, as the main source of her disaster.

Harriet had in fact no deeper plot than one which Nature devised. Before long she was to bear her second child, and she did not easily give up the hope that the event would bring the child's father back to her. The hope was slender enough by November 20th. " Next month I shall be confined. He will not be near me. No, he cares not for me now. He never asks after me or sends me word how he is going on. In short, the man I once loved is dead. This is a vampire." The child was born on November 30th, prematurely, and a week passed before Shelley had the news. He then called on Harriet, but the meeting was unhappy. Harriet describes the occasion and the child, Charles Bysshe : " an eight months' child, and very like his unfortunate father, who is more depraved than ever. . . . As to his tenderness for me, none remains. He said he was glad it was a boy, because he would make money cheaper. You see how that noble soul is debased. Money now, and not philosophy, is the grand spring of his actions." In the absence of diaries and letters we only see Shelley and Harriet together again on some days of April, 1815, when Charles Bysshe had to make a personal appearance in court during a case touching his father's property ; and then, as might be guessed, Harriet was now in a sweet and now in a disputatious mood.

Shelley might be right in his conviction that to be separated from Harriet and free of her sister's louder personality was a restoration of his identity, but within his new domestic life a fresh discomfort was already apparent. Sometimes Claire Clairmont was entirely agreeable and alluring, sometimes the opposite ; Shelley felt then that she was incapable of friendship ; but she was always present. From the first she had been hardly less interested in Shelley than Mary was, she was by nature possessive, and she did not mean to spend her life in Godwin's house. It was not easy to arrange that she should live anywhere else but with Mary, since her escapade in France made the Godwins unwilling to receive her on reasonable terms and she had no money. She began to fasten upon Shelley by her process of being sullen and sunny in turn and by accompanying him on his errands of difficulty and tediousness, as well as happier excursions. Mary viewed the absences of these two together with some impatience. Her diary for December 30th reads, " Shelley and Jane go out as usual. Read Bryan Edward's *Account of West Indies.* They do not return till past seven, having been locked into Kensington Gardens ; both very tired. Hogg spends the evening with us."

Whatever the day might bring to vex Shelley and Mary, they did not lose sight of the pleasures of the mind. Something was usually to be found in London to dispel their troubles for an hour or two, from exhibitions of art to exhibitions of animals ; though when they went to the theatre they did not admire the art of acting, the morality of the piece or the genius of Edmund Kean. New books, travels, lives, novels, poems were welcomed, though the welcome did not always last. The day after their return from Holland Shelley brought home from Hookham's the large book by Wordsworth, " The Excursion," but it would not do : Wordsworth was called, in the language of the new philosophy, " a slave," and Shelley soon deplored his downfall in an anticipation of Browning's " Lost Leader," ending,

> In honoured poverty thy voice did weave
> Songs consecrate to truth and liberty,—
> Deserting these, thou leavest me to grieve,
> Thus having been, that thou shouldst cease to be.

Other authors, however, remained true to emancipation. Shelley already had a regard for " The Empire of the Nairs " by Sir James Lawrence, a Utopian invention friendly to the anti-marriage precepts of Mary Wollstonecraft. He was not its only reader, or George Cruikshank would not have based a cartoon upon it called " The Court of Love ; or, an Election in the Isle of Borneo " with the Regent and Lady Hertford as the central figures. Mary's mother was a favourite author with Shelley and Mary at this time, and among their poets were Southey for his epics and Kirke White with his pensive imaginations on death and illness and the fate of sensitive spirits.

Insistent problems nevertheless made that late autumn rather like a bad dream. Bailiffs from what I have seen of them are not inhuman, but their attentions are awkward, and Shelley was on the run from them. He had to pawn his solar microscope for petty cash, to be away from Mary and to meet her stealthily : " Gray's Inn Gardens is a dangerous place, yet can you think of any other ? " " We can go into St. Paul's, where we can sit down." There was even a difficulty about dinner, which might have induced Dr. Johnson to include Shelley in his " Lives of the Poets " had the period been earlier. But on November 9th Mary was able to pack and leave St. Pancras to rejoin Shelley at 2 Nelson Square, on the south side of Blackfriars Bridge. The house has escaped structural damage from recent bombings. He had managed to stave off arrest, and was hoping to receive £12,000 for the reversion of Castle Goring ; it was a temporary calm, disturbed by new demands from Godwin's creditors, and a warning from Harriet—December 20th—that she would have to get her lawyer's assistance. But a more comprehensive security was now near.

The wonderful year 1815 came in. On January 5th the party went to Newman Street to see a statue called Theoclea, " a divinity " in Mary's opinion " that raises your mind to all virtue and excellence " ; next day Shelley took Claire to Garnerin's lecture on electricity, and on returning read aloud Coleridge's " Ode to France." Next they heard that Peacock was in gaol for a debt of £40 ; but the Sunday newspaper of January 8th brought news which made a great difference to their feelings. Near an announcement that the Right Honourable Lord Byron had married an heiress named Miss Milbanke was one that at Horsham Sir Bysshe Shelley, Bart., had died. All regret for him was lost in the prospect of the relief which Shelley would gain by his will, the reading of which he made sure of attending. Claire accompanied him to Slinfold, the next village to his own, and was left there while he hastened to Field Place. Sir Timothy had given orders that he should not be admitted ; he accepted the ban quietly and sat on the steps reading " Comus " in Mary's Milton. The family doctor came out, told him that his father was very angry with him, and noticed the signature in the book. John Shelley-Sidney, who liked him, emerged later and described the will as most extraordinary ; and that was all the information given to Shelley, except that his father's attorney would tell him more. He collected Claire at Slinfold and next day heard from Whitton that if he would entail the estate—in spite of his objections to entail—he would have the income of £100,000. In any case " the reversion of the settled estates " was his. His decision had to be made within one year.

For immediate income he could negotiate the sale of a minor estate to his father, who was willing, and who paid some of his debts and £1000 a year. The transaction was completed in June, and Shelley requested Sir Timothy's bankers to pay Harriet £200 a year besides £200 immediately against her debts. As he allowed Peacock a salary of £100 he soon became less rich than might have been hoped ; but then there was Godwin. Shelley was commonly believed to have bought Mary and Claire from him for £1500 the pair. It was incorrect ; but Godwin's demands make it look quite inexpensive. He took £1000 from Shelley that June and insulted him for not handing over £200 more raised, he said, for the occasion ; the occasion was one of many. With regard to the arrangement for Harriet's benefit, it might be thought that now a formal separation and agreement upon the care of the children would appear, but no document has been produced, nor I believe did Harriet ever sign anything of the sort.

Shelley was unwell that spring, and the trouble was diagnosed as consumption. We may marvel that anything of him was left to consume, but he was not inclined to think much of his appalling exertions, and the demands on his nerves. One thing there was during the spring of 1815 which might have cut him to pieces, had he guessed it, a by-product of the problem of Claire Clairmont. Claire, it has been mentioned, caused Mary annoyance by usurping Shelley while Mary herself, in the period before her first confinement, was to some extent a prisoner. Meanwhile T. J. Hogg had come on the scene again. " Perhaps he still may be my friend," Shelley noted on November 14th, " in spite of the radical differences of sympathy between us ; he was pleased with Mary ; this was the test by which I had previously determined to judge his character." Shelley had not confided in Hogg since the Bracknell days except for his letter after the continental tour, telling him of the summer's history and the glorious union with Mary.

Mary's first impressions of Hogg were unfavourable. They grew kinder, and Hogg took considerable pains that they should.

Before long he had made much the same proposals to her as he had once done to Harriet. She was a child, a Godwinian, sometimes solitary and often jealous—she did not feel any love for Hogg, but attentiveness and admiration were pleasing just then. Godwinian rules do not require that any person intimately concerned should be kept in ignorance of the situation, but Hogg behaved with the ordinary cautiousness of the seducer. Instead of being happy over this volunteer Mary was relieved when the whole position changed, as it did in May : Claire was persuaded to go away to Lynmouth, " The Maie and her Elfin Knight " could be together, and Mary heralded " our regeneration." She had had a grief which might not pass so soon as the episode just mentioned. Her baby, born in lodgings in Hans Place about February 22nd, a seven months' child, lived hardly a fortnight. " I think about the little thing all day," she wrote a month after the death of this little girl.

A comment on Hogg's pursuit of Shelley's loves was made by Shelley himself, without knowing how closely it applied, while he reviewed a novel published by Hookham as "The Memoirs of Prince Alexy Haimatoff," by John Brown, Esq. The author was Hogg, and the reviewer applauded him, yet protested against some worldly advice given to the prince by his tutor. "We cannot regard his commendation to his pupil to indulge in promiscuous concubinage without horror and detestation. The author appears to deem the loveless intercourse of brutal appetite, a venial offence against delicacy and virtue ! he asserts that a transient connection with a cultivated female may contribute to form the heart without essentially vitiating the sensibilities. It is our duty to protest against so pernicious and disgusting an opinion."

Upon Mary's recovery she and Shelley set out on a tour in the west country, and were at Torquay in June. Presently Shelley left Mary at Clifton while he hunted for a house by himself ; one was found in the district which so curiously drew him back, the country round Eton. He had even taken Mary for occasional escapes from London to the Windmill Inn at Salt Hill ; now he chose a furnished house at Bishopsgate not far from Old Windsor and Virginia Water, or Marlow where Peacock was living. As the days were fine and settled it was soon resolved with Mary and Charles Clairmont to visit the source of the Thames, and at the end of August they rowed away from Old Windsor. At Oxford Shelley led the way round his old haunts much as though nothing untoward had ever hurled him from them ; the Bodleian, the Clarendon Press (which was then in the Sheldonian building),

the colleges and the " very rooms " once assigned to Shelley and
Hogg. But it was at Oxford that Shelley now proved false to
vegetable diet and on Peacock's advice ate mutton chops. He
felt better, and the boat moved on to Lechlade—a place which
we may see much as Shelley knew it. At an inn he wrote the
poem " A Summer Evening Churchyard " which in view and
arrangement resembles some noble water-colour by the poetic
artists who at that time were also exploring this beautiful land.
Lechlade Church rises with grandeur from that scene of " Silence
and Twilight," subtly reflected in Shelley's calm, moved by
gentlest airs :

> Thou too, aerial Pile ! whose pinnacles
> Point from one shrine like pyramids of fire,
> Obeyest in silence their sweet solemn spells,
> Clothing in hues of heaven thy dim and distant spire,
> Around whose lessening and invisible height
> Gather among the stars the clouds of night.

Beyond Lechlade a proposal of Shelley's that they should proceed
by canal and river to the Falls of Clyde was defeated by the fees
of £20 required by the Severn Canal Company, and even the
source of the Thames remained uncaptured because of long
shallows and forests of water-weed. The whole delightful excursion lasted ten days, and left Shelley in rude health.

Silence and Twilight reappear in a long poem which Shelley
wrote after the inland voyage, in the new home by Windsor Park.
The Preface of " Alastor, or the Spirit of Solitude," is dated
December 14, 1815 ; the motto from the Confessions of Saint
Augustine is in remarkable contrast to that from Voltaire prefixed
to " Queen Mab," but Shelley's mind had lately gone towards
" divine philosophy." He had not done with the sceptical
writers, but " Religio Medici " had come his way. " Alastor "
was a title suggested by Peacock with his passion for Greek, and
signified an evil genius, the general meaning of the poem (to
which Shelley's contented life with Mary gave rise) being that
" self-centred seclusion " is punished by such a daemon of
ruin and frustration. At the same time " Alastor " is an elegy
uttered for

> a dream
> Of youth, which night and time have quenched for ever,
> Still, dark, and dry, and unremembered now.

It is also a narrative poem, and as such it has conspicuous
defects unless we agree that a tale by Shelley obeys no ordinary

rules. The theme is cloaked with description until it hardly
moves ; the poet's delight in the wonderful, which makes him
note in his diary Mary's fable that a cat eating roses becomes
a woman, overcomes him now and a new magical voyage leaves
the intellectual purpose forsaken too long. An imperfect command
of the diction is also betrayed in such details as the application
of an adjective, " wild," " strange," " solemn " and so on, until
particularity is lost. Having written " the vacant brain " he
writes " the vacant woods " and of one gazing " vacantly," within
a few lines. Nothing however could deprive the work of its
pervading beauty, its melancholy grace, to quote Wordsworth
from whom Shelley had been learning the still depth of poetry.
The invocation to " earth, ocean, air, beloved brotherhood " and
the " Mother of this unfathomable world " expresses the disciple-
ship in outlook and in terms grown classic elsewhere, " natural
piety " and " the deep heart of man."

If one were set to trace other masters in " Alastor " it could
be done, and in the list of English poets Shakespeare, Milton,
Coleridge and Landor would be found here as in Shelley's recent
reading. But Shelley was finding himself. He and we have
enjoyed other poets on oriental subjects, but they do not give us
the grandeur which, probably with thoughts of his friend J. F.
Newton, he imagines in " Alastor " :

> Among the ruined temples there,
> Stupendous columns, and wild images
> Of more than man, where marble daemons watch
> The Zodiac's brazen mystery, and dead men
> Hang their mute thoughts on the mute walls around,
> He lingered, poring on memorials
> Of the world's youth.

Other poets have excelled in the revealing of forest, rock and
river, but his tree-poetry is not the same : he may begin with a
reminiscence of Thomson's " Summer," he does not stay there :

> More dark
> And dark the shades accumulate. The oak,
> Expanding its immense and knotty arms,
> Embraces the light beech. The pyramids
> Of the tall cedar overarching, frame
> Most solemn domes within, and far below,
> Like clouds suspended in an emerald sky,
> The ash and the acacia floating hang
> Tremulous and pale. Like restless serpents, clothed
> In rainbow and in fire, the parasites,

Starred with ten thousand blossoms, flow around
The grey trunks, and, as gamesome infant's eyes,·
With gentle meanings, and most innocent wiles,
Fold their beams round the hearts of those that love,
These twine their tendrils with the wedded boughs
Uniting their close union.

It was from his own travelling that he drew this search of the
lonely soul, from his own dear Thames especially that he took
the setting ; the final fate of his wanderer was what might have
been his own; but the security which the wanderer denied himself
was now his. The mountain cataract and the whirlpool were
past, their far roar only mingled

With the breeze murmuring in the musical woods ;
Where the embowering trees recede, and leave
A little space of green expanse, the cove
Is closed by meeting banks, whose yellow flowers
For ever gaze on their own drooping eyes,
Reflected in the crystal calm.

It was a brief illusion, but a kind one.

"Alastor" was published in the ordinary way by Baldwin,
Cradock and Joy at the beginning of 1816, being the first real
appearance of Shelley among the poets available to the common
reader. He added to the main poem a few lesser ones and
translations and a version of the opening cantos of " Queen
Mab " with only a short passage on mitres and crowns to scare
anybody. A copy of the book was sent to Southey with an appeal
to him to regard it as a work concerning the human heart.
Perhaps Sir Timothy's copy also came from the author ; he took
the meaning of " Alastor " to be that Shelley still " wanted to
find out one person on earth the Prototype of himself." Mary
Mitford saw the volume splendidly bound in the library of Mr.
Perry, editor of *The Morning Chronicle*, who asked her for an
opinion on it. Callers interrupted her reading and her answer
was, " doubtless it was a very fine poem, only she never could tell
when she took up the book, where she had left off half an hour
before." The disadvantage would be felt by others who ventured
on a poem with hidden meanings under a classical title ; they
could make their way more easily through beautiful Mrs. Tighe's
" Psyche " which was in its fifth edition in 1816 than through
" Alastor " or its rivals. Among Shelley's own poems " Alastor "
remains hauntingly distinct in landscape and in movement; it
keeps its own spirit of solitude.

While the year of Napoleon's fall was waning life at Bishops-

gate was free from " events." Shelley's comment on Napoleon
was that he rejected him and his system but, now that he and
France were in the dust, the world was still not free, nor virtue
out of danger from

> old Custom, legal Crime,
> And bloody Faith the foulest birth of Time.

This sonnet was in time for the " Alastor " volume. The effect
of visits by Hogg and Peacock was to make Shelley turn from the
contemporary scene to his classical library, and the conversation
was generally about Greek authors, quantities and qualities.
Walking by himself beneath the oakwoods Shelley had other
thoughts and began to note them down. Having lately read Sir
Thomas Browne he agreed with his definition of a man's life, but
what could be done about it ? " If it were possible that a person
should give a faithful history of his being, from the earliest epochs
of his recollection, a picture would be presented such as the world
has never contemplated before. A mirror would be held up to
all men in which they might behold their own recollections, and
in dim perspective, their shadowy hopes and fears—all that they
dare not or that daring and desiring they could not expose to
the open eyes of day. But thought can with difficulty visit the
intricate and winding chambers which it inhabits. It is like a
river whose rapid and perpetual stream flows outwards ; like
one in dread who speeds through the recesses of some haunted
pile, and dares not look behind." This was the annihilation of
autobiography ; safer, to rejoin those thriving cynics Hogg and
Peacock and hear how Lucian painted society or which of the
variant readings in " Prometheus Vinctus " were to be preferred,
until the chessboard produced a silence. At the end of November
Sir Timothy's lawyer informed him that Shelley was acting under
an assumed name in Shakespeare at the Windsor Theatre, but
surely Peacock would not have missed the humour of it if it had
really been so.

Behind the Bishopsgate scene the cool beastliness of Godwin
tormented Shelley. The philosopher had played an Alastor to
the poet since the disclosure of his love for Mary ; he had reduced
it to mere lust, and refused to alter his tune. Tremendous letters,
before Shelley and Mary made off together, informed Shelley
that he had betrayed Godwin, and family life : " I could not fear
that the existence of your wife and child would be overlooked by
either of you—I could not have believed that you wd. sacrifice
your own character and usefulness, the happiness of an innocent
and meritorious wife, and the fair and spotless fame of my young

child, to fierce impulse of passion—I could not believe that you wd. enter my house under the name of a benefactor, to leave behind an endless poison to corrode my soul." The upshot was that the degraded benefactor must pay, and instead of ordinary acknowledgement be treated with disdain while he paid.

For the sake of his ideal Godwin and for the father of his beloved Shelley most patiently, courteously and ably went on explaining to his tormentor the situation of his estates—and paying. Even he could not remain all-enduring and uncomplaining for ever. " I lamented," he wrote to Godwin on March 6th, 1816, " over my ruined hopes of all that your genius once taught me to expect from your virtue, when I found that for yourself, your family and your creditors, you would submit to that communication with me which you once rejected and abhorred, and which no pity for my poverty or sufferings, assumed willingly for you, could avail to extort. Do not talk of *forgiveness* again to me, for my blood boils in my veins and my gall rises against all that bears the human form when I think of what I, their benefactor and ardent lover, have endured of enmity and contempt from you and from all mankind." Formerly Shelley had exulted in the duty of the man of fortune to befriend the man of genius ; he would be another Sir George Beaumont nourishing his Wordsworths and Coleridges ; the instance on whom he now tired himself caused little rejoicing. Under these shadows and with uncertainty about the actual application of his grandfather's will Shelley faced the year 1816. Godwin's negotiation was done partly by letter and partly through Turner, the lawyer married to Shelley's admired Cornelia.

On January 24th Mary brought Shelley a son who was named William, presumably after the author of " Political Justice." Shelley allowed himself a momentary revenge by writing to Godwin, " Fanny and Mrs. Godwin will probably be glad to hear that Mary has safely recovered from a very favourable confinement, and that her child is well."

The house on Bishopsgate Heath, very near the park gates as you entered the Great Park from Englefield Green, was one of Shelley's happiest resting-places. His friends and his books increased the comparative peace of mind which Mary had given him. He did not seek fresh acquaintances, but one with a poet's name is fortunately remembered by Peacock—old Dr. Pope, a Quaker, of Staines. First called in as a doctor, Pope returned as a friend. " He liked to discuss theology with Shelley. Shelley at first avoided the discussion, saying his opinions would not be to the doctor's taste ; but the doctor answered, ' I like to hear thee talk, friend Shelley; I see thee art very deep.'" Now Peacock began to take pleasure in Shelley's habit, the habit indeed of his period, of reading aloud, and then and afterwards heard him through " almost all Shakespeare's tragedies, and some of his more poetical comedies," not in the shrill discordant voice of his excited moods but with a low soft voice yet clear, " good both in tune and in tone."

X

GENEVA

LIKE many thousands of his countrymen Shelley had been an observer of the career in literature and in fashionable life of Lord Byron. Time was now to bring these two startling young men into contact, and to create a mutual respect which both, if they might review their lives on earth, might call in many ways their most invigorating and entertaining yet never easy friendship. In the spring of 1816 the " domestic circumstances " of Byron and whatever the scandal-lovers of the time knew or pieced together about them led to his leaving England for the last time. Like King Lear and with similar language he summoned his train together, comprising William Fletcher, Robert Rushton, a Swiss named Berger and John William Polidori, M.D. ; he took his carriage, copied from Napoleon's, with a library and a chest of plate ; and, what was more important, he took with him the inclination to continue his mighty poetic journal " Childe Harold's Pilgrimage." On April 25th, 1816, he embarked for Ostend, Flanders, the Rhine and the South. All the newspapers did their best or worst with this enigmatic self-banishment. Shelley could not miss it, but did not connect the remarkable news with his own future.

He had agitated Godwin by allusions to an " Italian scheme " which had in fact been discussed years before with Harriet. He decided to defer it again, but several reasons worked on him to make him give up the green retreat near Windsor ; and the failure of one of his plans in respect of his future property removed his reason for staying in England. He felt the strain of living as he and Mary were doing under bitter conventional judgment, fighting for every point. By this time Claire had made her way back into their household, increasing their anxieties. A new continental experiment was decided upon. The wonder is that when it was made a third lady was not of the party ; at the last moment Shelley in London was visited by a sympathetic incognita who had been captivated by " Queen Mab " and proposed escaping from her trivial though luxurious life in order to be always with its author. For once Shelley managed not to re-adjust his world on a chivalrous impulse ; nevertheless the lady did run away in the desire at least to be near him, and how all would have ended had she not died in Italy is hard to guess.

Shelley, Mary with William and Claire left Dover on their way to Geneva in the first week of May, 1816, and from Dover Shelley posted to Godwin one more long and careful letter, ending with a most generous tribute. " However what you erroneously call fame and honour separate us, I shall always feel towards you as the most affectionate of friends." The travellers did not much enjoy their journey through France, and passed through Dijon without a word for the food and wine of Burgundy. Rain, wind, snow accompanied them as they entered mountain country ; the scene grew spacious and sublime. Reaching Geneva they put up at Dejean's Hotel de l'Angleterre, Sécheron, and it was as if they had come from the wilderness " to the warm sunshine, and to the humming of sun-loving insects. From the windows . . . we see the lovely lake, blue as the heavens which it reflects, and sparkling with golden beams. The opposite shore is sloping, and covered with vines. . . . Gentlemen's seats are scattered over these banks, behind which rise the various ridges of black mountains, and towering far above, in the midst of its snowy Alps, the majestic Mont Blanc, highest and queen of all." A boat was quickly hired, and the days closed with moonlight on the waters.

Some ten days of this gentle life had passed when Lord Byron and his retainers arrived at " the well-known hotel." The excitement of Shelley and Mary at seeing him was great, yet not so great as that of Claire, who had her own most interesting reason for it. Byron was not a stranger to her, nor was he unadvised that she would be arriving at the Hotel de l'Angleterre. Some time earlier she had approached him as one of the committee of Drury Lane Theatre with a request to be allowed an opportunity as an actress, and though he was difficult to catch for an interview she at least succeeded in becoming his mistress. This triumph was kept a secret, and even now that she met Byron again in the presence of Shelley and Mary it seems to have remained one to them. Poor girl, she was not to find it much but dust and ashes in the end.

Byron was naturally in no mood to encounter the travelling Briton who would serve his slightest actions up in gossip or print, but the author of " Queen Mab " was different. Companionship began at once ; Byron also had the passion for a boat, and with him and Polidori the water-party in the evening continued famously ; all sometimes landed for a walk where the vine-dressers sang—all women, Mary noticed, with mostly harmonious though masculine voices. One night brought a thunderstorm of gigantic wrath which Mary reported in prose but Byron in memorable verse,

> How the lit lake shines, a phosphoric sea,
> And the big rain comes dancing to the earth.

At the end of May Shelley took his household from the hotel into a cottage on the far side of the lake, Campagne Chapuis or Mont Alégre. Byron remained at the hotel for another fortnight, but paid evening visits with Polidori to his new friends. Mary was never to forget his singing the Tyrolese Song of Liberty composed by Tom Moore as his boat went off in the gathering shadow one evening ; the moment was correctly Byronic, for the weather was changing and the wind rising. At length Byron came to live in a modern house, the Villa Diodati, separated from Mont Alégre by a vineyard ; here were fine trees, grand prospects of city, lake and mountain. After breakfast Byron would stroll to the cottage for a talk. Sailing excursions were frequent, and evenings when it was too wet to enjoy them outdoors were often spent in conversations in Byron's long saloon.

A voyage of some length was resolved upon by the two poets, who took with them a servant and two boatmen. Shelley told Peacock how he delighted in it all but praised it most " because then I first knew the divine beauty of Rousseau's imagination, as it exhibits itself in ' Julie.' " They set forth on June 23rd along the southern shore of the lake, and at Meillerie the spirit of Rousseau began to dominate Shelley's feelings ; he was informed to his delight that Louise, the beautiful Queen of Prussia, had elected to pass a night at the inn because of its associations with the romantic Frenchman. " Meillerie is the well-known scene," Shelley says, " of St. Preux's visionary exile ; but Meillerie is indeed enchanted ground, were Rousseau no magician. Groves of pine, chestnut and walnut overshadow it ; magnificent and unbounded forests to which England affords no parallel. In the midst of these woods are dells of lawny expanse, inconceivably verdant, adorned with a thousand of the rarest flowers, and odorous with thyme." A violent contrast befell them when they sailed on—a hurricane, which bewildered the boatmen. Byron took off his coat, Shelley did the same, " and we sat with our arms crossed, every instant expecting to be swamped." Shelley was no swimmer, and was vexed that Byron might risk his life to save him ; he strongly and coolly requested him to do no such thing, and planting himself on the locker grasped the rings at its ends and said he would go down in that position. The feat was not demanded of him ; the boat was brought, amid the congratulations of onlookers, into quiet water at St. Gingoux, and the travellers were soon admiring one of the outfalls of the Rhone.

It was not easy now for Shelley to tear himself from the pages of " Julie," but other subjects were at hand, above all the Castle of Chillon. The dungeons cast their clammy gloom on Shelley, but whereas he simply commented to Peacock on " that cold and inhuman tyranny which it has been the delight of man to exercise over man," Byron composed within a few days his dramatic tale " The Prisoner of Chillon." At Clarens all was Rousseau and his creations : " we gathered roses on the terrace, in the feeling that they might be the posterity of some planted by Julie's hand. We sent their dead and withered leaves to the absent." At Lausanne Byron gathered acacia leaves on the terrace whence Gibbon saw Mont Blanc after writing the end of " The Decline and Fall of the Roman Empire," but Shelley did not, " fearing to outrage the greater and more sacred name of Rousseau." This tour closed on July 2nd, and the poets resumed their usual work and play on the shore of their lake.

Byron left the next tour to Shelley and his ladies, who took the road towards Mont Blanc on July 20th ; at each halt Shelley described what they had seen in a letter to Peacock. Remembering that his friend had begun an astrological poem on Mr. Newton's zodiacal myths, to " assert the supremacy of Ahriman," Shelley from the Hotel de Chamonix offered him a thought : " Imagine him throned among these desolating snows, among these palaces of death and frost, so sculptured in this their terrible magnificence by the adamantine hand of necessity, and that he casts around him, as the first essays of his final usurpation, avalanches, torrents, rocks and thunders, and above all these deadly glaciers, at once the proof and symbols of his reign." Struck by the incessant unquiet movement of the Sea of Ice at Montanvert, Shelley had the sensation " that Mont Blanc, like the god of the Stoics, was a vast animal, and that the frozen blood for ever circulated through his stony veins." On the evening of the 27th the party called at Diodati and talked with Byron till midnight before regaining the cottage and the cradled William.

In a hut among the horrid grandeurs which suggested sinister deities Shelley signed his name in the book and merrily added an ingenious Greek hexameter defining himself as philanthropist, democrat, and atheist—qualifications not popularly connected with the influence of mountain scenery on the spirit. The entry did him more harm than he could fear ; " it was bad taste, to say the least of it," Byron remarked. Extended and inaccurate versions were obtained by Shelley's enemies in England and published. Southey was quickly on the spot ; he took a copy of the inscriptions, and on his return made use of it. In spite of his three attributes Shelley was as weak as other men when led by his womenfolk into a bazaar of souvenirs at Chamonix ; he growled but he produced the money for " some specimens of minerals and plants, and two or three crystal seals." He also acquired, in the manner of a country gentleman, " a large collection of all the seeds of rare Alpine plants, with their names written upon the outside of the papers that contain them. These I mean to colonise in my garden in England, and to permit you to take what choice you please from them." Peacock, who received this promise, was under instructions to find Shelley a permanent abode.

Conversations with Byron and Polidori were apt to run upon diablerie, superstition and magic. To include Polidori's name is correct since he actually took part, but he was not a valued contributor ; his vanity and envy spoiled the fellowship. Polidori yearned also to be among the poets, and his pushfulness reduced Byron to the plain justice of reading aloud a tragedy which he had made up, and one mysterious line of which survives,

'Tis thus the goitred idiot of the Alps.

The understanding between Byron and Shelley irritated the man until, defeated by Shelley in a sailing-match, he declared he had been insulted and threw out a sort of challenge. At this Shelley, who shared Sir Richard Steele's opinion that duels were criminal, was only amused, but Byron shrewdly took up the point. " Recollect," he said to the physician, " that though Shelley has some scruples about duelling *I* have none, and shall be at all times ready to take his place." Shelley was not sure that Byron was safe with such a medical attendant. Polidori's inner world was a dizzy one : Byron disturbed him one day as he prepared to take poison, an act which was only postponed a few years. It was due in Byron's opinion to his disappointed hopes of literary fame.

With or without this handsome eccentric the conversations grew. One evening all present had been reading a collection of ghost stories from the German, and then Byron recited a passage from Coleridge's " Christabel " which had not yet come to hand in its printed form. Byron remembered the unveiling of the bewitching Geraldine : " Behold ! her bosom " . . . At that instant Shelley was looking at Mary's bosom, and suddenly a story heard long ago flashed into his mind ; he jumped up and ran from the room. After a cold water treatment he explained that he had seen Mary like the Sussex woman of fable (or perhaps one pointed out to him as a boy) with eyes in her breasts, and had rushed out to break the spell. This was promising, and before the evening ended it was agreed that each of them should write a tale of mystery. The results of that decision will appear later.

As if the king of the ghosts had ordered it, on August 14th there came to Byron's villa one who had made a great stir in his time by romances and ballads of the supernatural. Many an evening at Field Place had been made unearthly by this man's publications. M. G. Lewis, M.P., author of " The Monk " and " Tales of Terror " was not gruesome in real life ; when Byron had seen him last the account given to Tom Moore was, " He is really a good man—an excellent man—he left me his walking-stick and a pot of preserved ginger. I shall never eat the last without tears in my eyes, it is so hot ! " But Lewis knew what was expected of him at a party and told five ghost stories which Shelley wrote down—" all grim," he remarked, using a favoured adjective.

The compositions due to the reading of " Fantasmagoriana " had varying fortune. Polidori wrote the life and death of a skull-headed lady who owed her condition to spying through a key-hole, and he took over from Byron the idea of a tale called " The Vampire "—a creature still admired. Byron began and dropped a thriller which was becoming vampirine, and burned another on the Belphegor into which he had mixed satire upon his marriage. He could have made a name with such prose tales, E. A. Poe not having yet arisen, but he directed his fancy away from them, and the immediate popularity of poems now written instead—" The Dream," " Darkness," an " Incantation " used in " Manfred "—confirmed his judgment.

Shelley hoped to turn his early experiences to account. In " Alastor " he mentioned having made his bed on coffins (in the vaults at Warnham church no doubt), in case death sent a ghost as a messenger ; at Eton he had roused the dame once by upsetting a frying-pan of witches' oils after midnight ; but he had had no real luck. He therefore had no story. Neither had Mary, who being the daughter of that assiduous author Godwin was ashamed of this failure. A story came. She listened to more talk between the poets on the principle of life, the revival of the dead, galvanism, the manufacture of a bodily form which might be warmed to life. Lying awake afterwards she seemed to see a man's form, " stretched out, and then, on the working of some powerful engine, showing signs of life." Next morning she knew that she had her story, and began it as a short story, but Shelley

required her to write it more expansively ; and so she proceeded
with " Frankenstein ; or, the Modern Prometheus."

The alternative title turns our minds to the ancient myth
which was often reviewed by the two poets. Byron was an old
student of the " Prometheus Vinctus " in which Aeschylus
summed existence in the contest between the supreme despot
and the benevolent rebel. At Harrow in 1804 he had translated
one or two passages from the Greek play, and later published these
exercises as relics of happy hours when he studied this and other
Greek plays thrice a year. Shelley was still reading " Prometheus
Vinctus " with an enthusiasm which moved Byron and gave him
energy. " The Prometheus, if not exactly in my plan, has always
been so much in my head that I can easily conceive its influence
over all or any thing that I have written." Byron now desired
Shelley to translate the play for him, and wrote an Ode on the
god, relating his singular doom to man's " sad unallied existence."

Similarly he went to work on a drama " of a very wild, metaphysical and inexplicable kind " with a hero resembling
Prometheus in his addresses to the elements and his resistance to
the soul's enemies :

> My past power
> Was purchased by no compact with thy crew,
> But by superior science—penance, daring,
> And length of watching, strength of mind, and skill
> In knowledge of our fathers—when the earth
> Saw men and spirits walking side by side,
> And gave ye no supremacy : I stand
> Upon my strength —I do defy—deny,
> Spurn back, and scorn ye !

Since Shelley had lately discerned the god Ahrimanes enthroned
among the glaciers, it is noteworthy that in this drama " Manfred"
Byron passes from a scene at the summit of the Jungfrau to a
terrific strife of wills in " the Hall of Ahrimanes."

At once, then, the presence of Shelley had produced new feelings about great subjects, new purposes in poetry, which Byron's
first real biographer did not overlook. Thomas Moore was not
constituted for Shelley's intellectual company, but even he has
to admit the effect of a few weeks of it on his eminent friend. He
remarks Shelley's mysticism, as he terms it, in the third Canto
of " Childe Harold," but is equally observant of another element
there : " Shelley omitted no opportunity of bringing the beauties
of his favourite writer [Wordsworth] under the notice of Lord
Byron," and thus supplying " the tinge, if not something deeper,

of the manner and cast of thinking of Mr. Wordsworth, which is
traceable through so many of Byron's most beautiful stanzas."
Byron described himself at Geneva as having been dosed with
Wordsworth physic even to nausea, but he read some of the
poems recommended with pleasure. In truth Shelley educated
Byron as nobody had done and induced him to conceive his
poems as a seer and nature-worshipper. For once, even though
not for long, Byron seemed steadily poised in a scheme of things :

> From the high host
> Of stars, to the lull'd lake, and mountain-coast,
> All is concenter'd in a life intense,
> Where not a beam, nor air, nor leaf is lost,
> But hath a part of being, and a sense
> Of that which is of all Creator and defence.

Causing this phase in Byron's poetry, Shelley himself wrote
little in Switzerland, but that little was of a noble substance. In
the voyage round the lake he planned the " Hymn to Intellectual
Beauty," as if to dispel the falsity of the supernatural of Diodati
conversation. In place of boyhood's search for ghosts and similar
necromancy he set " the awful shadow of some unseen Power,"
the spirit of beauty through man's world giving " grace and truth
to life's unquiet dream." Moore's general complaint against the
vagueness of his verse does not touch this clearly modelled shrine
to a mystery. " Mont Blanc " grew in Shelley's mind as he stood
on the bridge of Arve, delighting in conjecture upon what he saw
and described greatly ; but the poem culminates in a religious
thought,

> Mont Blanc yet gleams on high :—the power is there,
> The still and solemn power of many sights,
> And many sounds, and much of life and death,—

and there man perceived " the secret strength of things." Before
many years passed the lines were being quoted as Byron's.

On August 2nd, 1816, Shelley found a letter at Geneva from
his solicitor, P. W. Longdill, requesting him to come to England,
but he delayed. On his twenty-fourth birthday, two days later,
Mary gave him a telescope and sent up a balloon which instantly
took fire. The arrival of Monk Lewis made a diversion, and he
spoke not only of goblins but of his slaves in Jamaica whom he
had just visited ; it can be imagined how readily Shelley joined
Byron and Polidori in witnessing the codicil to Lewis's will, by
which the heir was required to treat the slaves as conscientiously
and humanely as the testator did. The last talk up at Diodati,

where Hobhouse had joined Byron, the last boat-excursion went by ; Shelley took charge of the third Canto of " Childe Harold " in manuscript, to be delivered to John Murray ; and so the inhabitants of the cottage left Geneva early on August 29th. On the way to le Havre they visited Fontainebleau and Versailles, where Shelley found the magnificence oppressive, and " the vacant rooms imaged well the hollow show of monarchy." A point puzzled him : " The people who showed us through the palace obstinately refused to say anything about the Revolution. We could not even find out in which chamber the rioters of the 10th August found the King." Shelley was himself to express the reason for this weariness over the past. The rest of the journey leaves one subject for a historical painter : Shelley in Rouen Cathedral before the tomb of Richard Coeur de Lion and his brother. Arriving at Portsmouth, Shelley was amused by the Customs officer who in the traditional manner turned over the pages of the " Childe Harold " manuscript in the hope of finding smuggled lace.

For his friendship with Shelley at Geneva Byron had to pay in the tattle of London society. The presence of Mary and Claire meant of course that he had in his house " two sisters as the partakers of his revels." Claire would probably have liked this to be more than true, but nothing is known of her at Diodati, though Byron hints that she was still his mistress there. Byron was an obvious sinner, but the knowing ones found the real villain in Shelley. The poetess of Hampstead, Joanna Baillie, reproved Walter Scott for trying to make her think better of Byron. " You will remember when I returned from Switzerland, having heard there that he was living with a gentleman and his wife on the banks of the lake, how ready I was to suppose he was in a respectable house. . . . But I wish I had been less ready. . . . Not long after I sent you my last letter, I learnt that this same gentleman and his wife were a married man who has run away from this country, and a girl whom he has seduced, and that their house was anything but a respectable one. This information did not come from Lady B. Oh ! why have you endeavoured to reconcile the world in some degree with that unhappy man, at the expense of having yourself considered as regarding all want of principle and the vilest corruption with an indulgent eye ? "

No home awaited Shelley and Mary in England ; Mary took the baby and his Swiss nurse Elise to Bath, and Claire went too. Her secret was probably out ; she was with child by Byron. To be near London and his lawyers Shelley stayed with Peacock at Marlow. They resumed their daily airings by boat or afoot, but

Shelley attended to business and among other things acted for
Byron in respect of the new manuscript of " Childe Harold,"
" The Prisoner of Chillon " and " Manfred." By Medwin's
account he carried out instructions firmly and demanded a good
price—" I got £2400," says Byron—with the consequence that
Murray " always entertained a spite against him for making the
agreement " and Shelley used the angry nickname " The
Murrain." He would never have fought so hard for his own
benefit. Reporting the transaction to Byron he sent him a
majestic exhortation on the subject of poetry : " I only know
that your powers are astonishingly great, and that they ought to
be exerted to their full extent." He had fancied that the French
Revolution would be a subject to ensure this, " a theme involving
pictures of all that is best qualified to interest and to instruct
mankind." Towards the end of September Shelley joined Mary
at 5 Abbey Churchyard, Bath, and the arrangement with Claire
as their housemate was in force again. Soon they would find a
house in some lonely landscape, and Byron would have to come
and stay. Meanwhile Godwin clamoured for £300, without which
he would not be able to finish his novel ; that Godwin should not
complete a novel was to Shelley a black outlook. He racked his
brains to find the money which his father and his own lawyer
were trying to prevent him from applying to such objects.

XI

HARRIET'S SHADOW

ALTHOUGH Shelley had witnessed many abrupt and usually corrosive changes in his existence he could hardly have expected the load of fate which the hours were now bearing towards him. His worship of Godwin had proved the gateway to his sweet and profound happiness, but with shadows numberless besieging it, from which actual tragedy was about to advance. The outward beauty, the courtesy, the idealism of Shelley were such that against all his own intention he was the occasion of hard emotional conflict and entanglement in others.

Godwin was of the opinion that Fanny, the daughter of Mary Wollstonecraft and Gilbert Imlay, was attracted to Shelley as were Mary and Claire, and Fanny's long letters to Mary often show a proprietary interest in him and in the circumstances of his life. Despite the distance at which she stood from his home she liked to feel that she helped to direct his affairs. Her own life was truly lonely. Neither Godwin nor his second wife wanted to hear about her private feelings ; so the long letters were written, partly *at* Shelley, and being only letters did not free her from dejection. Some prospect was opened for a month or two by an aunt in Ireland, Everina Wollstonecraft, who might take her for training as assistant in her ladies' school ; but while Shelley was in Switzerland Everina inspected her niece and rejected her.

On September 24th, 1816, Fanny saw Shelley for a little while in London. She passed on some gossip that Mrs. Godwin had picked up at Bracknell, urged him to supply Godwin with £300, and suspected Shelley of not being frank with her on his plans about that. They parted in Piccadilly, and Shelley caught no note of impending disaster except what he remembered in writing a small poem later :

> Her voice did quiver as we parted,
> Yet knew I not that heart was broken
> From which it came, and I departed
> Heeding not the words then spoken.

On October 9th, when Shelley was at Bath with Mary, a truly

alarming letter came from Fanny, which sent Shelley to Bristol to investigate ; the next day he went again and found out something ; on the 11th he journeyed to Swansea. Fanny was lying dead at the Mackworth Arms, a laudanum bottle and a farewell note beside her.

For this ending Shelley could not be blamed, but he could not escape a sense of blame, as though his life had necessitated the death of an innocent. To quiet his nerves he read Montaigne, for whom Byron had such liking, and he hoped to have served his far-off friend by reading the proofs of the new Canto. Murray however declined to let him see them, asserting that Byron had entrusted the task to the editor of the *Quarterly Review*. Mary, who could meet most troubles with intellectual labours, continued writing what was to be known in the twentieth century as " the book of the film." Claire played her piano. On November 20th Shelley sent Byron a long letter, desiring him to send some kind message to her, instead of some other sort which had lately come. " Her time approaches, and her spirits begin to fail." In spite of this, the letter does not show Shelley as in any grave unrest. He speaks calmly and critically of politics and literature. " We have no new things to tell."

But where was Harriet now with her two children ? In June, 1816, she had been consulting Peacock about her income. It may have been in the summer that she stayed in a cottage at Bracknell, perhaps to be able to talk things over with Mrs. Boinville ; of such a visit Shelley heard through Fanny during that last interview. Usually she had been at her father's house, 23 Chapel Street, though from the first she had felt gloomy under the restraint there ; seemingly she wrote from that address with signs that she was on good terms at home to J. F. Newton in June, 1816. Nothing in Shelley's letters until the end of November and beyond suggests that anything out of the ordinary was happening to her or that he apprehended any such thing. But in mid-December he was suddenly informed that Harriet was dead,— drowned.

It was commonly said afterwards that Eliza and John Westbrook behaved towards Harriet with something of cruelty ; when these imputations came to Shelley's knowledge, he did not accept them, writing to Eliza, " I cannot help thinking that you might have acted more judiciously, but I do not doubt that you intended well." What particular action he referred to is unknown. All that has hitherto appeared in print concerning Harriet's last days is uncertain and entangled. After prolonged consideration, and while we await the results of patient inquiry into the genuineness of several professed documents, I take Eliza's word that Harriet was living at her father's almost to the last. "To that house," writes Peacock, " her body was carried " ; and the tradition that she was drowned not in the Serpentine as is usually assumed but in the old Reservoir in the Park a few steps from Chapel Street may still be the truth.

I pass over accounts of inquests on a woman or women found drowned in the Serpentine in the first weeks of December, 1816, for there is nothing in them to make it quite clear that they touch the tragedy of Harriet. Nothing in them links up the case with the name Shelley or Westbrook. A lady known as Smith is mentioned, and in one way and another is soon taken to have been Mrs. Shelley ; she is then imagined to have lived with a groom called Smith, and then, with a painter and glazier named Benjamin Smith of 61 Mount Street who was buried on December 11th. That is truly incredible ; she could not have lived in open adultery with a well-known tradesman one minute's walk from her father's door. She was " on the town," they say—but she had £400 a year. In short, it would almost be easier to identify her with the Harriot Smith who died in 1831 and whose headstone may still be seen in the graveyard of Grosvenor Chapel. Again, her sister Eliza " murdered " her to get the whole of John Westbrook's property, for the old man was breaking up. But he was not, and he refrained from dying until 1835.

In *Records of Shelley*, 1878, E. J. Trelawny gave his reconstruction of this sad mystery, having perhaps heard Hogg, Hookham, Claire Clairmont and Peacock on the subject. "Harriet sought a refuge with her father. The father at last was confined to his room by sickness, and the sister refused her entrance there. . . It is too painful to trace her faltering steps. She made one effort to hold on to life. A man professed to be interested and to sympathise in her fate. He was a captain in the army, and was suddenly ordered to join his regiment abroad. He promised to correspond with her. Her poverty compelled her to seek a refuge in a cheaper lodging ; her former landlady refused to forward her letters to her new address. In this deplorable state, fancying that no human being could take the least interest in her, . . . she hastened into the Park, and threw herself off the bridge into the Serpentine." Trelawny showed Richard Edgcumbe some documents on Harriet's death ; he never published these, and they are now untraced.

Harriet's beauty and elegance may have attracted an admirer ; that might explain the sternness of her father and sister ; but even Trelawny's tale leaves much in doubt. The assumption that

Harriet committed suicide, however probable it is, and of long standing, is an assumption. Many young people talk easily of suicide and so did she once. In the last known letter to Catherine Nugent she asked, " Is it wrong, do you think, to put an end to all one's sorrows? I often think of it—all is so gloomy and desolate. Shall I find repose in another world? Oh grave, why do you not tell us what is beyond thee ? "

A news paragraph which *The Times* printed on Thursday, December 12, 1816, which might refer to Harriet, is available to all who have some notion of life in London at that date. Perhaps it was Thomas Barnes who saw to it that nothing more appeared, no more was made of a startling story, if indeed Mrs. Shelley was meant. " On Tuesday," said *The Times*, "a respectable female, far advanced in pregnancy, was taken out of the Serpentine River, and brought home to her residence in Queen Street, Brompton, having been missed for nearly six weeks. She had a valuable ring on her finger. A want of honour in her own conduct is supposed to have led to this fatal catastrophe, her husband being abroad." If Harriet's story was like others of that day of mistress-chasing it may easily be pictured how some romantic and careless soldier had persuaded her to live in " very private " lodgings as his wife,—not far from Knightsbridge Barracks—and the rest would follow.

The dates on letters purporting to be from Hookham and from Shelley, on the subject of the newly discovered disaster, have been tampered with, and I have therefore to add this reason to others for not using those papers. In any event it is probable that it was Eliza who informed Shelley by letter of the death of her sister, and that he replied from Bath and announced that he would come to London. Perhaps he had not thought much about Harriet's life with him since the autumn of two years before, when he consulted Basil Montagu on his plan of having her back with him and Mary, and was with difficulty dissuaded. It was too late to give Harriet a home now, but he was determined that her children and his should have one. It might not be agreeable to face the Westbrooks, but he would see. Probably his lawyer advised him to wait until Mr. Westbrook's lawyer answered a question about Ianthe and Charles. On the 17th, hearing that Eliza meant to keep the girl if not the boy, he twice called on her at Chapel Street without being able to see her ; he therefore wrote her a letter insisting on his claims as a parent, and sent Mrs. Boinville (who could have told us much about all these events) to speak of them more fully. But he returned to Mary alone.

The honour of Shelley is darkened by the heartlessness of

expressions attributed to him upon the death of his first wife. It is impossible not to withhold judgment until it is proved that they are genuine or counterfeit. The appalling love-story of the Madman in his poem " Julian and Maddalo " has been interpreted as a fragment of autobiography. Call it rather a poetic imagination, a sketch of insanity no doubt made possible by his own moods and passions. Now that Harriet was gone for ever he spoke of her on few occasions, one of which Peacock witnessed. The friends were walking in Bisham Wood when Shelley " suddenly fell into a gloomy reverie." They went on with hardly a word till Shelley remarked that he might well become a beerdrinker, since such people had a means of deadening their feelings. Next day he explained apologetically : " I was thinking of Harriet." With that disclosure a poem of November, 1817, may be connected, and would seem to be addressed to his early self, and the memories of Harriet and Fanny :

> That time is dead for ever, child !
> Drowned, frozen, dead for ever !
>   We look on the past
>   And stare aghast
> At the spectres wailing, pale and ghast,
> Of hopes which thou and I beguiled
>   To death on life's dark river.
>
> The stream we gazed on then rolled by ;
> Its waves are unreturning ;
>   But we yet stand
>   In a lone land
> Like tombs to mark the memory
> Of hopes and fears, which fade and flee
>   In the light of life's dim morning.

Harriet's notion that after all Godwin was her greatest enemy would have deepened had she foreseen how *he* would treat her memory. In January, 1817, he " had evidence " that she was unfaithful to Shelley ; he worked out a date ; in May he had " unquestionable authority " and sent the story round. Many years later Hogg produced the opinion that Peacock was Harriet's lover : the same man assured Trelawny that Harriet was perfectly innocent. What was Shelley's opinion ? In his legal battle for his children he would have found it valuable to establish what Godwin told him ; but he did not try. In after years Claire said that in Mary's belief Shelley left Harriet because she was in love with a Major Ryan and the child she was to bear in

December, 1814, was not his own. Nothing written by Shelley about his first marriage hints at this ; the few direct confidences of his from the year 1814 ascribe his leaving Harriet to other causes altogether ; and his record of his intimate life before and during his courtship of Mary, written in 1815 to Hogg, says nothing of Harriet's being in the least inclined to love any one else. In spite of " these stories of military men " the appearance of Ryan at dinner with the Shelleys at Cooke's Hotel in 1813 does not constitute adultery with Harriet.

I do not feel sure that Ryan was even a military man. Hogg describes how he met three or four times dining with the Shelleys at their hotel a distressed poet whose forecasts of suicide got Harriet's sympathy but presently wearied even her. More than one such poet named Ryan was looking for something to eat in London then. Shelley's visits to Dublin had made him an obvious mark for such applicants, and Harriet's mention of Ryan in her letters to Catherine Nugent is not at all effusive. Mary's journal in January, 1815, says that " Ryan " had written and called but neither she nor Shelley saw him. He may be the man who edited Colonel Stanhope's book about Greece and Lord Byron ten years later. When Godwin in May, 1817, attempted again to destroy the case for Harriet, he at least connected her name with a real soldier.

This matter needs to be examined. Godwin's letter to W. T. Baxter of May 12th is partly published : " The late Mrs. Shelley has turned out to have been a woman of great levity. I know from unquestionable authority, wholly unconnected with Shelley (though I cannot with propriety be quoted for this) that she had proved herself unfaithful to her husband before their separation." The suppressed passage alleged that she had lived openly with Colonel Maxwell, presumably the commanding officer of the 7th Dragoon Guards. On May 14th Godwin informed his wife, then in Paris, that he had written to Shelley " and introduced the story I had learned from Hill at the Exhibition the Monday before, which had so much disturbed me." His letter had been mainly on other subjects, he had expected an angry answer, but Shelley had replied placidly throughout. " As to Hill's story (I took care not to name my authority) he only said in a vague way that it was ' much exaggerated,' and that for the present explanation was superfluous."

Almost certainly the story sent to Baxter was the story " introduced " to Shelley, who knew perfectly well the circumstances which had been worked up, and dismissed the subject. But if Godwin *had* named his authority Shelley would have laughed what

Hogg calls his fiendish laugh ; for Hill would be Tommy Hill, the most open-mouthed old chatterbox in London, satirized by his friends again and again for his endless " I know it for a fact."

The object of Godwin was to get his family affairs into something like conventional forms as quickly as possible, and even gloss the free love of his daughter and Shelley with respectability. It was to be marriage, in any case—and Shelley was a son-in-law with several recommendations. Within the month of Harriet's death, the advice of Peacock and of Sir Lumley Skeffington, a fading dandy and writer of plays, was taken on the question of this marriage ; it appeared best to act promptly, and Shelley and Mary had their wedding on December 30th in one of Wren's city churches, St. Mildred's, Bread Street. Godwin and his wife circulated the news : here is Godwin informing a usually neglected brother. " My daughter is between nineteen and twenty. . . . I went to church with this tall girl some little time ago to be married. Her husband is the eldest son of Sir Timothy Shelley, of Field Place, in the county of Sussex, Baronet. So that, according to the vulgar ideas of the world, she is well married, and I have great hopes the young man will make her a good husband. You will wonder, I daresay, how a girl without a penny of fortune should meet with so good a match. But such are the ups and downs of this world." And this is Mrs. Godwin squaring things up for Constable the publisher. " My time and my thoughts have been employed to even a painful degree upon the question, so interesting to the comfort and the peace of this family, which I took the liberty to mention in confidence to you in our last interview. I have now the pleasure to announce that Mr. Godwin's daughter, Mary, has entered the marriage state with Mr. Percy Bysshe Shelley, eldest son of Sir Timothy Shelley, Baronet, of Field Place, Horsham, Sussex. We are now endeavouring to forget preceding sorrows, and to enjoy the flattering prospects which seem to present themselves. The young couple have been in town several weeks, principally under our roof, and my poor nerves begin to cry quarter from the bustle and feasting occasioned by the event."

Another event had come which, though it was the achievement of her own daughter, Mrs. Godwin could hardly be expected to announce ; it was not announced to her. On January 13th, 1817, the solitary Claire gave birth to a girl, the child of Lord Byron, whom she called for the time Alba (" Dawn " in modern style) but for whom the poet chose the name Allegra. The presence of this infant and absence of her father cast Claire more than ever upon the Shelleys, although one of the few blessings for which

Mary, thinking of a settled home, appealed to Shelley was that Claire should be out of it.

On his wedding day Shelley wrote to Claire (if the letter is genuine) that the bustle and feasting at Skinner Street seemed dreadful to him. " I am resolved to overcome such sensations—if I do not destroy them I may be myself destroyed." His marriage did not remove the heavy oppression of the dispute over his children. Eliza Westbrook, whose first reason for not giving up Ianthe was that it would be cruel to take the child from her usual surroundings, had not relied on her own unaided defences. She was going to see to it that Shelley did not have them. Had she not mothered them ? A document designed accordingly, headed " To the Right Honourable John Lord Eldon, Baron Eldon of Eldon in the County of Durham, Lord High Chancellor of Great Britain," was filed on January 8th, 1817.

The Lord Chancellor had formerly been a Fellow and Tutor of University College, Oxford, and might have heard there that Shelley was a dangerous young man ; the Complaint put before him by the lawyers of Eliza Westbrook and her father was calculated to make him believe it. The object of the paper was to place Eliza Ianthe Shelley aged three and a half and Charles Bysshe Shelley aged two under the protection of the Court of Chancery. Their father having become acquainted with " a Mr. Godwin the author of a work called Political Justice " and his daughter Mary had deserted his wife and unlawfully cohabited with her " and is now unlawfully cohabiting with her and has several illegitimate children by her." He avowed himself an atheist, was the author of " Queen Mab "—with Notes—and had " blasphemously derided the truth of the Christian Revelation and denied the Existence of God as the Creator of the Universe." This man intended if he could to get possession of the persons of the children " and educate them as he thinks proper." Mr. Westbrook had made provision for them on January 2nd by setting aside £2000 in four per cent bank annuities and appointing trustees.

The Complaint was supplemented by nine letters from Shelley to Harriet after he left her, a copy of " Queen Mab " and other exhibits. Nothing is known to have accompanied Shelley's Answer dated January 18th, in which it was claimed that after Ianthe's birth Shelley and Harriet " agreed in consequences of certain Differences between them to live separate and apart." He had not deserted her " otherwise than by separating from her as aforesaid." At her urgent entreaty he permitted the children to stay with her, though he would have liked to have had them under his own care and management, but he forbore because of

Harriet's wishes and their tender years. He intended to have
them and provide for their education at the proper time. He had
never abandoned or deserted them, and if they had been in the
custody of Eliza and John Westbrook it was against his consent ;
" they have been clandestinely placed in some Place unknown to
this Defendant " and the Westbrooks repeatedly refused to deliver
them up or say where they were.

He was not unlawfully cohabiting with Mary Godwin, having
married her. He had sent Harriet £200 to discharge her debts
in June, 1815, and arranged that she should receive £200 annually
by quarterly payments from Sir Timothy's bankers, out of his
annuity of £1000. As the father of the children he was their
natural guardian ; it was his duty and his right to have the
custody of their persons and the superintendence and management of their education. They " ought to be delivered up to him."

On this occasion the law's delays were not great, at first. Lord
Eldon took the case on January 24th. Shelley must have felt
apprehensions as he looked at the Lord Chancellor, whose
adversaries said that his eminent station was due to powerful
patronage ; and then, what a prosecutor of political libellers he
had been in his day ! The Westbrooks had engaged a man of
different outlook, tall thin Sir Samuel Romilly, known for his
recent proposals to reduce capital punishment and other humane
efforts. Shelley asked his companion Leigh Hunt if he could pick
out Romilly from the rest of the Bench, and Hunt at once did so
correctly ; he did not think it difficult, Romilly's look being so
earnest and intelligent. Shelley's counsel were Charles Wetherell,
Basil Montagu the friend of Coleridge and Lamb, and Bell. Of
Wetherell it was said, unjustly no doubt, that " he makes gigantic
efforts, but does little evil to his antagonists unless it be by chance";
Montagu's special greatness was in questions of bankruptcy ; and
Bell's " speeches were quite as unintelligible as his written
opinions, which when legible were extremely valuable."

Romilly emphasised the atheism in " Queen Mab " ; Montagu answered that it was not published and had nothing to do
with paternal rights. He made a fine speech, observing without
contradiction " that Deism, or the belief in a God separated from
any other faith, was notoriously the religion of almost all the
literati of Europe " ; but Eldon would not give a decision, and
ordered that further hearings should be in the Lord Chancellor's
private room, in Westminster Hall. He remarked that there was
no need to exhibit a young man's follies to the public, and Mr.
Wetherell was of the same opinion. Shelley in the days following
wrote a Declaration, venturing to define what was in the Lord

Chancellor's mind after the speeches against him : " not whether
I shall teach my children religious infidelity, not whether I shall
teach them political heterodoxy, but whether I shall educate
them in immodest and loose sentiments of sexual connexion."
Marriage in England was a mischievous and tyrannous institution,
but he had honoured the feelings of the community by marrying
Mary.

Lord Eldon revealed his mind on March 27th. He rejected
the possibility that Shelley would bring up his children without
instilling his own principles. " This is a case in which the father
has demonstrated that he must and does deem it to be matter
of duty which his principles impose on him, to recommend to
those whose opinions and habits he may take upon him to form,
that conduct in some of the most important relations of life, as
moral and virtuous, which the law calls upon me to consider as
immoral and vicious—conduct which the law animadverts upon
as inconsistent with the duties of persons in such relations of life,
and which it considers as injuriously affecting both the interests
of such persons and those of the community." He would not
therefore give Shelley his children ; but the Court would consider
plans for their education.

It did so, gradually ; and both the Westbrooks and Shelley
put forward plans, of which the Court at last approved Shelley's.
His counsel had excepted to the order that the children should be
sent to the Rev. John Kendall, a schoolmaster at Warwick. He
named instead as suitable persons an Irish doctor named Hume
and his wife, who lived at Hanwell, and sent in an inoffensive
curriculum. To them in August, 1818, the children were entrusted, and the arrangement held until the year of Shelley's
death. In 1823 Ianthe was placed under the guardianship of
Eliza and her father after all, and Charles went to his grandfather
at Field Place. Whether Shelley was allowed to see them again
between the Chancery case and his final departure from England
is not on record.

But the fierce hopes and fears under which he contended for
freedom represented in his children are recorded indelibly. His
emotion when the decree was against him was such that " he
never afterwards dared to trust himself with mentioning the
children to the friend who stood at his side throughout the
business, and who was the dearest friend that he had." His mind
was horrified not only at what had happened but at what might
happen ; for a passing observation from the Lord Chancellor
seemed to him to threaten that his boy William would also be
taken from him. Informing Byron that " tyranny, civil and

religious," was upon him, he mentioned this possibility (in July, 1817). In a poem to William Shelley imagined an escape across the sea with him and Mary in a small boat, and he was determined to try this if necessary.

Inevitably Shelley saw the Lord Chancellor as a monster. He might have considered him in a less hideous shape had he won his case ; perhaps he smiled at Eldon's own insignificance when, towards the end of 1817, his eldest daughter defied him and made off from his house to marry G. S. Repton, an assistant of the architect Nash. But with similar passionate vision to that of Cobbett and Hazlitt, Shelley viewed Eldon as the mask or machine of corrupt power, and his poetic, measured curse upon him is known to all who read him. 'The Lord Chancellor's very urbanity—he was extremely courteous even when he forbade the publication of the proceedings in the newspapers—was torture to Shelley. The main curse was in the form of a description of what the children were doomed to, but Eldon's expression of the painfulness of his duty did not escape :

> By thy most killing sneer, and by thy smile—
>   By all the arts and snares of thy black den,
> And—for thou canst outweep the crocodile—
>   By thy false tears, those millstones braining men,
> I curse thee—though I hate thee not.

Some years later, in the wonderful series of political caricatures signed H. B., Eldon was again and again depicted as the servile, smug and lachrymose creature whom Shelley had some reason to curse.

The Westbrook v. Shelley case did not pass without notoriety. Newspaper reports were given in spite of the confidential nature of the hearings, and they were on account of it rich in imagination. Public attention was to some extent diverted from the rights and wrongs of Shelley's children by the Lord Chancellor's decision to have them discussed in private. It was a habit of his on these occasions, and an opponent of such private hearings took the chance to renew his protest in a letter signed " Publicola," of great length, conspicuously published in *The Times*. An editorial article agreed with the correspondent, asserting " that however the rights of the parties applying to a court of law or equity are their own, yet the judicial proceedings upon those rights are public property."

XII

THE HAMPSTEAD SET

IT IS singular that the period of crowding miseries just traced was for Shelley also the period of his emerging into literary London. Hitherto he had been in the by-ways, despite Hookham's book shop (where he might run into Hazlitt without noticing) or Godwin's (whose clerks were observant of the lover and not the poet). At an early date he had met the editor of *The Examiner*, a journal which was growing in quality and variety ; he now resolved to submit his " Hymn to Intellectual Beauty " over his pseudonym " The Elfin Knight," found so often in the " Faerie Queene." Hunt did not know who the Knight was but he knew poetry when he saw it, and he announced that the " Hymn " would be printed at the first opportunity. This was in October, 1816 ; on December 1st, having seen more of Shelley's work and identified him as the Elfin Knight, Hunt honoured him with John Keats and J. H. Reynolds in the celebrated manifesto " Young Poets." These men, and Lord Byron in his new style, would reanimate English poetry.

Though he was discussed only briefly and described rather as an original thinker than a poet, Shelley felt that it was praise worth having. He showed his pleasure by sending Hunt a cheque either for Hunt's use or for the *Examiner's* fund to help " the distressed poor in Spitalfields," and by visiting Hunt at Hampstead. The sense of the meeting was expressed in Shelley's letter from Marlow on December 8th, 1816. " I have not in all my intercourse with mankind experienced sympathy and kindness with which I have been so affected or which my whole being has so sprung forward to meet and to return. . . . Let me talk with you as with an old friend." At once Shelley made time to deal with Hunt's difficulties. He baulked at nothing when he saw a chance of serving needy merit. For instance—a little later on—he called on Samuel Rogers the banker-poet, " introducing himself, to request the loan of some money which he wished to present to Leigh Hunt." Rogers was equal to refusing that but noted that " both in appearance and in manners Shelley was the perfect gentleman,"—and the young man talked of Lord Byron too in a very proper manner. However Shelley collected the money, his gift to Hunt, who was heavily in debt, came to £1400.

When a devastating letter summoned Shelley from Bath to London again it was to Hunt's cottage that he went, and on December 18th he wrote to Eliza Westbrook that Hunt would receive the children from her at any convenient time. This was not to happen, but soon afterwards Shelley brought Mary to the Vale of Health, where they enjoyed many easeful hours that winter. Hunt's idealism, vitality and accomplishments were truly a blessing to Shelley now : " I have firm friends here. I am not, as might have happened once, to be oppressed in secrecy and solitude." The cottage which John Keats had discovered with warm delight a little earlier was one which allured men of genius and men who honoured genius. Shelley found himself quickly domesticated among these picturesque people, even if they did not all like him or he like them. The uniting element was a regard for free beauty in life, literature, music and the fine arts. The little palace of art had its touches of tinsel and plaster, but Shelley was not in the mood to worry much about them.

Of the four poets who spent the evening of February 5th, 1817, in the little cottage at the Vale of Health, and who had probably passed earlier evenings together there, only one had yet made a name ; this was Leigh Hunt himself. He had sent forth his " Story of Rimini " as a specimen of new ways of poetical writing, and freedom in sentiment, in colouring, in movement and expression. He felt that he had a part to play in making English poetry more fluent and flexible, more gorgeous than it had latterly been, and this bright enthusiasm supported by his readings of Italian verse and his acquaintance with painting and music was part of his charm in conversation. John Hamilton Reynolds, who had seen Hunt as a leading figure in the pilgrimage to Parnassus, was ten years his junior ; he was an insurance clerk who had published several pieces in verse. One, a Byronic tale called " Safie," had brought him a friendly letter from Byron in 1814 ; his latest production (1816) was " The Naiad and Other Poems." Reynolds hardly knew whether he was wit or dreamer. His tastes led him to the theatre and the greenroom, to the prize-fight, to the club ; yet he haunted sylvan solitudes and mused on high romance. Before long he wearied of Hunt's company and grew sarcastic on his character, perhaps on Shelley's also. Shelley did not like him. Yet Reynolds could not help being an amusing and even exciting companion.

Failing to fulfil the promise acclaimed in Hunt's " Young Poets " Reynolds is chiefly remembered as the friend of one who did, John Keats. At the beginning of the winter, the schoolmaster of Keats, Charles Cowden Clarke, had brought his old pupil, all expectancy and enjoyment, to Hunt's cottage, and Keats was hailed unhesitatingly as a youth of glorious powers of mind and enchanting personality. Soon afterwards Hunt invited Godwin, Basil Montagu and Hazlitt to dine, and took the opportunity to announce the discovery of a genius ; he put before them a number of manuscripts which included the sonnet " On First Looking Into Chapman's Homer," and, Hunt says, these writings " were pronounced to be as extraordinary as I thought them." Keats therefore met Shelley and Mary with a sparkle of fame about him already.

The two young poets passed their time together amiably enough, but did not really harmonise. Keats was too young to apprehend that Shelley was living under an almost intolerable strain, and seems to have known nothing of his distresses ; besides he was a combative critic of human beings, enjoying the verbal caricatures in which Reynolds was so handy. Leigh Hunt, with his opportunities to observe the relations of Shelley and Keats in what was practically the family circle, describes them best : " Keats did not take to Shelley as kindly as Shelley did to him. Shelley's only thoughts of his new acquaintance were such as regarded his bad health, with which he sympathised, and his poetry, of which he has left such a monument of his admiration in *Adonais*. Keats, being a little too sensitive on the score of his origin, felt inclined to see in every man of birth a sort of natural enemy. Their styles in writing also were very different ; and Keats, notwithstanding his unbounded sympathies with ordinary flesh and blood, and even the transcendental cosmopolitics of ' Hyperion,' was so far inferior in universality to his great acquaintance, that he could not accompany him in his daedal rounds with nature, and his Archimedean endeavours to move the globe with his own hands."

Understandable dissatisfaction arose in Keats's mind when during one of their walks on Hampstead Heath—lanky Shelley and little Keats—Shelley advised him not to publish his early poems, which in fact were about to be handed in at Charles Ollier's office for the purpose. Even if the slightly older Shelley argued from experience and said that he regretted having rushed into print even with " Queen Mab," he was likely neither to persuade nor to please a rival poet, seizing the glittering moment. The great business of the Vale of Health coterie just then was to publish Keats's genius to the world. Shelley's friends Peacock and Hogg, who also visited Hunt, were not in favour of it. When they saw a sonnet by Keats and an editorial commendation in *The Examiner* of March 16th, so Mrs. Shelley reported, they

" were very much scandalised " and proposed " to petition against
the publication of any more." If Keats heard of their attitude he
might estimate Shelley by his austere friends.

Freedom of discussion, the rule at Hunt's cottage, does not
invariably leave mutual liking and esteem after it. In December,
1816, the tumultous historical painter Benjamin Haydon, a
familiar friend of Hunt and an old contributor to *The Examiner*,
was invited to dine and to meet Shelley. Haydon arrived late
and found his place opposite a " hectic, spare, weakly yet
intellectual-looking creature, carving a bit of broccoli or cabbage
on his plate as if it had been the substantial wing of a chicken."
It was a pity Haydon had not arrived later still. He was at this
period furiously clinging to orthodox Christianity ; he heard
the vegetarian opposite " saying in the most feminine and gentle
voice, ' As to that detestable religion, the Christian. . . .' " It
was deliberate, he felt ; he was intended to be the sport of the
evening ; he " resolved to gore without mercy." Over the dessert
" to it we went like fiends," and Shelley's heresies that the Mosaic
and Christian dispensations were inconsistent, that Shakespeare
was not a Christian were, according to Haydon, demolished by
Haydon. On these matters the artist was implacable ; even his
devotion to Keats grew cold at last through a suspicion of his
unbelief or mere speculation ; Shelley therefore in a moment
unwittingly acquired an enemy the more dangerous because
Haydon by temperament distorted minor annoyance into intolerable wrong.

Since Haydon was beginning to remove himself from Hunt
and his sophistications, Shelley and he did not meet many times ;
but he was not the only man in the circle who did not garland
all he saw there with love-knots. William Hazlitt, though he did
not have bad dreams over Shelley's disrespect for bishops and
the litany, was too much of a practical man to take the young
reformist seriously, or perhaps their similarities of impulse and
passion came too close. At least they sometimes forgot their
troubles in good talk. On the night of February 9th, 1817, they
sat until three in the morning, while a warm argument was held
" in favour of the Monarchy by Leigh Hunt and Coulson "—the
editor of *The Globe*—" and in favour of Republicanism by Shelley
and Hazlitt."

Years afterwards when Hazlitt was pressed for an explanation
of his writing Shelley down, he could or would give no better
reason than that he disliked his looks. Hazlitt was by profession
a portrait-painter, but his sketches of the Shelley whom he saw
are in words. Shelley had " a fire in his eye, a fever in his blood,

a maggot in his brain, a hectic flutter in his speech, which mark out the philosophic fanatic. He is sanguine-complexioned, and shrill-voiced. As is often observable in the case of religious enthusiasts, there is a slenderness of constitutional *stamina*, which renders the flesh no match for the spirit. His bending, flexible form appears to take no strong hold of things, does not grapple with the world about him, but slides from it like a river—

> And in its liquid texture mortal wound
> Receives no more than can the fluid air."

When Shelley's mortality had been proved beyond question, Hazlitt wrote again : " Mr. Shelley was a remarkable man. His person was a type and shadow of his genius. His complexion, fair, golden, freckled, seemed transparent, with an inward light, and his spirit within him

> so divinely wrought
> That you might almost say his body thought.

He reminded those who saw him of some of Ovid's fables. His form, graceful and slender, drooped like a flower in the breeze. But he was crushed beneath the weight of thought which he aspired to bear, and was withered in the lightning-glare of a ruthless philosophy."

Hazlitt might deplore, he could not ignore Shelley. He pondered upon him far more than over the quieter Keats. To Hazlitt Shelley was a psychological curiosity, and yielded a kind of unholy inspiration ; he was to write of Shelley with full eloquence even while he attacked the absurd egotism cramping such abilities and exaltations. Leigh Hunt was inclined to trace Hazlitt's strictures on Shelley to a grudge : Hazlitt had been angry to hear that Shelley had cut him up at Godwin's table. It is possible, for Hazlitt was exceedingly sensitive ; but the cause was deeper. Hazlitt excelled in studies of character, and like all great artists placed his lights and shades as he desired. Moreover he might himself digress from some sublimity into a personal foible or anecdote but he did not pardon the weakness in others ; as when in the full blaze of victory over the French Revolution and its results Shelley wasted time and words over his old topic of " introducing the domestic government of the Nayrs into this country as a feasible set-off against the success of the Borough-mongers."

Horace Smith, one of the City men who have made their mark in literature, and an old friend of Leigh Hunt, came to Hampstead to meet Keats and Shelley in the winter of 1816. They were as yet obscure but Smith was a celebrity, one of the authors of that recent collection of parodies, " Rejected Addresses," which everybody had read. Smith instantly agreed on the poetry in Keats's first manuscripts ; he as readily recognised the eminence of Shelley, of whom he had already formed an impression as man (" a grievously over-punished man ") and poet. Hunt arranged a meeting, and Smith gladly answered the call. For half an hour after his arrival he was alone with Keats : " to an observant eye Keats's looks and his attenuated frame already foreshadowed the consumption that had marked him for its prey. His manner was shy and embarrassed, as of one unused to society, and he spoke little." Then the maid brought in Mr. Shelley. " I beheld a fair, freckled, blue-eyed, light-haired, delicate-looking person, whose countenance was serious and thoughtful, whose stature would have been rather tall had he carried himself upright ; whose earnest voice, though never loud, was somewhat unmusical. Manifest as it was that his preoccupied mind had no thought to spare for the modish adjustment of his fashionably made clothes, it was impossible to doubt even for a moment that you were gazing upon a *gentleman*, . . . one that is gentle, generous, accomplished, brave." Out on the Heath Smith got Shelley to himself, and heard him talk brilliantly of Coleridge's " Kubla Khan " and of Plato, for whom his admiration was unbounded ; he compared parts of the Grecian's doctrines to those of the New Testament and dwelt on " the singular accordance between the scriptural narrative of the birth of Christ and the miraculous nativity attributed to Plato, 420 years before our era."

This was the heathenism which so enraged Haydon, and men less inflammable were at least uneasy when the strange newcomer insisted on talking of religions. A younger painter than Haydon, whose name perhaps Shelley did not catch—for he wrote to him later as if they were unacquainted—is an example. Joseph Severn is honoured for his friendship to Keats in a tragic extremity, and Keats was present when he met Shelley. Severn describes (the reader will pardon some repetition) the " tall, elegant but slender figure : his countenance painfully intellectual, inasmuch as it showed traces of his struggle with humanity, and betrayed the abstract gift of a high mind in little relation with the world. His restless blue eye seemed to dwell more on the inward than the outward aspect of nature. His manner, aristocratic though gentle, aided his personal beauty. Fine classical features, luxuriant brown hair, and a slightly ruddy complexion, combined with his unconsciousness of his attractive appearance, added to his fine exterior." Shelley's eyes made many people grow descriptive : Cowden Clarke calls them "intensely blue, with a gentle and lambent expression, yet wonderfully alert and engrossing ; nothing appeared to escape his knowledge."

Severn like Haydon fancied that Shelley, who was only seeking for a thoughtful disputant and a keen debate, was aiming at his personal convictions while he told Leigh Hunt that he meant to write a poem comparing Christ to a mountebank and the miracles to juggling. Severn interrupted ; the greatest men since Christ had been Christians, and the faith therefore stood above ridicule. This led to an examination of the religious denominations of great men, including Shakespeare : on this very unsteady ground they exchanged quotations till Keats and Hunt told Severn he had the better of it, and Shelley said he would write an essay on the matter. In his later life Severn found in Shelley's "Essay upon Christianity" what, apart from the flashings of a conversation, Shelley felt about Christ, and Mr. Gladstone explained to him that "Prometheus Unbound," towards which Shelley in 1817 was moving, was in all but name a Christian poem. Severn still had to get over his illusion that Shelley's talk had deprived or helped to deprive Keats of "the means of hope," a view which nothing written by Keats begins to justify. Keats had solely an aesthetic or poetic interest in Shelley, who for him might range through all theology for all eternity—his own study of the Bible was that recommended by Jowett : he read it like any other book. He would have hated to hear that his own views on religion were provided by any other mind.

Imperfect sympathies, then, happened at Hunt's cottage as elsewhere, but piano-playing, flute-playing, quartets, the news, new books, prints, casts, gems, pots of flowers, jokes and kindness made up a diversion which Shelley needed. The shocks which he had suffered and the postponements and perplexities of the Chancery suit demanded such a remedy. Friends and relations of Hunt dropped in freely, not all of them literary or political but all treating life as an endless adventure. Marianne Hunt and her sister Elizabeth came under Shelley's spell as women so often did, thought him perfect, and made him feel that the cottage was his. The eldest boy, Thornton, aged six, was sure that *he* owned Shelley. " He was as strictly a part of the family as any of our blood-relations, for he came and went at pleasure. I can remember that I performed his bidding equally with that of my father. . . . I found in Shelley a companion whom I better understood, and whose country rambles I was more pleased to share. . . . Shelley entered more unreservedly into the sports and even the thoughts of children. . . . I can remember well one day when we were both for some long time engaged in gambols, broken off by my terror at his screwing up his long and curling hair into a horn, and approaching me with rampant paws and frightful gestures as some imaginative monster." Given fine weather they would launch their paper boats on the Vale of Health pond, and Shelley was in this the master mariner after years of practice on the Serpentine, the Round Pond in Kensington Garden, Virginia Water, a pool at Bracknell and the Surrey Canal. Peacock was his only challenger. But Shelley was not able to limit his thoughts to the game or the pleasure of loading his little boats with half-pence for the boys to race after. He "playfully said how much he should like it if we could get into one of the boats and be shipwrecked,—it was a death he should like better than any other."

One snowy night the editor of *The Examiner* was returning from the opera and nearing his own door when he heard "strange and alarming shrieks, mixed with the voice of a man." The shrieks were those of a woman, the voice was Shelley's—and neighbours gave the popular interpretation of these circumstances. But they were wrong. The woman, who had come with her son to town while he appeared before a court of law, had been discovered by Shelley in a fit at the top of the Heath. He went from door to door for assistance, and was given only a harangue : " No, Sir : there's no necessity for that sort of thing, depend on it ; impostors swarm every where : the thing cannot be done ; sir, your conduct is extraordinary." In the short time available Shelley made a democratic reply, then brought the woman and her son with some difficulty down the footpath to the Vale of Health, and called a doctor. Next day he sent the couple comfort-ably home to Hendon ; and this, says Hunt, " was one of the most ordinary of his actions." If he went to the coach station he was likely to give away most of his money and travel outside or make his journey on foot.

His ability and will to look away from his own troubles and serve the cause of one or many others come out in his preparing a tract at this period. Not all the conversation at Hunt's was poetical, and the politician Shelley drew encouragement and in-formation there for this pamphlet, which he published annoy-mously early in March, 1817, through Charles and James Ollier. Their advertisement, March 7th, of two books together is almost a text for a contrast between two great poets : " This day is published, price 1s., A PROPOSAL for putting REFORM to the VOTE, throughout the Kingdom. By the HERMIT of MAR-

LOW. Also, in 1 vol. post 8 vo., price 6s. 6d. boards, Poems, By John Keats.

> ' What more felicity can fall to creature
>   Than to enjoy delight with liberty ? '
>   Spenser.—Fate of the Butterfly."

Shelley's plan was for a plebiscite, with the typical offer to subscribe £100 towards the expense, timed to be useful to a meeting of reformists at the Crown and Anchor Tavern. Shelley supplied Ollier with a list of persons and clubs to whom copies should be sent in England, Wales and Scotland ; the list indicates that his extant correspondence by no means covers the whole of his labours in the cause of liberal opinion, organisation and action. A single name among these recipients of the " Proposal " denotes the hopeful perseverance of his mind in the search for the men whose co-operation might benefit society. Perhaps nobody now has heard of Mr. George Ensor ; but Shelley, in the weeks after being expelled from Oxford, had followed that mild Irish nationalist on " National Education," and had traced his ideas through subsequent disquisitions. In 1816 *The Examiner* had reviewed with fullest approval Ensor's book " On the State of Europe," wherein the dangers of monarchy and despotism were expressed exactly as Shelley would desire. Ensor was also a determined public opponent of the propositions of Malthus on population. Shelley's " Proposal " reached the *Quarterly Review*, and was included in a list of books prefixed to an article on deplorable political opinions but not discussed in it.

XIII

MARLOW

IT APPEARED to Shelley that however the law might dispose of his claim to the children he could now settle down at least until he should be summoned to occupy Field Place, and, as his father was still taking his place in the House of Commons, that might be some time yet. In Peacock's company he had grown fond of the riverside country round Great Marlow, not far from his old haunts at Bracknell—though Mrs. Boinville had not lately shown the old friendliness. He found that a pseudo-gothic dwelling with pointed windows and battlements, Albion House in Marlow, was to be let, took it on a lease for twenty-one years, and furnished it well ; one room " large enough for a ballroom " became his library adorned with great casts of Apollo and Venus. Shelley also took the lease of four acres of meadow adjoining the house. At about the time when his Reform pamphlet was issued he moved in, with Mary and the boy, Claire and Byron's daughter, the Swiss *gouvernante* Elise, a cook and Harry the gardener and handyman.

But the number of inhabitants at Albion House in Shelley's reign was usually larger than that, for it was his way to invite all friends. The Hunts, a numerous tribe, were accommodated whenever they pleased. Godwin was an early guest, and was taken on the river while all talked of novels and perfectibility. Hogg would often come, and Peacock, " to drink his bottle " even if Shelley was away. Horace Smith came ; Cowden Clarke enjoyed one visit ; but Keats did not appear. " I refused to visit Shelley," he wrote in October, " that I might have my own unfettered scope," and he explained later to Cowden Clarke that Shelley had invited him to make one of his household. The opportunity was not roughly set aside by Keats, but he feared that the latitude even of Shelley's arrangements would not leave him a free agent.

This was indeed to have been a happy period, and the pseudonym on Shelley's political pamphlet, " The Hermit of Marlow," sums up his dream of a peaceful nook there in the beloved Thames Valley. There he would husband his resources, help the needy, observe the world at will, talk, write, entertain genius, find Nature ever changing and ever beautiful, love and be loved in his home. Something of the intention was fulfilled. When hostile people, noticing not only Mary and Claire in his house but now and then other London ladies, said that it was an odd sort of hermitage, they did not upset him. Leigh Hunt says that he passed his days very like a hermit, rising early, walking and reading before his meagre breakfast, writing and studying most of the morning. A dinner of vegetables, conversation with his friends, another walk, and reading to Mary until ten o'clock completed his ordinary day. Peacock says more of Shelley's walking. It was thirty-two miles to Tyburn turnpike but they would often cover them afoot by field path and highroad and after a night or two return the same way. Every notable place within sixteen miles of Marlow was visited, particularly the scenes sacred to the great Republicans, Cromwell, Hampden and Milton. And of course Shelley kept a boat, the *Vaga*, and was often sailing or rowing between Maidenhead and Henley.

His physical tirelessness was admired by young Thornton Hunt who went on the river with him. His love of flowers delighted Thornton's aunt Bessy, a capable botanist, who watched him hastening home from his rambles " with his hat wreathed with briony, or wild convolvulus ; his hand filled with bunches of wild-flowers plucked from the hedges as he passed, and his eyes, indeed every feature, beaming with the benevolence of his heart." Horace Smith, one of his wisest friends, remembered one of these excursions especially—it was his last wandering with the poet. Among woods like green cloisters they talked, as on their first walk, of religion. With kindling looks, striding on more and more urgently and swinging his arms to and fro, Shelley uttered his thought : to attempt a view of the Deity as a person, or imagine the Deity otherwise than as the spirit of the universe, was presumptuous, for the finite cannot grasp the infinite. Systems of religion must die, all but one—the religion of nature ; and though human nature might not be absolutely perfectible, it might be improved almost without limit, evil not being inherent in our creation but accidental.

All this was enchantment to Horace Smith who had escaped for a brief holiday from the different speculations of the Stock Exchange. He did not himself see religion quite as Shelley did, and these were Utopian dreams not to be consummated on earth, but he listened to them with profound emotion. The woods round their steps took the aspect of a vast natural cathedral, the quiet earth seemed listening also to the enthusiast, the blue sky between the tree-tops smiled upon him : " a solemn reverence began to mingle with my admiration of the singular youth by my side."

S.   F

Looking at the gleaming countenance and the slender energetic body, he thought of all he knew about Shelley—his genius, his intellectual light, his philanthropy and self-denial, the courage and grandeur of his soul, " combined with a feminine delicacy and purity, and an almost angelic amenity and sweetness." This, he almost fancied, was " a spirit from some higher sphere " come to earth with word of a new golden age and the manner in which it could be most quickly attained.

Shelley in the ordinary way acted as matter-of-fact angel, since the overthrow of Napoleon had brought no golden age to his poor neighbours. Leigh Hunt treated him, he said, as if he were " some antient and wrinkled, but good-natured grand-uncle," instead of " the most imprudent of mankind." His relief measures show the tradition of Field Place as well as his own kind heart. Somehow he produced a bag of coins on Saturday nights and doled them out to distressed persons, especially widows and children. For the cold weather he distributed blankets and sheets, stamped SHELLEY in large lettering so that they should not be easily " negotiable." He went from cottage to cottage giving amateur medical advice and supplies of soup, and Mary ascribed to this visiting his severe attack of ophthalmia. A little girl named Polly Rose was given a second home at Albion House. Altogether he was " living like a country gentleman on a small scale," but he worked in other ways to improve the Englishman's condition far beyond his local tour. Not every country gentleman was a political freelance.

On a November day in 1817 he read in his newspaper that the Princess Charlotte, daughter of the Regent, had died in childbirth; and that three artisans who had taken part in a small insurrection in Derbyshire had been executed for high treason, with all grimness. The first of these events was dwelt upon as a national calamity ; Shelley did not think of it so ; it was the second which appeared to him to be one. Grief for the Princess, he wrote in a new pamphlet, was essentially a private thing ; an amiable young lady was dead. But by the execution of Brandreth, Turner and Ludlam the British nation suffered incalculable bereavement. In imagination, with the drum of a funeral march in his sentences, he followed them to the grave ; it was the funeral not only of three men but of British Liberty. What Shelley was saying was also urged in successive articles in *The Examiner* ; Hunt was moved to poetry by the death of the beautiful Princess, but protested against the suppression of topics quite as painful and important. Shelley's " Address to the People on the Death of the Princess Charlotte " with a motto from Leigh Hunt's *Reflector* —" We pity the plumage, but forget the dying bird "—was quickly given to his new publisher Ollier, but Ollier would hardly run the risk of being connected with it. Shelley's first edition of it has vanished, but some years after his death the pamphlet came out more or less in facsimile of that printing and had some circulation, though by then it was a ghost from far away.

A much greater work was disturbing Ollier, reformist though he was—one of Shelley's long poems on the tribulation and glory of man. The birthplace of this design was the cottage of Leigh Hunt, if Medwin reports Shelley rightly as saying that " Laon and Cythna " was written in competition with " Endymion " by John Keats. At that date Hunt—himself wandering along in a melodious mythological poem called " The Nymphs "—often promoted poetical contests, but usually suggested short productions on a set subject. Shelley and Keats apparently entered for a race with longer ones, the time limit being six months. The reading public was showing an appetite for narrative poems, and both writers set to work to supply them ; thus far at least they shared their thoughts, but it is clear why Keats preferred not to stay at Marlow. Beginning in April, 1817, he completed " Endymion " in rather more than the time proposed, but " Laon and Cythna " was being printed already. Augustine Birrell couples both works in a comparison with Browning's " Sordello," equally " difficult to read and for the same reason—the author's lack of experience in the art of composition."

Shelley certainly wished his bewildering poem to be generally admired ; he says as much in the preface. " I have chosen a story of human passion in its most universal character, diversified with moving and romantic adventures, and appealing, in contempt of all artificial opinions or institutions, to the common sympathies of every human breast." He presented a love romance with a hero, a heroine, and the course that never did run smooth. He inwove the theme of human emancipation and fearful war against tyranny, with startling changes of fortune and extremes of misery and blessedness. The original alternative title, " The Revolution of the Golden City : a Vision of the Nineteenth Century," shows him locating the action in the Byronic regions about Constantinople, and his hero and heroine were modern Greeks whose campaign and journeys might to some extent be charted on a map like those of the poet in " Alastor." To some extent they could be seen as living in the material world, as in the battle scenes where, in the classic style of artillery bombardment,

> Far overhead, ships from Propontis keep
> A killing rain of fire.

Or again Laon proposes that Cythna shall be taken to a free country of measureless possibilities,

Nay, start not at the name, America !

Such touches of reality marked a poem, the aura and quality of which were not real ; and in a review Hunt said reluctantly but roundly, as though in reply to a spoken question by his friend, " The work cannot possibly become popular." Canto I, which Shelley thought introductory, stood in its complication between almost all conceivable readers and the great romance. The poet discovered himself perhaps in the year 1812, " when the last hope of trampled France had failed," contemplating the sea in a golden dawn which was suddenly blotted out by a tempest, then watching an Eagle and a Serpent fighting on high until the vanquished Serpent fell. It was now evening and the tormented sea grew calm ; the poet went down the cliffs and found below a Woman of supreme beauty with a little boat, its prow made of moonstone. The wounded Serpent, so enormous earlier, came to rest in her bosom ; she invited the poet to voyage with them, and as they sailed she told her history and interpreted the Serpent and the Eagle. Few could have understood the interpretation, few were Shelleyan enough to comprehend the growing web of idea and narrative, spun in unfamiliar hues to a tune of flowing, lulling numbers.

Yet the age of Shelley, of Blake, of Joanna Southcott and John Martin was the age of visions. A catalogue of poems defined by their authors in that word would be long and impressive. Readers who could be patient with the obscure significances of " Laon and Cythna " might well feel in its inventions that Shelley was a wonder of the age. Whatever it meant, the combat of the Eagle and Serpent was depicted with profuse energy, daring fancy, burning belief. Even when many poets and painters were creating strange architecture the Temple reached by the boat with the moonstone prow was a new and stupendous imagining ; the occurrences in the hall of ten thousand columns, while the Woman faded and Laon and Cythna became visible, were indeed magical. Throughout his twelve Cantos scene and deed of the same nature burst forth from Shelley's mind with little interval except for philosophical conversation. The ultimate turn of events was not the least surprising, as it was the most beautiful. Laon and Cythna were defeated and burned under the Tyrant's eye, but death came as another life. The dead child of Cythna was the plumed Seraph who steered a new and yet lovelier boat towards them ; a new voyage of enchantment brought them to the Temple of the Spirit.

The poem might also win a few sensitive readers by the subtle and delightful expressions of external nature which Shelley could now give. It was his to experience the elemental circumstance in which we live with peculiar, sweet, sharp and various excitement. The effect of tyranny on Laon's country which he described included the deadening of such responses among the enslaved : none in that régime wandered forth to see or feel

> Earth, our bright home, its mountains and its waters,
>   And the ethereal shapes which are suspended
> Over its green expanse, and those fair daughters,
>   The clouds, of Sun and Ocean, who have blended
>   The colours of the air since first extended
> It cradled the young world.

But of several products of adventurous genius in this poem two remain to be selected here.

For all our wealth of love poetry nobody before Shelley had quite told the mystery and far country of love's physical union. When " public hope " had been for the time taken from Laon and Cythna, his deep understanding represented them finding a haven in this " tumult and tenderness." His picture of their bridal-night in the autumn hills stands alone in its rendering of a universal and wonderful thing which has been passed by in silence by most other English poets. The other achievement is Cythna, who has been pointed out as the first " new woman " in our poetry. It is she rather than Laon who is impelled by a passion and empowered with an intelligence for reforming the world. Feminine as she is, fair as the fairest and unsurpassed in woman's love, she is the leader of political justice. This supremacy is illuminated when, just as Laon expects immediate destruction by the sabres of the Ottomans, Cythna comes into the battle like an avenging angel on " a black Tartarian horse of giant frame " and carries Laon away to the mountains—

> borne beyond pursuer,
> And we are here.

The composition of " Laon and Cythna " kept Shelley solitary in the summer of 1817 many mornings—in his library, in his boat among the islets of the Thames, on a seat high up in Bisham Wood. He seems to have hoped that the old-established firm Messrs. Longman would publish it, for they were just enjoying the huge success of a wild oriental tale in verse, the " Lalla Rookh " of Tom Moore ; and he desired that Moore's opinion on his opening cantos might be obtained. Moore sent a kind and encouraging letter, but in the end Shelley paid for the printing and Ollier and another firm appeared as publishers. The book had been advertised as ready in *The Times*, and the first few copies had been sold when Ollier took fright. The Deity, Kings, Priests had been so freely treated that all concerned in the book risked a costly prosecution for blasphemy. Even Hunt, who was in an invidious position, since it was he who had desired Shelley to assist Ollier in his enterprise by making him his publisher, had his fears. After one magnificent letter of protest Shelley grew gracious as usual, invited Ollier to Albion House and spent a day with him modifying the text. Some of the changes show how sweetly reasonable Shelley could be. He had made one of his characters parody Addison's endlessly quoted " See how a Christian can die " with

> Therefore shall ye behold
> How Atheists and Republicans can die.

That was changed. The title itself became " The Revolt of Islam," and the re-issue went out accordingly ; but a greater change was that Shelley dropped " one circumstance intended to startle the reader from the trance of ordinary life." His hero and heroine in the revised version ceased to be brother and sister. In the end Shelley himself took great trouble to call in copies of the unrevised poem. Too late, of course. His enemies had already acquired this proof that he was a worshipper of incest.

In the third Canto Laon heard a low cry from Cythna bound by the tyrant's men :

> " My mien grew calm and meek,
> And grasping a small knife, I went to seek
> That voice among the crowd."

The action caught Hunt's eye as characteristic of Shelley himself ; the words became a pleasantry between them. " On which," Hunt would write in a letter, " Shelley looked meek, and taking forth a pen," etc. ; Shelley would report some satirical verses of his as full of *small knives*. The friends had a humorous as well as imaginative understanding. Shelley could trust Hunt to pick up his literary allusions, as when he described his " languishing into hate " against Mrs. Godwin with a parody on Pope's " Dying Christian's Address to his Soul." Probably the same woman was being execrated when Shelley asked, " Hunt, we have love-songs, why should we not have hate-songs ? " And he wrote one or two, but left more unfinished ; his friend did the same. Not only Hunt but Keats noticed Shelley's pleasure in nonsensical applications of

> For God's sake let us sit upon the ground,
> And tell sad stories of the death of kings.

Once in the Hampstead stage to town the other occupant " was
an old lady, who sat silent and stiff after the English fashion ; he
startled her into a look of the most ludicrous astonishment by
saying abruptly, ' Hunt,

> For God's sake let us sit upon the ground,' etc.

The old lady looked on the coach-floor, as if she expected to see
us take our seats accordingly."

Association private and public with the writers and proprietors
of *The Examiner*, together with his reputation and literary appearances, drew on Shelley the fire of the big gun set up to protect
inherited ideas, the *Quarterly Review*. Nowadays no parallel exists
to this extraordinary conservative periodical as it then was. Its
adverse sentence was heard far and wide. Hunt and Shelley
alike served among its targets, but Shelley's turn really came,
after an interval, when " The Revolt of Islam " was condemned.
It is curious that the writer of the article, a schoolfellow of
Shelley, was a nephew of the poet whose " Ancient Mariner " he
knew by heart ; and that Shelley received some of the odium
stored up against that poet. The Rev. George Coleridge had long
trained J. T. Coleridge in disapprobation of the family's man of
genius and of " specious argumentation " which wore down
moral sense and led to systems of fallacy and deception. For the
Quarterly's onslaughts upon reformist poets this training was
excellent, and Uncle George laid down the review with solemn
satisfaction at the " Christian pummelling " of Hunt and his
" compeer or rather co-fiend Shelley," whose private life or a
distortion of it the reviewer took as part of his subject-matter.

The co-fiend was able to find entertainment in the performance. " They say that ' My chariot-wheels are broken.' Heaven
forbid ! My chariot, you may tell them, was built by one of the
best makers in Bond Street, and it has gone several thousand
miles in perfect security. What a comical thing it would be to
make the following advertisement :—' A report having prevailed,
in consequence of some insinuations in the *Quarterly Review*, that
Mr. Shelley's chariot wheels are broken, Mr. Charters, of Bond
Street, begs to assure the public that they, after having carried
him through Italy, France, and Switzerland, still continue in
excellent repair.' " And further, " I was amused, too, with the
finale ; it is like the end of the first act of an opera, when that
tremendous concordant discord sets up from the orchestra, and

everybody talks and sings at once. It describes the result of my battle with their Omnipotent God ; his pulling me under the sea by the hair of my head, like Pharaoh ; my calling out like the devil who was *game* to the last ; swearing and cursing in all comic and horrid oaths, like a French postilion on Mount Cenis ; entreating everybody to drown themselves ; pretending not to be drowned myself when I *am* drowned ; and lastly, *being* drowned." Not many years would pass before a gentle idealist named Arthur Henry Hallam gave " The Revolt of Islam " to a friend destined to be Dean of Canterbury, who in turn gave it to his beloved as a wedding-present, " this treasure of sweet song."

The composition, revisal and preparation for the press of so extensive an imaginative work as " The Revolt of Islam " might have exhausted a mind of more than common powers, but Shelley quickly planned other long poems. " Rosalind and Helen " and " Prince Athanase " can be regarded as partly due to an artistic necessity. Shelley had been long confined to the "stanza of Spenser (a measure inexpressibly beautiful)," and the time came for a change of movement and tune. " Rosalind and Helen," which will be noticed again further on, was in a metre developed from that so delightful to Shelley and others in " Christabel." " Prince Athanase " is in *terza rima*. It was too much like a new version of " Alastor " to interest Shelley fully, and it did not pass the stage of an outline—again a romantic hero's voyage in search of ideal love, his disappointment and death, his discovery in death of the One he sought—with some mighty fragments. These have something of biography in them. The Prince is a Shelleyan spirit, though Shelley warns us that the analysis grew morbid : the Prince's friend is Dr. Lind once again, talking of Plato—or a wise veteran very like him : and what is left of the vision of the One surely speaks of Mary Godwin. Here occur passages in Shelley's angelical manner on spring and on all-vivifying love, to make us regret the failure of the whole impulse :

> Thou art the radiance which where ocean rolls
> Invests it ; and when heavens are blue
> Thou fillest them ; and then the earth is fair,
> The shadows of thy moving wings imbue
> Its deserts and its mountains till they wear
> Beauty like some bright robe. . . .

But the year 1817 was not one of unspoiled retirement. Besides the principal poem then written it was unlikely that much could be completed. Some vestiges of a poem on " Otho " remain, calling up the figure of Shelley at his library table with the

Roman historians open before him. "To Constantia Singing" may be the memento of one of the performances of Claire Clairmont, who had had some training from one of the fashionable Corris. This musical and dramatic young lady was generously supported ; on April 17th Shelley was ordering (on a post-obit unfortunately) a cabinet piano, to cost from fifty to seventy guineas. It was made by Joshua Kirkman of Carnaby Street (whose improvement in grand pianos had been praised by the Regent) under the direction of so fine a musician as Vincent Novello, and was much liked at Albion House, where Leigh Hunt, possibly the best pianist among the poets of England, often played on it.

Claire Clairmont, who was now familiarly known as First Lady, was well content to remain with the Shelleys and had indeed no other solution for the problem brought about by her brief intimacy with the now contemptuous and distant Byron. She appeared to thrive on her troubles, and visitors would be struck by her strong feelings, lively temper, social talents and brilliant looks. Mary was neither in her most thoughtful or beautiful form ; she grew pale, neglected her clothes, and seemed intent upon disagreeing with whatever was proposed ; this peevishness was imitated by small William. In fact Mary, besides the task of running Albion House, was undertaking too many things at once for a girl so young. In May she achieved the difficult object of completing "Frankenstein," and went to town to arrange publication—but it must be anonymous. Like other popular books "Frankenstein" was rejected by more than one publisher, first John Murray, then Ollier, possibly Taylor & Hessey. Mary's next literary employment was to prepare for the press under Shelley's editorship the travel journal which Hookham and Ollier published late in 1817 as "A Six Weeks' Tour." It was much like other travel books of the time, except in the splendour of some of the description.

Throughout the Marlow year Shelley wrote to Byron in the hope that the father of Claire's child would do something useful about her ; "She continues to reside with us under a feigned name. But we are somewhat embarrassed about her. We are exposed to what remarks her existence is calculated to excite. At least a period approaches when it will be impossible to temporize with our servants or our visitors." Alba, naturally, was happy enough where she was, and that was generally on the nursery floor with William, "talking a most unintelligible language together" and "amusing themselves for hours in the most sociable way." On the whole, Byron wished Alba to be sent out

to him in Italy, but he made no arrangements for her safe convey-
ance, unless Shelley brought her himself; and Shelley had that
possibility often in his mind.

On September 2nd Mary gave birth to a daughter who was
named Clara Everina. The event gave no more trouble than was
expected ; but Shelley's " languor and increasing illness "
alarmed Mary and he was ordered off to London to consult a
good physician—namely William Lawrence, eminent as an eye
surgeon. He prescribed rest and a change. Marlow in the
nineteenth century was " a negative sort of place," and Mary
began to feel that in spite of the long lease of Albion House,
which was damp enough to mildew the books in the library, they
ought to move. But where ? For the first time Mary found her
man of genius wanting in decision. He listened affectionately
to her reasonings and agreed that they should leave Marlow for
Italy or perhaps the coast of Kent ; he requested her to make the
choice. Looking through the haze of money troubles Mary
hardly saw how it could be Italy, but Shelley asserted that " the
Italian sun will be the best physician."

Still the frosty hand of Godwin threatened any such plan. It
was not until December that Shelley could face him with the
news that a journey to Italy was scarcely avoidable if he were
not to perish of consumption, for that was suspected as his illness.
Godwin had no interest in Shelley's illness, and continued to bait
him over the sums of money raised and to be raised for his debts.
Shelley refused to let this inconceivable father-in-law drive him
silly or deflect him from the Italian scheme, the date of which
remained very uncertain. At least he caused to be inserted in
The Times of December 16th the following advertisement :
" BUCKS. GREAT MARLOW.—To be LET, furnished, or unfurnished (or the Lease and Furniture, which is modern and new,
to be disposed of,) a HOUSE, containing a good dining-room,
library 36 feet by 18, drawing-room 30 feet by 18, study, 5 best
bedrooms, 2 large nurseries, each 30 feet by 20, water closet,
6 or 7 attics, convenient offices, good garden and pleasure-ground,
with immediate possession ; 4 acres of land may be had. Apply
personally, or by letter, post paid, to Mr. Madock's, carpenter,
Great Marlow."

The sunny side of his life there had been more than Mary was
apt to allow. " Beautiful walks, uplands, valleys, wood, water,
steeples issuing out of clumps of trees, most luxuriant hedges,
meads, cornfields, brooks, nooks and pretty looks "—so a guest
painted the surroundings in June, 1817. Idlings in the garden on
the mound and the rustic seat under the trees with vistas of hay-

fields and sheepwalks, outings to Bisham Woods or Medmenham Abbey were always to be had. One summer day was given to a ramble through the grounds, the ornamental buildings and shaded walks of Cliveden, and a tea-party on the river below. The lonely boat tied to its willow below the tumbling-bay served Shelley's poetry well. Yet the felicity was not to last. " Transactions " called Shelley away too often, even had he been in perfect health. The Chancery suit was not yet at an end. Among minor business, Shelley had to try and dispose of a manuscript work by Claire, which had no luck ; but he succeeded in finding a publisher for " Frankenstein "—Messrs. Lackington, Hughes—and by the end of September was assisting Mary in the correction of proof sheets. He supplied the preface in which he claimed for the book a purpose not usually noticed by its readers, " the exhibition of the amiableness of domestic affection, and the excellence of universal virtue." It was announced, as " a work of imagination," for issue on January 1st, 1818.

XIV

DEPARTURE FROM LONDON

THE MONTHS of October and November, 1817, found Shelley very often in London, and Mary was obliged in spite of her loneliness to warn him at least once not to return, since his creditors might pounce on him at home to arrest him. One creditor found him there, but did him no harm. This was Munday, the Oxford bookseller, who went away leaving an order for some copies of " The Revolt of Islam." Shelley had time enough in the end to distribute his blankets and pensions, and receive more visitors at Marlow. One was the father of Mary's Scottish friend, Isabel Baxter, now married to an old schoolmaster and brewer named Booth. Mr. Baxter to his surprise found Shelley's personal life so frugal, sound and fine that he endeavoured to reconcile Isabel with her discarded friend. Mary invited Isabel to Italy. These advances infuriated Booth, who forbade his wife and father-in-law to have anything to do with the Shelleys. Feeling the distress of his wife Shelley made a characteristic attempt to restore the situation ; but one wishes that he had been spared the bother of treating with such creatures as the little bullying Booth.

Against such reckonings of human nature Shelley could set his fuller knowledge of Horace Smith ; one incident gave him an immediate pleasure in this friendship. Hearing that Leigh Hunt's affairs were critical Smith sent him a banknote and " a letter full of delicacy and cordiality, making it a matter of grace to accept." Shelley witnessed this ; he commented, " I have only to say to Horace Smith that I want a hundred pounds or two, and he would send it without any eye to its being returned ; such faith has he that I have something within me beyond what the world supposes, and that I could only ask his money for a good purpose." Again, " I am afraid he must think me a strange fellow ; but is it not odd that the only true generous person I ever knew, who had any money to be generous with, should be a stockbroker ! " His voice rose in his enthusiasm : " And he writes poetry too ; he writes poetry and pastoral dramas, and yet knows how to make money, and does make it, and is still generous ! " When Shelley was abroad Smith could not do too much for him in practical ways ; and at Shelley's death, so Miss Smith told

172

Thackeray's daughter, he found that he had paid £150 in postages and small commissions which he never asked Shelley to repay.

It was probably in amicable competition with Shelley that Smith wrote his long poem " Amarynthus the Nympholept," but no doubt exists on another and briefer contest. At the close of 1817 Shelley and Smith wrote sonnets on Ozymandias, both being attracted by the progress of Egyptian exploration. Its results were familiar to them both in the rooms of the British Museum or even as they walked along Piccadilly in the hieroglyphical façade of the Egyptian Hall. The sonnets differ considerably, and Horace Smith only allowed the ruined statue of Ozymandias one " stupendous Leg " ; he closed however with a dream of the future which Shelley sometimes knew—of London gone the way of Babylon.

The same widespread excitement over colossal statues, pyramids and deserts can be felt underlying another sonnet competition held at Leigh Hunt's, who had moved to 13 Lisson Grove, Paddington, on February 4th, 1818. The players that day were Shelley, Keats and Hunt, and it has usually been held by judges of sonnets that Hunt won ; he was contented to remember the three friends in their diversion and that the three sonnets appeared somewhere in print together. The subject was " The Nile " and its treatment by each poet throws light on the several dispositions and thinkings of these men. To Hunt the great river gave not only a vista of the " young world " and the laughter and genius of Cleopatra, but the symbol of fruitful progress and " our own " course of doing good. To Keats the theme meant the contrast between prevailing dreaminess in thinking of the Nile as a desert flood and the assurance that it was as pleasant and verdurous a river as any of ours. But to Shelley the dual character of the Nile, causing rich growth and causing plague, resembled the ambiguous nature of progress :

> Beware, O Man—for knowledge must to thee
> Like the great flood to Egypt ever be.

By this time a new tenant for the house at Marlow had signed an agreement. On February 6th, Shelley and Mary played their last game of chess in Albion House, and a few days later their household had left the village. In spite of calumny their name lingered there for many years, recalling many good works. Not even Shelley's first action as a villager—the abrupt dismissal of a gardener for lopping a noble holly tree—had prevented that fair reputation. Cowden Clarke, revisiting the neighbourhood, was told by one of the richer residents that " they all considered

Shelley a madman." He had asked for it by declining to pay
calls ; and when he went into the town he had a book in his
hand and read it as he went. Such local friends as he made were
not rich—the brothers Tyler, for instance, men who worked in a
draper's business and used their minds—and these were in the
majority.

Shelley's arrival in town was celebrated, as it happened, by
Horace Smith in *The Examiner* with a sonnet to the author of
" The Revolt of Islam." It contained these lines :

> The heart that could conceive so bright a day
> Is proof that it may come ;—therefore shall they
> Who live on tears and darkness, steep each tooth
> In poison'd gall to make that heart their prey ;
> But thou shalt smile and pity, giving thy youth
> To glorious hopes, and all-defying Truth.

On February 10th Shelley and Mary were in their box at the
Opera for *Don Giovanni*, and of other nights there that of the 24th
gave them *Figaro*. For some time past Shelley had been inclining
towards that which made an immeasurable extension in his
poetical methods—an experience in music. He had of course
heard airs by Mozart often enough, especially at the Vale of
Health ; but in April, 1817, the already celebrated *Don Giovanni*
produced for the first time in London aroused a vast enthusiasm,
made even William Hazlitt happy, and induced Peacock to take
Shelley to an early performance. Shelley was for a time uncertain
if it was comedy or tragedy but yielded to the music and the
action. He liked *Figaro* even more ; in fact he became " an
assiduous frequenter " to whose box Leigh Hunt often looked up
for unspoken communications with the " thin patrician-looking
cosmopolite " and the " sedate-faced young lady " with the great
forehead and white shoulders " unconscious of a crimson gown."
The profusion and the unity attainable in opera by a genius
exulting in his mastery enthralled Shelley, and he felt the quality
expressed by Hazlitt : " Mozart's music should seem to come
from the air, and return to it." Next time he set forth on a long
poem his spirit would be aided by the spirit of this music ; we
may be sure that the versatility, delicacy and array of the ballet,
with recollections of his admired Mlle. Milanie, would also
accompany his creative thought. She excelled in a joyous little
fable called " The Return of Spring " in which she was Cloris,
carrying a rose, which Zephyr (M. Baptiste) made many aerial
attempts to steal away from her ever escaping.

Together with Shelley at the Opera in 1817 and 1818 we must

see him at the theatre, outgrowing a prejudice, sometimes with Peacock and sometimes with Hunt. Peacock says that *The School for Scandal*, which was to Edward Fitzgerald the perfection of comedies, was no fun to Shelley, but merely an unbaring of the heartlessness of society. He was better pleased in studying the acting of Miss O'Neil, an Irishwoman whose noted Juliet had earned her one of Hazlitt's critical portraits ; later on he had turned censorious and ironical about her. " There is a *fleshiness*, if we may say so, about her whole manner, voice, and person." But when she played Bianca in *Fazio* by an Etonian of Shelley's day, the Rev. H. H. Milman, Shelley agreed with Hazlitt's other words, " Her great excellence is extreme natural sensibility ; that is, she perfectly conceives and expresses what would be generally felt by the female mind in the extraordinary and overpowering situations in which she is placed. In truth, in beauty, and in that irresistible pathos which goes directly to the heart, she has at present no equal, and can have no superior." The deep impression was to be of importance to Shelley the writer in course of time. He could surely provide a part superior to Bianca for so excellent an actress of the abrupt and passionate.

In London, with Italy as the near prospect, Shelley and Mary had something of a final holiday. They visited the Indian Library and the Panorama of Rome, the Casts from Phidias, the Elgin Marbles and the pantomime, which was *Harlequin Gulliver* with its grand scene of the cornfield of the giants. They did not miss the Apollonicon, described by Dr. Percy Scholes as " the most elaborate barrel organ ever built," in its own house in St. Martin's Lane ; it had cost £10,000, and six players could perform upon it at once ; but it was undecided whether Shelley went for the sake of the music or the miracles of machinery. Their lodgings were at 119 Great Russell Street, some twenty doors along from Tottenham Court Road on the left hand ; the landlady's name, strangely enough, was Godwin ; but we hear of many evenings elsewhere, at Hunt's, Horace Smith's, Vincent Novello's in Oxford Street with intervals of organ music.

Peacock, Hogg and Keats were at Hunt's with them on February 11th, but by the cruelty of fate no note of the conversation exists. The first two would come to supper in Great Russell Street, and William Godwin got that far ; but one living close by who would have been as welcome as his writings did not come. Charles Lamb had seen Shelley once, was tormented by his voice, and since then had heard dark allegations against him. A Mr. Bramsen dined with the Shelleys on February 15th ; he was an author who travelled in Egypt and other countries with the eldest son of Sir John Maxwell. As usual the duties of friendship did not keep Shelley from activities legal, literary and religious. His money affairs and other matters were partly entrusted to his unselfish Horace Smith. He wrote an article on Peacock's classical poem " Rhododaphne," intended for *The Examiner* and announced there without result. An evening at Drury Lane for a new comedy, " The Castle of Glyndower," was almost wasted. In the third act the occupants of the pit made a vast disturbance. The Manager asked leave to continue. " The two next acts, to the evident perplexity of the performers, were hurried through like two or three scenes of dumb show, in the teeth of one unceasing storm of groans, hisses, and cat-calls." On March 9th, 1818, William and Clara Everina Shelley were taken to be christened at St. Giles in the Fields, and so was Claire's and Byron's child Clara Allegra. Not a single journalist caught this unusual opportunity. The day after was one of packing and farewells, with Hunt and his wife in attendance. Godwin came in the evening ; Peacock, ready for his supper, arrived from the first performance in England of *The Barber of Seville*.

The Mary Lamb noticed in Mrs. Shelley's diary as calling was really Dr. Lambe's daughter, not Charles Lamb's sister ; and to a great age she recollected " Shelley seeing her downstairs to the door behind the man carrying boxes ready corded for the next day's departure for Italy." At last Shelley, not yet in health, fell into a deep sleep, and the Hunts would not have him disturbed before they took their leave.

The family and the servants had to be early on the road next morning, going the way of Chaucer's pilgrims through Ospringe to Canterbury, and thence to Dover, which they saw at the end of the day in the darkness with its many twinkling lights. They lodged at York House. The hurricane which had passed over England a week before with ruin in its track, bringing down trees and chimneys in London and blowing wayfarers into the Thames, was not quite spent ; and on March 12th they woke to find the Straits in such commotion that they held a conference about embarking then or waiting. When they ventured in the *Lady Castlereagh* they were blown across in two hours and forty minutes to Calais, where they put up at the Grand Cerf Hotel.

It may be due to the disappearance of family papers that among Shelley's latest doings in England nothing shows him making an attempt to see either his family at Field Place or his children and Harriet's. These may have been at Warwick, and were certainly much under the watch and ward of Eliza Westbrook whom Shelley would not be able to approach even through

Mrs. Boinville. This lady had decided against him. Eliza never let go of Ianthe Shelley. She herself married Robert Farthing Beauchamp of Tetton House, Somerset, at St. George's, Hanover Square, in the month of Shelley's death, and in 1823 became one of Ianthe's legal guardians. A notice of her wedding in *The Examiner* was probably intended to meet Shelley's eye ; it never did. If it had been her original aim to see Harriet safely married into a county family, she secured that as nearly as possible in 1837 when Ianthe became the wife of Edward Jeffries Esdaile of Cothelstone House, a little way from the home of the Beauchamps. Esdaile was descended from a Lord Mayor of London whose portrait Reynolds painted and from William Esdaile, banker and collector of prints and drawings. Ianthe lived until 1876, and her children well knew the stately and unusual old lady with her man-servant and lady companion who took such an interest in them all. Eliza had inherited John Westbrook's property—he left £60,000—and was easily equal to the situation. Ianthe's brother did not live with her, nor did he live long. Sir Timothy received him and gave him something of the love he had once felt for Percy Bysshe Shelley ; he had him taught Latin by the same clergyman, Mr. Edwards, now vicar of Warnham, as he had chosen before. He sent him to Sion House Academy at Brentford. But when the boy died of consumption in 1826 the old man ordered that he should be described on the memorial tablet in Warnham Church simply as grandson of Sir Timothy and Lady Shelley.

The Shelley who departed from England in March, 1818, was beginning to be a public character. He had been recognised as a poet of original tone, style and subject, fertile in mighty visions such as the age was expecting from its artists, abounding in expressions sublime and beautiful. He was known and feared for his reputed views, even for his real ones—absurd, abominable, yet some morning (God forbid) they might become part of the presaged uprising of " the mob." Of his personal habits and acts many a wicked whisper was going round. It was certainly an exaggeration that he had murdered his first wife, but epicures of crime were most unwilling to hear that he had not. Occasionally someone would speak up in public for Shelley, but then it could hardly be in any quarter except where his associates were supposed to be of the same hell-fire club. The Lord Chancellor, who was later on to be horrified by Brougham's sitting on the woolsack in an overcoat and top boots, had obviously been horrified by Shelley or he could not have made the resounding decision that he must not have his own children with him. Nevertheless

Shelley's last days in London were not disturbed by any incident
arising from these causes ; he was not expelled thence in any sense
but one : his own sense that however delightful the face of
England's capital was, behind it lay terrible chaos.

Shelley in March, 1818, left behind him a city which he had
known as few know it, which he had even enjoyed, but which
sent with him a sort of ghost ; he sketched the emanation later in
stanzas beginning

> Hell is a city much like London.

The conclusion was,

> So good and bad, sane and mad,
> The oppressor and the oppressed,
> Those who weep to see what others
> Smile to inflict upon their brothers,
> Lovers, haters, worst and best,
>
> All are damned—they breathe an air
> Thick, infected, joy-dispelling :
> Each pursues what seems most fair,
> Mining like moles, through mind, and there
> Scoop palace-caverns vast, where Care
> In throned state is ever dwelling.

After half a century this note of doom was to be caught up and
reverberated by a poet who called himself Bysshe Vanolis in one
of London's profoundest poems, " The City of Dreadful Night."

XV

BYRON ONCE MORE

FROM Calais the Shelleys took "the most direct road for travellers hastening to Switzerland or Italy," and paid no particular attention to the French country on the way. They stayed one night at Saint Omer, little dreaming that a century afterwards it would be crowded with British soldiers, the allies of the French. The landscape thence to Douai was avoided as dismal, and it was not noticed that Rheims had a cathedral. The dangers of the road were much more in their minds, but after Chalons-sur-Marne the way was smoother, and the wine country with its hills pleased the eye. By the time they reached Lyons, it was March 22nd, 1818, and the sky was blue and bright. " The heat in this city to-day," Shelley wrote to Hunt, " is like that of London in the midst of summer. My spirits and health sympathise in the change."

To beguile the time for himself and Mary and Claire he read from the lectures of Augustus Schlegel, which had been translated by the editor of *The Morning Chronicle*, and were setting many discussions going upon the principles of taste and the history of literature. He enjoyed Charles Lamb's " Rosamund Gray," republished with other writings by Lamb over Ollier's imprint. He also read Hunt's new volume of poems, " Foliage," in which honour was done to himself and his opinions, and enjoyed the poetical fancies of " The Nymphs," which is indeed a little gallery of the graces. He would have liked to find himself in Hunt's study talking over the felicities and the faults of the piece ; but the spirit of the south called strongly. Looking from the riverside at Lyons towards Mont Blanc, all had memories of Geneva, and the moonrise over the Alps deepened them. Shelley wrote to his old companion of the moonlit lake, Lord Byron, who about the same time was writing to Hobhouse in England, " A clerk can bring the papers (and, by-the-bye, my *shild* by Clare, at the same time. Pray desire Shelley to pack it carefully), with *tooth-powder, red only*."

The next main move begun on March 25th was for Milan, and the route lay through the valleys of the Alps. It crossed the frontier between France and the dominions of the King of Sardinia, and there Shelley's books were inspected with knotting

179

of brows ; but the censor at Chambery let them pass. At Les Echelles the imagination of Shelley was stirred by what appeared as a proper scene for one of his heroic figures, the Prometheus of Aeschylus. As he contemplated the caverns in the precipices, the ice and snow on the mountains, the " walls of toppling rocks," he seemed to see what Aeschylus describes, " the winged chariot of the ocean nymphs " ascending those else inaccessible scarps. On the 30th the travellers dined on Mont Cenis, where Shelley called the mountains " God's *corps de ballet*, of which the Jungfrau is Mademoiselle Milanie." Thereafter the blossoming serenity of the season made them all happy. Again Shelley expressed his natural unity with the state of the weather : " I depend on these things for life ; for in the smoke of cities, and the tumult of human kind, and the chilling fogs and rain of our own country, I can hardly be said to live."

Once more Shelley's new chapter was opening with high coloured prospects. On arrival at the first Italian town, Susa, the initial letter might have been drawn by Mary from the antiquity they visited in the sunset : " a ruined arch of magnificent proportions, in the Greek taste standing in a kind of road of green lawn, overgrown with violets and primroses, and in the midst of stupendous mountains, and a *blonde* woman of light and graceful manners, something in the style of Fuseli's Eve, were the first things we met in Italy." From Susa they travelled to Turin and had time there for the opera, but Milan was where Shelley meant to pause and consider more lasting arrangements. He found that city very agreeable and Mary also liked it. Still it was his desire to spend the summer in something like the way that he had enjoyed in 1816, and the Lake of Como promised to gratify him so. He took Mary on a little tour of the Lake early in April, and two or three houses were inspected, including Pliny's Villa. Mary's account of the scenery is briefer than Shelley's but shares the same enchantment ; nevertheless the decision not to live in what he called its divine solitude was probably taken because of her desire for society.

Shelley wrote Peacock one of his landscape letters in the style of the period, at which he was now a master ; but he had grown willing to include appreciations of man's work as well as nature's. The white cathedral of Milan, about which I have heard a new generation speak in boredom, drew from him a splendid eulogy : " the effect of it, piercing the solid blue with those groups of dazzling spires, relieved by the serene depth of this Italian heaven, or by moonlight when the stars seem gathered among those clustered shapes, is beyond anything I had imagined architecture capable of producing." He left a word about his movements there which has been remembered by many pilgrims : " There is one solitary spot among these aisles, behind the altar, where the light of day is dim and yellow under the storied window, which I have chosen to visit and read Dante there."

From Peacock and Hunt and indeed from London itself Shelley had learned to enjoy the theatre and the opera, and he took his opportunities during these early Italian days. Even at Lyons his party had gone to the Comédie and found it very amusing. At Turin they snatched the time for an opera which was made less intelligible because the audience talked throughout, but at Milan something better rewarded them, " a most splendid exhibition." Shelley was not much impressed by the opera itself, but by the " ballet, or rather a kind of melodrama or pantomimic drama," the subject being *Othello*. Though no Mlle. Milanie was there to fascinate him, the whole thing struck him as being " much superior to anything of the kind in England, indeed . . . wholly unlike anything represented on our stage, being a combination of a great number of figures grouped with the most picturesque and even poetical effect, and perpetually changing with motions the most harmoniously interwoven and contrasted with great effect." And all this, he found, sent him home with the sense of having been a spectator of true tragedy.

The direction of his mind which these things show is visible accordingly in what he was meaning to write in 1818. He speaks of " many literary schemes," and we know of some stately ones, all dramatic, which did not come to anything. First there was a tragedy on the madness of Tasso, his adventures and misfortunes ; " I have taken the resolution to see what kind of a tragedy a person without dramatic talent could write." It has been suggested that he gave up this design when Byron's " Lament of Tasso " came into his hands—a dramatic soliloquy taking up the main interests of the theme. Another project was to dramatize the Book of Job, which Shelley always read so intently ; and even less of this is extant in the poetical works than of the Tasso. A modern " Timon of Athens " remained as an attractive dream. Of " Charles the First " however, the editors have collected most spirited scenes and sketches. A fifth mighty plan, to which we shall come, is found in most libraries in its full achievement.

Byron, who had been a little earlier than Shelley to hear Rossini's opera of *Othello*, when it was performed at Venice, now draws nearer Shelley's own story. The letter written from Lyons to the " new illustrious exile " had been on the subject of Allegra, and this troublesome subject continued to be imposed upon Shelley ; the demand of Byron, in response to more letters, was that Claire should hand the child over. She was aware that Allegra's worldly prospects depended on her doing this, and yet was reluctant ; apart from maternal instincts, she was disturbed by gossip concerning Byron's foolhardy life at Venice. Shelley, trying to do his best for her as the child's mother, and putting her case before Byron with the utmost strength and courtesy, received the irritable reproaches which usually meet persons in his situation. Allegra was sent off with her nurse to Venice on April 28th, and on May-day the Shelleys themselves left Milan for Pisa, where if not in some place near it they were to spend the summer.

First impressions of Pisa were not good, and they did not stay many days. Mary says that the speedy move from the town was due to the sight and sound of convicts in the streets, chained together in pairs under the eyes of armed guards, sweeping and pulling carts. The town was large but had long been scantily inhabited. " Its deserted streets and sombre aspect," wrote an admirer of Shelley, " remind one of the precincts of the colleges of Oxford and Cambridge, during the vacation ; and the sight of a professor or student, gliding along, adds to the resemblance." The Shelleys had a letter of introduction to Mr. and Mrs. Gisborne at Leghorn, which was so great a contrast to Pisa in its modern activity and throng, and they went to present it. Mrs. Gisborne had been one of the ladies whom William Godwin had wished to marry, after which she had become Mrs. Reveley and the mother of a boy named Henry, and after her husband's death she had married again. Mr. Gisborne was a merchant, not the most successful of the class, and a studious and peaceful man. Henry Reveley, who was eighteen years old, had been trained as an engineer and, like his father, had some talent as an architect. Such were the new acquaintances of the Shelleys, and they became some of their most sensible although not always co-operative friends. With his customary superlatives Shelley wrote to Peacock that Mrs. Gisborne was " the sole attraction in this most unattractive of cities. We had no idea of spending a month here, but she has made it even agreeable."

Shelley made his own reconnaissance of the next of their homes, the Baths of Lucca, and early in June Mary was glad to be in a house there among the wooded heights. There were countless walks, the only sound was " the running of the river in the valley below," and a servant named Paolo did everything choicely even if he cheated. Shelley and Mary read Ariosto (" *sometimes* a poet "), and in the evening took their way into the woods ; but he occupied himself also in translating the " Sym-

posium " of Plato, for want, he said—since he looked on translation as not a very creditable task for those who could write their
own works—for want of something better to do. Moreover he
wished Mary to understand the culture of the Athenians. The
translation took him ten days. It has helped a host of readers
as he meant it should help Mary. It was accompanied by an
essay, left imperfect but extensive enough to point out Shelley
as a magnificent lecturer on the classical ideal ; curiously enough
this prose ode to the age of Pericles ends with Shelley's admitting
the great improvement in the position of woman in later society.
To that extent Lord Eldon might have written it.

Even if Shelley's version of the Symposium had never got
further than his writing-desk it would have been one of the
excellent preparations for his coming glorious performances in
poetry. Most of these preparations were outdoor pursuits. One
day in June he and Mary rode to the Prato Fiorito or Flowery
Meadow on high among the Apennines, and the cicala played
them all the way to that kingdom of the sweet jonquils. There
were other rides amid the forest scenery, " lighted home by Venus,
Jupiter and Diana." Shelley found for himself a waterfall under
a crag, and after reading his book on the rock he jumped into
the clear cold pool, and sometimes crept up the torrent like a
young eel on a mossy weir. But his dearest adventure was simply
watching the changing and eternal heavens above him, their
gathering thunderstorms, their delicate gossamer clouds and white
woolpacks, their sheet-lightning and their nightpiece of moon
and stars.

With all this, Shelley could be persuaded to take a look at
human beings, and he gave the Casino a trial. Here also the
mind of the poet discovered what it had been attracted to since
1817—the grace of the dance. The women, he reported, were
" far removed from anything which the most liberal annotator
could interpret into beauty or grace," but then, " it is well that
it is so, for these dances, especially the waltz, are so exquisitely
beautiful that it would be a little dangerous to the newly unfrozen
senses and imaginations of us migrators from the neighbourhood
of the pole. As it is—except in the dark—there could be no
peril." He might allude to England as the Arctic circle, but even
in his exultant possession of nature in the Apennines he found
himself half wishing for the comfortable old place where Peacock
was still taking the girls out on the river. " I have seen nothing
so beautiful as Virginia Water—in its kind. And my thoughts
for ever cling to Windsor Forest, and the copses of Marlow."

By this time " Frankenstein " had been published, and

attacked in *The Quarterly Review* ; still, it was too exciting a book to be left at that. Shelley, who was not to see it become a sort of household word, or know that it would be quoted in parliament by a Prime Minister, was well pleased with its general reception. Mary, who appears to have taken little notice of the publication and the effects, now found among Shelley's papers the manuscript of something begun by him while she was busy with writing " Frankenstein." She pressed him to complete the story in verse, " Rosalind and Helen," which had an imaginative source in her own severance from her dearest Isabel Booth. He went to work, introduced the tale with a scene on the shore of the Lake of Como, but prefixed a few sentences betraying his lack of conviction about the composition. The forms of persecution or injustice which Shelley had seen ready to descend on one holding such opinions as his own, the tragic joys of acting in the light of those opinions make up the story. Its chief merit is the canonisation of love spiritual and physical as harmonious and undivided. The sinuous verse fittingly attends this most truthful and human revealing, particularly in the passage beginning

> I know not how, but we were free ;
> And Lionel sate alone with me,
> As the carriage drove thro' the streets apace ;
> And we looked upon each other's face ;
> And the blood in our fingers intertwined
> Ran like the thoughts of a single mind,
> As the swift emotions went and came
> Thro' the veins of each united frame.
> So thro' the long long streets we passed
> Of the million-peopled City vast
> Which is that desert, where each one
> Seeks his mate yet is alone,
> Beloved and sought and mourned of none ;
> Until the clear blue sky was seen,
> And the grassy meadows bright and green,
> And then I sunk in his embrace,
> Enclosing there a mighty space
> Of love.

The first accounts of Allegra now transferred to Byron's villa were that " they dress her in little trousers trimmed with lace and treat her like a little princess." Byron's other interests in Venice, however, did not fall in with the art of bringing up a small daughter, and Claire received letters from the nurse Elise which called for some action by her. As usual this meant Shelley, and he took Claire on a difficult errand on August 19th, 1818 ; it had at least the benefit of a first view of Florence. The late masterly Poet Laureate Robert Bridges, walking in his hill garden with its view over Oxford, was known to observe that Florence offered no such wonderful sight. Shelley had seen Oxford, as we know, but he would have disagreed. He sent Mary a letter worthy of the occasion, worthy even of his breakfast at the inn in this surpassing city : " figs—very fine—and peaches, unfortunately gathered before they were ripe, whose smell was like what one fancies of the wakening of Paradise flowers." Yet his letter is not all in this tone. It begins with the muddle of Claire and Allegra. The plan was that Shelley should go and talk Byron over without letting him know that Claire had left Lucca : " the worst of this plan is, that it will not succeed, and that she will never be quite satisfied that all has been done." Later on Shelley is not sure that Mary either is quite satisfied about life in general. " If you love me you will keep up your spirits and at all events tell me truth about it." The postscript is endearing : he has been reading " The Two Noble Kinsmen," which Mary knew, and he cuts short the long scholarly discussions of the authorship. " The whole story wants moral discrimination and modesty. I do not believe that Shakespeare wrote a word of it."

Allegra, as her mother knew, was not actually living with Byron but in the house of the English Consul at Venice, R. B. Hoppner —an intimate friend of the cross-grained editor of *The Quarterly Review*. When Shelley and Claire came to Padua, Shelley was to have gone on by himself, but women change their mind, and Claire had decided at the last moment to call with him at the Hoppners'. How this might appear to Shelley's disadvantage she failed to consider. She was courteously received and in a few minutes her " little Ba " was in her arms. Shelley took himself off for the difficult interview with Byron, whose attention wandered. His kindest self almost came to the fore, though he only said he would not necessarily abandon Allegra if Claire took her altogether. In the end he offered Shelley a house which he rented of Hoppner at Este, and where the child might come on visits ; and then, glad to change the subject, he invited Shelley to ride with him on the Lido—" a long sandy island which defends Venice from the Adriatic." Both had passages of autobiography to deliver as they rode. Byron asked about Harriet, presumably having heard the versions which were given by haters of Shelley and his creed. He had read Hunt's " Foliage," transmitted by Shelley earlier, and re-named it " Folly-age," having decided that such Hampstead neo-classicism was not adult poetry. Delighted

with Byron's cordiality and the apparently happy issue of the
Allegra negotiations, Shelley at once wrote to Mary asking her
to hasten to Este and enclosing £50 for the purpose. " I have
done for the best—and my own beloved Mary, you must soon
come and scold me if I have done wrong, and kiss me if I have
done right." At all events he could commend Mrs. Hoppner,
" who is so good, so beautiful, so angelically mild, that were she
as wise too, she would be quite a Mary ; but she is not very
accomplished. Her eyes are like a reflection of yours."

The summons to Este for Claire's benefit reached Mary just
when she could have done without it, for the Gisbornes had
arrived as her guests ; she had entreated them to come and take
away her loneliness, and they had bestirred themselves. However,
on August 31st, having packed and settled the household business
once more, she started out for Este. The long process of getting
there was held up a day at Florence by the passport officers, and
the journey was especially trying for the baby Clara. This anxiety
had not lessened when on September 5th Mary took her bonnet
off at the Casa Capucini. The child continued ill, and the
position was not made simpler by the illness of Claire also ;
Shelley went hither and thither seeking to be useful. At length
he wrote from Padua that he was arranging for his wife and
child to be in Venice, and would meet them at Padua on the
24th ; Mary would have to start on this journey at half-past
three in the morning. She did as he wished, and now Shelley
was as deeply disturbed as she by the condition of the baby. At
Fusina passports were demanded—they had been forgotten ; but
Shelley was not to be stopped and on arrival at Venice went off
for Dr. Aglietti. The doctor was out, and when Shelley had
made his way to the inn he found Mary with another physician,
who could only say that Clara was past hope. She died and was
buried the next day on the Lido.

Clara's mother remembered her face as being like Shelley's.
" She died," Shelley wrote, " of a disorder peculiar to the
climate." The blow fell from the glorious sky which had seemed
to portend blessings only. Shelley and Mary found what consolation they could in going on with their friendships, readings
and sightseeings ; and during September they lived at Este.
Byron was affable and sympathetic, entrusted Mary with his
" Mazeppa " to transcribe for him, and gave Shelley the experience which thousands of people would have paid a mint of
money to have at that period—to hear him read his own poems.
The fourth canto of " Childe Harold " and the first of " Don
Juan " are particularly mentioned. Looking about him as he

came and went in Venice, Shelley did not bring off one of his great pen-pictures for the whole city, but in a few words he drew one of its characteristic objects with a power derived from his recent disaster. " The gondolas themselves are things of a most romantic and picturesque appearance ; I can only compare them to moths of which a coffin might have been the chrysalis. They are hung with black, and painted black, and carpeted with grey ; they curl at the prow and stern, and at the former there is a nondescript beak of shining steel, which glitters at the end of its long black mass." He did not know that these black vessels had been so by law since the fifteenth century. For the public life of the city, he had no good word : " A horde of German soldiers, as vicious as and more disgusting than the Venetians themselves, insult these miserable people." Hitherto he had scarcely found anything to praise or even to respect in the Italian character.

At Este the garden stretched to the foot of a ruined castle, the home of owls, bats and Echo. Behind rose the Euganean hills ; in front lay " the wide flat plains of Lombardy, in which we see the sun and moon rise and set, and the evening star, and all the golden magnificence of autumnal clouds." A vine-trellised walk led Shelley from his hall door to a summer-house where he read and wrote. But the spirit of the place and time and of his own life after its series of sudden calamities is perpetual in his poem entitled, in his unpretentious way, " Lines Written Among the Euganean Hills." A day's excursion in the neighbourhood of Arqua gave the impulse to this musical meditation.

The reader of eighteenth-century poetry may hear, or think he hears, some reminiscence of a much-loved landscape poem in Shelley's own ; " Grongar Hill" by John Dyer, the work of one who was both poet and painter, may have helped in the choice of the clear-flowing metre and the method of producing in words the illusion of a panorama. The vagueness of which Shelley had been guilty in earlier picture-writing has been exchanged for the graphic certainty made familiar by the older poet of the hills. The mythological forms stand in the scene as in some rich embellished engraving, seen without disbelief by the eye of tradition ; for a worthy view of Venice the water-city, we need hardly seek further :

> Beneath is spread like a green sea
> The waveless plain of Lombardy,
> Bounded by the vaporous air,
> Islanded by cities fair ;
> Underneath Day's azure eyes

> Ocean's nursling Venice lies,
> A peopled labyrinth of walls,
> Amphitrite's destined halls,
> Which her hoary sire now paves
> With his blue and beaming waves.
> Lo ! the sun upsprings behind,
> Broad, red, radiant, half-reclined
> On the level quivering line
> Of the waters crystalline ;
> And before that chasm of light,
> As within a furnace bright,
> Column, tower, and dome, and spire
> Shine like obelisks of fire,
> Pointing with inconstant motion
> From the altar of dark ocean
> To the sapphire-tinted skies ;
> As the flames of sacrifice
> From the marble shrines did rise
> As to pierce the dome of gold
> Where Apollo spoke of old.

This detail from the picture is at once simple and sumptuous, and the presence of the artist finishing his work with a lonely joy in it, utterly devoted to it, is manifest. But the 373 " Lines " altogether are not confined to such a happiness in art. They are partly an autobiographical audit, as the beginning proclaims,

> Many a green isle needs must be
> In the deep wide sea of Misery,
> Or the mariner, worn and wan,
> Never thus could voyage on.

Shelley still hopes that such islands await him and those he loves, and not the haven of death which might be reasonably expected, since death appeared to have a horrible liking for his neighbour-hood. The poem also includes his thought, historic and prophetic, on the fate of Venice, on the university of Padua, on freedom and tyranny ; and in its completed shape it brings a rhapsody on Byron at Venice. He declares that as Shakespeare's glory dwells for ever by the Avon, so shall that of this new " tempest-cleaving Swan " be everlasting in Venice even if all else there is over-whelmed. A bold prediction, even for Shelley !

From time to time Shelley was to deify Byron the master poet in this manner, no matter what he might say of him or think of him in his character and conduct. It is as though he had transferred to him the intellectual wonder with which he had

contemplated Godwin—yet he never lost it in regard to that
man who in all affairs was his dreary plague. Shelley might
himself have been an entire nobody, have written nothing at all,
when he detached his feelings from what a scurrilous author
called " The Real Byron " and allowed himself to adore the
genius and volcanic energy of the poet. This was a vision which
he lived, and which makes him spiritually comparable to William
Blake, seeing in strange immensity.

Nobody has left more scathing comments on the weaknesses
and absurdities of Byron's nature than Shelley. Before the end
of 1818 he sent Peacock a few remarks on " Childe Harold,"
asserting that it was written in a spirit of " self-willed folly, in
which he hardens himself " ; that the source of the contempt and
desperation expressed there, supposed a sublime one, was in truth
merely sordid. " The Italian women with whom he associates
are perhaps the most contemptible of all who exist under the
moon—the most ignorant, the most disgusting, the most bigoted.
. . . He is heartily and deeply discontented with himself ; and
contemplating in the distorted mirror of his own thoughts the
nature and the destiny of man, what can he behold but objects
of contempt and despair ? . . . I do not doubt, and for his sake
I ought to hope, that his present career must end soon in some
violent circumstance." The substance of this was not of Shelley's
making. When Lady Blessington was exploring Byron's haunts
she found that " a thousand stories are told of his low amours,
and reckless associations, while a resident at Venice," and
remembered how when she talked with Byron his early memories
of the place had seemed to awaken a sort of horror of it in his
mind. Latterly the Venetians have talked of him as eccentric
rather than depraved, and his ghost swims home from the
evening parties along the canal to the Palazzo Mocenigo, pushing
a board before him with a lantern on it.

Yet in the summer-house at Este Shelley wrote of Byron in
his other mood of hero-worship and even more, much as when
King Lear was fascinated by the fantasies of the supposed Bedlam-
beggar. Besides the poem just considered, the enthusiast produced
a lengthy narrative in the rhymed couplet called " Julian and
Maddalo," names concealing very slightly his impressions of
himself and Byron. These impressions are diffused in the poem,
which opens with the rides and discourses of the poets on the
Lido, but compact in the preface. Maddalo, taken for all in all,
" is a person of the most consummate genius, and capable, if he
would direct his energies to such an end, of becoming the re-
deemer of his degraded country. . . . His passions and his powers

are incomparably greater than those of other men ; and instead of the latter having been employed in curbing the former, they have mutually lent each other strength."

As there were two Byrons in Shelley's mind, there are two Shelleys in ours, and " Julian and Maddalo " includes them both. It is a duality. It opens with freely rippling conversational verse, in which the scene, the ride, the two speakers, the child Allegra and the talk are brought to life as firmly as any realist could desire. This is the Shelley who might be the most charming and capable man in any company, observant of all ordinary things and speaking with the easiest elegance. Then the poem veers away from Julian and Maddalo into the unstable world of the third main character, a madman pent in the grim black building pointed out by Maddalo during the sunset. Of all asylums this on the little island of S. Servolo, amid the incessant lappings of dull waters, was generally seen by travellers with most dismay. In the madman's outpourings against a false woman, and his wordings of the agony of love, some have detected a version of Shelley's own inner attitude to Harriet. The identification will not work out that way, but the study of the abyss which Shelley unfolds here is not less bewildering. He makes his madman speak of venom and poison, and " plagues of blistering agony " ; and it is not so distant an imagery from what might suit the moments in his own life when he acts or speaks in a sort of distraction. The lines

> *Me*—who am as a nerve o'er which do creep
> The else unfelt oppressions of this earth

have pardonably been quoted often enough as though they were Shelley's definition of himself and not his madman in the hiss of the Adriatic storm.

In the annual called " The Forget-Me-Not " for 1837 can be read a tale by R. Shelton Mackenzie, LL.D., which may explain how Shelley came to let his study of Byron and himself pass into an emotional history of one made insane by unhappiness in love. This tale, " Julian and Leonor," is prefixed with a declaration that it is founded on fact ; " the circumstances are not wholly unknown in Rome and Venice, nor the dramatis personæ in England." The main scene is the same madhouse seen from the Lido at Venice. The main character is an Englishman, a cultured idealist whose physical beauty is not all effaced by his affliction ; and the occasion of his losing his reason is the enforced retirement of his Italian love to a convent. But she escapes, comes to him again, and succeeds in restoring him to sanity and quiet life.

Before this even, his story has become a popular legend with the boatmen of the Lido. Its resemblances to Shelley's poetical tale are sufficient to suggest that he or Byron might have heard a version from them.

Three years after "Julian and Maddalo" Shelley wrote a short poem exceeding anything written by him in 1818 to show his idolatry of Byron's greatness ; and possibly no tribute ever paid by a poet of the first order to another man of genius is quite so self-effacing. If only for the sake of biography, as an evidence of the difficulty presented by an element in Shelley's personality, this sonnet is now correctly transcribed :

LINES TO ———

If I esteemed you less, Envy would kill
Pleasure, and leave to Wonder and Despair
The ministration of the thoughts that fill
    My mind, which, like a worm whose life may share
A portion of the Unapproachable,
    Marks your creations rise as fast and fair
As perfect worlds at the creator's will,
    And bows itself before the godhead there.

But such is my regard, that, nor your fame
    Cast on the present by the coming hour,
    Nor your well-won prosperity and power
Move one regret for his unhonoured name
Who dares these words,—the worm beneath the sod
May lift itself in worship to the God.

The same wonder is expressed in similar metaphor in a letter to the no doubt slightly puzzled Mr. Gisborne. If Shelley was content as an artist in poetry to be nothing while Byron was everything, he yet had ambitions as a philanthropist, and he was convinced that anything which might exhort Byron to use all his gifts was a service to the world.

XVI

A THREE-YEARS CHILD

IN OCTOBER, 1818, Shelley had made up his mind to go further south for the winter, visiting Florence and Rome and settling until the spring at Naples. Some last conversations with Byron sped the month, at the end of which it fell to Shelley to take Allegra from Claire and leave her with her father. Well laden, his carriage moved out of Este on November 5th, and it moved all the slower "through deep and clayey roads." Somehow Shelley was reminded of home and the Weald of Sussex, and he made some shrewd observations on the farms and farmyards as they passed, very much as his father might do. On the 7th he enjoyed a tour of the great library at Ferrara, with its illuminated manuscripts, its relics of Ariosto and Tasso—these last making him write to Peacock as a graphologist. " The handwriting of Ariosto is a small, firm and pointed character, expressing, as I should say, a strong and keen but circumscribed energy of mind ; that of Tasso is large, free, and flowing, except that there is a checked expression in the midst of its flow, which brings the letters into a smaller compass than one expected from the beginning of the word. It is the symbol of an intense and earnest mind, exceeding at times its own depth, and admonished to return by the chillness of the waters of oblivion striking upon its adventurous feet. You know I always seek in what I see the manifestation of something beyond the present and tangible object ; and as we do not agree in physiognomy, so we may not agree now." Peacock might have agreed that Shelley's own handwriting announced the swift, piercing and upsoaring nature of his thought.

Two days later Shelley began an enormous letter from Bologna. He writes as one who has done his duty by scanning a large picture gallery, and he describes a number of the paintings with intelligent thoroughness. One of them suggested a protest against some of his own writings : it was a Guercino, and the subject was " the founder of the Carthusians exercising his austerities in the desert. . . . He was clothed in a loose dress of death-coloured flannel, such as you might fancy a shroud might be, after it had wrapped a corpse a month or two. It had a yellow, putrified, ghastly hue, which it cast on all the objects around, so that the hands and face of the Carthusian and his companion were jaundiced by this sepulchral glimmer. Why write books against religion, when we may hang up such pictures?" After this satisfactory outburst he rode next day to a chapel of the Madonna in the mountains, and his activity as a tourist may be measured by his going out for a moonlight walk through Bologna the same night.

In the midst of his picturesque discoveries his English memories occasionally sprang up. The Roman bridge at Rimini reminded him of Waterloo Bridge, new in his time and destroyed so complacently in ours, and advancing upon Rome he was pleased with the Campagna di Roma, and called it a "flattering picture of Bagshot Heath." Rome itself, though on this journey he had only a week for it, stirred him profoundly ; and every day the party visited the Forum and the ruin of the Coliseum. " In Rome, at least in the first enthusiasm of your recognition of ancient time, you see nothing of the Italians." He found the English burying-place near the walls, at the foot of the pyramidal tomb of Cestius, and took an immediate liking to it. The sight of galley-slaves at work on the ruins was distasteful, but Shelley looked beyond the moment, and began a tale called " The Colosseum." In it occur the following words spoken by an old man : " ' It has happened,' said he, with a deep and suffering voice, ' that men have buried their children.' "

Shelley went forward from Rome by himself, and his first moments in Naples were marked by the terribly near view of a murder in the street. After that he selected lodgings for his family, and found very good ones, comfortable and overlooking the sea, with only the royal gardens, their flowers, statues and vases, between. The end of the year was approaching, but here they would all be delighted, as Mary certainly was when she brought the others along. The street scenes were endlessly gay ; all was paper lanterns, laughter and marketing and guitar-playing. " The climate," Shelley wrote, " is delicious. We sit without a fire, with the windows open, and have almost all the productions of an English summer." Excursions were soon provided. They could see Vesuvius from the garden but naturally would not rest content with that. For the last stage of the ascent, " Mary and I mounted mules, and Claire was carried in a chair on the shoulders of four men, much like a member of parliament after he has gained his election, and looking, with less reason, quite as frightened." The marvels of the mountain appeared even grander after the sun went down, and Shelley obtained a number of verbal photographs for Peacock, but returned home

" in a state of intense bodily suffering " and angry with himself at having spoiled the outing for the others.

Pompeii was the inspiration of another topographical letter to the classic-minded Peacock, and one which should have been printed locally for the use of other British visitors. It would have brought Shelley more money than his poems. The city as he refashioned it in his prose from the remains was nearly a perfect place. Even the tombs gladdened him. " How unlike ours ! They seem not so much hiding-places for that which must decay, as voluptuous chambers for immortal spirits." We see the group of Shelleyans sitting under the portico of the temple of Jupiter, lunching on oranges, figs, medlars and bread, and enjoying a scene which made Shelley sigh for that from the Acropolis of Athens. Had he by some miracle of time and place seen *that*, he would have sped on in desire for something yet more noble, beautiful, luminous and chromatic. Still, he gives a sparkling picture of the view towards Sorrento from Pompeii on December 22nd, 1818, at midday, over the basket of fruit ; and " every now and then we heard the subterranean thunder of Vesuvius ; its distant deep peals seemed to shake the very air and light of day, which interpenetrated our frames, with the sullen and tremendous sound."

Such pleasures of the imagination and such days in the open —and sometimes over the waves in the sun—might be supposed to assure Shelley's happiness while he lived at Naples ; but the tone of the minor poems which he was writing denies that he was enjoying life. He hid some of them from Mary, who when she came upon the manuscripts in later years was sadly confused, and tried hard to explain the glooms therein. It was true that " at this time Shelley suffered greatly in health. He put himself under the care of a medical man, who promised great things, and made him endure severe bodily pain, without any good results." The physical cause was great ; was there anything more ? " One looks back with unspeakable regret and gnawing remorse to such periods ; fancying that, had one been more alive to the nature of his feelings, and more attentive to soothe them, such would not have existed. And yet, enjoying as he appeared to do every sight or influence of earth or sky, it was difficult to imagine that any melancholy he showed was aught but the effect of the constant pain to which he was a martyr."

The most famous of the poems in which Shelley privately confessed his despair is headed " Stanzas written in Dejection near Naples." He may have read Coleridge's poem from similar depths of frustration, but his own lament has nothing like the

upwelling power and ultimate hope of that ode. He writes with
a subdued beauty preluding Verlaine, but as one with small
wish to emerge from his shadows, for

> now despair itself is mild,
> Even as the winds and waters are ;
> I could lie down like a tired child,
> And weep away the life of care
> Which I have borne and yet must bear,
> Till death like sleep might steal on me,
> And I might feel in the warm air
> My cheek grow cold, and hear the sea
> Breathe o'er my dying brain its last monotony.

Unquestionably the past refused to be past with him, and burdened
him with all its accumulated weight ; but we perceive that the
next events were also responsible for his dejection. Like Robert
Burns, looking forward he could not see, but he feared. Some
condition existed in his life at Naples in December, 1818, which
has not been clearly mentioned and may not now be traced
exactly but which obliged even this most courageous of men,
young as he was, to doubt his continued endurance.

Writing to the Gisbornes in 1820, Shelley uses the words " my
situation at Naples in December, 1818," as though he lived there
in some more than commonly troublesome dilemma. His servant
Paolo, in revenge for his dismissal, had by that later date attempted
to extort money from Shelley by threatening to accuse him of
some disgraceful crimes. Paolo did in fact run about with his
story, which was that Claire was Shelley's mistress and at Naples
gave birth to his child ; the child was instantly seized by Shelley
and consigned to the Foundling Hospital. The nurse Elise, whom
Paolo had seduced and under pressure from the Shelleys married,
took the same tale to the Hoppners. " Claire had no child at
Naples," said Mary, who could hardly have overlooked the detail
if she had ; but in his letters of 1820 to the Gisbornes Shelley
sends news more than once of a child in whose existence he was
in some manner concerned, " my poor Neapolitan," " my
Neapolitan," " my Neapolitan charge." This was a little girl,
who died in the summer of 1820, causing Shelley to say, " It
seems as if the destruction that is consuming me were as an
atmosphere which wrapt and *infected* everything connected with
me."

Who was this infant, and why did Shelley, as it is now known
that he did, register himself officially as the father ? " She is to
come to us as soon as she recovers "—but she did not recover ;

Mary must have known all about her. The lady who left every-thing in order to be near Shelley and who died in Naples has been conjectured to have been the mother, and to have entrusted the baby to him in her last hours. Even if nothing decisive is ever brought to light on these veiled matters, it can hardly be wrong to see beyond Shelley's dejection, under the fairest outward circumstances of his winter at Naples, a reason for its extremeness, and a reason of this kind. He was to bear one more burden which must increase the malignant power of his enemies ; and when Paolo, found guilty of more cheating than even Shelley could put up with, was sacked at last and went off with his new wife Elise, at the beginning of 1819, it must have been with apprehension as well as relief that Shelley saw them go. Milly the girl from Marlow remained, unimpressed by the odd style of these foreigners and falling in love with all the Englishmen she saw ; it is regrettable that she has left no Reminiscences of her years with the Shelleys.

In Naples Shelley went on with his inspection of paintings ; at home he had not entirely ignored the exhibitions and he knew something of the fashionable artists, but Italy quite changed his occasional glance into a connoisseur's survey. His remarks are not limited to connoisseur language, and of Michael Angelo's "Day of Judgment" he said, "a kind of ' Titus Andronicus ' in painting, but the author surely no Shakespeare." No Dante either; for "he has no sense of beauty, and to want this is to want the sense of the creative power of mind. What is terror without a contrast with, and a connexion with, loveliness ? How well Dante understood this secret." The habit of examining pictures was, I think, coming into Shelley's intellectual action not only when, like the retired colonels and the dilettanti around him, he was passing sentence on cried-up canvasses. It was sharpening his poetry, making him perfect and enrich the details, as in this stanza :

> He mocked the stars by grouping on each weed
>   The summer dew-globes in the golden dawn ;
> And, ere the hoar-frost languished, he could read
>   Its pictured path, as on bare spots of lawn
> Its delicate brief touch in silver weaves
> The likeness of the wood's remembered leaves ;

as in this comparison,

> As when the black storm hurries round at night,
>   The fisher basks beside his red firelight ;

or this,

> Like the dark ghost of the unburied even
> Striding athwart the orange-coloured heaven.

The last special expedition made by the poet from Naples
was to Paestum, sixty miles south. He made his usual prose
picture of the mountain and sea scenery on the way, and of the
architecture when they reached it through the violet-scented air.
On this journey they found that even in Italy it could rain cats
and dogs, and the wildness in the air was such as Shelley could
feel with particular sympathy, while they rode in the carriage
before the break of day. " The night had been tempestuous, and
our way lay by the sea sand. It was utterly dark, except when
the long line of wave burst with a sound like thunder beneath
the starless sky, and cast up a mist of cold white lustre." A
few days later the carriage drawn by " our own horses " was
conveying the party to Rome, where they were to stay three
months.

At last Shelley found that Italian people were not wholly
impossible. " We see something of Italian society." The women
were illiterate but alluring—" a kind of gentle savage." He saw
two of the highest beauty within a month, though their talk was
undistinguished. Of the eyes of ladies like these, he felt that
" though good and gentle, they want the mazy depth of colour
behind colour, with which the intellectual women of England
and Germany entangle the heart in soul-inwoven labyrinths." If
there are not enough mysteries in Shelley's biography, this
possibility of an adoration for some German poetess is available
to future writers. Sometimes the Shelleys went in the evening to
the house of a Roman lady, who wrote, painted and entertained,
named Signora Dionigi. There they met a queer learned creature
who passed as a colonel and was a parson, Robert Finch, and
were amused with his eccentricities ; but their English acquaintances were very few. Those who came to the Signora's evenings
said nothing throughout, and chose the moment to make for the
door all in a body. Lord Guilford called on the Shelleys in their
lodgings on the Corso. He was a noted traveller, and his ruling
passion was the renaissance of Greek culture. He only called
once. Sir William Drummond, whose metaphysical writings had
been much read and esteemed by Shelley, and who was an
exceptionally capable man as well as hospitable, also called—
once. More than one person in England was doing his best to
make Shelley's career of villainy familiar to the English abroad,
and supplement the hints of reviews and newspapers.

The sense of ostracism was painful even to Shelley : "if I were *alone* I should laugh ; or if I were rich enough to do all things " ; but Mary would have been happier not to be barred out of the social game. Even Colonel Finch with his stories of his intrepidity and his militant mustachios was better than nothing. A strong attempt was made to capture the Gisbornes for coming months. Meanwhile Mary, who had as a child received drawing lessons from John Linnell, the friend of William Blake, was learning to paint and of course seeing the glories of Rome. Both she and Shelley shared the popular excitement at Holy Week when the Emperor of Austria came to Rome, and however Shelley's political soul darkened at what this might imply he got as many tickets for the *festas* and *funzioni* as he could. Fireworks, illuminations, the Pope performing the ceremonies at St. Peter's, all gave them the same pleasure and enchantment as if they were children still.

But Shelley was easily disenchanted by other sights. Again he saw, in the square of St. Peter's, about 300 fettered criminals, chained, guarded by squads of soldiers with loaded muskets, dully hoeing the weeds between the flagstones. " The iron discord of those innumerable chains clanks up into the sonorous air, and produces, contrasted with the musical dashing of the fountains, and the deep azure beauty of the sky. and the magnificence of the architecture around, a conflict of sensations allied to madness. It is the emblem of Italy—moral degradation contrasted with the glory of nature and the arts."

These last had drawn from him a descriptive letter begun on March 23rd in his fullest manner of delight. It would be hard to detach details from so well linked a composition, but the ruins of Rome will scarcely find so impassioned a tourist again. Shelley includes in his scroll of glowing prospects and exquisite facsimiles a solitary being who can and must enter these pages. " I walk forth in the purple and golden light of an Italian evening, and return by star or moonlight, through this scene. The elms are just budding, and the warm spring winds bring unknown odours, all sweet from the country. I see the radiant Orion through the mighty columns of the temple of Concord, and the mellow fading light softens down the modern buildings of the Capitol, the only ones that interfere with the sublime desolation of the scene. . . . This walk is close to our lodging, and this is my evening walk." His admiration was only restricted at St. Peter's, which he thought from the outside " inferior in architectural beauty to St. Paul's " and from the inside an exhibition of " littleness on a large scale." We must wish that he had lived to discourse on St.

Paul's and Christopher Wren, pen in hand, with something of his Italian maturity in the criticism of architectural beauty.

High if not highest on the list of Shelley's Roman treasures were the Baths of Caracalla, huge chambers with towers and recesses which he described in the manner of a mountain range ; and besides the labyrinthine vastness and variety of the work itself the prodigality of nature had brought there a wilderness of trees and plants such as he was formed to fall in love with. As he traced the paths upward through the branches of myrtle, bay and fig he discovered one " little mossy lawn, surrounded by the wild shrubs ; it is overgrown with anemonies, wallflowers and violets, whose stalks pierce the starry moss, and with radiant blue flowers, whose names I know not, and which scatter through the air the divinest odour, which, as you recline under the shade of the ruin, produces sensations of voluptuous faintness, like the combinations of sweet music." Here was a little kingdom waiting for him, and at once he had a new study under the spirit-giving blue sky of spring not less beautiful than that at Este. Among the writings which he had begun at Este, one was understood by him as a true and destined work, and he brought his manuscript for the continuation here above the world upon the Baths of Caracalla. The title of the work, " Prometheus Unbound," had been chosen at Este, and the first act completed at Naples. By April 6th, 1819, he had added two more acts and at that moment was inclined to think the whole lyrical drama stood before him in its final state. With very little interval he turned his attention to another drama of an almost equally difficult kind but very different in style and action.

Thus the devotion of Shelley to the art of which, still a very young man, he was attaining the mastery, and the blessed chances which gave him for the time a perfect place of work, had defeated the bedevilment which had soured the air of Naples for him. Yet the suspicions which his health often reawakened and the advice of the doctors, for whom he had such a reverence even if they turned out now and then to be human in erring, moved him to look for another residence. First it was to be on the Bay of Naples, at Castel del Mare, and the migration was fixed for May 7th ; but after all it was not tried. Mary was expecting another child and the physician on whom she relied would be either at Pisa or Florence at the important time ; moreover young William was not very well and would do better in summer in some cooler place. At the end of May therefore the plan was a house at the Baths of Lucca, perhaps the Baths of Pisa. But before anything had been settled, a new and crushing affliction broke in upon Shelley and Mary.

William Shelley had begun to be quite a character, and talked away in three languages as merrily as fond parents could wish. His name at home was Willmouse and Willman. He had a complaint not unusual with children, a trouble usually driven out with the simplest medicine ; and then suddenly, early in June, he became seriously ill. Dr. Bell was an able physician by any standards, but could not check the illness, a high fever. Shelley passed sixty hours without sleep in watching over the boy, who at one stage when hope had vanished appeared to regain some hold on life, then slipped away, and died on June 7th. He was buried in the Protestant cemetery which Shelley had seen with a deep tranquillity on his first visit to Rome.

What this loss meant to Shelley may be told in his own words on the boy's promise. " He had lost all shade of ill-temper, and had become affectionate and sensible to an extraordinary degree, his spirits had a very unusual vivacity—it was impossible to find a creature more gentle and intelligent. His health and strength appeared to be perfect ; and his beauty, the silken fineness of his hair, the transparence of his complexion, the animation and deep blue colour of his eyes were the astonishment of every one. The Italian women used to bring each other to look at him when he was asleep." William was three and a half years old. He was the subject of memorial verses both by his father and his mother, Shelley thinking of him in life on the quiet sands of the sea with his

> mingled look of love and glee
> When he returned to gaze on thee,

and in death as undying, partaking the life of the flowers and shining grasses of the burial ground.

Mary's lines are to some extent an epitome of all their travels since William's birth :

> He dwelt beside the Alps, or gently slept,
> Rocked by the waves o'er which our vessel swept,
> Beside his father, nurst upon my breast,
> While Leman's waters shook with fierce unrest.
> His fairest limbs had bathed in Serchio's stream ;
> His eyes had watched Italian lightnings gleam ;
> His childish voice had, with its loudest call,
> The echoes waked of Este's castle-wall ;
> Had paced Pompeii's Roman Market-place ;

Had gazed with infant wonder on the grace
Of stone-wrought deities and pictured saints
In Rome's high palaces :—there were no taints
Of ruin on his cheek—all shadowless
Grim death approached—the boy met his caress,
And while his glowing limbs with life's warmth shone,
Around those limbs his icy arms were thrown.

. . . .

No grief upon thy brow's young purity
Entrenched sad lines, or blotted with its might
The sunshine of thy smile's celestial light ;
The image shattered, the bright spirit fled,
Thou shin'st the morning star among the dead.

The intention of removing from Rome was strengthened by
the wish to be away from the daily scenes associated with the dead
child, and before many days they were at Leghorn near the friendly
Gisbornes. It is true that Shelley often said dry things about Mr.
Gisborne—" a man who knows I cannot tell how many languages,
and has read almost all the books you can think of ; but all that
they contain seems to be to his mind what water is to a sieve."
Still, Gisborne had liberal opinions reflected from those of his
wife, and Shelley made the best of him on that account. With
the Gisbornes he enjoyed a new book which came out to him
from England, one which he had every reason to welcome, for it
was " Nightmare Abbey " by his friend Peacock ; and in one of
the characters he perceived a witty and good-tempered caricature
of himself. Probably he had got some previous hint of this
inclusion, for the first thing he says of the book after mentioning
his delight is, " I think Scythrop a character admirably conceived
and executed." Had Shelley done nothing else but supply the
original for Peacock's droll study he would not have lived in vain.

Scythrop Glowry in the novel is nearer to Shelley in life, so
far as the sketch goes, than official biography. He is a perfectly
accomplished member of society but of a romantic and speculative
disposition. He is highly liable to fall in love. Upon losing Miss
Girouette he retires to his lonely, but not too lonely tower, and in
the evening sits reading " The Sermons of Werther " on a mossy
stone under a canopy of ivy—" with an owl in it." His zeal for
metaphysical romance and romantic metaphysics, his " passion
for reforming the world " replaces his sorrow, and he publishes a
treatise promising, in his view, to arouse the nation ; but the
sale ends at 7 copies. He is undaunted. " Seven copies have been
sold. Let me find the seven purchasers of my seven copies, and

they shall be the seven golden candlesticks with which I will illuminate the world." This as we have seen is the precise method of Shelley in his earlier phase as a reformist. For his scientific recreations the character of Scythrop offers a parallel : he has some mechanical genius, and with the aid of a dumb carpenter makes models of cells and secret passages.

Now comes his cousin Marionetta, a lovely young lady in whose supposed graces of person and light unromantic conversation some have noted an impression of Harriet. Before long the enraptured Scythrop is addressing her in his tower, " Let us each open a vein in the other's arm, mix our blood in a bowl, and drink it as a sacrament of love. . . ." Marionetta promptly darts away ; and in any case Scythrop's father wants him to marry Miss Toobad, just then finishing her education in a German convent. His longing for the mysterious is answered one evening when he finds in his tower a figure concealed in a black cloak, who is revealed as a dazzling beauty, and hails him as the reformer and the author of " Philosophical Gas ; or, a Project for a General Illumination of the Human Mind." She seeks his protection, he lodges her in the secret rooms he has built, calls her Stella and commends her attitude to liberty and the German drama. But she is found by old Mr. Glowry. She is none other than Celinda Toobad. Both she and Marionetta renounce Scythrop. Shall he renounce them ? No. " I cannot renounce either. I cannot choose either. I am doomed to be the victim of eternal disappointments ; and I have no resource but a pistol." Needless to add the novelist finds the way out, and the last scene shows Scythrop ordering the butler to " Bring some Madeira,"—a wine which we do not know that Shelley often touched.

The comedy could not have come at a better moment for Shelley's spirits—though he insisted on " looking deeper " into it and commending Scythrop's ardours as " the salt of the earth." He was well repaid for having found for Peacock a passage in Ben Jonson to stand as motto to the novel. He pleasantly reported from the little country house near Leghorn that he had a study there in a tower, something like Scythrop's. In fact it was an eyrie of glass whence he could see the sea, with its islands, Gorgona, Capraja, Elba and Corsica on one side and the Apennines on the other. He was an absolute salamander, for in fine weather nobody but himself could endure the heat of this turret, but he wrote vigorously in it. However, it was not here that he did for " Prometheus Unbound " what he felt to be necessary to its whole movement and culmination.

The delay in adding the fourth act may not have been entirely due to the number of other writings which Shelley was now producing. He had just discovered an author who filled his mind with a new quality. Possibly it was when his doctor advised him to go to Spain for the winter that he took to learning Spanish from Mrs. Gisborne, and the next thing was that he was reading some of the plays of Calderon and estimating them as approaching Shakespeare's. He thought, when he had enjoyed twelve of them, that Calderon was like Shakespeare " in the rare power of inter-weaving delicate and powerful comic traits with the most tragical situations, without diminishing their interest."

Such consolations as these were granted him in a period when Mary could not rise from her miseries, but an old torment returned : William Godwin could not even avoid writing irony to his daughter for being grief-stricken " because a child of three years is dead." Shelley requested him to send her some milder message, but Godwin only told her that her hope of remaining on terms with her father was to make Shelley pay some more money. This was too much even for Shelley, who remembered that Godwin had had £4700 from him, and he wrote to Leigh Hunt, " He heaps on her misery—stiff misery. I have not yet shewn her the letter—but I must. I doubt whether I ought not to expose this solemn lie ; for such and not a man is Godwin. But I shall as is our custom (I mean yours and mine) err on the side of patience and endurance. . . . I have bought bitter know-ledge with £4700. I wish it were all yours now."

XVII

"AS FROM A TOWER"

UP IN his hothouse at Villa Valsovano, sometimes pausing to note the songs of the peasants below, or to follow the course of tremendous storms striking in waterspouts out at sea, Shelley devoted himself with extraordinary strength of mind to his literary work. The principal part of his programme was the blank-verse play in five acts called *The Cenci*, conceived at Rome when a friend gave him a manuscript version of this abnormal tragedy— " a detailed account of the horrors which ended in the extinction of one of the noblest and richest families of that city during the pontificate of Clement VIII, in the year 1599." The giver of the manuscript has been thought to be Count Stendhal. In brief the story was the murder of an incestuous and inhuman father by the daughter, Beatrice, with the law's savage revenges ; and when Shelley and Mary had seen Guido's portrait of Beatrice at the Colonna Palace, he was profoundly affected, taking her to have been " one of the loveliest specimens of the workmanship of nature." The Cenci Palace, vast and gloomy and in great part retaining the appearance which it had in the sixteenth century, spoke also to his imagination.

Coming that way thirty years later Charles Dickens was similarly moved. " The portrait of Beatrice di Cenci is a picture almost impossible to be forgotten. . . . She has turned suddenly towards you ; and there is an expression in the eyes—although they are very tender and gentle—as if the wildness of a momentary terror, or distraction, had been struggled with and overcome, that instant ; and nothing but a celestial hope, and a beautiful sorrow, and a desolate earthly helplessness remained. . . . The guilty palace of the Cenci : blighting a whole quarter of the town, as it stands withering away by grains : had that face, to my fancy in its dismal porch, and at its black blind windows and growing out of the darkness of its ghostly galleries. The History is written in the Painting ; written, in the dying girl's face, by Nature's own hand. And oh ! how in that one touch she puts to flight (instead of making kin) the puny world that claims to be related to her, in right of poor conventional forgeries ! "

In every way this history of a kind of martyrdom was waiting for Shelley's poetic and moral commemoration, now that he had increased his genius with so much observation of the past as it yet showed in Italy. Above all he was moved to utter something of an elegy, since no English author had done this, in honour of the heroism of Beatrice Cenci—the feeling that the dead may not be beyond the influence of just honours was not unknown to him. " What may atone, O ever injured shade ? " was a verse he knew. As he told Peacock, in writing this play he did his best to leave out of the case all " peculiar feelings and opinions " of his own, to represent the characters and their world as in their time. He proceeded with the livelier confidence because he had made a mental note or two during his nights at the play in England. Miss O'Neil would be the very person for the part of Beatrice, and Edmund Kean should have acted the unholy old Count Cenci—" but that is impossible." The disadvantage of the piece, which he did not shuffle over, was the unpopularity of incest on the London stage ; yet he used all his skill to avoid precise allusions to the crime, and to keep an audience in its seats.

" The Cenci," as literature, has another disadvantage. If he hoped (and he did) to become a successful dramatist in the year 1820, it was an indispensable condition that he should put on one of the endless pseudo-Elizabethan or at least post-Elizabethan compositions which were in vogue then and for years afterwards. He would have to stick to the general form, rhetoric and grouping which make the spirits droop in contemplation of those hollow dramas—*Fazio, Bertram, Mirandola, Virginius, Ethelstan* and all the tribe. Certainly he was right in claiming that his play was superior to all of them, with the now neglected exception of Coleridge's *Remorse*—but, like Keats on whom the same theatrical ambition had fastened, he was working in a debased kind. Let us suppose that someone had been admitted to his Scythropian tower who could discern this at that date and had entreated Shelley to think it over—not to wear the dowdy old costume, but find a fresh style and attire for his play of Beatrice : what a rejection he would have ensured for it at the great theatres, and what a play posterity would possess ! As it was, Shelley went ahead with echoes of Beaumont and Fletcher and Ford and Webster and even the perpetrator of *Fazio* in his head, and with Lamb's *Specimens of the Dramatists* at his elbow—an anthology meant to display the poetry of Shakespeare's rivals and memorable in that respect, but productive of too many sickly emulations.

With innocent diligence Shelley even copied some situations which are best in their proper home—*Macbeth* for instance. He contrived a banquet at which things went all wrong, and the guests began to make for the exit ; his murder scene is almost a proof that Shakespeare's own ghost walks :

Beatrice   O fear not
What may be done, but what is left undone :
The act seals all.
                    Enter Olympio and Marzio.
                    Is it accomplished ?
Marzio   What ?
Olympio Did you not call ?
Beatrice   When ?
Olympio   Now.

The conclusion of Shelley's tragedy is reckoned masterly, for the touches of nature there, on the verge of death,—

                        Here, Mother, tie
My girdle for me, and bind up this hair
In any simple knot ; ay, that does well.
And yours I see is coming down. How often
Have we done this for one another ; now
We shall not do it any more.

It owes too much to Webster's Duchess in a like extremity, asking that her little boy may be given some syrup for his cough, and to Lear requesting the gentleman to undo a button ; but it appears too late as the human touch in Beatrice.

In making the principal characters Shelley shows less scholarship and more audacity. The Count with his insatiable cruelty and yet his trust in God—*his* God—is a strong study. Much of him even is transferred from Lear—the curse on his daughter for example, which he delivers kneeling, not forgetting to wish her a thankless and thwart child. Beatrice has several splendid speeches assigned to her, and at times resembles the portrait which Shelley meant to have as the frontispiece to the book in a calm, sweet and all-enduring straightforwardness. She speaks like a great lady though young. Mr. St. John Ervine regards the play altogether as a proof that Shelley could write for the stage, and " knew the tricks of the theatre trade by instinct,"—such tricks as suspended intensity. He finds a sardonic humour in it of the kind that is called Shavian, and certainly the side remark of the Pope as he pronounces sentence on the Cenci family is bitterly amusing :

            " Parricide grows so rife
That soon, *for some just cause no doubt*, the young
Will strangle us all, dozing in our chairs."

Giving up the idea of a frontispiece as an extravagance, Shelley, had 250 copies of *The Cenci* printed at Leghorn, and he sent the text to Peacock who was desired to submit it to the managers of the two great theatres. It was considered necessary that the authorship should be closely concealed, not only because of the *Quarterly* reviewers and others in public positions but because of that pocket battleship Eliza Westbrook. If it were known to be Shelley's, he thought that she " alone would hire enough people to damn it." Henry Harris, who had taken the management of Covent Garden in succession to his highly popular father, regarded the crime of Count Cenci as an insuperable objection, and would " not even submit " the part of Beatrice for Miss O'Neil's perusal; he invited the writer to send a tragedy on some other subject. Miss O'Neil's marriage finished all prospect of Shelley's providing her with a less embarrassing opportunity. She became the wife of an Irish M.P. in December, 1819, and gave up acting.

In course of time, at a period when people of this century assume that the Victorians, in their appalling prudery, were all clothing the legs of chairs, a trial performance of *The Cenci* was given. The date was May 7th, 1886, at the Grand Theatre ; and 3000 persons applauded the noble acting of Herman Vezin and Alma Murray. Miss Murray thus fulfilled the ambition of her life, and received not only immense acclamations but a locket from Lady Shelley with a miniature of Beatrice and a wisp of Shelley's hair in it ; Robert Browning wrote to assure her she was " the Poetic Actress without a rival " ; but she answered an inescapable question about the play firmly. " How do you think it would be received by an ordinary English audience, if played at a regular night performance ? " " I hardly think it suitable for performance, except under special circumstances. It is too *ideal* and too *terrible* for ordinary occasions." If the play were regarded otherwise than " ideally " it was open to such criticisms as W. S. Landor had made. " Scene 3 is beyond all credibility— A feast to celebrate the death of his children ! and given to the nobility of the land, many of them good men." Beatrice was, to him, equally incredible ; her adjurations were all hollow, her song ill-timed, and so on. Yet Desdemona also sang a song in a tragic hour ; and Shelley was more subtle in his theory of the nature of imaginative drama than Landor in his lusty hurry perceived.

The next imaginative work written by Shelley grew from the fact that when he looked forth from his tower he did not only see the southern sky, sea and land. Late in August, 1819, he wrote to Peacock, " I most devoutly wish I were living near London.

. . . My inclinations point to Hampstead ; but I do not know whether I should not make up my mind to something more completely suburban. What are mountains, trees, heaths, or even the glorious and ever-beautiful sky, with such sunsets as I have seen at Hampstead, to friends ? Social enjoyment, in some form or other, is the alpha and omega of existence. All that I see in Italy . . . is nothing ; it dwindles into smoke in the mind, when I think of some familiar forms of scenery, little perhaps in themselves, over which old remembrances have thrown a delightful colour. How we prize what we despised when present ! So the ghosts of our dead associations rise and haunt us, in revenge for our having let them starve, and abandoned them to perish."

There was one English ghost whose living name he never allowed himself to write, but Harriet was not all the England in his mind, nor was his mind's eye only upon his personal praeterita. His desire to see old friends was of course great, as was his pleasure when a portrait of Leigh Hunt arrived after a year's delay, being a copy of the upper part of a chalk drawing by Wildman. " It is almost yourself," he wrote, " and we sate talking with it, and of it, all the evening. There wants nothing but that deepest and most earnest look with which you sometimes draw aside the inner veil of your nature when you talk with us, and the liquid lustre of your eyes." It was to Hunt, remembered in this manner of comprehension, that Shelley wrote the dedication to *The Cenci*, and in that specimen of gracious encomium he spoke of the " patient and irreconcilable enmity with domestic and political tyranny and imposture which the tenor of your life has illustrated."

Tyranny's operations in England were among the things appearing to Shelley in the south, and while he was at work on his play the newspaper—he received the very useful one edited for continental readers by Galignani of Paris—suddenly announced these in a hateful and violent form. A meeting of reformists in Manchester on August 16th had been pronounced illegal, and in the end, to disperse the crowd, a cavalry charge was made and a number of English workpeople were killed and wounded. It was the action angrily called Peterloo, from its being held in St. Peter's Field, and it looked to Shelley like the prelude to a revolution, though he reasoned that this would not break out in full until a financial crisis occurred. He hoped that even at the distance of Leghorn his vision might be of value to his country in what might become a merciless civil war. There is the beat, the roar, the singleness of a march of immense forces in his " Mask of Anarchy," the poem which he composed as a directive to the leaders of labour; and in sending it for publication to *The Examiner* he was well aware that in the north of England that journal was read with attention by groups of working men. Had Shelley ever decided to live in Yorkshire or Lancashire and talk with as well as write for his "Men of England" there, he would very probably have kindled an enthusiasm or led a movement which would have surprised the government.

To these working men he wished victory, and what they wished for themselves—a just return for their skill and labour; but he would have them fight their war with the wise self-control preached in the Sermon on the Mount. Passive resistance was the campaign he saw victorious, if all who were in serfdom would make common cause. His proud ballad makes most lays of labour sound like begging and snuffling. The Mask opens with a flaming light on the types of tyrants, and nobody can complain if Shelley took some personal satisfaction in giving Lord Eldon a place among them and in generalising the fate of Ianthe and Charles:

> His big tears, for he wept well,
> Turned to mill-stones as they fell.

> And the little children, who
> Round his feet played to and fro,
> Thinking every tear a gem,
> Had their brains knocked out by them.

Having created a magnificent pageantry of the Anarchs riding with their skeleton commander through England to Westminster, Shelley turned to the other side—the slaves whose half-starved drudgery and enforced darkness of mind were the basis of the surfeiting and privilege of the upper orders. "Men of England, heirs of Glory," he called them, and he bade them

> Rise like Lions after slumber
> In unvanquishable number,
> Shake your chains to earth like dew
> Which in sleep had fallen on you—
> Ye are many—they are few.

But he would have them rise with reverence for the "old laws of England," which he knew better than most heirs to baronetcies:

> And if then the tyrants dare
> Let them ride among you there,
> Slash, and stab, and maim, and hew,—
> What they like, that let them do.

> With folded arms, and steady eyes,
> And little fear, and less surprise,
> Look upon them as they slay
> Till their rage has died away.

It is not wonderful that John and Leigh Hunt, who between them spent several years in prison and many hundreds of pounds in the cause of reform, did not risk publishing this republican challenge at this stage in their paper ; but when the Reform Bill had proved that public feeling had moved in the direction pointed out and prophesied by Shelley, Leigh Hunt at once published the manuscript with an eloquent preface. By that time Shelley had been dead ten years. Now that he has been dead over a century, " The Mask of Anarchy " makes perhaps a more urgent call on the intelligence and feelings of men than ever, for though the particulars of the war between insolent and implemented oppression and unambitious, sensitive lives must ever change, the doctrine of bloodless, revengeless resistance in which he believed is unalterably right, as it is angelically difficult.

The manuscript of his political poem had not been dispatched long before a fresh instance of the misused power which Shelley abominated came to his notice. This time it was religious intolerance which set him writing, but it was of a piece with the other aggressions upon liberty in England. A humble and no doubt tedious publisher named Richard Carlile who had republished Tom Paine's " Age of Reason " and other free-thinking pamphlets was tried for blasphemous libel and sentenced to three years imprisonment and a fine of £1500 ; the jury is said to have been openly enraged with his line of defence, namely, that the scriptures were not of divine origin ; and Shelley perceived that the defendant had been fastened upon because he was a poor man. The wealthy Deists whom he enumerated were too strongly entrenched to be attacked. On this occasion Shelley's protest was in prose, intended to appear in *The Examiner* . and on December 2nd Leigh Hunt referred to " your political songs and pamphlets, which we must publish " ; but the Letter on Carlile remained unprinted. It is a fine piece of argument, a summary of Shelley's thoughts on the Tories, and a proof of his interest in the Deists. Here occurs his opinion of Tom Paine as " that great and good man." Reconsidering all the news from England in 1819 Shelley wrote the strenuous sonnet beginning " An old, mad, blind, despised and dying king " which ends in an expression of his hopefulness in spite of all the aspects of evil ; these, he said, from useless princes to Christless religion and an obsolete Senate

> Are graves, from which a glorious Phantom may
> Burst, to illumine our tempestuous day.

Those who take Shelley for a fantastic optimist should remember that " may."

In October, 1819, Shelley was at Florence, " where we have taken pleasant apartments for six months." The loss of his aerial study did not spoil his productive energy ; he had compensations. " The fields his study, nature was his book " might be his motto as well as that of other poets ; and one day in a wood along the Arno near Florence—the remoter part of the much frequented Cascine—the unrest in the universe around him marking the change of season worked in him to the extent that he wrote a poem of the highest strength and beauty. The " Ode to the West Wind " may be compared with the Stanzas written at Naples at the end of the previous year, since it records a sense of exhaustion and mortality in the author. He remembers that once, in boyhood, he was almost as swift as the wind, but now he prays for reanimation.

> Oh, lift me as a wave, a leaf, a cloud !
> I fall upon the thorns of life ! I bleed !

Already he thinks he sees the attritions of age in himself :

> Make me thy lyre, even as the forest is :
> What if my leaves are falling like its own ?

Notwithstanding these sighs the Ode is a proof that he was capable of poetic force and zeal beyond the range of any of his contemporaries in 1819. The storm-wind was not more momentous than his invocation, and flashing conception of his meaning to mankind. This selection of nature's mighty phenomena as his poetical world is found again soon after in a Chorus of Spirits singing of heaven, its

> deep chasms and wildernesses
> And green worlds that glide along,
> And swift stars with flashing tresses,
> And icy moons most cold and bright,
> And mighty suns beyond the night,
> Atoms of intensest light ;

all which, again, he imagines in a drop of dew, and calls all as frail and impermanent as that.

The Shelleys lived in Florence at the Palazzo Marino, 4395 Via Valfonda. The church of S. Maria Novella was their local landmark. But we know most of him as a haunter of the Uffizi Gallery, annotating sculpture and painting, worshipping the grace which the Greeks could create from all subjects. A painting then attributed to Leonardo da Vinci but now excluded from his works, the Medusa, was appreciated in a poem, as if Shelley knew that Walter Pater would supply the prose later on. Well he caught the significance of the symbols in this picture of horror. Thus occupied, or on his rounds in the Cascine woods, he hardly made any new acquaintances, and no unexpected incidents checked his intellectual diligence for some weeks unless the arrival of the *Quarterly* with an attack on his character was one. At that he was partly amused, partly inclined to exact an apology from the editor or a public show of evidence for the charges made. Occasionally his banking problems made him anxious, since as usual he had found new objects for his benevolence.

After being five months, " hateful months," without a child, Mary was glad to bring into the world on November 12th, 1819, a fine little boy, who was called Percy Florence. He got through the cold winter splendidly and grew fat. This child was destined to become the most delightful of men, whose tastes and endeavours from the amateur theatre to steam yachts and photography reflected in a gentle light and on a small scale the manifold enthusiasms of his inspired father. The newest of these was working up at the date of small Percy's birth. Shelley had suggested to Mrs. Gisborne's son, Henry Reveley, the plan of building a steamboat to ply between Marseilles, Genoa and Leghorn. In July, 1819, the steamship *Savannah* of 350 tons had crossed the Atlantic in 26 days, and it was time that the Mediterranean should be brought up to date. Reveley naturally took charge of the practical side of the scheme, and Shelley acted as the patron, finding money for the work as fast as he could, and encouraging the workmen. On the day of Percy's birth Reveley sent Shelley a glowing account of the casting of " both the steam cylinder and air-pump." Shelley already saw himself aboard the vessel on the day when she would put in at Leghorn to astonish the waiting multitudes on the quay.

And just at this time Shelley won a new acquaintance who soon passed by but had as deep and beautiful an effect upon him as any one whom he ever met for so short a time. The measure of this is in the lyrical poems which he was enabled to add to lasting literature. The newcomer can hardly have been unknown to him by report already. Sophia Stacey was the daughter of Flint Stacey, brewer, banker and mayor of Maidstone, who died in November, 1802 ; she then became the ward of Shelley's uncle

and aunt the Parkers ; and now she was travelling with " a little
old Welshwoman," Miss Corbet Parry-Jones, as her companion.
The fashionable round which she fully enjoyed did not prevent
her from falling under the spell of the recluse-like Shelley when
she took apartments at the same boarding-house in Florence. She
had heard what a remarkable being he was, and she found it all
true. Soon he was teaching her Italian every day, and when the
problem of finding a second name for the child Percy was mentioned she proposed " Florence " and it was approved.

Sophia was a wide-eyed listener to Shelley's talk on the
established church, love, liberty, death, music and books ; played
the harp, and sang very sweetly ; could join in all his family
and Sussex recollections. He was enchanted, and said so in
melodious verses. " Thou art fair and few are fairer " is a
confession of a charmed hour, and the stanza is identical with
that of the " Voice in the Air " in " Prometheus Unbound "
adoring the spirit of love through all creation ; it looks like an
amplifying of what Shelley felt as he heard young Sophia sing.
Several other songs are recognisable as part of the Sophia idyll,
and when at the end of the year she went her way to Rome he
presented her with Leigh Hunt's *Literary Pocket-Book* for 1819
containing his copies of some of these pieces : " An Anacreontic "
(" The fountains mingle with the river "), " Time Long Past "
and " Goodnight." And if the position seemed what is called
dangerous, probably Shelley himself made the complete comment
in the little piece headed " To ——,"

> I fear thy kisses, gentle maiden,
> Thou needest not fear mine ;
> My spirit is too deeply laden
> Ever to burden thine.

Sophia went her way, but her presence in Shelley's home in
November and December, 1819, filling his heart with music and
daybreak, may well have had a big share in setting him free from
his increasing gloom over English political events and in cue for
the fourth, lyrical and irresistible act now added to " Prometheus
Unbound." That had been written just before Sophia's departure.

Any one else but Shelley, or a select few of richest genius,
would have thought it enough to have written just then a work
which he hardly notices in his course, although he sent Mary's
transcript to Hunt on November 2nd, 1819. It was " not bad,"
he said later, though " perhaps no one will believe anything in
the shape of a joke from me."—" Shelley had no sense of humour."
—The incredulity has persisted, but " Peter Bell The Third " is a

humorous poem of the first order. It is a joke, but it is a tremendous one ; it is parody, but as in the instance of Mr. Sassoon's " Daffodil Murderer " the parodist often ceases to tread the path of imitation and forgets himself into original and spontaneous poetry.

Reading his *Examiner* when it had come all the way to Florence Shelley was entertained by two reviews, which gave him the chance of his own performance. The first of them, which had been sent in anonymously by Keats, welcomed in an artful way a burlesque on Wordsworth's poetry called " Peter Bell." The irreverent author, whose name was withheld, was J. H. Reynolds, and he had anticipated Wordsworth's own poem " Peter Bell " by a few days ; that was the subject of a dashing article by Leigh Hunt in the next *Examiner*. Shelley had for some time looked on Wordsworth as a turncoat, heard of his efforts in election campaigns for the diehards, and took the signs to be that the Lake Poet was paying the price for deserting his principles by becoming appallingly dull ; under these circumstances the " Peter Bell " joke might be continued.

The resulting poem, which occupied six or seven days in composition, is frequently a parody on Wordsworth or an irony on his career ; nevertheless it is not limited to his dispraise. As a critical study of him, fragmentary as it is, it is brilliant ; the power of Coleridge to make Wordsworth a poet is here expressed with grimness but with subtlety. The beauty of Wordsworth's own poetry has not often been reflected more delicately :

> But Peter's verse was clear, and came
>   Announcing from the frozen hearth
> Of a cold age, that none might tame
> The soul of that diviner flame
>   It augured to the Earth :
>
> Like gentle rains, on the dry plains,
>   Making that green which late was gray,
> Or like the sudden moon, that stains
> Some gloomy chamber's window-panes
>   With a broad light like day.

Thus Shelley anticipated the verdict of later years on Wordsworth's value as an antidote to the scientific spirit, a healing power. Yet the figure of Peter is really used by Shelley as a means of introducing the wider topic of spiritual subjection to the Devil, presiding over the condition of England. The Fiend's address is one that Shelley had had many opportunities to study

on his walks with Harriet—flunkeydom, Grosvenor Square : and
it is the dark sublime of the poem when not only that residence
but the town as a whole is presented in glowering panorama.
The resemblance of Shelley's mind to Byron's comes out here,
and it is hard to say which of them was the more satirical and
unescapable observer of the London scene, from which profusion
one vignette only may exemplify Shelley's vision—the types to
whom he guessed many Harriets had fallen victims :

> Things whose trade is, over ladies
>   To lean, and flirt, and stare, and simper,
> Till all that is divine in woman
> Grows cruel, courteous, smooth, inhuman,
>   Crucified 'twixt a smile and whimper.

Death, the Devil, Hell, Sin, Grace, Damnation, Double Damnation—these headings alone elevate the spacious theatre wherein
Shelley exhibited his puppet Peter ; but he was not allowed to
do so as speedily as he wished. Ollier saw no money, and much
bother, in such a publication.

In an article replying to the *Quarterly* on himself and Shelley
Hunt declined to make direct observations on what was being
alleged against his friend, " leaving him when he returns to England to take such notice or otherwise of his calumniators as may
seem best to him." Though Shelley could make out a plausible
comparison between London and hell, the winter of 1819
threatened to drag him thither on business, and the bitter thing
was that it was mainly Godwin's business. It would be necessary
for him to go alone and with as much secrecy as he could ensure.
But the thought of this journey to England was not caused solely
by a new impact of obligations incurred for the relief of Godwin's
endless wants. Shelley, not being Old Moore enough to foresee
that his father would live for a quarter of a century longer, was
forced to bear in mind the daily possibility of finding himself
the new Baronet and hastening to Field Place to superintend the
widespread estates. His brother John was still a child ; should
Sir Timothy die, no prospect of a substitute appeared there.

Among Leigh Hunt's private recommendations to Shelley,
one was that he should have his portrait painted ; and in 1819
something was attempted in this way. " Let Shelley," his friend
wrote, " plant himself opposite the artist, glancing neither to the
right hand nor the left, and look him straight forward in the face,
and if a spirit came down from the planet Mercury, to sit still a
little, and look at me, the thing could not be finer." The daughter
of Shelley's Dublin friend J. P. Curran was now painting in

Italy, and she agreed with Hunt's prescription of the attitude in her portrait of Shelley begun at Rome. Unfinished as it is, it has been the best known portrait of the poet since it was first engraved in 1833—perhaps indeed, apart from the Droeshout Shakespeare, the best known effigy of any English poet.

Amelia Curran certainly saw Shelley as a spirit and gave expression to what she saw, the objection being that he was a man and one on whose countenance much hard experience had been recorded. The portrait has a luminous and phantasmal beauty, but was so little like the life that it has only escaped being thrown away by Shelley's wife by a lucky chance. For closer resemblance, we may remember that Sophia Stacey found one in a bust of Lucius Caesar in the Naples Museum. Another attempt to portray Shelley was made in the first days of 1820 by Mr. Tomkins who also boarded at Louisa du Planti's Palazzo, and he remembered that Shelley sat to him wearing a fur-collared cloak ; but the fatality overhanging Shelley portraits did not spare this. It is lost. We are left to make our own pictures of the man out of the ideal one by Amelia Curran, the unbeautiful yet perceptive bust by Marianne Hunt, the verbal descriptions, and the portraits of Shelley's brother and sisters.

Meanwhile in Rome Bartolini's studio was filled with portraits of the English. Elderly gentlemen with " double chins, resembling the breast of the pelican," portly matrons with purchased luxuriant tresses, " young ladies with compressed waists, and drooping ringlets, looking all like sisters ; and young gentlemen, with formal faces and straight hair," were being immortalised there. Byron in due course sat like the rest to Bartolini for his bust.

Shelley's fur cloak was not a fancy costume. Even he cursed the cold snap at Florence at the beginning of 1820 as infernal. He had started up a new piece of writing, something from " the great sandy desert of politics," in other words " an octavo on reform," but he did not feel like hurrying it on in such a temperature. " Prometheus Unbound," which he declared to be " the best thing I ever wrote," was by now all on the way to Ollier and the press. His physical pains increased upon him, and he was easily persuaded that Florence was not the right place for him, whereas at Pisa he could consult " the celebrated Vacca." On January 26th with Mary, Claire, the baby and attendants he went by boat on the Arno towards Pisa, and they arrived in the evening and put up at the best inn, the Tre Donzelle.

XVIII

"PROMETHEUS UNBOUND"

WHEN Mary Shelley's first novel was entitled *Frankenstein ; or, the Modern Prometheus*, the alternative title referred to a legend which is prominently given and explained in Bacon's *Wisdom of the Ancients*, much read by the Shelleys. Prometheus in that tale made a man of clay, as well as parts of animals, and in order to keep him alive stole up to heaven with a bundle of twigs, kindled it at the sun's chariot and returned with this vital fire. This parable was not quite the view of Prometheus which made many of the authors of the romantic age dwell upon his name, nor did they pay much regard to the crimes also charged against him in old fable—his cheating Jupiter at a sacrifice, his attempt to deflower Minerva, his rejection of Jupiter's gift to men of perpetual youth.

We see the Prometheus of modern romantic poetry first in the early writings of Goethe, appearing in fragments of a drama and an ode of sure power ; and the light which the ancient figure bears at this stage is more like that of the human soul. He defies Zeus not in matters of bull-hides stuffed with bones but in the theory of life. There are no gods but what man creates for his belief ; there is no terror, no comfort from them, save in reflection of man's world ; the human race must itself supply its divine standards. So Goethe presented Prometheus and what the myth signifies in 1774.

About fifty years later S. T. Coleridge in a lecture to the Royal Society of Literature tried to interpret the Prometheus of Aeschylus, and he was humorist enough to admit that he was leading his audience through " the holy jungle of transcendental metaphysics." He made many excellent observations, and of the masterpiece of Aeschylus he said : " It is more properly tragedy itself in the plenitude of the idea, than a particular tragic poem. . . . In the Greek we see already the dawn of the approaching manhood [of nations]. The substance, the *stuff*, is philosophy, the *form* only is poetry. The Prometheus is a *philosopheme*." Coleridge provided a key to the figures employed in it ; the fire that was stolen from heaven was pure reason in man ; Prometheus was Idea ; and even Io, who rushes in distractedly under the sting of a supernatural Gadfly, is mundane religion, while Juno is the

217

political priesthood. However these explanations might stand,
the great message of Prometheus was that " Nature, or Zeus, as
the νόμος 'εν νομιζομένοις can only come to a knowledge of herself
in Man."

Between Goethe's ode and Coleridge's lecture Shelley was
intervening in 1818 and 1819 with a Prometheus not altogether
uncongenial with theirs. He knew the play by Aeschylus as well
as they, and was as much drawn to the gospel which it delivered
to the race of men at any period. He knew that Aeschylus had
written a Prometheus Unbound, based on a turn of events which
would damage the nobility of that gospel as he took it to be. For,
after setting the example of unassailable and absolute resistance
to tyranny and brutality, Prometheus in the ancient sequel
accepted deliverance as payment for a service which he was
able to do for Zeus. " In truth," says Shelley, " I was averse
from a catastrophe so feeble as that of reconciling the Champion
with the Oppressor of mankind." It would destroy the glory
of moral courage for which only Prometheus appeared to have
been imagined or rather re-imagined by the Greek poet. Then
by what stroke in a new drama on the subject might Prometheus
be set free ? He was still chained and clamped on a precipice
in the Caucasus, still visited by " heaven's wingéd hound "
tearing his heart ; what might end the torture and leave Prometheus in all his majesty, " the type of the highest perfection of
moral and intellectual nature " ?

Shelley had his answer. He was aware that he had in his
reach a work of a new sort and was ready to invent or adapt
every kind of contributory novelty for it. In a manner he went
back to his old favourite Thomas Gray, whose lines he had by
heart :

> The boast of heraldry, the pomp of power,
>   And all that beauty, all that wealth e'er gave,
> Awaits alike th' inevitable Hour.

The ending of the combat between Zeus and Prometheus was
indicated in the last three words especially. But Shelley's
imagination and the nature of his lyrical drama clothed that
plain thought of the triumphs of time in his own strange way.
Among the persons of the drama he introduced one, emanating
" rays of gloom," called Demogorgon, and it is he who coming
in the car of the Hour dethrones Zeus and ends that despotism.
Readers of Spenser and Milton would remember him lurking like
a cunning old conger

> Downe in the bottom of the deepe *Abysse,*

most obscure, most intractable and dreaded of deities. Not only
did Shelley bring about the freedom of Prometheus by means of
Demogorgon, taking action when the mysterious forces with him
collectively called "the Hour" were at their point; it is to him
that he entrusts the song or speech of honour to Prometheus at
the end of the tale, though Demogorgon to the last remains "as
darkness."

To show the conflict between Prometheus and Zeus in full
was not Shelley's business; Aeschylus had written the one play
necessary to do that; but for some part of its course Shelley's
play recites and varies the legend shaped by his predecessor. At
the same time he discloses his Prometheus as one terribly aware
of the miseries heaped on those in the modern state of society
who wished to live in freedom from its conventions. For this
Shelley employs the furies to torment Prometheus with the
apparition of

> a youth
> With patient looks nailed to a crucifix.

Such was the Christ in whom Shelley believed, and for whom as
a man he had a passionate devotion. It is nowhere seen more
clearly than in the cry of Prometheus to this historic figure of
unselfishness like his own:

> Remit the anguish of that lighted stare;
> Close those wan lips; let that thorn-wounded brow
> Stream not with blood; it mingles with thy tears!
> Fix, fix those tortured orbs in peace and death,
> So thy sick throes shake not that crucifix,
> So those pale fingers play not with thy gore.

What had happened to the teachings of this youth?

> I see, I see
> The wise, the mild, the lofty and the just,
> Whom thy slaves hate for being like to thee,
> Some hunted by foul lies from their heart's home,
> An early-chosen, late-lamented home,
> As hooded ounces cling to the driven hind;
> Some linked to corpses in unwholesome cells;
> Some—Hear I not the multitude laugh loud?—
> Impaled in lingering fire.

These expressions are figurative, conveying the problems of
political justice which he had so often defined in other terms,
and the whole play is a web of allegorical allusions.

The liberation of Prometheus grows on the view with progress of radiant expectancy and happy augury until the Hour has brought the scene itself. Hercules then unbinds the captive with few words ; and from that time the personal Prometheus is not represented in the distinct manner of the opening. Not he but the change in the world consequent on his inestimable and crowned endurance is the ultimate aim of the play. At first Shelley was content to close it with the third act and with the long announcement of the Spirit of the Hour, commissioned to go round the world sounding a mystic shell to all that lives. That speech is of much beauty, intellectual and humane ; yet it must have been Shelley's opinion as he reconsidered the work that it inclined too much towards a speech at a reformists' meeting to end such a lyrical drama. The reformed world was certainly outlined there, by a decisive mind : not with the extremist impossibility which is imputed to Shelley :

> The painted veil, by those who were, called life,
> Which mimicked, as with colours idly spread,
> All men believed or hoped, is torn aside ;
> The loathsome mask has fallen, the man remains
> Sceptreless, free, uncircumscribed, but man
> Equal, unclassed, tribeless, and nationless,
> Exempt from awe, worship, degree, the king
> Over himself ; just, gentle, wise ; but man
> Passionless ?—no, yet free from guilt or pain,
> Which were, for his will made or suffered them,
> Not yet exempt, though ruling them like slaves,
> From chance, and death, and mutability,
> The clogs of that which else might oversoar
> The loftiest star of unascended heaven,
> Pinnacled dim in the intense inane.

Feeling that the victory of Prometheus should not be concluded in that way, as if he had been writing a political poem and nothing more, Shelley presently caught the music which inspired the appropriate ending. It must itself be jubilant, aerial, adventurous—and the fourth act appears to have been his equivalent of a ballet, springing from all he had enjoyed of spectacle, dance and music in the two years or more before the play was written. Right through " Prometheus Unbound," of course, the illusion of something like a theatre with hardly any limit to its possibilities of movement, costume, lighting and colouring, melody and instruments of music had been created. The twentieth century might have seen Shelley, had anything of his family fortunes been spared to him, using all his ingenuity on the

production of the piece, so as to bring before the bodily eye and
to the ear such conceptions as multiply in it :

Ione.   O, sister, look ! White fire
          Has cloven to the roots yon huge snow-loaded cedar;
          How fearfully God's thunder howls behind. . . .
Panthea. See where the child of Heaven, with winged feet,
          Runs down the slanted sunlight of the dawn—

or, more curiously invented still,

Fury.   The beauty of delight makes lovers glad,
          Gazing on one another ; so are we.
          As from the rose which the pale priestess kneels
          To gather for her festal crown of flowers
          The aerial crimson falls, flushing her cheek,
          So from our victim's destined agony
          The shade which is our form invests us round,
          Else we are shapeless as our mother Night.

In the final act, masque, dance and air and chorus are created
with all delight, to speak for the Promethean plan better than any
homily could however gracious ; and from the first notes which
sound like a bugle-horn in the forest, and were so intended, to
the time when "the stream of sound" sinks so that Demogorgon
may speak the praise of the Titan, Shelley's imaginary stage is
an enchanting entertainment. It might be enough delight if we
merely watched these lovely coloured motions, drank in these
cadences and liltings and lived in these rhythms which like a
young Prospero he conjures together. But Shelley intended much
more than revels, and it is difficult to come to the end of what he
has embodied of passionate thought within these princely pageants.
In an interval Ione and Panthea see bewildering forms in the
forest which are probably the emblems of Shelley's scientific
notions. They are visions, but not without a place in the waking
world, and those who know Blake's drawings will be prepared
for them. One is that crescent chariot of which the wheels are
clouds azure and gold and in which sits, guiding the chariot
with a quivering moonbeam,

                   a wingéd infant, white
Its countenance like the whiteness of bright snow,
Its plumes are as feathers of sunny frost,
Its limbs gleam white, through the wind-flowing folds
Of its white robe, woof of ethereal pearl.
Its hair is white, the brightness of white light

> Scattered in strings ; yet its two eyes are heavens
> Of liquid darkness, which the Deity
> Within seems pouring. . . .

This white child with the thunderstorm eyes may be the spirit of electricity.

Then comes something stranger, ringing with harmonies as it speeds,

> A sphere which is as many thousand spheres,
> Solid as crystal, yet through all its mass
> Flow, as through empty space, music and light :
> Ten thousand orbs involving and involved,
> Purple and azure, white and green and golden,
> Sphere within sphere . . .
> With mighty whirl the multitudinous orb
> Grinds the bright brook into an azure mist
> Of elemental subtlety, like light.

Here I imagine we have something like " the circle of the sciences," the advance of man's knowledge in a vast number of interdependent subjects, enabling him to resolve the material world into its elements. Within the orb dwells another phantom child, the Spirit of the Earth, from whose starred forehead a ray pierces the depths of land and water, unbares the secrets there, points out the vestiges of life once magnificent in forms long extinct.

The astronomer in Shelley joins with the bright lyrist in the imagined interplay of moon and earth, which even for him is a remarkable episode—for nobody else could have dreamed so of the love between those two, and he writes as though it was an easy thing to present. It is the utmost assertion in all his writings of his creed of love, one and the same whether felt by man and woman or by whatever is, and while we hear with wonder the voices of his " lamps of heaven," and confess that they are the imaginary voices of nature, we know that human wooing has never been more beautifully remembered :

The Moon

> Thou art folded, thou art lying
> In the light which is undying
> Of thine own joy, and heaven's smile divine ;
> All suns and constellations shower
> On thee a light, a life, a power
> Which doth array thy sphere ; thou pourest thine
> On mine, on mine !

The Earth

I spin beneath my pyramid of night,
Which points into the heavens dreaming delight,
Murmuring victorious joy in my enchanted sleep ;
As a youth lulled in love-dreams faintly sighing,
Under the shadow of his beauty lying,
Which round his rest a watch of light and warmth doth keep.

The Moon

As in the soft and sweet eclipse
When soul meets soul on lovers' lips
High hearts are calm, and brightest eyes are dull ;
So when thy shadow falls on me,
Then am I mute, and still, by thee
Covered ; of thy love, Orb most beautiful,
Full, oh, too full !

" My best poem." Shelley had given all he knew as man and
artist to its creation, and among the rest he had brought for the
blessing of his fellows the spirit of delight which we hear he could
shed upon his intimates in his daily affairs, but which in his
poetry is often overcast. Whether this was the outcome of his
finding for a time such a paradise in Italy, and notably that
fragrant solitude in the ruins of the Baths of Caracalla, or sheerly
of his realising the privilege of his genius to call man forth from
his smoky and dissonant occupations rather than help to impress
his worries more deeply into him, " Prometheus Unbound " is
the song of pleasure which its title would imply. It was by no
means Shelley's fond error to assume that the world will ever
be one vast valley of Avilion, one age-long summer afternoon,
or that lyric and bergamasque can be the condition of humanity ;
and so he leaves it at the fall of the curtain to Demogorgon to send
us home with his true meaning. Eternity, he says, will again
in her manifold workings release evil. When that comes we must
reassume empire over the enemy even as before, by the spells of
gentleness, virtue, wisdom and endurance. Prometheus is gone,
but his way to victory is perpetual ; there is no other way.

The appeal of Prometheus as a symbol of human history, at
the opening of the nineteenth century, was very vivid, and among
the evidences one is appropriate here. When Leigh Hunt heard
from Shelley in the summer of 1819 that the great poem was in
progress, he replied that he had himself been thinking lately of
writing on " Prometheus Throned," and was well content to
leave the subject in better hands. Hunt might yet be proud to
have been Shelley's contributor in a small degree. He had

published a few years earlier a mask called " The Descent of Liberty" in which the dancing measure adapted to lyrics was pleasantly used, and when Shelley wrote

" Ah, sister, Desolation is a delicate thing "

he caught up one of his friend's metrical varieties. In a poem called " Power and Gentleness " also Hunt had previously expressed something of the Promethean creed of " life, joy, empire and victory."

Turning to the fortunes of " Prometheus Unbound " on its way to becoming one of the new books of 1820, we find the author writing to Charles Ollier on March 6th and again on March 13th in some anxiety—had the manuscripts arrived ? Shelley's Italian years were spoiled by incessant anxiety on matters of the sort. However, Ollier received the copy, with no notion of his privilege, and was requested by Shelley to print it in good style, with fine ink and paper, as being the favourite. A high distinction of appearance belongs to all books published by Ollier during his brief partnership with his brother, and the " Prometheus Unbound " volume was brought out with its share of that ; but the errors of the press were numerous. The " Ode to the West Wind," that " To Heaven " and several other short poems were included in the volume, which has duly received recognition as one of the most illustrious single collections of verse ever issued in England. Shelley requested Ollier to let him hear how it was received. Then he asked that only abusive notices should be sent, apart from the friendly tributes which such friends as Hunt and a few others might print. The formula for Shelley in the reviews was beginning to be stereotyped, and any volume by him would probably be discussed at more or less length with no difference from this formula :—a man of uncommon powers and detestable principles. But Theodore Hook at least noticed the title of Shelley's lyrical drama :

" Shelley styles his new poem ' *Prometheus Unbound* '
And 'tis like to remain so while time circles round ;
For surely an age would be spent in the finding
A reader so weak as to pay for the binding."

The original forecast of Shelley himself was that not more than twenty readers would pay for copies at all.

That suspicion was stirred by his candid sense of the abstruseness of his poem. To this day it exacts from the reader a sustained and informed intentness failing which it becomes a luminous haze, and few perhaps have the necessary time and period knowledge for elucidating its multitude of hints to the imagination. Mary Shelley was not far wrong when in 1839 she commented, " It requires a mind as subtle and penetrating as his own to understand the mystic meanings scattered throughout the poem. They elude the ordinary reader by their abstraction and delicacy of distinction, but they are far from vague." Except for several of the lyrics, it is probable that " Prometheus Unbound " is generally taken to be a poetical cloudland, richly tinted and far-floating but too insubstantial to be more than a passing show. There are however many passages which will be quoted for a long time yet as the prophecies of the coming race.

It may not be unconnected with the publication of Shelley's great poem that in the Royal Academy exhibition of June, 1821, a picture entitled " The Deliverance of Prometheus " was shown. The artist was that tireless reader Henry Fuseli, aged 80, and this was the first paper sketch of his to be publicly exhibited. He had drawn his " Prometheus Vinctus " already. His conception of the surroundings of the unchained Titan was not like Shelley's which is full of fierce yet exquisite beauty ; Fuseli saw them as one unbroken blank desolation. Lovers of coincidence may care to know that while Shelley's work was being published, Beethoven's " Overture to Prometheus " was being performed on the Apollonicon of Messrs. Flight and Robson, which Shelley had paid his shilling to hear before leaving England. Louis Cazamian points out something more striking. At almost the same date as that of the composition of Shelley's " lyrical drama," Beethoven was composing his " Choral Symphony."

XIX

PISA, AFTER ALL

IN SPITE of the dullness which was the steady quality of Pisa when the Shelleys first saw it, they were back again and they began to grow a little fond of the town ; for one thing it was an economical life that they lived in their rooms on the Lung' Arno, and Mary reported, " For the first time in our lives we get on easily, our minds undisturbed by weekly bills and daily expenses." As for the surroundings, Shelley found that they took some hold on him. Later on when Byron expected him to agree that the sunsets at Venice were incomparable, he disagreed : " Stand on the marble bridge, cast your eye if you are not dazzled on its river glowing as with fire, then follow the graceful curve of the palaces on the Lung' Arno till the arch is naved by the massy dungeon-tower, forming in dark relief, and tell me if anything can surpass a sunset at Pisa." Here Shelley consulted Vacca, " the most famous surgeon in all Italy " and a hearty infidel, and received the advice to give up his bottles of medicine ; but he should go to the Baths of Lucca at the end of May.

There was little to interrupt these quiet days in Pisa unless it were some disturbing letter from the outside world. They could call on one or two friends who understood their way of living well, and the names of Mr. and Mrs. Mason appear in their letters. These excellent people were in reality Mr. Tighe and Lady Mountcashell, who had been placidly living together for so long that any irregularity in their union was quite forgotten. Mrs. Mason was a lady of noble and serene presence, many accomplishments, and a steady cheerfulness and confidence in life. Mr. Mason was not unlike her in tastes and ways. It is thought that Mrs. Mason was the original of the lady who made so beautiful a garden in Shelley's fanciful poem " The Sensitive Plant," written during these last months of winter at Pisa in 1820. At first glance it appears to be a floral fairy-tale, but on inspection the Shelleyan touch of dissembled autobiography is revealed— certainly not exact self-portraying, but the suggestion. If we think of it as a reverie, the drifting soft metre may seem the best for it, but the poem is comparatively languid. Shelley falls into the error of heaping up his imagery, and, overlooking the effect of the best things, of letting them be jostled by weaker ones. The

loveliness of flowers notwithstanding this has had few such poets,
—Ruskin wrote in 1837 that " every one who is about to lay out
a limited extent of garden, in which he wishes to introduce many
flowers, should read and attentively study, first Shelley and next
Shakespeare,"—and the contrasting pervasion of decay after the
lady's death is by a strong painter of the sinister.

Shelley continued to paint it, speedily beginning another
longish piece called " A Vision of the Sea." It was never completed, but what there was of it earned some praise when it was
published in the *Prometheus Unbound* volume. A similarity to
the visions of Goya, or to passages in Melville's " Moby Dick,"
comes out in this tale from the frontier of madness ; a tale of
dead crews, tigers breaking loose from the ship's hold, a woman
of heavenly beauty aboard the wreck and a bright child on her
bosom, a combat of a tiger with a sea-snake, a blue shark ravening
the tiger, and a sudden boat with marksmen levelling at the other
tiger. And still borne by a fragment of the wreck the strange
woman holds on:

> Death, Fear,
> Love, Beauty are mixed in the atmosphere,
> Which trembles and burns with the fervour of dread
> Around her wild eyes, her bright hand, and her head
> Like a meteor of light o'er the waters ! her child
> Is yet smiling, and playing, and murmuring . . .

What does all this portend ? Some have interpreted, since Shelley
so generally includes a second meaning ; yet I believe that it is
no more than what his title defines. He had a day when these
oddly assembled pictures rose to his mind, as the face that the
sea wears among the inhabitants of time—a portrait at an unusual
angle. Probably then, we may know what his nervous constitution was from such inedited conception of the terrible, or
from a single frightful imagining :

> The tigers leap up when they feel the slow brine
> Crawling inch by inch on them ; hair, ears, limbs and eyne
> Stand rigid with horror ; a loud, long, hoarse cry
> Bursts at once from their vitals tremendously.

These acute moments in Shelley's being were balanced by the
calms which his letters depict. Nothing could be less like them
than his way of telling Leigh Hunt about Mrs. Mason : " You
will think it my fate either to find or to imagine some lady of 45,
very unprejudiced and philosophical, who has entered deeply
into the best and selectest spirit of the age, with enchanting

manners, and a disposition rather to like me, in every town that
I inhabit." And when his cousin Medwin writes of illness and of
good company in Geneva, his reply is : " I hope if they come to
Italy I may see the lady and your friend. Though I have never
had the ague, I have found these sort of beings, especially the
former, of infinite service in the maladies to which I am subject ;
and I have no doubt, if it could be supposed that any one would
neglect to employ such a medicine, that the best physicians
would prescribe them, although they have been entered in no
pharmacopeia." He even enjoyed a grumble, and it was not
surprising if he grumbled about Ollier as a publisher—but he
gave it up : " In fact they are all rogues. . . . Perhaps we ought
to regard an honest bookseller, or an honest seller of any thing
else in the present state of human affairs, as a kind of Jesus
Christ. The system of society as it exists at present . . . So far
the Preacher."

It is certain that Shelley could never be long utterly separated
by his brightest Muses from the rather solemn attractions of " the
system of society." Why he was busy in April, 1820, on the topic
of Agriculture I do not know, unless he was preparing himself for
installation as the squire of Field Place ; or the information may
have had some bearing on his new political work, "A Philosophical
View of Reform." Opening with a sketch of the nations where
already " the new philosophy " was operative or challenging,
from America to India (and he even put in a good word for the
missionaries) and the just-founded negro republic of Liberia, he
reasoned that by a similar process England had reached a crisis,
moved by a desire of change from institutions unequal to the work
of providing happiness of mind and body for the people.

Very soon he was explaining how the national debt had been
begun and why. " The rich, no longer being able to rule by
force, have invented this scheme that they may rule by fraud."
To that had been added the thing which Cobbett denounced so
thunderously—the deceitful contrivance of paper money, and a
" new aristocracy " had established itself, an " order of drones " ;
not great landowners and eminent merchants on whose power
the country's export and import trade depended, but " attornies
and excisemen and directors and government pensioners, usurers,
stockjobbers, country bankers, with their dependents and descendants. These are a set of pelting wretches in whose employment
there is nothing to exercise even to their distortion the more
majestic faculties of the soul." Shelley had a professional objection
to these. " They poison the literature of the age in which they
live by requiring the anti-type of their own mediocrity in books,

or such stupid and distorted and inharmonious idealisms, as alone have the power to stir their torpid imaginations."

In sum, because of the unequal distribution of the products of labour—and those meant " all property "—Shelley maintained " that the majority of the people of England are destitute and miserable, ill-clothed, ill-fed, ill-educated." Reform must come, but not the reform of Malthus (limiting the parenthood of the poor) to which he directed some flaming disgust. Shelley had a plan, involving the liquidation of the National Debt : " such a gentleman must lose a third of his estate, such a citizen a fourth of his money in the funds ; the persons who borrowed would have paid." On other questions he was for proceeding less abruptly, on universal suffrage and on votes for women for example. Whether we look upon the wiser and sounder parts of Shelley's little book or upon the outbursts of indignation and detestation, it all stands as an achievement to make us love him ; to wonder moreover at the range of the man who could on the same day write his ethereal poems and these philanthropic essays exhibiting so much of firm grasp on the situation of capital and labour.

The " View of Reform " waited a hundred years for publication *in extenso*, and lacking encouragement from his friends in London Shelley did not quite fill up some of the blanks in his manuscript. He was occupied with a sort of a parallel work in verse, his long " Ode to Liberty," for which the news from Spain gave an impetus. It became a historical sketch of the subject, in which there is more rhetoric or thinner use of his accustomed metaphorical idea than fresh poetry. When it appeared in the *Prometheus Unbound* volume, the fear of a prosecution caused the word " king " in the lines

> Oh, that the free would stamp the impious name
> Of KING into the dust

to be represented by four asterisks. The *Quarterly* reviewer, quoting the lines, increased the asterisks to six in the hope that pious readers would perceive Christ was intended.

It was in a happier hour that Shelley composed the song of " The Cloud " from which generations of readers have caught a delight. So familiar is it now that we do not always notice how original it is. Had any earlier English poet identified himself thus with a natural object and written in the first person of such a creation—" I bring fresh showers for the thirsting flowers " ? or had any one written a complete lyric rhythmically corresponding throughout to the changeful movement of the thing described ?

To the first question a forgotten poet named Thomas Heyrick

in the seventeenth century gives an answer ; his poem on a humming-bird, for instance, is in the first person,

> The *Indians* me a *Sunbeam* name,
> And I may be the Child of one.

For the rest, there is more in the poem than a song and dance of an immortal cloud, for Shelley at his maturity rarely expressed outward forms without allusion to some universal and permanent idea. So here his cloud is the messenger of a scientific under-standing. The poet's way of thinking is signalled more than once in a special word,

> I pass through the *pores* of the ocean and shores ;
> I change, but I cannot die ;

and

> the winds and sunbeams with their *convex gleams*
> Build up the blue dome or air ;

the scientific allusion is elsewhere made in a symbolic figure. Lightning, the pilot of the sailing cloud-castle, is

> Lured by the love of the genii that move.
> In the depths of the purple sea ;
> Over the rills, and the crags, and the hills,
> Over the lakes and the plains,
> Wherever he dream, under mountain or stream
> The spirit he loves remains.

It is Shelley's conjecture of the electrical element in nature, and that too has a connection with his theory of love in the physical world—an emanation from something still more sublime.

In " The Cloud," the laughing cloud, Shelley speaks for the sense of brilliant, careless revel in nature, and might be called the humorist of the sky ; he was very soon to add a new lyric with a similar exhilaration and defiance to dullness in it. The opportunity arose through a holiday near Leghorn, where the house of the Gisbornes who were away on a visit to England was at the service of the Shelleys. Even the view from the windows was enough to have inspired him : " the enormous chain of the Apennines, with its many-folded ridges, islanded in the misty distance of the air ; the sea, so immensely distant, appearing as at your feet ; and the prodigious expanse of the plain of Pisa, and the dark green marshes lessened almost to a strip by the height of the blue mountains overhanging them. Then the wild and unreclaimed fertility of the foreground, and the chestnut trees. . . ." On an evening stroll through this foreground Shelley heard his old friend the skylark carolling overhead, as in Buckinghamshire, and up sprang his poetry to meet the bird. This poem too has been so long a classic that it may not always be considered in its newness. Again Shelley has found a metrical form answering to the subject, the short lines of his stanza seeming the swift climb of the lark, the long ones the circlings and poisings of the bird in fullest music. The many similes attempted are light-hearted, not sober truths—nothing will do taken by itself, but from the rapid series some impression of this " sprite or bird " may be made. It is a conversation poem, an improvisation, and a record of the moment ; we may see the author and his wife in that lane, spell-bound awhile, then returning to earth—but the last words are of the poet's problems : he with all his books and his music can never find such a skill as this bird's. Half that gladness would make him the wonder of the age.

At Pisa indeed Shelley had been very much the student of literature, and in Claire's opinion had qualified as one of " the *odd* English " then resident : " Shelley, who walks about reading a great quarto *Encyclopaedia*, with another volume under his arm." Probably he was improving his mind on the subject of mechanics in order to follow intelligently all the preparations for Henry Reveley's steamboat ; he mentions mathematical studies with Mary, who was inclined however to spend her time on learning a system of shorthand. Other oddities at Pisa were Mr. Dolby, aged 70, who rejoiced at having escaped at last from England and also went about, singing as he went, with his pockets stuffed with books ; Mr. Tighe or Mason, who planted potatoes in pots ; and one more celebrated man. Walter Savage Landor was both odd and illustrious, but he had resolved to see nothing of his countrymen, above all Shelley, concerning whose depravity he had been informed by Sir James Mackintosh—a philosopher. He, also, knew for a fact that Shelley had driven his first wife to her death. Later on, in prose and verse, Landor paid homage to the young poet whom he began to fancy he *had* known a little, and who (he believed) had defended " Gebir " against the satire of Byron. But somehow or other Landor had been provided with " a detailed narrative of all the circumstances of Shelley's first marriage and its disastrous issue," from " a source unhappily only too authentic," and he turned from Shelley's alleged offer of a visit with distrust.

In spite of local isolation Shelley continued to owe his worst moments to William Godwin. With extreme loyalty to an ideal he wrote on May 26th to the Gisbornes in London, " Our anxiety about Godwin is very great, and any information that you could give a day or two earlier than he might, respecting any decisive event in his law-suit, would be a great relief. . . . You know that added years only add to my admiration of his intellectual powers, and even the moral resources of his character." On his side Godwin delivered himself deliberately to his new audience of damning hints against his son-in-law ; and duly the question came round to a present supply of cash. Would Gisborne advance £400, with Shelley as the ultimate debtor ? Shelley, advised of this plan, wrote to Gisborne accepting his fate if Gisborne approved. " I could impose one condition alone. If you perceive that the money will not fulfil its object, or that you cannot enforce the intended appropriation of it, I entreat you to refuse to lend it at all. You know my situation ; you know Godwin's implacable exactions ; you know his boundless and plausible sophistry. On the other hand, if you can effect this compromise, the benefit would be great."

Gisborne may not have been a clear-minded man in business, but he detected something shady in Godwin's transactions, and the disappointed old hunks sent one more poisonous letter to his daughter. Her nerves had been so shaken by earlier ones that she had asked Shelley to intercept such attacks, and he did so now. He replied, and if Godwin had not been the singular machine that he was this reply must have brought about some reform. Shelley explained not only that Godwin's behaviour to his daughter was inhuman but that on simplest grounds of financial wisdom he ought not to receive a new loan. The son-in-law's general position was, " I have given you within a few years the amount of a considerable fortune, and have destituted myself for the purpose of realising it of nearly four times the amount. Except for the *good will* which this transaction seems to have produced between you and me, this money, for any advantage it ever conferred on you, might as well have been thrown into the seas. Had I kept it in my own hands this £4000 or £5000 and administered it in trust for your permanent advantage, I should have been indeed your benefactor. The error, however, was greater in the man of mature age, extensive experience, and penetrating intellect than in the crude and impetuous boy."

For all this Godwin was inseparable from Shelley's life to the end, and he did not tire of informing anyone who would listen that Shelley had engaged to clear him of debt. Among the latest letters of the poet, one to Mrs. Godwin shows Shelley maintaining his decision to keep Mary clear of the argument, to raise no more funds for Godwin by the process of burdening his estate or his income, and yet to find him some money. He was at the time trying to borrow £400 from Horace Smith for Godwin's benefit, but Godwin had anticipated him in applying to that generous but watchful man. The cynic may discern in the action taken against Count Cenci by his daughter Beatrice in the play something like Shelley's momentary wish concerning Mary's stony-hearted father. It would however be impossible to fit the play to the Godwin story, since Mrs. Godwin the second is so competent a confederate of Godwin in his snug career of " pecuniary embarrassments." Let who will follow Shelley in reverencing the intellect of Godwin, foretold

> to stand
> Among the spirits of our age and land,
> Before the dread tribunal of *to come*
> The foremost.

Let Godwin be believed in claiming for himself, enlightened by the conversation of Coleridge, " my theism, . . . a reverent and soothing contemplation of all that is beautiful, grand, or mysterious in the system of the universe." But it is a relief to Shelley's biographer to come to the point when he and his destructive ingenuity of greed may be dismissed from a story quite calamitous enough even without him. The last word on him may be an echo of himself, if Basil Montagu reported the incident accurately. When word was brought to him that his wife Mary Wollstonecraft was dead he said to the servant, " What evidence have you of the fact ? "

The poetical prophecy quoted earlier is from the lovely rhyming letter to Maria Gisborne in London sent by Shelley from her house at Saint Elmo in July, 1820. It is the most precise picture of himself and his ways that he ever wrote, and is an answer to those who, fixing on episodes in his life, are afraid that he had no humour. This quality plays through the poem, but so commixt with others that the whole is a serious work. The principal laughing matter is Shelley's occupation of Henry's engineering shop, where he affects to be an ignoramus, among

> Great screws, and cones, and wheels, and grooved blocks,
> The elements of what will stand the shocks
> Of wave and wind and time.

In fact, he says, *he* is the real Archimage, sitting there

> Plotting dark spells, and devilish enginery,
> The self-impelling steam wheels of the mind

Which pump up oaths from clergymen, and grind
The gentle spirit of our meek Reviews
Into a powdery foam of salt abuse.

As for his occasional dreams of returning to England—no. He calls up the night life of London in a flash, and then he turns to his surroundings at the moment, the green caverns of foliage, the fireflies over the cornfields, the contadino's and the nightbird's songs from the distance ; and the moonlight is all that London has in common with his Italian paradise.

But the firm of Shelley and Reveley was never to carry the passengers who might go from this Paradise as far as Marseilles. The young engineer did not finish the job. He called Shelley to blame for this, because he had required the engine to be built on too huge a scale. The house planned by Shelley's grandfather near Worthing had suffered from the same touch of the gigantic. The Gisbornes supported Henry in his abandoning the work and disposing of the materials. Probably Shelley lost money on the whole experiment, but it does not appear to have been that side of it which made him suddenly lose all patience with his friends and write of them in that fierce-sounding strain usual in his moods of frustration. It was an aristocratic dialect, and with it may be remembered the panegyrical fluency of his moments of satisfaction. In a letter to Claire Clairmont who was at Florence as a governess (the part which she played at intervals through life), Shelley spoke of the Gisbornes in imitation of a famous sentence in " Gulliver's Travels " : " The Gisbornes are people totally without faith. I think they are altogether the most filthy and odious animals with which I ever came into contact." On the same day however, he wrote to John Gisborne asking him about Arabic grammars, dictionaries, manuscripts and teachers.

The temporary absence of Claire was overdue. Mary had become impatient with her again, and Shelley's task of keeping some balance between them had not grown easier. The uneasy household was transferred in August, 1820, to escape from the great heat in Leghorn, to the Baths of Pisa, where it was almost as hot ; and on August 12th, leaving the two girls to explore the city of Lucca, Shelley took a day off. He made his way up the Monte San Pellegrino, and came thence with the form and spirit of a new poem in his mind, as, to quote from it, " on blind Homer's heart a winged thought." In three days he composed " The Witch of Atlas " in the stanza called *ottava rima*—a long poem. There is a Fay in Spenser's " Faerie Queene " who

had the skill
Of secret things, and all the powers of nature,
Which she by art could use unto her will,
And to her service bind each living creature,
Through secret understanding of their feature.
Thereto she was right faire, when so her face
She list discover.

Shelley's years of delight in the " Faerie Queene " lead to the
conclusion that this same Fay was the " wizard lady " whose
secrets and arts are disclosed in " The Witch of Atlas." He wrote
his poem in the spirit of deep caprice which had entered into
some of his recent pieces, and with a feeling of stage illusion,
carnival, masquerade. His theories of the physical (and electrical)
universe, of love and life, of good and evil, and tyranny and
freedom are interwoven with the poem, yet with a holiday care-
lessness, and even with some stanzas in a comic vein. Altogether
his object was to please all minds that might be willing to receive
a far adventure for its beauties and inventions, and catch here
and there some slanting light on things as they are.

When he showed the poem to Mary, she could not enjoy it.
At the time she was in a melancholy state, at no time was she
particularly able to take pleasure in insubstantial humour. She
found fault with the theoretical part of the poem and the absence
of any plot and characters needed for a plot, and made her
objections to the whole " upon the score of its containing no
human interest." The failure of the " Witch " with this first and
most prized audience made Shelley quite unhappy, and he
addressed to Mary those stanzas which now stand as prologue.
They contain words as painful as any that he ever suffered himself
to use, often though he mentions his unpopularity as a poet :

O, let me not believe
That anything of mine is fit to live !

It is here that he speaks of his " dressing " his Witch in her light
flowing garment, a term which admits us to his mind while he
worked on the piece ; and he adjures us not to unveil her—to
analyse the fable into a plausible set of prose meanings, in spite
of which the scientific background and data have been cleverly
traced out by Mr. Grabo. Mary would not have blamed him,
if he cared to expend his time thus ; but she did not change her
opinion about the poem.

Without a pause Shelley hastened into the writing of a new
Ode, occasioned by " the intelligence of the proclamation of a

Constitutional Government at Naples," but complicated by the fact that his impressions of Baiae and Pompeii were demanding poetical utterance. The " Ode to Naples," as it stands, begins with two Epodes, an arrangement which is against all the rules, and the detail is a sign of the perplexed mind of the artist. In particular the majestic and lucid passage on "the City disinterred" appears to be misplaced ; a separate poem was the only fair treatment of such a motif, not a combination with other matters. The acclamation of the liberators at Naples is not all equal to it, and might have won Shelley a university prize for a poem on a set subject. This will have been the Ode to Liberty which he was reading to Mary, Claire and Mrs. Mason on August 24th, 1820, in his house at the Baths of San Giuliano, when an unexpected accompaniment was struck up beneath the windows by droves of pigs brought for sale at the fair.

Not a bit disconcerted Shelley likened their chorus to the frogs in the comedy of Aristophanes, and soon went on to say how such a chorus of pigs would help in a mock drama on the political situation in England. Perhaps he remembered a piece of satire by Professor Porson, which had been reprinted in 1818 in *The Examiner*, called " A New Catechism for the Use of the Natives of Hampshire ; Necessary to be had in all Sties." There the people of Britain were represented as so many hogs at the mercy of their hog-masters. Shelley's talk on these lines met with the party's approval and at once he began operations. The situation was not in itself especially interesting to him. George IV was trying to disburden himself of Queen Caroline, and at length it came to a trial : " Lord Castlereagh placed the ' Green Bag ' on the table of the House of Commons, demanding in the King's name that an inquiry should be instituted into his wife's conduct." Shelley's antipathy to the ex-Regent meant that he would be favourable to the Queen's cause, but his first comment was, " What silly stuff is this to employ a great nation about. I wish the King and Queen, like Punch and his wife, would fight out their disputes in person." But already he had some notion of a pseudo-classical satire on the business, and when chance had presented him with a resonant chorus he was delighted to write it.

" Oedipus Tyrannus, or Swellfoot the Tyrant, a Tragedy in Two Acts " would probably be named more frequently and even recommended for reading but for several disadvantages. The first is that it was written by Shelley. From any other hand it would be appreciated as a vigorous and resourceful burlesque— and it contains passages as witty, versification as entertaining as W. S. Gilbert in general gives us ; but the rumour that Shelley cannot make a joke has gone on through the years, and the main part of his poetry is not humorous. Next, the circumstances and personalities on which his diversion depends have been practically forgotten, and even the Green Bag with its agitating secrets means nothing, no more than the Budget of twenty years ago or the massacre of Amboyna. Moreover Shelley's play is a parody on Greek drama, and that was in large measure the reason for his taking so much trouble with it ; but classical amusements have not been flourishing well while the nature of education has changed.

The public men who are caricatured by Shelley in this performance include, besides George IV of course, Castlereagh and Eldon. Since the Chancery proceedings much had happened to Shelley, but nothing to reconcile him with the power of that legal Lord who is made to say,

I.

Went to the garret of the swineherd's tower,
Which overlooks the sty, and made a long
Harangue (all words) to the assembled Swine,
Of delicacy, mercy, judgement, law,
Morals, and precedents, and purity,
Adultery, destitution, and divorce,
Piety, faith, and state necessity,
And how I loved the Queen !—and then I wept
With the pathos of my own eloquence,
And every tear turned to a millstone which
Brained many a gaping Pig.

But Castlereagh and oratorical ornament receive attention. On his proposing to prove the Queen's innocence " by pouring on her head this mystic water," the contents of the Bag, there is common consent, voiced thus :

First Boar. Excellent, just, and noble Purganax,
Second Boar. How glorious it will be to see her Majesty
Flying above our heads, her petticoats
Streaming like—like—like—
Third Boar. Anything.
Purganax. Oh no !
But like a standard of an admiral's ship,
Or like the banner of a conquering host,
Or like a cloud dyed in the dying day,
Unravelled on the blast from a white mountain ;
Or like a meteor, or a war-steed's mane,

Or waterfall from a dizzy precipice
Scattered upon the wind.
First Boar.   Or a cow's tail.
Second Boar. Or *anything*, as the learned Boar observed.

If Shelley would forgive such a judgment, a gustier dramatic
energy animated " Oedipus " than is found in " The Cenci." Its
occasion releases more of his habit of mind and knowledge of life
than the loftier aimed tragedy. The wording is strong and, the
temptation to abstract symbols being away, we hear a master of
ordinary affairs in almost every line. This is the man who had
he been called upon to superintend agricultural properties and
the interests of country towns and village would have known what
he was looking at and whether things were thriving. The comparison with Byron is sustained by the piece—Byron, ranging in
his verse from mysteries of biblical antiquity to the many realisms
of fashionable or plebeian life in *Don Juan*. These two men were
indeed made to converse with the widest and closest mutual
understanding—so long as Byron was not playing for safety.

The idealist Scythrop in Peacock's " Nightmare Abbey "
published a pamphlet of which seven copies were sold, and that
is the extent of the sales of Shelley's " Oedipus Tyrannus." At
least, it was published, and that can be said of few of Shelley's
writings at that period. Horace Smith took it to J. Johnston of
Cheapside, who produced it " for the author," without disclosing
who was the author ; on being threatened with an action by an
alderman Johnston surrendered the numerous copies remaining.
The City, led by " heroic Wood," as Charles Lamb called him,
might be on the side of the Queen, but Shelley was unlucky in
his publisher's address—since in December, 1820, a " loyal, that
is ministerial, address was sent to the King from the ward of
Cheap."

Shelley's indestructible resolution to strike back at authority
turned despotic comes out in his story during 1820 in more ways
than one. It strengthened the regard he had for young John
Keats, victimised by the Journals established to protect the ruling
class and annihilate any dissentients. He was not a complete
worshipper of every word that Keats wrote, nor of the kind of
miscellaneous beauty-gathering which Keats sometimes accepted
as poetry ; but he had never lacked attention to his friend's
progress, literary or personal. On reading " Endymion " at
Leghorn in August, 1819, Shelley found it hard to get through,
yet " full of some of the highest and the finest gleams of poetry "
—and he requested Ollier always to send his own publications to

the author. In May, 1820, he told Ollier that Keats was " going to show himself a great poet ; like the sun, to burst through the clouds, which, though dyed in the finest colours of the air, obscured his rising." Then the Gisbornes were able to send news of the young man. He was under sentence of death from Dr. William Lambe, whom Shelley had formerly known and consulted ; consumption had gone too far ; and, as if that were not enough, he had burst a blood-vessel.

On receiving this black news, and recalling how mercilessly Keats had been reviewed in company with most of those who used to meet at Hampstead, Shelley sent him a letter perfect in its kind—unless it resembled too much that of a judicious old uncle and adviser. Still, it was an invitation in which Shelley was seconded by Mary, to Pisa for the winter, and—" you ought at all events to see Italy, and your health, which I suggest as a motive, might be an excuse to you. I spare declamation about the statues, and the paintings, and the ruins—and what is a greater piece of forbearance—about the mountains, streams, and the fields, the colours of the sky, and the sky itself." To this unexpected letter Keats replied with a degree of hopefulness on August 16th, when he knew very little about his immediate plans except that he would have to go to Italy for the chance of survival and expected to go without a companion. He described Shelley's letter, when next he wrote to Charles Brown, as " of a very kind nature," and in his reply he showed that he really was glad of it, but could not at once be definite upon the arrangements. Recovering slightly, he decided to go to Rome for the winter, and to call on Shelley in the spring. The Gisbornes carried his letter and " a fine piece of poetry " back to Italy, but before Shelley received them a letter from Leigh Hunt had informed him of Keats's intentions.

These two letters between Shelley and Keats have long been famous as revealing in brief the characteristics of two poets. Shelley had resumed his literary talk with Keats by mentioning that he had re-read " Endymion," with " a new sense of the treasures of poetry it contains, though treasures poured forth with indistinct profusion," and he added, " In poetry I have sought to avoid system and mannerism. I wish those who excel me in genius would pursue the same plan." Keats in answer stands on the defensive ; he wished that Shelley might curb his magnanimity, and be more of an artist and " load every rift " of his subject with ore. Though he daily expected his copy of " Prometheus Unbound " he would have preferred that Shelley should still be working on the manuscript. It is noteworthy that each writer had in mind the long poems of the other, since in short ones their way of expressing a sentiment with fewest but richest touches was not widely different. The " Ode to Autumn " and the " Ode to the West Wind " are alike examples of choice and full-sailed art, where each word and intonation does its duty.

Almost certainly Keats would have enjoyed some new lyrics which Shelley wrote with a particular object during 1820. Mary had been varying her writing of novels with the composition of short verse plays, " Proserpine " and " Midas," and in the course of these she needed some lyrical interludes. She was in the favourable position of being able to command Shelley to supply them. For the first piece he wrote the fable of Arethusa and Alpheus with splendid life and grace, as well as a song in Ben Jonson's manner to be sung by Proserpine gathering flowers. For the second he gave the contention of Apollo and Pan, in which Midas made the unlucky decision ; and most of us would have done the same as Midas. Such delightful new music as Shelley invented for Pan might well charm even beyond the high, wise and full-toned verses of Apollo. It would not be surprising if " The Two Spirits : an Allegory " among the 1820 poems was also intended for a situation in a drama, and in this Shelley achieves a metrical deliciousness beyond even the song of Pan. The stanzas rejected or excluded are a sign that Shelley was artist enough for anything—if he curbed his magnanimity.

> Some say when nights are dry and clear,
> And the death-dews sleep on the morass,
> Sweet whispers are heard by the traveller,
>   Which make night day :
> And a [silver] shape like his early love doth pass
> Upborne by her wild and glittering hair,
> And when he awakes on the fragrant grass,
>   He finds night day.

This year Shelley received advice from a poet very different to Keats, and of another kind altogether ; I say he received it, but that depends on the chance of his reading the magazines or on the author's sending him a copy. From what we know of Bernard Barton the Quaker poet, who had a country bank and would therefore be on Shelley's black list for a start, a copy must have been sent to the exile ; Barton had previously tackled Byron with his poetic attempts. " Poems " by Bernard Barton contained " Stanzas Addressed to Percy Bysshe Shelley "—with a footnote, " No one can more admire the genius of this highly-gifted man, than I do ; but, in exact proportion to my admiration, is the regret I feel, for what I consider as the perversion of powers so rare, the misapplication of powers so splendid." The aspiring Quaker in the Stanzas reasoned that Shelley had delighted in

> Forests, and lakes, the majesty of mountains,
>   The dazzling glaciers and the musical sound
> Of waves and winds, or softer hush of fountains ;

but knowledge and feeling came from the invisible. Milton had described what happened to people who plucked forbidden fruit ; and those who indulged " visions of unutterable things " were doomed to barren disappointment. Many pure and bright spirits had ended " in stoic apathy, or starless night " who could have died much respected had religion been their nourishment. " Ere it shall prove too late, thy steps retrace." This invitation to Christianity has a simple sweetness which contrasts with most of the contemporary public allusions to Shelley's spiritual future.

He was at the time concerned more with his prospects in this world. His cousin Tom Medwin, who had arrived from Geneva, had broached a scheme. Medwin claimed to have a friend, very wealthy, " who will be at Leghorn next spring, and who designs to visit Greece, Syria, and Egypt in his own ship. This man has conceived a great admiration for my verses, and wishes above all things that I could be induced to join his expedition. How far all this is practicable considering the state of my finances I know not yet." This was written by Shelley at Pisa on October 29th, the house at the Baths of San Giuliano having been flooded by the River Serchio. The new house at Pisa on the Lung' Arno was the Palazzo Galetti, and Shelley's study was next to Medwin's room ; it was too soon for him to take this as a disadvantage. He had not yet heard Medwin's stories " of the interior of India," on which that amiable waster was to float through society or out of it for another half century. Like Hogg, Medwin had the merit of being a chess-player, and even more the merit of knowing that Shelley was a poet.

XX

ACQUAINTANCES AT PISA

THE CITY of Pisa, as has been seen, had its share of foreign eccentrics and literati, but it did not lack home-grown ones, and with some of them the Shelleys had become acquainted. The first reported in her letters to the Hunts by Mary was a professor of physics named Francesco Pacchiani, whom the other Pisans believed to be mad. He enjoyed the notoriety. He was a thinker, a praadoxer and a being who " did wander everywhere." Mary was charmed with the beauty of his language as he talked ; it seemed one was listening to the idiom of Boccaccio or Machiavelli. And yet Pacchiani affronted Shelley by telling a grubby story. For a time he was a favourite, but his noise and boasting grew wearisome, and he earned the title " Our Black Genius." Pacchiani, although he was a priest, was a nimble scamp living by his wits, and Mary collected stories of his ingenious thieving.

The next hero was Tommaso Sgricci, a man almost of Shelley's age and a poet—but his special talent was that of improvising poetic drama. The art was popular, but Shelley believed that this was the greatest of the *improvisatori*. He was present with Mary more than once at the theatre when Sgricci delivered a tragedy extempore, " Iphigenia in Tauris " for example. With what seemed miraculous fluency Sgricci poured forth ideas and words, and acted his scenes and characters, to an audience of university students and foreigners. The Pisans did not come, and Shelley told the wonder-worker that he appeared in Pisa as Dante among the ghosts. Sgricci was rumoured to have led an irregular life, but that was not a displeasing thought to Mary as she encouraged him to speak of his inspiration and indeed to give her a private display of his intellectual brilliance. He did not gain a permanent place in the family circle. Shelley heard him say things to the discredit of the Neapolitans, or the people of the Kingdom of Naples—those who might soon rise and vindicate freedom ; and Shelley could not forgive even an *improvisatore* for such base talk.

Of far higher meaning to Shelley was the discovery, through the bustling Pacchiani, of a young lady whose situation was in some ways like that of Harriet at the boarding-school on Clapham Common years before. The Contessina Teresa Emilia Viviani, a girl of nineteen, was kept as a *pensionnaire* in the Conservatorio of St. Anna not so much for the protection of her morals as to keep her out of the way of her mother's lover. Her sister had been removed to a safe distance from him in another establishment. Claire, Mary, Medwin and Shelley were all fascinated by their first meetings with Emilia Viviani so caged up (though it did not escape Claire's notice that she carried on various love affairs from the cage). She was a beauty in a classical style, reminding Medwin of " a Greek Muse in the Florentine gallery," and her eyes were like those of Beatrice Cenci in the picture. Moreover, so far as the Shelleys were judges of Italian writing, her letters and other small compositions presented a lofty mind in a pure and delicate style.

And this beautiful and intelligent girl was confined to a convent !—lodged in a little room with a few sticks of furniture, some cheap prints of saints, a waxen Gesu Bambino in a glass case, and a cracked mirror. Shelley was soon in a state of indignation, rapture and romance, which was not diminished by the fact that Emilia could sometimes get out for an evening walk. He first met her on or about December 5th, 1820, and it was not until April that he emerged from the ethereal dreams into which the Emilia of that sudden revelation had bewitched him. It is beyond me to call his feelings by the word too often profaned, and even amid his dreams he himself was cautious on the point : " I see Emily sometimes ; and whether her presence is the source of pain or pleasure to me, I am equally ill-fated in both. I am deeply interested in her destiny, and that interest can in no manner influence it. She is not, however, insensible to my sympathy, and she counts it among her alleviations. As much comfort as she receives from my attachment to her, I *lose*." Shelley was writing (January 16th, 1821) to Claire, and after his reference to Mary's jealousy he continued, " There is no reason that you should fear any mixture of that which you call *love*. My conception of Emilia's talents augments every day. Her moral nature is fine —but not above circumstances ; yet I think her tender and true —which is always something. How many are only one of these things at a time ! So much for sentiment and ethics."

The personal story of Emilia was connected with that of her English friends through 1821 and later, even if the ideal light had faded from her. In spite of her resistance to Shelley's making a goddess of the girl Mary was her visitor until May, 1821. Shelley, sympathising with the victim of society if going no further than that, looked forward to Emilia's finding a husband— and yet he feared it. In September she married, but he still regarded himself as in some manner her guardian, and it was only an application for a large loan which ended the friendship. The married life of Emilia was not happy, and when Medwin revisited her at the age of thirty-five she was ill, solitary and in want.

All this might be no more than the innumerable small sketches of experience in the margin of Shelley's life had Emilia not kindled his mind to the radiance which remains in his poem " Epipsychidion." There may be many opinions on its meaning, even on its value as a poem ; there cannot be much debate about its being a record of an inimitable personality. When he had written it, and in the process thrown aside a number of poetical reasonings and communings associated with the theme, Shelley sank down suddenly from his exaltation. He saw himself as one of the fools of time. Emilia, poor thing, was a girl with the full share of feminine helplessness, fickleness, dullness—how had he come to transform her into the supreme and soul-enchanting majesty of his poetical Emily ? He sent the poem to Ollier, to be printed anonymously in a small edition, but with a word of explanation : it " should not be considered as my own ; indeed, in a certain sense, it is a production of a portion of me already dead ; and in this sense the advertisement is no fiction." For he had equipped the poem with some preliminary sentences attributing it to one who had " died at Florence, as he was preparing for a voyage to one of the wildest of the Sporades."

At the same time he announced that the poem was one of those which do not need the circumstances shadowed in the symbols to be known in order to be comprehended by the right reader. When a man of Shelley's power sends forth, in prose or verse, a set of strange enigmas, however they may be employed for his own central theme, others will do a great deal to extract their interpretation ; and though Shelley warns us again against " undressing " his poem, he also gives the impression of having deliberately played the Sphinx towards the curious. The title is a challenge. It may be equivalent to " a manual of the soul " —echoing the seventeenth century " encheiridion." But the first lines open the series of autobiographical riddles :

> Sweet Spirit ! Sister of that orphan one,
> Whose empire is the name thou weepest on ;

and the " orphan one " is the daughter of Mary Wollstonecraft, who possesses the name Shelley. No one will solve all the puzzles that follow, unless a key to them has been left by Shelley in papers yet unexamined, but the Moon of his life is certainly Mary, the Sun Emily, and we may apply the other lines on his loves to one and another of the women seen in this narrative. Yet, who in real life was the Tempest who when the Moon was in eclipse so stirred him ; who was the Comet for whose return he appeals in graceful idealisms—to share the sky with the Sun and Moon ? It is evident that Shelley's short life had been more varied with passionate aspirings than the biographies register ; and above all we encounter in " Epipsychidion " one form in a pre-Raphaelite colouring and surroundings whose actuality must have been of acute importance to Shelley but is otherwise concealed. For in his youthful quest for the woman who should answer to his conceptions of woman's heavenliness, he came upon one of a terribly different kind :

> There,—One whose voice was venomed melody
> Sate by a well, under blue nightshade bowers ;
> The breath of her false mouth was like faint flowers,
> Her touch was as electric poison,—flame
> Out of her looks into my vitals came,
> And from her living cheeks and bosom flew
> A killing air, which pierced like honey-dew
> Into the core of my green heart.

A well, or fountain, may be Shelley's clue to the place where this false love was met—for it is a metaphor for a source of learning and the arts.

At the time of writing his poem he was so strongly under the impression that his search for the dreamed-of woman was now complete as to say so without disguise :

> At length into the obscure Forest came
> The Vision I had sought through grief and shame . . .
> I knew it was the Vision veiled from me
> So many years—that it was Emily.

To her he proceeded to offer a kind of eternal summer honeymoon, and at all events a triumphant union of souls ; even so, at last he closed on a simple term which simplifies the perplexities of his poem and gives it all a significance beyond even his worship of Emily : " for I am Love's."

" Epipsychidion," one of two poems which Shelley was known to regret writing or issuing, has a hurry and flow, together with some want of determined and distinctive language, which suggest that he was trying to do what he heard Sgricci do. It has the air of a glittering improvisation. He sends image flying after image, for example, in attempting to catch for the future some semblance of his " youth's vision thus made perfect." It becomes an imaginative conjuring trick ; and he only ends it with a sigh,

> I measure
> The world of fancies, seeking one like thee,
> And find—alas ! mine own infirmity.

For the pervading spirit of his poem, he found a prototype in Dante's Vita Nuova ; and for the mysteriousness and its share in bringing his beloved's pre-eminence into the attention of posterity his model was Shakespeare's Sonnets. The versification shows that he had inevitably taken more of Keats's " Endymion " into his poetical life than he could know. For the circumstance that he wrote parts of the poem also in Italian verse no explanation is necessary. Ollier published " Epipsychidion " in 1821, and the literary world was completely unaffected. Nobody could remember the title long enough to call at the bookseller's for a copy.

Shelley was not the only poet on the premises at Pisa. Tom Medwin was there. " Besides writing poetry he translates," Mary wrote, wishing he would take himself off ; for whatever she or Shelley happened to be doing Medwin would interrupt by reading out something good by himself or it might be by another. " He is Common Place " personified. Nevertheless he had been writing verses and inducing Shelley to help him with them and the question of publishing them. Shelley did his best with Ollier and so Medwin was on the eve of a debut. His " Sketches in Hindostan and other Poems " published in May, 1821, received no more attention than " Epipsychidion." But perhaps Medwin's rival poet was really John Taaffe, the Irishman who according to Shelley sent Mary two guinea pigs with a letter ending, " O, that I were one of those guinea pigs, that I might see you this morning ! " Count Taaffe (for he claimed that title) was at least amusing by accident—he " rides, writes, invites, complains, bows, apologises." His great work was a translation, accompanied by a commentary, of Dante, in which Shelley happened delightedly upon the line,

> I Mantuan, capering, squalid, squalling.

But Shelley yielded to Taaffe's requests and forwarded specimens of the work already printed at Pisa for the consideration of Ollier, and he spoke highly of the value of the commentary on Dante to " all foreigners and most Italians."

It might be that Taaffe was not a real count, but Mary's catalogue of new acquaintances in the winter of 1820—1821

included an undeniable Prince and Princess. These were Prince
Alexander Mavrocordato of Greece and his cousin Princess
Argyropoli. The Prince, a short gentleman with protracted
whiskers, was in exile, but his heart was set upon the liberation of
his country ; in spite of that virtue and his proficiency as a student
of many subjects, including botany, Shelley put him privately in
the same class as Taaffe and Medwin. " A vessel has arrived,"
he wrote in June, 1821, " to take the Greek Prince and his suite
to join the Army in Morea. He is a great loss to Mary and
therefore to me . . . but not otherwise." Mary had been learning
Greek from the Prince in return for English lessons, and she found
him as charming a person as he was clever in learning. Naturally
his delight in the tidings of a revolution in Greece, at the beginning of April, 1821, was well supported both by Mary and her
husband ; yet do what he would Shelley was very much the
Briton in meeting this promising personality, and his turban. " I
reproach my own savage disposition that so agreeable accomplished and amiable a person is not more agreeable to me."

That was not for general circulation ; and the public version
of Shelley's feelings towards the young man appeared thus :

To His Excellency
PRINCE ALEXANDER MAVROCORDATO
Late Secretary for Foreign Affairs to the Hospodar of Wallachia
THE DRAMA OF HELLAS IS INSCRIBED AS AN
IMPERFECT TOKEN OF THE ADMIRATION,
SYMPATHY, AND FRIENDSHIP OF
THE AUTHOR.

" Hellas, a Lyrical Drama," was composed later in 1821, but
may conveniently be noticed at this point. " It is a mere im-
provise," Shelley declared—a form of leading article on the news
of the day, but written with the " Persae " of Aeschylus in mind ;
and the object was of course to contribute some encouragement,
and rouse enthusiasm, to the cause of Greek freedom. In its way
" Hellas " is magnificent, though it was written from the fragmentary information in continental newspapers ; but Shelley so
writing at full speed was not lacking in imaginative poetry, the
shaping spirit. His old friend (and Medwin's) Ahasuerus, the
Wandering Jew, is called up anew so that he may help to awaken
the sense of destiny ; his moody eloquence has certainly deepened
since he came on and was driven away into the twilight of
ghosts in " Queen Mab." Mahmud, the Macbeth of Islam, even
if he is " vexed by the wise mad talk of the old Jew," is not

denied the stature of a dynast, or the mixture of human nature.
The poetical relief map outspread in particular by the irruption
of messenger after messenger swiftly announcing " the images of
ruin " is immense and thrilling. War finds in Shelley an artist
with something like the scope of his life-long follower Thomas
Hardy :

> Ten thousand cannon
> Lie ranged upon the beach, and hour by hour
> Their earth-convulsing wheels affright the city ;
> The galloping of fiery steeds makes pale
> The Christian merchant ; and the yellow Jew
> Hides his hoard deeper in the faithless earth.
> Like clouds, and like the shadows of the clouds,
> Over the hills of Anatolia,
> Swift in wide troops the Tartar chivalry
> Sweep ;—the far flashing of their starry lances
> Reverberates the dying light of day.

As he fashioned his drama, Shelley took his speed from the
inward assurance that the Greeks would free themselves from the
Turkish tyranny, but heavy shadows fell across the sunbright
future. He could only gather at the time of writing that British
policy would range his country on the side which he wished to
see defeated. This alliance, he felt, might and must defer the
dawn of liberty over Hellas, and towards the close of the work
his sense of the misery that it would mean to a generation found
a voice in saddened choruses. From this mood he rose to that
emotional final chorus which to many is the one thing that
matters in " Hellas " :

> The world's great age begins anew,
> The golden years return ;
> The earth doth like a snake renew
> Her winter weeds outworn :
> Heaven smiles, and faiths and empires gleam
> Like wrecks of a dissolving dream.

A song of victory. Even so, there could be no victory in his
feeling unless it marked the end throughout the world of such
bloodshed, ravage and bedevilment as he had been delineating.

> O, cease ! must hate and death return !
> Cease ! must men kill and die ?
> Cease ! drain not to its dregs the urn
> Of bitter prophecy.

> The world is weary of the past,
> Oh, might it die or rest at last.

What bitter prophecy did Shelley mean ? He had hinted at it in an earlier stanza, imploring that we might have no more " tales of Troy," penned in massacre:

> Although a subtler Sphinx renew
> Riddles of death Thebes never knew.

If he had seen the scientific war which had been developed by the year 1945 he would have been indescribably distressed, but he would not have been taken by surprise.

The political situation in the near East gave Shelley a new interest in his own " Revolt of Islam," and on February 16th, 1821, he wrote to Ollier inquiring if a second edition was to be expected. It was not ; but he had a desire to make many corrections in it and entirely to recast one part of it. New editions of Shelley were not yet wanted, yet before long one of his productions did reappear, and against his will. For some years he had not set eyes on a copy of " Queen Mab," but now one of the sharp-eyed knaves who made a living by piratical publishing in London reprinted it for general circulation. Shelley was half amused to see it advertised, was even grateful to William Clark for omitting " a foolish dedication to my late wife, the publication of which would have annoyed me " ; but evidence was soon forthcoming of the help that this edition gave to his detractors and slanderers. He felt moreover that, after ten changeful years, he was no longer the author of a poem written (as he said) " in the most furious style, with long notes against Jesus Christ, and God the Father, and the King, and bishops, and marriage, and the devil knows what." But his main wish was " to protest against all the bad poetry in it." Shelley was not an assiduous writer of Letters to the Editor, and his example in the *Examiner* on this matter was unusual for him—skilful of course ; but the injunction against the pirate for which he now applied to Chancery was not granted.

Neither authors nor reviewers can govern the fate of what has once got into print. " Queen Mab " was neither so poor a poem as Shelley's memory told him, nor so dangerous as his enemies wished to paint it. A generation later it was almost respectable, and we may catch sight of it in the hands of many peace-loving people—Tennyson's brother-in-law, for instance, who on a summer holiday in France, coming to a dull place called Nerondes, decided that " the surrounding flat country presented no inducement for a ramble, so I took repose in the poetic groves of Shelley, and was deep in ' Queen Mab ' when the hour of five was struck by the church clock."

Shelley was not so occupied with the works and the affairs mentioned in this chapter as to be without certain " high and new designs in verse ; but they are the labours of years, perhaps." He alluded to some already imagined poems on the grand scale, which we cannot identify with anything remaining, projected or attempted, in his later pages. He had by him at the beginning of 1821 the first sketches for a historical tragedy, " Charles the First," towards which he had been and still was reading histories of England in the times of Laud and Clarendon. This play had been announced in the *London Magazine* of January, 1821, with great expectations—had not Shelley already treated the public to a " powerful " drama ? and Ollier had even proposed to pay Shelley something for the copyright. But " Charles the First " was to Shelley only a practice or a parergon. " My thoughts aspire to a production of a far higher character," he again declared, " but the execution of it will require some years. I write what I write chiefly to inquire, by the reception which my writings meet with, how far I am fit for so great a task, or not."

The clues to this foreshadowed book's nature are few and dim. Shelley was studying Arabic " for a purpose," and enduring Medwin as a fellow-student until the ex-officer ran off in pursuit of an English girl aged fifteen ; but this language study may have been a preparation for the travels beyond ordinary limits which Shelley was longing to try. His request to Ollier to send him books on the Peninsular War accords with his brief note on a drama about Napoleon, with spirits as well as men as the characters. This would have been a considerable undertaking, but not what Shelley would call a great one. Another request looks more in that direction : he asks for " the most copious and correct history of the discoveries of Geology. If one publication does not appear to contain what I require, send me two or three." In June, 1821, he fears that one of his boxes has come to grief : " it contained a chaos of the elements of ' Charles I.' If the idea of the *creator* had been packed up with them, it would have shared the same fate ; and that, I am afraid, had undergone another sort of shipwreck." It may then have been an epic or miracle-play on Genesis and earlier which had arisen, though far on the horizon, to his inward sight.

Among the books which Ollier sent out to Shelley, a new magazine was instantly attractive. It was called *Ollier's Literary*

Miscellany, to be published occasionally, and although the contributors were anonymous their abilities were conspicuous. Shelley was struck with an essay on German drama (containing an appreciation of Shelley himself) by Julius Hare of Cambridge, and even more with a masterpiece of ironical argument called " The Four Ages of Poetry." He soon knew that this was the work of T. L. Peacock, and was not long in coming to the rescue of the art which he lived for. Ollier invited him to be a paid contributor to the Miscellany, but his declining the payment lost him nothing since no further numbers were published, and the first part of his answer to the tomb-maker of poetry though dispatched to London on March 20th, 1821, did not reach the reading world until 1840. By that time the controversial occasion whence it grew was out of date, and Shelley's piece appeared as it had been modified for possible publication in another periodical by John Hunt.

Peacock, who was now an official at the East India House, wrote his " Four Ages of Poetry " as if the desk's dead wood had begun to dry the last of romance out of him. His argument was, in brief, that poetry was a primitive thing, and that as ages proceeded its glories died away. The age in which he was writing was, from this point of view, the age of brass. Poetry was out of date, and accordingly poets were overshadowed by men of some service to humanity. Though the writer was not wholly serious in this verdict, he had been forming his opinions from his observation of what men of intelligence were reading : " moral, political and physical science have entirely withdrawn from poetry the attention of all whose attention is worth having." All this came to Shelley as a congenial challenge, but in truth he needed very little incitement to produce an essay on poetry. He admired Coleridge's " Biographia Literaria." He had been taking his opportunities in the prefaces to his own works, the " Revolt of Islam," " Prometheus Unbound," " The Cenci "—prefaces glowing with his intellectual intensity, his zeal for the spirit of the age in its best literary embodiments, and his worship of the arts.

It was not only Peacock's impiety at that shrine which aroused him. He was for ever reading whatever he could get by or about Sir Philip Sidney, who in 1581 wrote " An Apologie for Poetrie " in reply to some Elizabethan detractors of it ; and by Francis Bacon, whose " Advancement of Learning " extols it. He accordingly wrote his paper in a vein of eloquence resembling that of those exalted minds with their wide views of life and letters, and he announced it to Peacock, " You will see that I have taken a more general view of what is poetry than you have, and will perhaps agree with several of my positions, without considering your own touched. But read and judge ; and do not let us imitate the great founders of the picturesque. Price and Payne Knight, who like two ill-trained beagles began snarling at each other when they could not catch the hare."

Shelley's " Defence of Poetry," or rather the fraction of it which we have, is illustrious because of the number of utterances in it which have long been regarded as criticism alike true and beautiful. They shine in the treasury of thought upon this subject : " Poetry lifts the veil from the hidden beauty of the world, and makes familiar objects be as if they were not familiar." " The cultivation of poetry is never more to be desired than at periods when, from an excess of the selfish and calculating principle, the accumulation of the materials of external life exceeds the quantity of the power of assimilating them to the laws of human nature." " It is the perfect and consummate surface and bloom of all things ; it is as the odour and the colour of the rose to the texture of the elements which compose it, as the form and splendour of unfaded beauty to the secrets of anatomy and corruption." These and numerous other conclusions, divested of the style in which Shelley moves so easily, are such as a fine critic himself unpractised in the composition of poetry might give ; the " Defence " has the additional attraction of containing passages on the writer's own experience as a poet. " The mind in creation is as a fading coal, which some invisible influence, like an inconstant wind, awakens to transitory brightness. . . . When composition begins, inspiration is already on the decline, and the most glorious poetry that has ever been communicated to the world is probably a feeble shadow of the original conceptions of the poet." By inspiration Shelley had come to feel that he meant the tide of the time, the spirit of the age, nature's surrounding genius intermittently surging through individuality. " Poets are the hierophants of an unapprehended inspiration ; the mirrors of the gigantic shadows which futurity casts upon the present ; the words which express what they understand not." Possibly in the continuation Shelley would have included, what the reader misses in his magnificence and his philosophical criticism, some close discussion of particular poems and questions of what is and is not poetry in instances of writings ; he clearly mentioned an intention of justifying what is always the " modern " experiment of bringing the manners and opinions of the day into the poet's concerns, or perhaps fresh terms—as when Mr. de la Mare writes genes and chromosomes into his spirit-songs.

His preoccupation with long poems did not shut out the inspiration to lyrical verses in the first half of 1821. Some of these confess a depth of sadness to which he had hardly sunk hitherto—they are brief but mighty. For once he appears to be in the mood which in later days made Hardy give to the watching Moon the opinion that everything was " a show God ought surely to shut up soon." What did the future offer, what was the record of Time?

> Unfathomable Sea! whose waves are years,
>   Occan of Time, whose waters of deep woe
> Are brackish with the salt of human tears !
>   Thou shoreless flood, which in thy ebb and flow
> Claspest the limits of mortality,
>   And sick of prey, yet howling on for more
> Vomitcst thy wrecks on its inhospitable shore ;
>   Treacherous in storm, and terrible in calm,
>   Who shall put forth on thee,
>   Unfathomable Sea ?

When he heard the news of the death of Napoleon, which happened in May, 1821, Shelley wrote in another manner of the history of the world. The news arrived on a splendid morning and, moved by the contrast between this scene and the gloomy importance of the ex-tyrant, he devised a dialogue :

> " What, alive and so bold, O Earth ?
>   Art thou not overbold ?
>   What, leapest thou forth as of old
> In the light of thy morning mirth ? . . .
> What, Mother, do you laugh now he is dead ? "

To this,

> " Who has known me of old," replied Earth,
>   " Or who has my story told ?
>   It is thou who art overbold."
> And the lightning of scorn laughed forth
> As she sung, " To my bosom I fold
> All my sons when their knell is knolled,
> And so with living motion all are fed,
> And the quick spring like weeds out of the dead."

The whole highly original poem may be considered as a pointer to the kind of work towards which Shelley would have turned had his time been longer.

His time had seemed within a few seconds of closing on April

16th. The lure of the waters was not less for him now than when
he rowed his boat on Warnham ponds, and since the Arno in
summer was exceedingly shallow, he enlisted Henry Reveley's
aid in adapting a small craft " such as the huntsmen carry about
with them in the Maremma, to cross the sluggish but deep streams
that intersect the forest." In the broad canal to Pisa this boat
with its big sail was suddenly upset, and luckily Reveley knew
what to do. He had a very sensible candidate for rescue, and
when he told Shelley (who still could not swim) to be calm and
quiet in the water the answer was, " All right ; never more
comfortable in my life ; do what you will with me." This mishap
came late on a moonlight night. When Reveley had added to
the rescue of Shelley that of the boat, the drenched sailors
knocked up a farmer's family and were treated with bustling
kindness, vast fires and loads of food.

One of the party who shared the adventure was among the
newest and best of Shelley's acquaintances at Pisa, to which place
he was preceded by the praises of Medwin. He must indeed have
set eyes on Shelley before, for Edward Ellerker Williams (to give
him his full name) had been at Eton a short time during Shelley's
schooldays. Since then Williams had seen a good deal of the
world. At first he was in the navy, then he took a commission
in the army, and was sent to India. A consequence of this was,
besides his meeting with Medwin, that he came to the rescue of
a beautiful girl whose original name was Jane Cleveland, and
whose family was well known in the Indian army. She had been
married to and fortunately abandoned by another officer. When
after many wanderings they arrived in Pisa at the beginning of
1821 Edward and Jane were known as Mr. and Mrs. Williams
and were the happiest of married people. They had come with
the particular object of knowing Shelley, and Edward in his
generous manner soon reported that the poet deserved all
Medwin's laudations : " Shelley is certainly a man of most
astonishing genius, in appearance extraordinarily young, of
manners mild and amiable, but withal full of life and fun." On
his side Shelley was quietly pleased with Ned Williams and his
liking the things and ways of looking at things which he himself
liked. Williams was able to draw and paint, and that alone was a
recommendation ; but besides he was writing a poetical play
called " The Promise : or A Year, a Month and a Day." Duly
Shelley responded to the invitation to revise it, and he did more
—he contributed a version of his lyric " Epithalamium." As for
Mrs. Williams, Shelley was for months uncertain whether he
liked her or not. By degrees she attained as safe a place in his

regard as her husband had taken from the first, and he began to confide in them both a feeling all too like that which he had expressed at Bracknell seven years before.

Mary was no longer the answer to all life's problems. She could no longer attempt to make Shelley think that she was. Her references to Shelley's infatuation with Emilia are not effusive but they are unmistakable ; she treated that matter as a sort of a blight on their private life, and wanted it removed. At best she looked on it as a farce from which her husband might not emerge without being seriously fooled. This aloofness caused Shelley to complain to his good-natured friends in the strain of the verses, beginning " The serpent is shut out from Paradise," of the cold home and the indifference to which he returned from the happiness of friends. In spite of this Mary has described the summer of 1821 as a pleasant time when she and Shelley were living again at the Baths of San Giuliano, and the Williamses at the village of Pugnano four miles off. The boat which had been capsized was now much improved and carried them unfailingly on their visits along the canal, where the trees dipped their boughs into the waters, the ephemera darted on coloured wings to and fro and after dark the aziola (" little downy owl ") made the shades melodious.

Of those days in special Shelley made no poem, but he leaves us a considerable portion of that which was to describe a day's voyage shared by Williams and himself. Even in its disorderly state " The Boat on the Serchio " stands among the favourite poems of Shelley, partly because of the opening which leads the dawn on over the boat sleeping on the stream, " like a beast, unconscious of its tether " (a time and circumstance strangely neglected by our poets), and partly from the fresh sketches of the conversation and bustle of the crew. The importance of tea in Shelley's life has nowhere been more curiously stated ; it is almost the only thing in which he resembles Dr. Johnson. He now had to stow aboard their supplies of this luxury ; a delicate operation.

> With a bottle in one hand,
> As if his very soul were at a stand,
> Lionel stood—when Melchior brought him steady :—
> " Sit at the helm—fasten this sheet—all ready ! "

XXI

THE FATE OF KEATS

IT HAS been noticed that when Mr. and Mrs. Gisborne returned to Italy in the autumn of 1820 they carried " a letter and a fine piece of poetry " from John Keats to Shelley. When Leigh Hunt used those words in writing to his friend in the south he may have meant the volume entitled " Lamia, Isabella, and Other Poems " published for Keats in July, 1820 ; at any rate that volume was in Shelley's hands in October. If Hunt was hinting that one poem in it was so fine that the rest did not compete with it he anticipated Shelley's immediate enthronement of " Hyperion." The book contained besides the pieces named in the title the " Eve of St. Agnes " and a series of odes which have been the delight of countless readers, but Shelley did not take much notice of them or he did not write down his comments ; and some of the rest agreed not at all with his conceptions of poetry. What he selected with a passion of approval was the fragmentary " Hyperion," with its epic quality and its parable of a universal necessity,—a mastering, severe but vital change.

Greatly moved and inspired he renewed what may be called his crusade for Keats. He prepared a long letter to Gifford, the editor of *The Quarterly Review*, urging him to reconsider the harsh style in which one of his critics had assailed Keats, to look at " Endymion " again (Shelley pointed out some of the fine passages), and above all to give his mind to " Hyperion " which, so an Advertisement informed the reader, had been left incomplete because the *Quarterly's* reviewing had disheartened its author. If Shelley on second thoughts did not send this letter, he counted on " Hyperion " as the means of winning over some who had condemned Keats and of confirming the faith in him of others. More than once he called Peacock's attention to a composition which a classical scholar might especially enjoy ; and he sent Claire Clairmont the book with " Hyperion " as the outstanding subject, and wrote to Mrs. Hunt about it, and in brief was Shelley *monté*.

The zeal which he was showing was warmed by the accounts he had heard of the state produced in Keats by the *Quarterly's* hostile criticisms. In the letter to Gifford he said that, according to his information, they had acted terribly upon the poet ; " the first effects are described to me to have resembled insanity, and it was by assiduous watching that he was restrained from effecting purposes of suicide. The agony of his sufferings at length produced the rupture of a blood-vessel in the lungs, and the usual process of consumption appears to have begun." In 1825 a friend of Fanny Brawne, Keats's betrothed, noted what she also said on this : " She and his sister say they have oft found him, on suddenly entering the room, with that review in his hand, reading as if he would devour it—completely absorbed—absent, and drinking it in like mortal poison. The instant he observed anybody near him, however, he would throw it by, and begin to talk of some indifferent matter." If Shelley was mistaken in his reckoning of the damage done to Keats by critical brutality, it is clear that there were sufficient reasons for his error and for the similar indignant errors of Hazlitt, Byron, William Hone and many others. The editor of the *London Magazine* had put the point of view quite simply in the number for September, 1820, by calling it a disgrace to the period " that a dastardly attempt should have been made to assassinate a poet of power " like Keats.

Meanwhile where was Keats ? On November 11th, 1820, Shelley asked Mrs. Hunt this question. " I am anxiously expecting him in Italy, when I shall take care to bestow every possible attention on him. I consider his a most valuable life, and I am interested deeply in his safety. I intend to be the physician both of his body and his soul, to keep the one warm, and to teach the other Greek and Spanish. I am aware indeed, in part, that I am nourishing a rival who will far surpass me ; and this is an additional motive, and will be an added pleasure." Having discovered that Keats's ship would arrive at Naples, Shelley had acted already on the information. Keats was there at the beginning of November and in the words of his fellow-traveller Severn he " received a letter from Shelley, then in Pisa, urging him to come northward, and be the guest of him and his wife ; a most generous letter, and the second he had received from that fine poet and noble man. But our plans were already fixed, and all our arrangements made for an immediate departure for Rome." It was at Rome that Keats died on February 23rd, 1821, but Shelley had not been able to find out much about him and this event did not come to his knowledge until mid-April. One of his earliest actions was to inform Byron, and in doing so Shelley did not spare the Reviewers whom he held responsible for a tragedy of genius destroyed.

Shelley might think that he had at length awakened Byron to a better or a sweeter feeling towards Keats. The frantic disgust which Byron had been showing over the young poet's attempts,

and especially the " Lamia " volume, is very faintly sounded in
his letter to Shelley of April 26th : " Though I differ from you
essentially in your estimate of his performances, I so much abhor
all unnecessary pain, that I would rather he had been seated on
the highest peak of Parnassus than have perished in such a
manner. Poor fellow ! though with such inordinate self-love he
would probably have not been very happy." Here was a gleam
of hope ; and Shelley never gave up the intention of bringing
Byron over. " I am always battling with *the Snake* "—so Byron
told Medwin, using one of his nicknames for Shelley—" about
Keats, and wonder what he finds to make a god of, in that idol
of the Cockneys ; besides, I always ask S. why he does not follow
his style, and make himself one of the school, if he thinks it so
divine." Byron progressed at least far enough towards Shelley's
position to pay tribute to the sublimity of " Hyperion," though
his famous stanza on Keats's death is saturated not with the pity
for which Shelley asked but with the contrast between his own
intrepidity and the problem of poor little people who die of
adverse criticism.

In the preface to a poem on Keats which he began writing
soon after the shock of the news from Rome Shelley also alludes
to a contrast ; speaking of the Reviewers, he said that " these
wretched men know not what they do. They scatter their insults
and their slanders without heed as to whether the poisoned shaft
lights on a heart made callous by many blows or one like Keats's
composed of more penetrable stuff." The incessant malediction
which, however mixed with conventional words on his endowments, Shelley had received and was receiving in the public
prints, was much in his mind on this occasion. He was determined to find out who the persons were who were shooting at him
behind the cover of anonymous journalism, and at Keats. " I
hear " (June 11th, 1821), " that the abuse against me exceeds all
bounds. Pray, if you see any one article particularly outrageous,
send it me. As yet I have laughed ; but woe to these scoundrels
if they should once make me lose my temper. I have discovered
that my calumniator in *The Quarterly Review* was the Rev. Mr.
Milman. Priests and eunuchs have their privilege."

Thus from the beginning " Adonais : an Elegy on the Death
of John Keats " was not a simple and continuous poem on that
ending or that poet. It was sure to be involved with a view of
Shelley's fate as a poet, and even a premonition of his wearying
of the world at last and escaping where Adonais was. The very
thought of Rome and the Protestant Cemetery was as an invitation
to eternity, by way of that charming green ground which Shelley

before this had a parent's reason in his heart to see with tears and with faith,

> Where, like an infant's smile over the dead,
> A light of laughing flowers along the grass is spread.

The theme of Keats's immortality became a longing, the thought of his being free from the patchwork of time for the completeness outside it rose above the tale of his slaughterers and the assembly of his mourners. Of all the complicated lives of which we have word Shelley's was the most complicated ; of all swift hopes and felicities his changed most rapidly into remorse ; well then might he be captured with the glory of a coming simplicity :

> The One remains, the many change and pass.
> Heaven's light forever shines, Earth's shadows fly ;
> Life, like a dome of many-coloured glass,
> Stains the white radiance of Eternity,
> Until Death tramples it to fragments. . . .

In another manner " Adonais " turned while Shelley was writing it into a composition less single and concordant than he had expected. The spirit in which he began to write was largely the legacy of ancient Greece, and his intention was to make a modern English poem in imitation of it. He had been familiar since he was a pupil of Dr. Keate at Eton with the bucolic poets Theocritus, Bion and Moschus ; and had in part translated, probably when he was living with Leigh Hunt, Bion's Elegy on the Death of Adonis. The first line of " Adonais " is practically a literal translation of the first line of that. The motto to the preface of " Adonais " is a quotation from the Elegy of Moschus over the grave of Bion ; and it led to a minor inconsistency in Shelley's poem. For, having accused the enemy of murdering Keats by " piercing his innocent breast," Shelley remembers his Greek model in the stanza beginning " Our Adonais has drunk poison." The unequalled picture of the quick dreams coming to love and lament their lifeless poet is amplified from that of the Loves trying to revive Adonis in the idyll of Bion. These are instances of Shelley's classical intention which could be multiplied ; but he did not remain confined to his scholarly though exquisite field. Such constraint could not be kept once his ardent philosophy seized on the elegy ; for the Greek poet mourning his friend and rival could only say that man the strong and the wise has not even the prospect of the flowers and herbs, which come another summer, but sinks into an interminable death. Shelley's view agreed rather with Pope's dying Christian : " let me languish into Life."

He lives, he wakes,—'tis Death is dead, not he.

In a letter to Mr. Gisborne Shelley speaks of his Elegy as " a highly-wrought *piece of art* "—a term which Byron also uses in a similar way—and it may be he refers to the ingenious and delicate manner in which he had composed variations on the type of Greek threnodies now noticed. The artist who was so perfectly ready to serve the demand of the impassioned man was able to work in many other ways in " Adonais." Some parts of the poem appear designed as a verbal illusion of funeral statuary, comparable in effect with the memorials then being set up by men like Chantrey and Westmacott. The forms that come round the body lying in " deep and liquid rest " in the " twilight chamber " are done in marble if words may so persuade :

> One from a lucid urn of starry dew
> Washed his light limbs as if embalming them ;
> Another clipped her profuse locks, and threw
> The wreath upon him, like an anadem,
> Which frozen tears instead of pearls begem ;
> Another in her wilful grief would break
> Her bow and wingéd reeds, as if to stem
> A greater loss with one which was more weak ;
> And dull the barbéd fire against his frozen cheek.

Occasionally the verse recalls a subject or a tone in the poetry of Keats, without any announcement as a rule ; though " Thy spirit's sister, the lorn nightingale " is distinct enough. The comparison of Adonais to

> a pale flower by some sad maiden cherished
> And fed with true-love tears, instead of dew,

would send many afresh to " Isabella." Shelley is remembering both the " Ode on a Grecian Urn " and " The Eve of St. Agnes " in writing—I speak of the character of the verse itself—

> Whence are we, and why are we ? Of what scene
> The actors or spectators ? Great and mean
> Meet massed in death, who lends what life must borrow,
> As long as skies are blue, and fields are green,
> Evening must usher night, night urge the morrow,
> Month follow month with woe, and year wake year to sorrow.

How highly wrought " Adonais " was, and how Shelley endeavoured in this work to satisfy Keats's own demand and " be more of an artist " than ever, the relics of his labour upon it illustrate well. Much of Shelley's rough drafts has vanished, but besides the poem in its finished form (which Ollier did not venture to publish without omissions) a quantity of studies and trial pieces is in existence. Some are given in the ordinary editions, by no means all. These discarded stanzas and verses particularly show how Shelley strove to make the procession of living poets to the grave of Keats more representative than it is in the published form. There he is limited to the rather unimpressive total of four, with " others of less note." The four are Byron, Moore, Shelley himself and Leigh Hunt, all of course masked in the pageantry of the poem. Byron was not, as we know, likely to attend this ceremony of adoration and grief even in an imaginative sense ; and Moore, though able to shed a tear over the harp that hung silent on Tara's walls, was unconcerned over the broken lyre of Keats. Yet Shelley hoped for these supporters in the long run ; and from his rejected pages we may interpret that he would have shepherded others in, Coleridge perhaps, Wordsworth, Charles Lamb. The first two of these became admirers of Shelley, so far as his poetical gift was concerned, rather than Keats ; and Charles Lamb had already written and published without signature a review of Keats's last volume which had itself the grace and colour of a poem, and which also replied to the destructiveness of certain Reviewers.

The main objection to " Adonais," in respect of what it contains, is that which can be made against " Lycidas." As in Milton's poem the person mourned, Edward King, does not receive a great measure of precise remembering, so the biographer's Keats is left vague by Shelley. The " moving pomp " crowds him out of many stanzas. What does the objection matter when so exalted and so incorruptible a memorial is raised to the spirit of a man, and to the spirit made active and purposeful by that man ? Nothing could be written of Keats's brief and unquenchable career to enclose the essence of it all more permanently than the stanza on his reception by souls of young poets dead and gone :

> The inheritors of unfulfilled renown
> Rose from their thrones, built beyond mortal thought,
> Far in the Unapparent. Chatterton
> Rose pale,—his solemn agony had not
> Yet faded from him ; Sidney, as he fought
> And as he fell and as he lived and loved
> Sublimely mild, a Spirit without spot,
> Arose ; and Lucan, by his death approved :
> Oblivion as they rose shrank like a thing reproved.

Nevertheless, Shelley was well aware that another kind of

memorial to Keats would be of service to his name and work and to the cause of simple justice in literature. In sending " Adonais " to Joseph Severn, and on several other occasions, he inquired after Keats's papers and whatever biographical materials were to be collected, since he was much inclined to publish the rest of Keats's writings with a memoir and a critical essay.

This, however, was a side issue. To judge by the number of times that " Adonais " is mentioned in Shelley's letters, he was more eager to see this poem find a large and enthusiastic audience than any he had written. Completing it in early June, 1821, he hastened into Pisa and had it printed " with the types of Didot," and was distributing it among friends while the London edition was being arranged. Byron took refuge from the main point in talking about Shelley's other works and applauding " Prometheus Unbound." Peacock received his copy. Horace Smith praised the poem and reassured Shelley over the apprehension that it was excessively metaphysical. Medwin was pleased with it. Leigh Hunt called it " the most Delphic poetry I have seen a long while." Severn probably wrote Shelley an appreciative letter, though to his friend Charles Brown he was reasonably critical—on his own level. " I find many beauties in it, but is it not a pity so much beauty should be scattered about, without the balancing of lights and shades, or the oppositions of colours ? In this poem there is such a want of repose, you are continually longing to know what he will be at. It gave me great pleasure as a tribute to poor Keats's memory." In the end it won Severn the friendship of Mr. Gladstone.

But " Adonais " when Ollier at last displayed the London edition had no general success, and Shelley was not blind to the fact. Equally he did not easily give up the dream of a new edition, containing his critical essay—but when he had an impulse to write that, he was unable to find his copy of the volume with " Hyperion " in it. From Severn he had the promise, which came to nothing, of a portrait of Keats. The emotion and chivalry which had compelled him to write " Adonais " were not of a nature to disappear under any lets and hindrances, and were freshened when he received some details, too late for his book, of Keats's last hours. Among these he read that Keats had wished to have for the inscription on his tomb, " Here lies one whose name was writ on water," and again he was prompted to write verses on the immortality of Adonais ; these, however, only survive as a brief fragment with uncertain readings. In fact, the poetic promise, fate and triumph of Keats were to be part of Shelley's thinking until the very last moments of his own mortality.

XXII

BYRON RECAPTURED

IN A HIGHLY entertaining work entitled " Narrative of Lord Byron's Voyage to Corsica and Sardinia, during the Summer and Autumn of the year 1821," we soon come upon anecdotes of one of Byron's company aboard the *Mazeppa*, a regrettable character named Percy S——. It appears that off Corsica the yacht ran into a tremendous storm, which Byron faced with a calm heart. But " Percy S——, who heretofore made no secret of his infidelity, and whose spirits we thought no danger could ever appal, appeared to have lost all energy, and the horrors of approaching death made him weep like a child. Those names which he never before pronounced but in ridicule, he now called upon in moving accents of serious prayer." When all appeared lost Byron sat in his trousers only, resigned to his fate : Percy S—— " lay at his feet in a state of insensibility," and was removed to his cabin. Danger over, he emerged, and Byron as he shook hands with him quoted, pointedly, these verses,

" Cowards die many times before their death,
The valiant never taste of death but once."

The reclaimed infidel, after " a glass of rum and water, warm," soon became " the same free-thinking, thankless dog as ever," and at dinner his Lordship " threatened to compose an elegy on the death and resurrection of Percy S——."

Subsequently S. wrote a poem descriptive of St. Fiorenzo, in bad French, but " it flattered the governor's vanity " ; and this was as well. The day before the *Mazeppa* was due to sail, he and a Mr. Denzell were out in a boat which was overturned in a squall. They clung on for four hours till " P—— S——, exhausted, had quitted his hold and was sinking ; saved as by a miracle he declared that he should be drowned if he remained with the yacht, and resolved to stay at St. Fiorenzo until he could get a passage to Venice.   Lord Byron laughed at the superstition of an avowed infidel, but did not try to dissuade him from his resolution—he was an eccentric being and much attached to his Lordship, who had treated him with great kindness for several years."

This voyage was imaginary from start to finish. But the lives

of Byron and Shelley were again drawn together in the summer
and autumn of 1821. At this time Byron was living at Ravenna,
having exchanged his Venetian antics for a quiet domesticity
with Countess Guiccioli, daughter of Count Gamba. The Count's
house at Ravenna was near an ancient forest, the Pinetum ; and
of the Gambas it is written that they " might have well been
called the Osbaldistones of Italy ; they were all sportsmen
according to their knowledge, which consisted of hunting a slow
pointer, who stood woodcocks and partridges equally well,
through the forests and vineyards." They were perfectly contented with Countess Guiccioli's being separated from her old
husband and living with Lord Byron, who had his splendid
apartments in Guiccioli's house. The lady had a bright complexion, blue eyes, auburn curls, a merry laugh, and a cultivated
mind ; she was of small stature and like Mary Shelley had legs
too short in proportion to her frame, " thus sacrificing grace to
strength." She was twenty years old in 1821.

Shelley, who had been whirling about to Leghorn on Claire's
business and to Florence in search of a house for Horace Smith,
returned to the Baths of Pisa on August 2nd only to receive
another demand for his friendly services. Byron wished him to
come at once to Ravenna. Shelley arrived there on August 6th,
having escaped injury when he was flung out of the light carriage
over a hedge ; he got in at ten at night and sat up talking with
Byron until five in the morning. The crisis which had induced
Byron to send for him was this : for political reasons the Gambas
had been expelled from Papal territory, Countess Guiccioli had
taken refuge in Florence, and Byron was wondering where he and
she should go next. The Guiccioli and her brother were proposing
Switzerland, and though Byron was full of doubt about that retreat
with all the English gossips in it he hardly knew how to reject
the desire of his mistress. For himself he much preferred Tuscany,
and Shelley was only too willing to see him established there ;
when therefore Byron requested him to write to the Guiccioli
and reason her out of the Swiss emigration, Shelley though a
stranger to her did his best in his best Italian—and at some length.

His eloquence carried the day. The Guiccioli replied, with
many compliments to the poet of whom she had heard so much,
that Switzerland was off—and would Shelley in his goodness be
certain not to leave Ravenna without Byron ? Shelley did not
literally promise this, but it was sufficient that he had made up
Byron's mind for him : he " is immediately coming to Pisa. He
will set off the moment I can get him a house. Who would have
imagined this ? " It was August 16th. Matthew Arnold who

likened Shelley to a beautiful but ineffectual angel could hardly
have acted more promptly than Shelley did now—admittedly
with Mary to help him—since within ten days the finest palace
on the Lung' Arno was at Byron's disposal. " Conclude," wrote
Byron on the 26th, " for the house then forthwith. I wish that
there were two more *stalls*—for I have eight horses. We are in
all the agonies of packing. . . . If my furniture be not sufficient
pray engage for some more—and if any money is necessary—
draw on me at sight ; you had better *clinch* the Padrone of the
palazzo—lest he rise in his price or play some trick with some
others of the hectic English. . . . Do the essential and I will approve
and sanction yr. proceedings."

Many things in Shelley's visit to Byron at Ravenna were
delightful or diverting to him, and above all the personality of
Byron. He found the hero improved since 1818 " in genius, in
temper, in moral views, in health, in happiness " ; it was not
possible to agree with his judgments on poetry but to hear him
talk about it was a piece of luck. Shelley noticed that Byron's
critical creed was one which, if Byron wrote in obedience to it,
would lead to mediocre work, and which his fine poems and
passages contradicted ; but " Marino Faliero," another of the
five-act tragedies, bore signs of the danger in it. Byron read
Shelley parts of the play, and, a very different matter, the fifth
Canto of " Don Juan." This sent Shelley into glories. " It sets
him not only above, but far above, all the poets of the day—
every word is stamped with immortality. . . . It fulfils, in a certain
degree what I have long preached of producing—something
wholly new and relative to the age, and yet surpassingly beautiful.
It may be vanity, but I think I see the trace of my earnest exhorta-
tions to him to create something wholly new." Talk on these and
other topics went on till six in the morning, but then in Byron's
house even Shelley resigned himself to getting up at midday.
Byron breakfasted in the afternoon, they talked or read till six,
went for a ride through the pine forests, dined at eight and so to
talk again. One of Byron's characteristics could not have been
missed by any visitor. Countess Guiccioli found it very comical,
and would tell a good story about it. For Michaelmas Day Byron
regularly resolved to have a roast goose, and bought one ; but
by the time he had fattened it for a month the goose and he were
such friends that the bird did not come to the table, and another
was bought. At last he possessed four pet geese which travelled
in cages under his carriage. Shelley's catalogue of Byron's zoo
(" besides servants "), omitting geese, includes " ten horses, eight
enormous dogs, three monkeys, five cats, an eagle, a crow and a

falcon ; and all these, except the horses, walk about the house, which every now and then resounds with their unarbitrated quarrels, as if they were the masters of it." Shelley supposed that this list was complete, but as he departed " met on the grand staircase five peacocks, two guinea hens, and an Egyptian crane. I wonder who all these animals were before they were changed into these shapes."

Enjoying so much at the Guiccioli-Byron palace, Shelley had only been in it a few hours when a matter came to light which almost turned everything to bitterness. Byron had been approached by R. B. Hoppner on the subject of Shelley's private life, and advised to drop him. The story accepted by the Hoppners as Elise brought it was the one already mentioned : Claire was Shelley's mistress, their baby had been born in the winter of 1818 and was instantly sent away to the Foundling Hospital at Naples, they had united in insulting, neglecting and beating Mary Shelley. These allegations, when Byron heard them in 1820, had not appeared to him improbable : " The Shiloh story is true no doubt " (Shiloh being one more nickname for Shelley), " it is just like them." He was willing to think that Claire had had more than one love-child. Now, in August, 1821, he may have changed his mind, and at least he did Shelley the justice of letting him know what was being said and believed by others. The scandals were observed by Shelley to have a deeper source than he could trace and to have the object, in the end, of " depriving us of the means of security and subsistence."

Something must be done to defeat them. Shelley sent his wife a summary of what he had heard and a request that she should write a letter, which he would forward, to Mrs. Hoppner, refuting the charges. This letter would be shown to Byron. Meeting the crisis with all her powers of explanation and candour Mary made a solemn request of Mrs. Hoppner that she should " reject as false every circumstance of Elise's infamous tale." It cannot be known if this letter was ever read by the Hoppners, since it was found by Hobhouse with the seal broken among Byron's papers after his death. Byron had promised Shelley to send it to the slanderers with his comments. Shelley's own last comment on the Hoppners and their craven enmity was "So much for nothing." But what they symbolised to him was far more important. It was the world, as Shakespeare had repeatedly referred to it in the Sonnets—the cold, wise, inspecting, credulous, mocking world ; and the wilderness seemed the only remaining hope. " I would retire with you," he wrote to Mary, " and our child to a solitary island in the sea, would build a boat, and shut upon my retreat the floodgates of the world. . . . Good, far more than evil impulses, love, far more than hatred, has been to me, except as you have been its object, the source of all sorts of mischief." An alternative to this solitary island, which was not likely to be found, occurred to him : to form and be closely connected with " a society of our own class, as much as possible in intellect, or in feelings. . . . Our roots never struck so deeply as at Pisa, and the transplanted tree flourishes not. . . . We must do one thing or the other—for yourself, for our child, for our existence."

It has been noticed that Byron in writing to Shelley's enemies called him " Shiloh." The explanation of that name is a key to Byron's harsher feelings about Shelley. It was widely known as the name of the Infant whom the piteous prophetess Joanna Southcott was to bring into the world—the much advertised modern Messiah.

At Ravenna Shelley made a tour of the ancient buildings, and closely examined the portrait in relief on Dante's tomb. The half-closed eye reminded him of that scamp Pacchiani. In the library he saw, and had enough technical experience to appreciate, specimens of the earliest printed books. Besides riding he accompanied Byron in pistol-practice, and was almost as good a shot at the pumpkins as his host. But the affairs of his friends were never out of his mind for long. He paid a visit to Claire's daughter in the convent, and found her grown tall and slight for her age, graceful in movement, full of religious names and words, and obviously taking after both her father and mother in her wild freedoms. " Before I went away she made me run all over the convent, like a mad thing. The nuns, who were half in bed, were ordered to hide themselves, and on returning Allegra began ringing the bell which calls the nuns to assemble. The tocsin of the convent sounded, and it required all the efforts of the prioresses to prevent the spouses of God from rendering themselves, dressed or undressed, to the accustomed signal. Nobody scolded her for these *scappature*." What would this imp become ? Shelley perceived in the child " the love of distinction and vanity, and this is a plant which produces good or evil according to the gardener's skill."

Another matter in which Shelley's philanthropy was needed originated with Lord Byron and suited Shelley's notion of forming a congenial group of sensitive people at Pisa. In 1818 Byron had told him that he wished Leigh Hunt would come to Italy, and if it was want of money that kept him away he would lend him £400 or £500 for the journey. Intricately and daily con-nected with the conduct and property of *The Examiner*, Hunt had been unable to act upon this ; but on August 26th, 1821, Shelley was in a position to send him another invitation. Lord Byron " proposes that you should come and go shares with him and me in a periodical work, to be conducted here ; in which each of the contracting parties should publish all their original compositions, and share the profits. He proposed it to Moore, but for some reason or other it was never brought to bear. There can be no doubt that the profits of any scheme in which you and Lord Byron engage, must from various yet co-operating reasons be very great. As for myself, I am, for the present, only a sort of link between you and him." On this occasion Byron did not offer the journey money and Shelley felt it impossible to ask him for it but hoped to borrow it from Horace Smith—who, after all the preparations for him, was not coming to Italy.

The project of a journal of this independent and powerful character was magnificent, whether it should be entitled *Hesperides* or something simpler ; but nobody concerned looked into its possible disadvantages. Byron's desire to have a Review of his own, more or less, was natural and admirable, but such schemes must be put into action through many practical arrangements. Leigh Hunt ought to have seen this, and certainly he informed Shelley of the problems which his leaving the *Examiner* office in 1821 would create ; his brother John, the quiet and sensible partner in the paper, was in prison for a new political libel, and there were other complications. Hunt could not forecast that upon his leaving the work to John he would be regarded as forfeiting the editorship and depriving himself of that permanent income ; nor that the Byron whom he would find in Italy had changed from the joyous youth who dined with him in the Surrey Gaol in 1813. There were other things in the near future, menacing the twinkling promise of the intended Review, which he cannot at all be blamed for not foretelling.

Shelley was a lure strong enough to make Hunt give up pros and cons and decide on a voyage to Italy. The editor of *The Examiner* with his wife and six small children was expected at Pisa any day in November, 1821. Hunt had written both to Shelley and Byron that he would be happy to engage in the great periodical ; and he was to receive for his travel £200 for which Shelley had given Byron a bond. Byron had assigned to the Hunts the ground floor of the Casa Lanfranchi which he and the Gambas had now taken, and he had paid the upholsterer's bill ; the furniture, good but plain and cheap, was chosen by Shelley, who put in what he himself was accustomed to have. Mary and he had in fact made sure that everything needed for the Hunt household was there ready, except bedding, and a woman cook of the country was already appointed and waiting in their own house. But the Hunts did not arrive in November, nor December. The wintry seas were in commotion and Mrs. Leigh Hunt was no sailor.

By way of substitute for Leigh Hunt Shelley now had Medwin in Pisa again, a bachelor still, and a scribbler. On November 20th Shelley took him over from the new lodgings to be introduced to Byron at the Lanfranchi palace ; the ghost of old Lanfranchi, according to Shelley, was unquiet, and walked at night. A bulldog posted at the top of the stairs knew Shelley and let them pass. Byron was cordial, and conversation began ; he gave Shelley part of a manuscript to read, called " Heaven and Earth," and spoke of Shelley's great rage for a boat. This introduction was very much what Medwin was looking for ; he had become acquainted with the greatest genius in Europe and by jotting down his conversations he would one day be enabled to publish a book at once famous and lucrative. The only date of a conversation in it is that just mentioned, but Medwin deserves some credit for collecting so much about Byron and Shelley in however disorderly a way.

Many of Medwin's bits and pieces do not need any date more precise than the winter of 1821, and they are at least all we can get of the good talk which flowed so freely when his distinguished friends were together—trifles, oddments, teasing but informative. Byron would contest Shelley's views on Christianity—call him " a Protestant—you protest against all religions " ; or discuss the perfect ode—and Shelley contended for that by Coleridge beginning " Ye clouds that far above me float and pause " ; or mention that Lady Byron had once written him a letter beginning " Dear Duck," which Shelley said would look odd in Italian, " Anitra Carissima." On the matter of reading Dante, Shelley remarked that it was unfavourable to writing because of the superiority of Dante's poem to all possible compositions. Byron urged him to translate Goethe's " Faust," but Shelley declared that the translator of " Wallenstein " was the only man living who could venture upon that, and he had already written to Coleridge but in vain. A curious reminiscence occasionally turned up, such as that of the lady who fell in love with Shelley for his verses ; or the offer to Shelley by Hookham of a large sum if he would prepare for the press the novel which caused so much gossip, called " Glenarvon," by Lady Caroline Lamb.

In November, 1821, Edward and Jane Williams returned to Pisa and found accommodation on the ground floor of the Shelleys' dwelling, the Tre Palazzi. Shelley quickly set Edward to work with him, as an amanuensis, on a work which had been in progress or in abeyance for some years—a translation of the " Tractatus Theologico-Politicus " of Spinoza. It was Williams also who transcribed " Hellas " for dispatch to Ollier, and the work must have stimulated him to look for a new dramatic theme himself, which he found in the biography of Pope Celestine V and Boniface VIII. The fate of authors is as uncertain as any other ; Williams who wrote so much and had the encouragement and testimony of Byron, Shelley and other noted literary people is only represented in print by the diary which he kept with gentle regularity. While these poets, dramatists, translators, Boswellians were so busy, the women had their usual household affairs and some entertainments. Countess Guiccioli proved to be a pretty girl with a kind heart, and Jane Williams was more and more admired. In the evenings all would meet sometimes to hear Shelley read poetry ancient or modern. Mary resumed her water-colours.

The tranquillity which these occupations may rightly ascribe to the period was disturbed on December 12th by one of the semi-tragic incidents in which Shelley was so often involved. It came to his knowledge that a man—he was actually a priest—who had committed sacrilege was to be burned at the stake at Lucca ; and he immediately determined to prevent this execution. His idea was to appoint Byron as commander of an amateur squadron of horsemen who should charge into Lucca at the proper moment, rescue the condemned man and carry him across the frontier. Byron upon reflection thought that " to save him by any means but *remonstrance* is of course out of the question," and fortunately for Shelley and the rest of the intended party of liberators even remonstrance proved unnecessary. Taaffe sped to Lucca to find out what was really happening, and before many hours Shelley was able to inform Byron, " The design which certainly had been in contemplation of burning my fellow-serpent has been abandoned, and he has been condemned to the galleys." Even Shelley accepted the theory that punishment of some kind was due to a man in holy orders who had stolen the sacramental cup.

The Pisa circle was more inclined to remember a less heroic occurrence concerning Byron and Shelley. On Christmas Day Byron, who made Countess Guiccioli laugh by his mingling abuse of England with a reverence for English customs, gave a full-sized dinner to his men friends, and before they went in they happened to be talking of longevity. Byron offered Shelley a bet of £1000 that Lady Noel would outlive Sir Timothy ; in other words, if he came into his estate before Shelley he would pay Shelley £1000, and *vice versa*. Shelley at once accepted this wager, as Sir Timothy would on all grounds have wished him to do. It was a serious bet ; and on January 22nd, 1822, Lady Noel died and Byron became much richer. He had however also become exceedingly close on money matters, though this was a temporary passion, and he failed to pay the £1000 ; we do not hear of this from Shelley ; but Williams and Medwin as witnesses of the wager were unfavourably impressed, and regarded Byron as neglecting a just debt. The surviving interest in the matter is rather that Shelley had no objection to betting. With his love of pistol-shooting, riding, yachting, billiards, and his knowledge of hare-hunting and fox-hunting besides the business of the farm, it shows him as a competent country squire. It is not hard to picture him instead of his young brother John as one of the stewards at the horse-races once held in St. Leonard's Forest.

But it was for Byron's benefit that he was playing this part in Italy ; and it was a contribution to the relief of his own spirits which Byron's society brought, " after the dreary solitude of the understanding and imagination " in which he had been living. And there were present vexations. Writing on the last day of 1821 to Claire at Florence, Shelley spoke of the illness of Mary which gave her sleepless nights, of his own pains and depressions, of the great gales which had strewn the shores of the Mediterranean with wrecks. " You may imagine, and I am sure you will share, our anxiety, about poor Hunt. I wonder and am shocked at my insensibility, that I can sleep or enjoy one moment of peace until I hear of his safety." He had had word of Hunt's ship the *David Walter* in the Bay of Biscay.

During the latter months of 1821 Shelley found it difficult to complete the short poems for which he still had beginnings and sketches. One attempt called " Ginevra " looks like a tale in verse suggested by reading Leigh Hunt's " Story of Rimini " and Keats's " Lamia," though the episode was derived from a guidebook to the antiquities of Florence. It reflects Shelley's willingness to look on marriage as a fatal mistake, but it is a half-told tale, and a surprise ending was probably in his mind ; much like that which Leigh Hunt produced years afterwards in the admired play, "A Legend of Florence," based on words in Shelley's poem,

> One step to the white deathbed,
>   And one to the bier,
> And one to the charnel,
>   And one, oh where ?

Another fragment from Shelley's study in 1821, faintly recalling
Keats's " Isabella, or, The Pot of Basil," is a portrait of himself
endeavouring to recapture delight, so elusive in the love of human
kind, in the forms of nature.   Perhaps in cold fact it was Mary
who placed a zucca in a vase on the window-sill, but in the poem
Shelley himself found the plant looking like the image of despair
on the riverside, and brought it to his room where he watched
its revival in

> Strong leaves and tendrils, and its flowers fair
> Full as a cup with the vine's burning dew,
> O'erflowed with golden colours.

Here too it appears likely that out of the greyness of the first part
of the poem a symphony of triumph was to break forth, but the
piece was never finished.

As for the future and its action, Shelley had not got any further
than headquarters at Pisa.   His travels in Arabia beyond the
reach of the postman had receded from his fancy.   He had
thought of becoming one of those picturesque Englishmen who
have been in the political employment of Indian princes, and had
consulted Peacock on this only to be told that these things were
after all an official arrangement, only open to " the regular
service of the East India Company." The old idea of following
earlier Shelleys to America was not wholly lost to view but was
not quite what he was after.   Thus he had a sense of wasting his
time and powers, and it is discernible in his not perfecting his
poems : " I wish I had something better to do than furnish this
jingling food for the hunger of oblivion, called verse, but I have
not."   Moreover across the way there was a poet whose progress
at once drew Shelley's limitless admiration and increased his self-
abasement. Byron's " Cain " was now published.   It appeared
to make any pre-adamite poetry by Shelley or by any one
superfluous. He and Mary thought it Byron's finest production ;
Mary described it as " a revelation " ; and Shelley found in it
such absolute genius making speed unwearied that he pondered
anew on the sublime paradox of that unconfinable spirit and that
earthbound man.   For himself, his mind was " like an overworked
racehorse put into a hackney-coach."

XXIII

BYRON RECONSIDERED

THE NEW YEAR, 1822, did not bring any immediate change. "Our party at Pisa is the same." Every week, besides miscellaneous meetings, Byron gave a dinner, which went on till three in the morning, and Shelley watched the others " making themselves vats of claret, etc.," but he thought that their host was seen at his best throughout these evenings. New books were often to be borrowed as John Murray's parcels reached Byron at the Lanfranchi Palace. Shelley was impatient for proof sheets of his own " Hellas," and began promising " Charles the First " for the spring ; it would be superior to *The Cenci* as " a work of art." He meant also to bring out his translations of the Homeric Hymns, which had accumulated since 1817.

Into the set of literary exiles a new figure suddenly arrived— one who during his wanderings had determined to pass some time with Shelley and with Byron. He was a man of Shelley's own age but not very like him. Edward Trelawny, the younger, son of a lieutenant-colonel, had never shown any desire to attend to the family interest in Cheshire ; he had had other adventures, which in his mind were for ever blended with many that he had imagined. He had one capital qualification for whirling about the world, though he did not think it at all adequate—an income of £500 a year. The impressions that he made at first on Shelley were not so marked as those he made on Mary, who, though she was unaware that Trelawny had had two wives already, described him with enthusiasm : " a kind of half Arab Englishman whose life has been as changeful as that of Anastasius and who recounts the adventures of his youth as eloquently and well as the imagined Greek . . . he is a strange web which I am endeavouring to unravel . . . he is six feet high—raven black hair which curls thickly and shortly like a Moor's—dark grey expressive eyes, overhanging brows, upturned lips and a smile which expresses good nature and kindheartedness—his shoulders are high like an Orientalist—his voice is monotonous yet emphatic and his language as he relates the events of his life energetic and simple— whether the tale be one of blood and horror or of irresistible comedy. His company is delightful for he excites me to think

and if any evil shade the intercourse that time will unveil—the
sun will rise or night darken all." Trelawny in fact was an
English eccentric, inclined to dramatise himself but naturally
moving in mysterious ways. In a sense he did little ; he took
part in the campaign for Greek Liberty a year or two after
meeting Byron, but afterwards did not help to make history.
His job was merely to *be* the many-travelled legendary man who
amused, shocked, excited and alarmed Victorian dinner-parties
and roared down all who did not please him.

Trelawny's stories, which Mary Shelley began to hear in
1822, were not unlike those of Othello, except that some of them
have been investigated. The principal thing about them was
that they passed the time very well if time was hanging heavy,
and Mary's might be ; but Shelley did not find it so as a rule.
He looked on Trelawny as a sailor with the sailor's rapture in
yarning, a sturdy and valuable man to have in Pisa for the
Byron programme. Trelawny had been consulting Williams
about his becoming one of " the Pistol Club," and was to be
welcomed in the plans and preparations for new boats and
voyages. Hardly had he rejoined his friends in their lodgings
when Shelley came in, tall and thin, mild-looking and beardless,
wearing " a black jacket and trousers, which he seemed to have
outgrown." He had a book with him, which was the plays of
Calderon, and on this he began a delightful monologue ; then he
was gone again, speedily to reappear bringing Mary along. Next
day Trelawny was escorted as Medwin and Williams had been
past the bulldog on the Lanfranchi staircase into Byron's billiard-
room. If he was disconcerted by the commonplace passages in
Byron's talk (for he shared the common fallacy that a poet must
always be talking poetry), he was astonished at the " passiveness
and docility " with which Byron paid attention to Shelley.
According to Trelawny Shelley could remonstrate with him on
his attitude to his literary work and arouse no wrath ; but then
" Byron knew him to be exempt from the egotism, pedantry,
coxcombry, and more than all, the rivalry of authorship, so that
he was the truest and most discriminating of his admirers." For
his part Byron revealed his sense of Shelley's worth by tossing
to him such letters as Tom Moore and others were busily writing
with the intention of detaching his Lordship from his degenerate
company.

The appearance and autobiography of Trelawny gave Byron
an idea. The English in Italy were exceedingly fond of amateur
theatricals ; now, he could call on some really promising talent.
They should perform *Othello*, with Trelawny as hero, to all Pisa

as audience, in the Lanfranchi Palace. Iago would be taken by
Byron, Cassio by Williams, and (how properly cast again !)
Roderigo by Medwin. Mary Shelley should play Desdemona
and Jane Williams Emilia, and it seems that some rehearsing
began ; but Madame Guiccioli persuaded Byron not to proceed.
Shelley, though he was not included in the cast, had an idea of
his own. He began a play about an Enchantress " living in one
of the islands of the Indian Archipelago " who " saves the life of
a Pirate, a man of savage but noble nature "—so, the chief parts
were already assigned to Jane and Trelawny—and was to include
sundry love situations, an Indian youth, and others. The fragments which remain are notable for many surprisingly beautiful
verses intended to be spoken by the Enchantress on the subject
of a plant in a vase. The plant grew and trailed over garden and
lawn and woodland and pool so wonderfully as to leave the drama
itself far behind ; and once more the Pisa Club was disappointed
of its theatricals. We may equally say that we are cheated of the
best flower-poem in English, but Shelley was not at his best at
the time in finding a terminable form for his floating world of
wonders.

Occasionally he looked over the scenes of " Charles the First "
which he had written, and wished he could write more ; the
completed play would have been in the conventional form, but
was already marked by a bolder and stronger dramatic diction
than *The Cenci*. Resolved to have a Fool in the piece, Shelley
nevertheless produced a fool of his own—and in the talk of the
King, Queen and this creature Archy while the rainbow shines
above them and London city there are the highest beauty and
prophetic intensity. All the characters, though only beginning
to unfold, have a sharpness of definition which promised a true
play ; but Shelley could not restrain his love of copious speeches
and thronging metaphysical exaltations.

His mind at this time was more stirred by the contemplation
of the grand works of others than by the chances of any to come
from himself, and his infinite pleasure in Goethe's " Faust " was
revived by the chance that Claire Clairmont was studying
German. He encouraged her to make a translation of the
masterpiece, which would meet Byron's desire to have one by
him. The arrival of a volume of illustrations to " Faust " increased his zeal. These pictures, the work of a Dresden artist
named Moritz Retzsch, who also published his etchings illustrating
Schiller and Shakespeare, are acute and striking though they grow
monotonous seen in quantity. They won a reputation through
Europe. Shelley was moved by one of them in particular, which

represents Faust and Margaret kissing in the summer-house—" I only dared," he says, " look upon [it] once, and [it] made my brain swim round only to touch the leaf on the opposite side of which I knew that it was figured." Accompanying the etchings by Retzsch he found a correct but spiritless translation of the scenes depicted, and although he sent Coleridge a request through Gisborne that he would come into action and make such pale efforts superfluous, Shelley soon devoted some days to trans-lating other scenes himself. The results justified him. Among his selections of the version the Walpurgisnacht was his big achieve-mnet, and when J. S. Blackie's translation of " Faust " appeared in 1834, one of several inspired in part by Shelley's example, a note said, " This is the glorious Brocken scene immortalized by Shelley." Blackie made a general suggestion with which Shelley would have been still more gratified. The intellectual, questing, homeless, unwearying character called Faust had " of late been rendered quite familiar to the English reader of poetry, by two very extraordinary intellectual phenomena—Byron and Shelley. Both these spirits, however different in many respects, are one in this, that they were equally English Fausts of the nineteenth century. And the admiration which both of them are known to have had for the great work of the German bard, would be sufficient proof of the identity, did not every page of their works bear witness to the same truth."

The differences between Byron and Shelley had never been unrecognised by either of them, and the friendship which existed between them was haunted by the strangest rumours or shadows of sudden catastrophe. It might have been a friendship in a play by John Webster. Shelley certainly did not wish to see it fly asunder on any account, but he was willing to risk much at the suit of Claire, on the subject of Allegra's future. In February 1822 he told Byron that it would be best for the child to be taken from the convent and placed in the institute at Lucca, but on this matter at least Byron would take no advice from Shelley or from any one else connected with Allegra's mother. In fact he was so inflammable that Shelley felt the subject could not be re-opened with him ; and to make matters worse Claire was inclined to solve her problem by a scheme of snatching Allegra from the convent and (with Shelley's help, of course) keeping her in some secret place. If in her wild one-track way she should do this Shelley saw himself inescapably confronted by Byron with a challenge.

Claire did not readily give up her dream of a rescue and an escape, and Shelley was still trying to talk her into sense on March

20th. " Your latest plan about Allegra seems to me in its present form pregnant with irremediable infamy to all the actors in it except yourself ;—in any form wherein I must actively co-operate, with inevitable destruction. *I would not* in any case make myself the party to a forged letter. I *could not* refuse Lord Byron's challenge ; though that, however to be deprecated, would be the least in the series of mischiefs consequent upon my pestilent intervention in such a plan. I say this because I am shocked at the thoughtless violence of your designs, and I wish to put my sense of this madness in the strongest light. I may console myself, however, with the reflection that the attempt even is impossible ; as I have no money."

But Allegra's mother was not the only cause of hazardous discord between Shelley and Byron. The proposed periodical was cause enough. Byron did not always treat the preliminary warnings from his sycophants at home as lightly and contemptuously as he could appear to do in Pisa ; and he had realised that Leigh Hunt, if he had dropped his employments in London for his call to the South, would be an expensive experiment in Italy. We gave signs of wishing himself out of the periodical scheme before it got any older ; and then in a moment he swung round. On March 2nd Shelley informed Hunt that Byron was once again expressing the greatest eagerness to establish the journal and the greatest confidence in Hunt as his associate, with renewed indifference to the disapproval of Tommy Moore. Pleased as he was with this reassurance Shelley could not count much on its permanence, and he had not much faith in Byron so far as his own affairs went. Both he and Mary allude to some part played by Byron in the calumnies which the Hoppners had helped to circulate—something more active than a mere failure to deny them. Shelley had moments when he saw Byron's character, apart from his mental glories, as a dark menace, and he wrote again to Claire, " It is of vital importance both to me and to yourself, to Allegra even, that I should put a period to my intimacy with L. B., and that without *éclat*. No sentiments of honour or justice restrain him (as I strongly suspect) from the basest insinuations, and the only mode in which I could effectually silence him I am reluctant (even if I had proof) to employ during my father's life. But for your immediate feelings I would suddenly and irrevocably leave this country which he inhabits, nor ever enter it but as an enemy to determine our differences *without words*."

It was for several reasons a bad moment for any such extrication, but another relief was possible : Williams on February

18th laid a wager with Shelley that Byron himself would quit Italy before six months. The summer would bring a change from this Pisan coterie, so attractive and so nerve-racking. Williams and Shelley began looking for houses on the Gulf of Spezia, which long before had impressed Dr. Smollett as a capital harbour for the English navy, and which Shelley had already visited with other and vaguer appreciation. At first it was the business of the house-hunters to find a place for Byron as well as themselves and Trelawny, but their failure did not matter in the end, since Byron gave up his intention. The social and literary diversions at Pisa went on. Trelawny was very regular at Lord Byron's house, but said that he felt like shouting with joy when he withdrew from the sessions of the cynical wit, heard the heavy iron-plated door's echo die away and adjourned " to the hospitable and cheerful abode of the Shelleys." The Pirate was never tired of watching Shelley's studious habits. He had not come across this sort of man before, though he himself was a steady reader ; but Shelley ! " He set to work on a book, or a pyramid of books; his eyes glistening with an energy as fierce as that of the most sordid gold-digger who works at a rock of quartz, crushing his way through all impediments, no grain of the pure ore escaping his eager scrutiny." The poet would sometimes take up a massive work on a scientific subject and deliver an epitome of it in simple language, a feat which Trelawny greatly admired.

At the same time he had an itch to drag Shelley away from all this ivory-tower incubation and to educate him in " real life," which for Trelawny included swimming. One day " I was bathing in a deep pool in the Arno, and astonished the Poet by performing a series of aquatic gymnastics, which I had learnt from the natives of the South Seas." Shelley was then enjoined to dive in and at least try floating ; but instead he lay on the bottom " like a conger eel " and was pulled out by the expert. He commented that he had not been over eager to be pulled out. " It's a great temptation ; in another minute I might have been in another planet." Shelley did not profess to know anything about the next world, but he knew what Shakespeare meant in writing of " this muddy vesture of decay." At Leghorn Trelawny led his friend to the docks and aboard a Greek cargo-boat, the *San Spiridione*, the crew of which in their immemorial fashion were squatted about the deck playing cards and munching food and looking very wild men. Digging at Shelley as the author of " Hellas," Trelawny asked him if the scene realised his idea of Hellenism. " No ! but it does of Hell " ; and Shelley probably

thought so still more when it came to having a pipe of tobacco
and some coffee with the skipper who—the low wretch—did not
support the revolution because it disturbed his trade. The next
lesson was better, though the mate of the American clipper to
which Trelawny hustled Shelley along insisted on offering a chew
of Virginia tobacco and a peach brandy, and a glass of grog came
up too. The mate, having defined the Greek vessel as " a bundle
of chips going to hell to be burnt," invited the Englishmen to
drink to the memory of Washington and the prosperity of the
United States. Shelley adorned this ceremony with a short
eulogy on Washington and a poem on his excellences.

Perhaps Trelawny was delighted to hear of Shelley getting a
little more real life on March 24th, 1822. Byron's party, diminished through Medwin's departure from Pisa, were returning from
their evening ride outside the town ; Byron, Shelley, Count
Gamba, Taaffe and Captain Hay, the ladies following in a
carriage. Sergeant-major Masi, a dragoon, who had been having
a few drinks, decided to annoy them by galloping through their
midst ; and on Taaffe's suggestion Byron and Shelley pursued the
man and Shelley caught up with him first. The sergeant-major
ignored their cards and magnificently declared, in the style of
his rank, that he arrested the whole lot of them ; a fight began
and the attacker struck at Shelley, " who took off his cap, and
warding the blow from the sharp part of the sabre, the hilt struck
his head and knocked him from his horse." A second slash as
he was on the ground was parried as best it could be by Captain
Hay with his cane. Masi then made off but outside the Lanfranchi
Palace had the poor luck to encounter one of Byron's servants
who speared him with a pitchfork. After some discussions with
the police, affidavits and plenty of exaggerated accounts the affair
was generally forgotten, and the sergeant-major indignantly
recovered. Shelley's final annoyance through the affray was
caused by Claire Clairmont's letter on it : he replied, "Don't be
so ready to blame. I imagine that there may be some more temper
and prudence in the world besides what that little person of yours
contains."

The incident near the Porta alle Piagge was of more interest
to the governor and the police of Pisa than Shelley knew. They
had been inspecting some of Byron's publications for evidence of
his seditious politics, and a spy named Torelli working for Austria
was equally observant. His description of Shelley's share in the
affray confuses him with Captain Hay : " In the confusion Masi
sliced the nose of an Englishman, said to be a captain, who
passes for a poet, and, among other eccentricities, prides himself,

as though it were an heroic action, on having had the epithet
atheist added to his name in his passport." Depositions were
taken, and a clerk named Lapini who had the duty of interrogating
Byron read a published account of him and took note that he had
murdered one of his mistresses and mounted half her skull as a
drinking cup. Lapini was correspondingly relieved when Byron
received him with every kindness ; but the whole town knew
that Byron had mounted two small pieces of field artillery for use
in emergencies at the door of his room. In all seventy witnesses
were examined. Torelli wickedly adds that while the affray was
being thus investigated, " Byron, contrary to his wont, caused
alms to be distributed to the poor at the door of his palace." The
servant Battista was banished from Tuscany, and the authorities
with all politeness postponed their intention of getting rid of one
or more of their mad Englishmen in the same way.

Occasion soon arrived for a greater sympathy between
Shelley and his friend Claire. She had been tragically right in
her fears that Allegra where she was placed might have small
chance in the event of an epidemic. It came, and typhus carried
the child off on April 19th, 1822. The news reached Shelley on
the 23rd just after Claire, who had been staying in Pisa, went
off with Mr. and Mrs. Williams for more househunting on the
shore of Spezia. Once again Shelley was compelled to take charge
of a painful situation. He resolved that Claire, who was speedily
to return to Pisa, must not be there in the vicinity of Byron for a
moment more than was unavoidable ; and when on the 25th she
returned, and there was news of an empty house at Lerici, he
told her nothing about Allegra but sent her off again with Mary
and Percy. The furniture was packed and sent by boat ; and
not only did Shelley get all this done, but he persuaded Mr. and
Mrs. Williams too to set off without losing a moment, all going
to Casa Magni, Lerici. Even then he did not at once disclose to
Claire what had happened to Allegra but when she showed an
invincible purpose of returning to Florence he broke the news.
In whatever else concerned her Shelley undertook the discussions
with Byron, who had been informed of Allegra's illness, apparent
improvement, and death ; and he was successful, in spite of an
embittered letter sent to Byron by Claire without his knowing
how she had written, in obtaining for her a portrait and a lock
of hair as mementoes of her child.

Though this removal to Lerici has the look of an escape from
a trying situation it was indeed only the summer migration which
would have been made in any circumstances. Shelley had not
tired of Pisa, however Byron's waywardness and obstinacy ex-

hausted him. The death of Allegra had brought him anxieties
and difficulties from which he needed rest, and he confessed to
Byron that at last he was too weak to ask Claire whether she
had any more wishes concerning Allegra's funeral. The signs of
Shelley's being inclined to take some rest, contrary to his usual
ways, had been increasing.

It is to this necessity that the growth of his dependence on
Edward and even more on Jane Williams is to be attributed.
They were " serene people, and alone." In January, renouncing
his first impressions, he had described Jane as " more amiable
and beautiful than ever, and a sort of embodied peace in the
midst of our circle of tempests." Delighting in her music, he
wrote to Horace Smith in Paris and asked him to buy without
delay a " good pedal harp," which he intended as a present for
her ; and when his friend Smith disappointed him, Shelley gave
her a guitar which has survived as the most famous of musical
instruments connected with our literature. The guitar was
accompanied with the graceful and yet ingenious lines in which
he compares himself and his friends to Ariel, Miranda and
Ferdinand, " The Tempest " being much in the thoughts of all
these wanderers at Pisa. Within the poem, the classical reader
may enjoy the art with which Shelley unites a melodious remembrance of Catullus's lyric on a sailing-boat to his other themes,
and all may admire the poetic use of the circumstance that the
guitar was made of Italian pinewood.

Not only could Jane allay Shelley's tormenting thoughts with
her singing and playing ; she had, or he believed she had, a gift
of hypnotism which made him write " The Magnetic Lady to her
Patient." In that poem it is easy to observe the fresh tempest
which smouldered on the horizon of the peace created by Jane ;
for it is without disguise an autobiographical poem. The substance of the mesmeric lady's utterances quoted in it is that she
does not love the patient, she can never be his, but is happy
that she has a healing power to bestow upon him. The patient
in his reply admits that his sufferings are not ended altogether,
but

" What would cure, that would kill me, Jane ;
    And as I must on earth abide
    Awhile, yet tempt me not to break
        My chain."

One day early in February, a day uncommonly gentle and
reviving, Shelley, Mary and Jane went for a long walk in the
pine forest of the Cascine near Pisa, and his poems commemorat-

ing that day are as clear and charming as when the details were
new in his feelings. " The Invitation " is spontaneous and eager,
" The Recollection " is naturally softer in tone and touched with
the sense " no more " ; but it is a melody of peace—and the
word is recurrent in the poem. No lyric in our language contains
such serenity, pure calm and radiant leisure. It seems overheard
from another world, almost like that one of reflection in the pools

> In which the lovely forests grew
>> As in the upper air,
> More perfect both in shape and hue
>> Than any spreading there.
> There lay the glade and neighbouring lawn,
>> And through the dark green wood
> The white sun twinkling like the dawn
>> Out of a speckled cloud.

So long as Shelley was able to write these " minor poems " he
needed not to be perturbed that his large designs were proving
stubborn. But since the note of discontent intruded into " The
Recollection " even, and Mary was beginning to be discussed as
the origin of it, Shelley was at some pains that she should not
read his verses. The paper containing " The Recollection " was
inscribed outside, " To Jane : not to be opened unless you are
alone, or with Williams."

What especially disheartened Shelley in his relations with
Mary is of course hidden, and why she smiled so seldom, but he
mentioned briefly the antagonism between her love of society and
his love of solitude. She even went to church at Pisa, only to hear
Dr. Nott preach some sermons against atheists. On being
questioned about his aim, the preacher denied that he had had
any local Englishman in his eye. It was not in Shelley's nature
to quarrel with Mary over going to church no matter what the
sermon was, but it was a symptom of her finding a life of her own ;
and in later years, reconsidering the comparative coldness that
had affected her marriage, she did not avoid a charge against
herself ; wishing much to express her devotion to Shelley she had
yet become unable to disperse a habit of hardness. The affection
in her heart had been unable to find a voice. And he had fallen
into something of lovelessness towards her, not necessarily so deep
as in his stanzas,

> When the lamp is shattered
>> The light in the dust lies dead,—
> When the cloud is scattered
>> The rainbow's glory is shed ;

yet discernible in his growing isolation. As she reviewed the position she did not remember, and it is too easily forgotten, that both of them were of the race of artists ; both were pursuing inner designs which demanded much of them ; that like Shelley she herself was married as much to the intellectual life as to a person.

If Shelley was in love with Jane, Mary did not perceive it ; she too had become attached to her in her own emotional way, she also took walks with Jane, and while they hunted for the first violets she looked upon her friend as

A violet by a mossy stone
Half hidden from the eye.

Mary foretold that when Leigh Hunt arrived Jane and he would sing duets enchantingly. At moments Mary even rose to the height of admiring Jane's housekeeping. This open-mindedness was to be more severely tested at Lerici ; but to Mary the move had a compensation, since Trelawny, who had gone to Genoa on a matter of boat-building, would be coming to Lerici for long visits in the summer.

Byron and Shelley had both commissioned a friend of Trelawny, Captain Daniel Roberts, to build them boats, but of different dimensions—" an open boat for Shelley, and a large decked one for Byron." Williams, rather to the amusement of the Pirate with his limitless seafaring experience, had brought out from England the section of a boat as a model, and Shelley had united with him in complete adoration for " this toy." On these lines and no others should Shelley's boat be built ; and when Roberts and the Italian builder in the government yard at Genoa were of another opinion they were given no encouragement. Trelawny in spite of his critical objections gave judgment that Shelley's boat was fast and strongly built. She was named by Byron the *Don Juan*—" we must suppose the name," Shelley observed, " to have been given her during the equivocation of sex which her godfather suffered in the harem."

And it was a name which so long as it recalled the poem then in progress could not but please Shelley, who had written of " Don Juan " to Byron the previous October, " It is a poem totally of its own species, and my wonder and delight at the grace of the composition no less than the free and grand vigour of the conception of it perpetually increase. . . . Nothing has ever been written like it in English, nor, if I may venture to prophesy, will there be, without carrying upon it the mark of a secondary and borrowed light." Trelawny's fear that Shelley was afraid of real

life hardly agrees with Shelley's canonisation of a poem so crowded
with that material—but Trelawny was ready to assert that Byron
had seen scarcely more than Shelley of man as he is. In fact,
nobody but Trelawny had ever " seen life." (He had served
some years in the Navy, leaving it " at the early age of 19, incapable of further exertions, in consequence of a wound he
received.")

XXIV

THE BOAT

IT WAS on May-day, 1822, that the Shelleys and Williamses took possession of the Casa Magni at the fishing village of San Terenzo. This house as Trelawny describes it was more like a boathouse or bathing-house than a place to live in ; its ground floor was used, when it was used, for storing tackle and produce ; upstairs it had a saloon and four small rooms ; and, Trelawny notes, " there was one chimney for cooking." But the veranda faced the sea and was indeed at the sea's edge. Behind the house was a wood, and an array of mountains. No road led to San Terenzo, only paths ; and for provisions it was necessary to market at Sarzana beyond the River Magra. If Sarzana failed you could try Lerici. The scene has been modified since, the Casa Magni no longer starts up in sullen eminence among the buildings, and San Terenzo has its autobus service.

One of the first things which Shelley and Williams did was a very sensible one ; indeed, they had made sure of it when they were this way before. They struck up a friendship with Signor Maglian, the harbour-master of Lerici, a married man on whose sympathy and experience they would often have to depend. The immediate benefit was that instead of paying £300 to the Customs on their furniture or else sending it back to Pisa as it was packed they were permitted to have it delivered at the house, and the house became temporarily an official depot for it. Among the monuments at Lerici there ought to be one to the said harbour-master. Even with furniture the fortress-like house did not please Mary, who speaks of the whole situation much as if Shelley had carried out his old plan of flitting into the uttermost parts of the earth. Her feelings were depressed by the fact that she was expecting another child. But the sea itself, now almost as much an occupant of the house as the two families, entered into her soul. Great was its beauty in sunshine and calm, but she arrived when gales and squalls embroiled the bay, and the roaring of wind and wave all night long made Williams think of the firing of heavy artillery. The village people appeared fiercely elemental, and at all hours Mary heard their wild songs and shouts along the beach.

To her husband and Williams nothing was really troublesome, apart from the heavy task of letting Claire know of her bereave-

ment ; and that became simpler because she came into the room
while they were considering how to tell her best. She guessed
what the secret was. After this the principal question was when
the *Don Juan* would arrive. Another boat helped to fill the interval
and to suggest dreams of voyages ; but a dream of another nature
occurred to Shelley on May 5th. Williams and he were watching
the moonlight on the surf below them, and Shelley was complaining of his nerves, when more than once Shelley thought he
saw a naked child, Allegra, rise from the sea and clap her hands
in joy, smiling at him. Williams understood this as the result of
a conversation in which both had been more melancholy than
usual ; but Mary might have something else to say of it. She
had not seen this phantom, but from the moment of coming to
Lerici " an intense presentiment of coming evil brooded over her
mind." In the apparition of Allegra we may discern Shelley's
self-questioning ; if he had not allowed Byron to take her away
from the home in which he had almost paternal authority over
the child, could she have come to such an untimely end ?

On the evening of May 12th Signor Maglian was with the two
Englishmen as they walked on the terrace when a strange sail
was descried coming round the point. It belonged to the *Don
Juan*, brought by Mr. Heslop and two English sailors from Genoa,
and they spoke well of her. Without delay Shelley and Williams
gave her a trial, and Williams wrote in his diary, " We have now
a perfect plaything for the summer." Shelley sent his congratulations almost at once to Roberts : " She is a most beautiful boat
and so far surpasses both mine and Williams's expectations that
it was with some difficulty that we could persuade ourselves that
you had not sent us the *Bolivar* by mistake. I do not know how
I can express, much less repay, my obligation to you for having
sacrificed so much of your time and attention as must have been
requisite to produce anything so complete." To Trelawny he
wrote, " Williams declares her to be perfect, and I participate
in his enthusiasm as much as would be decent in a landsman.
We have been out now several days, although we have sought in
vain for an opportunity of trying her against the feluccas or other
large craft in the bay ; she passes the small ones as a comet might
pass the dullest planet of the heavens."

For this boat, the arrival of which was unwelcome to Mary and
to Jane though they held their peace, one of the young sailors was
retained, and a smaller landing-craft was built by Shelley and
Williams. The materials were canvas and reeds, the boat was
$8\frac{1}{2}$ feet long and $4\frac{1}{2}$ feet broad. The first passenger in this tiny
vessel was Jane who, after a frightening trip in the *Don Juan*,

on June 12th, was put ashore by means of it. This boat was called the *Sandalino*, and there is something of mystery over the final name of the larger one. By Byron's orders *Don Juan* had been painted on the mainsail. The Shelleys had thought of *Ariel* as the name, but accepted the other ; yet it could not remain so coarsely inscribed. It was treating the beauty as a coal barge. After resisting all available chemicals the inscription was defeated by being cut out, but the boat remained the *Don Juan*.

Within a few days the boat had made an illusion of the classical mythology for her navigators, who sailed out to an island the existence of which they had not hitherto known, and which they named the Siren's Rock ; for they heard, " at the time we were beating to windward to weather it, a sort of murmuring, which, as if by magic, seemed to proceed from all parts of our boat, now on the sea, now here, now there." It was due to a certain small cord in the rigging, but it had a charm. " As we approached it ceased ; and again, as we stood off, it recommenced its song." It was with some difficulty that they succeeded in tacking at the last moment and escaping shipwreck on the Siren's Rock.

Many gallant voyages followed the arrival of their little boat, and Shelley regained his best health. Inwardly he was not well. The proximity of Jane was a blessing and an ordeal. He could be critical of her, and take sides with Mary when there was a small war over saucepans : " It is a pity that any one so pretty should be so selfish." But these disturbances passed, and in general Shelley saw Jane as one more goddess : she is the inspiration of his report on life at Lerici sent to Gisborne on June 18th. " I like Jane more and more, and I find Williams the most amiable of companions. She has a taste for music, and an elegance of form and motions that compensate in some degree for the lack of literary refinement. You know my gross ideas of music, and will forgive me when I say that I listen the whole evening on our terrace to the simple melodies with excessive delight. I have a boat here. It cost me £80, and reduced me to some difficulty in point of money. However, it is swift and beautiful, and appears quite a vessel. Williams is captain, and we drive along this delightful bay in the evening wind under the summer moon until earth appears another world. Jane brings her guitar, and if the past and future could be obliterated, the present would content me so well that I could say with Faust to the passing moment, ' Remain thou, thou art so beautiful.' "

Three poems besides those previously mentioned are the principal windows into Shelley's heart under the spell of Jane.

One of them expresses his pure contentment while he listened to
her music :

> Though the sound overpowers,
> Sing again, with your dear voice revealing
> A tone
> Of some world far from ours,
> Where music and moonlight and feeling
> Are one.

Another is the record of his musings on the terrace one evening
when Jane had gone indoors ; what, in cool reason, was this
Elysium ? The sight of the fisherman on the rocks with his lamp
to lure the fishes and his spear to destroy them was a figure of
his life ; but those unthinking victims rising to the flame were
happier than he. The other poem, for it cannot be attributed
to any other relationship at this date, arises from a moment in
which Shelley had revealed his enslavement by Jane, and would
have kissed her. Though she had forbidden him, she was too
well aware of his nature and his tribulations to be merely shocked
or indignant ; she was perplexed, for there was nothing that she
could do for his peace beyond what was daily done in the course
of friendship. Infinitely contented with Edward and her babies,
she had nothing to wish for. But she could not simply end or
cancel the situation, and Shelley wrote probably next day,

> We meet not as then we parted,
> We feel more than all may see ;
> My bosom is heavy-hearted,
> And thine full of doubt for me :—
> A moment has bound the free.

To suppose that the whole of Shelley's life at Lerici was set
to this music would be to forget his increasing command of
himself, his natural cheerfulness, his valuation of friendship and
the active life which serious affairs as well as recreations required ;
it would be to overlook the conspicuous aphorism in the letter of
June 18th to Gisborne, " I think one is always in love with
something or other ; the error, and I confess it is not easy for
spirits cased in flesh and blood to avoid it, consists in seeking in a
mortal image the likeness of what is perhaps eternal."

The hopes of Mary, that Percy might have a brother or sister
to grow up with, were ruined by her sudden illness of June 9th.
It was nearly the end of her, but Shelley made use of brandy,
vinegar, ice and resolution and the professional doctor arrived to
find her improving. Yet it was Shelley who unintentionally

delayed Mary's convalescence. The anxiety over her worst hours and a day of over-fatigue committed him to a night of terrible visions, in which he alarmed every one. In her account of this Mary includes other strange happenings, more like ghost visits than the dreams which made him scream that night. He had lately seen the phantasm of himself on the terrace, and it said, " How long do you mean to be content ? " More difficult to explain was an apparition of him seen by Jane, passing her window on the Terrace and repassing, without a coat ; Trelawny was talking to her at the time, but he saw nothing, nor had Shelley himself been anywhere near. Jane was greatly shaken, and might well be, seeing that she was not of a psychic type.

Almost as queer things were apt to happen to Shelley in " real life " in 1822. A sultry calm one evening forced him and Williams to row their boat in to the beach at Massa, which alarmed the guard, and since this worthy could not read he proposed to keep them waiting till his superior returned from another village. Shelley replied that he would do so at his peril, whereon two old muskets were produced ; so Shelley and Williams prepared their pistols. This incident closed without their having to use them, but serves as a reminder that life in Italy could now and then become quite idiotically unsafe. The law was still busy with the affair of the dragoon at Pisa, and as usual Shelley was principally concerned with the fear that the man who might have hurt or destroyed him might have to suffer.

On June 13th Trelawny and Roberts brought the impeccably handsome *Bolivar* into Lerici bay, and found the proprietors of the *Don Juan* so pleased with their boat that he had to be censorious. Their ambition was laughable : they had a feeling that the Mediterranean was too confined a lake for their master-piece, and wished they could be on the Atlantic " with plenty of sea-room." Naturally when Trelawny went for a sail with them he observed serious deficiencies, but it seems far from likely that by this time Shelley could not steer even if he had a volume of Plato with him. Williams indeed was a better navigator, but " over-anxious and wanted practice." When Trelawny was delivering his homilies the pair of them were regrettably indiffer-ent, and Shelley tried to head him off with a pun. After the Pirate's technical exposition of their errors and the consequence in a squall (" we should have had to swim for it ") Shelley said, with an eye on the pigs of iron serving as the *Don Juan's* ballast, two tons of it, " Not I : I should have gone down with the rest of the pigs in the bottom of the boat."

S.   K

Trelawny stayed long enough to pick up one or two anecdotes about Shelley which as he grew old became elaborate. One was supplied by Jane who had been out in the dinghy with Shelley when he made one of his not unusual remarks about solving the great mystery. As she had brought her two children with her, it is improbable in the extreme that he meant it seriously, but Jane commented that it was dinner-time, and they returned. Trelawny adds that Jane craftily secured this by making Shelley promise to write " the words for the Indian Serenade," but those had been written nearly three years before.

It was Shelley's customary protestation in these summer days that he was writing very little. Some reasons for it other than psychological ones appear in the letters of 1822. He had lost faith in Ollier as a publisher, and had even decided to have nothing more to do with him on whatever terms or for whatever apology ; certainly Ollier was a most unbusiness-like member of the Trade, and might seem to Shelley only to become active when he could ruin the text of his productions in the cause of conventional safety. But who else was there among London publishers who would be associated with the name of the Atheist, or take more trouble than Ollier over unsaleable books ? As yet John Hunt, a fearless and honoured Reformist, was only interested in publishing periodicals. In the end—by April, 1822—Shelley was obliged to give in : " I suppose I cannot escape from this thief Ollier ! " and had he known it Ollier's first venture in publishing was coming to a close. But, if this annoying problem was not a strong dissuasion from his writing new works, the repeated signs that he was an unpopular author had had some effect even on Shelley's mounting spirit. On June 18th he was in the mood to admit it. " It is impossible to compose except under the strong excitement of an assurance of finding sympathy in what you write. Imagine Demosthenes reciting a Philippic to the waves of the Atlantic. Lord Byron is in this respect fortunate. He touched a chord to which a million hearts responded."

We receive from him then under the date 1822 a total of poetry which is not so considerable, and from his own point of view the lyrics on his personal life would hardly count. They would be classed as *deliciae*, though the majority of lovers of poetry fasten on them rather than on great projects of the intellectual imagination. Of these one more was in Shelley's mind through the first half of the year, and it kept him busy even aboard the *Don Juan*. He did not complete it, but the extensive fragment in existence is of such pith and point that it challenges all his earlier

completed works on a big scale. This is " The Triumph of Life."
Little is known of the first indications of this great poem. At Pisa
he could see Orcagna's painting " The Triumph of Death "
and in the poets of Italy he could find Triumphs of Love and
other ruling passions. The observer will know that he owed
something of it to the Vision of Dante, and a little to Chaucer
from whose works he had occasionally read aloud on Pisa evenings.
Within the form and the detail, the debt was only to life itself,
which he had now had more time to study, and which in Trelawny's company he had been induced to watch in its most
unlovely and seemingly undirected confusion. In years gone by
his topic would have been the political systems or the religious
and moral superstitions which he then regarded as the sources
of human frustration ; now he was searching beyond those into
a further plane of problems—the nature of our coming hither
and going hence.

Here we have in a long poem the new kind of poetry which
in short form he had exhibited on hearing that Napoleon was
dead. When Williams first met Shelley he wrote to Trelawny,
" His ordinary conversation is akin to poetry, for he sees things
in the most singular and pleasing lights : if he wrote as he talked,
he would be popular enough." This was wisely said, and Shelley
was becoming capable of writing as he talked, with the necessary
selection and variation. He was reducing the idealisms, though
they had had the colours of the rainbow, which for some years
appeared to him as the substance of a poem with a theory, and
meeting the reader more nearly half-way and submitting to him
the objects of which he would discourse rather than their shadows.
In this development he did not, could not abolish the visionary
and the marvellous thoughts and their mysteries which were his
above all the poets of his age. His new poem contains abstractions
of glorious effluence, but they are even more alluring than their
predecessors because they are not profuse but set in contact with
presentations of the actual.

And of this later class, within " The Triumph of Life," a
study of Napoleon is one—Napoleon regarded as an item in the
tremendous throng following the splendid and appalling chariot
of which we guess the name. More striking still is the figure of
Rousseau, who had once appeared to Shelley as the master mind.
The whole passage introducing him is impressive :

> Struck to the heart by this sad pageantry,
> Half to myself I said—" And what is this ?
> Whose shape is that within the car ? And why ?—

I would have added——' is all here amiss ? '
But a voice answered, ' Life ! ' I turned, and knew
(O heaven, have mercy on such wretchedness !)

That what I thought was an old root which grew
To strange distortion out of the hill side
Was indeed one of those deluded crew,

And that the grass, which methought hung so wide
And white, was but his thin discoloured hair,
And that the holes he vainly sought to hide,

Were or had been eyes :—' If thou canst, forbear
To join the dance, which I had well forborne ! '
Said the grim Feature (of my thought aware.)

' I will unfold that which to this deep scorn
Led me and my companions, and relate
The progress of the pageant since the morn ;

If thirst of knowledge shall not then abate,
Follow it thou even to the night, but I
Am weary.' Then like one who with the weight

Of his own words is staggered, wearily
He paused ; and ere he could resume, I cried
' First, who art thou ? ' ' Before thy memory

I feared, loved, hated, suffered, did and died,
And if the spark with which Heaven lit my spirit
Had been with purer nutriment supplied,

Corruption would not now thus much inherit
Of what was once Rousseau, nor this disguise
Stain that which ought to have disdained to wear it ;

If I have been extinguished, yet there rise
A thousand beacons from the spark I bore.' "

It may be that Shelley's long familiarity with Goethe's "Faust"
and the May-day Night revelry equipped him to describe the
dance of men and women about the chariot, but nothing can
lessen the command with which he creates that allegoric picture
and its significance of our lives in one aspect. Poets in England
have not often spoken of this aspect, leaving it to satirists ; but
who in a metropolis, in the way of the world, has not seen what
Shelley here symbolises ? He and the painters of France have
the honesty which gives art its terrible inescapability ; or may we
again use the name of Goya to show what Shelley in 1822 had in
his reach ?

To savage music, wilder as it grows,

They, tortured by their agonising pleasure,
Convulsed, and on the rapid whirlwinds spun
Of that fierce Spirit, whose unholy leisure

Was soothed by mischief since the world begun,
Throw back their heads and loose their streaming hair ;
And in their dance round her who dims the sun

Maidens and youths fling their wild arms in air
As their feet twinkle ; they recede, and now
Bending within each other's atmosphere,

Kindle invisibly—and as they glow,
Like moths by light attracted and repelled,
Oft to their bright destruction come and go,

Till like two clouds into one vale impelled,
That shake the mountains when their lightnings mingle
And die in rain—the fiery band which held

Their natures, snaps—while the shock still may tingle ;
One falls and then another in the path
Senseless—nor is the desolation single ;

Yet ere I can say *where*, the chariot hath
Passed over them, nor other trace I find
But as of foam after the ocean's wrath

Is spent upon the desert shore ;—behind,
Old men and women foully disarrayed
Shake their gray hairs in the insulting wind,

And follow in the dance, with limbs decayed,
Seeking to reach the light which leaves them still
Farther behind and deeper in the shade.

These passages are in such dark colouring that we must ask whether in this, the last of his long poems, Shelley was offering a modern version of " The Vanity of Human Wishes " ; William Hazlitt assumed immediately that the title was just one more of Shelley's paradoxes ; was Hazlitt right ? and was the Triumph to be interpreted in an ironical sense ? Had the culmination of " Prometheus " been overshadowed by such a criticism of our world ? Most of the fragment is in the form of a summing-up by Rousseau, and it closes with a dreadful sadness concerning the effects of the ghastly dance. At that point the poet speaks again : " ' Then, what is Life ? ' I cried." There the fragment as it is usually printed ends, but a few more lines have been found, in which Rousseau begins to speak of some mortals who were or will be happy. This is only a slight clue to the unwritten or lost part of the Triumph, but it may not be wrong to see in it the hinge of the poem, swinging away from all that mortality, rushing on in its passions and ambitions and with a creed of materialism, must undergo, towards a hope and a mastery. In an artistic sense Shelley was unlikely to leave his poem as a monotony ; he had taken such pains to impress upon his readers the utter misery and waste of humanity that we suspect him of having a reasoned surprise in store and a reserve of inspiration for an antiphony, to lift the view of life out of all the turbulence and false and fatal flame into a majesty of spirit. For this ascension, it may be, he had been recently reading the scientists of whom Trelawny had heard him speak book in hand, but his solution of the as yet baffling riddle would have included other parts besides that of the inheritors of his hero Francis Bacon. At any rate no missing manuscript which we can think of in the annals of our poetry would be better worth finding than that which Shelley was about to write at the end of June, 1822.

XXV

THE DEEP

ON THE afternoon of June 13th Leigh Hunt was happy, after more than four years, to be almost in touch with Shelley at last. " The queen-like city of Genoa, crowned with white palaces, sat at the end of the Gulf, as if to receive us in state ; and at two o'clock, the waters being as blue as the sky, and all hearts rejoicing, we entered our Italian harbour, and heard Italian words." He quickly wrote a letter to Shelley, addressing it to Pisa,—and this slight delay was to have serious consequences. Replying on June 19th Shelley said that he would have come to Genoa had he heard sooner. Even then on June 24th he and Williams got the *Don Juan* ready for the voyage and Williams was about to weigh anchor when Mary had a relapse and there could be no going away till she had recovered. Shelley told Hunt to look out for the white house with arches near Lerici, as his ship went on to Leghorn, or to arrange with the captain to approach and fire a gun or send up a rocket—" we would instantly come alongside." Hunt's passage from Genoa to Leghorn began on June 28th.

No doubt exists of the joy which Shelley felt at the coming of his old friend. " A thousand welcomes, my best friend, to this divine country ; high mountains and seas no longer divide those whose affections are united. We have much to think of and talk of when we meet at Leghorn ; but the final result of our plans will be peace to you, and to me a greater degree of consolation than has been permitted since we met." So he wrote, and so he was determined things should succeed, but he was not sure that the periodical for which Byron had formerly proposed Hunt's collaboration would be fruitful. Writing to Horace Smith on June 29th he referred to his need of making " some arrangements " for Hunt with Byron, but saw in the future the breakdown of the alliance—" for I, who could never have been regarded as more than the link of the two thunderbolts, cannot now consent to be even that." As for himself, he only wanted to go on living at Lerici, and to have the summer indefinitely prolonged, but he confessed that Mary had not the same predilection for the place.

Hunt was taking his first look at the harbour of Leghorn when he saw a seafarer with a " knight-errant aspect, dark, handsome, and mustachio'd," standing on the deck of a speckless yacht

called the *Bolivar*. It was Trelawny, who was looking out for
Shelley's friend, and having been told by Byron that Hunt was
" a gentleman in dress and address " found him that and more.
The conversation was spirited, and Hunt characteristically
pleased with the intended literary syndicate, the " land of beauty
and song," and above all the expectation of seeing Shelley again.
Next day (apparently) Hunt found his way to Lord Byron, who
had moved out of Pisa with his mistress and Count Gamba to a
country house at Monte Nero ; the hot weather was the ostensible
reason but Gamba had been given the official hint to remove
himself from Pisa. In blazing heat Hunt tramped through the
dusty suburbs to " the hottest-looking house I ever saw," and he
was exceedingly unfortunate in the moment of his arrival on
other accounts. A brawl had just occurred between Byron's
servants and those of Gamba over a suspicion that Gamba was
conspiring with Byron in some manner to defraud them, and
Gamba himself had been slightly wounded. The assailant was
dismissed, and made his way to Shelley who in sheer disgust
gave him some money since nobody else would possibly do anything for him ; but this was not the end of the matter. The
police took notice of it, and Gamba was ordered to quit Tuscany
in three days—an order which Byron must look upon as implying
or in honour requiring his own departure ; and although the
time limit was extended, Hunt could well understand that it was
an emergency most unfavourable for consultations on the all-
promising journal. The spy Torelli was aware of some sort of
projected journal : his report was that Byron " is expecting
another English poet, a certain Smith, and they intend to start
a newspaper against the Italian Government, which is to be
printed in England, and bring them in much money. This will
be something far worse than Lady Morgan's book :—a weekly
satire directed chiefly against Austria, whom they call the usurper
of Italian freedom. This should be seen to."

After the affair of the stabbing and a drive in Byron's barouche
(" we met the police-officer ") Leigh Hunt returned to Leghorn,
brought his family and luggage ashore, and put up at a hotel.
At four in the morning of July 1st Williams was altering the
topsails of the *Don Juan* in the bay outside Casa Magni, and
Shelley was preparing to leave with him for Leghorn, picking up
Roberts at Lerici. He did not find it easy to get away. Mary was
still ill, and twice or thrice called him back, threatening to go
with Percy to Pisa if he did not quickly return. The *Don Juan*
behaved perfectly, and brought them to Leghorn, almost fifty
miles, in seven hours and a half—but it was then half-past nine

in the evening, and the quarantine men had gone home. The voyagers anchored close to the *Bolivar*, borrowed Byron's cushions and slept on their boat.

Next day Shelley and Hunt met at last. The moment (which Hunt's eldest son watched with a serious wonder) was picturesque. " What a moment it was ! I had often wondered to see men embrace, and disliked the custom ; but I found, on this occasion, how quickly great emotions dash aside preconceived judgments. My friend's manners had as little of the foreigner in them as mine ; and yet the moment he entered the room, the mutual impulse was so strong upon us, that we rushed as heartily together as a Pylades and Orestes ; and both, in separating, were in tears." The recollection is Leigh Hunt's, worked into a novel in which he drew a character from Shelley. On looking more steadily upon the man whom he had not seen for four years, he observed that these years and their cares had made their physical alterations. " Why the devil should they be able to spoil a face like his, and for no good to anybody ? He did not look older at first sight. I had always noted that there was something of an invincible juvenility about his face, except in the eyes ; and the air and the southern sun had embrowned him. But on observing narrowly, the youthful smoothness of his face was gone ; the temples seemed beaten in ; the forehead had wrinkles in it ; and his glossy brown locks were now dullened and mixed with grey. He also stooped as he sat. His person, however, seemed as noble as ever, when he stood up, or walked about. His step was as firm ; and his eyes were finer than I ever saw them."

With all reasonable speed Shelley installed Hunt and his family at Pisa in the ground floor of the Lanfranchi Palace, and explained to him how Byron had prevented him by a generous action from making the present of the furniture himself. He also touched on the uncertainty which he was sorry to feel concerning Byron's general frame of mind ; but Hunt was to have a direct chance to share the feeling almost at once. Byron had come in to Pisa on his own difficult affairs, and was upstairs probably thinking of anything but those of the Hunts. He may well be forgiven for wishing that the suggested journal had never been spoken of, but Shelley thought that his reception of Mrs. Hunt when she was ushered into his presence was " most shameful. She came into his house sick and exhausted, and he scarcely deigned to notice her ; was silent, and scarcely bowed. This conduct cut Hunt to the soul." Byron no doubt had not fully realised until he actually saw Mrs. Hunt what the journal would mean in personal responsibilities. Almost immediately after this

ominous meeting, so excellently had Shelley organised the day
that Vacca himself arrived to see Mrs. Hunt. He decided that
her case was hopeless ; that she was in a decline ; and on the
supposition that he might yet be mistaken gave Hunt particular
advice on her treatment—but he did not keep back his real
opinion. Marianne was to live until 1857 but Hunt, not being
gifted with the eye of providence, was thrown into misery.

The agitation of Byron on other subjects was what would be
expected. " His first idea," Shelley wrote to Mary on July 4th,
" was to sail to America, which has been changed for Switzerland,
then to Genoa, and last to Lucca." Trelawny, who had hoped to
have the fun and possibly the profit of " transporting the *Bolivar*
overland to the lake of Geneva," had suffered under the series
of plans, and was now kicking his heels ; but Hunt's case was
worse. He was relying entirely on the scheme of the journal and
had no money left. " Lord Byron," Shelley wrote, " must of
course furnish the requisite funds at present, as I cannot ; but
he seems inclined to depart without the necessary explanations
and arrangements due to such a situation as Hunt's." In a short
note to Jane Shelley said that he was returning to Leghorn that
night and would urge Williams to sail home alone with the first
fair wind : " I have thus the pleasure of contributing to your
happiness when deprived of every other, and of leaving you no
other subject of regret but the absence of one scarcely worth
regretting." And on the same day Williams made a celebrated
final note in his Journal : " Fine. Processions of priests and
religiosi have for several days been active in their prayers for
rain : but the gods are either angry or nature is too powerful."

Shelley was bent on persuading Byron to make clear and firm
agreements on behalf of Hunt, and told Mary that he would
hardly be at home as soon as Williams, but the point was to be
decided on July 5th ; meanwhile Byron offered the copyright
of his satire on Southey, " The Vision of Judgment," for the first
number of the journal, and if this held good all was well. Yet
Shelley was unable to leave for Lerici on the 5th, and on the 6th
Williams was writing to Jane from Leghorn concerning the delay.
" I have been kept day after day, waiting for Shelley's definite
arrangements with Lord B. relative to poor Hunt, whom in my
opinion he has treated vilely. A letter from Mary, of the most
gloomy kind, reached S. yesterday, and this mood of hers aggravated my uneasiness to see you ; for I am proud, dear girl,
beyond words to express, in the conviction that *wherever* we may
be together you could be cheerful and contented. . . . What can
I do ? Poor S. desires that I should return to you, but I know

secretly wishes me not to leave him in the lurch. He too, by his manner, is as anxious almost to see you as I could be, but the interests of poor H. keep him here ; in fact, with Lord B. it appears they cannot do anything,—who actually said as much as that he did not wish his name to be attached to the work, and of course to theirs."

It cannot be wondered at that Shelley appeared to Hunt to have less hope than formerly or that he was willing to speak clearly about Byron's character. He told Hunt to be as punctilious as he was himself in giving Byron his title : it was best for everybody. Once Hunt had printed a dedication and a poem to " my dear Byron," but it had been a tactical error. Shelley mentioned that Byron had asked him once if he did not feel a greater respect for the rich man of the present company than for any other ; and while he stuck to his adoring opinion of Byron's natural powers asserted that he never made you laugh to your own content. But they had other subjects, and on Sunday, July 7th, they took a rest and enjoyed some of these ; and the afternoon was passed in exploring Pisa. Hunt had overlooked the Leaning Tower in his first excitement. Some dry jokes of Hogg's imported by Hunt made Shelley laugh to his content perhaps not, for leaning against the wall in the passage outside the inn Shelley laughed till it hurt. Among other friends he spoke with great regard of Horace Smith. While they listened to the organ in the cathedral Shelley said, " What a divine religion might be found out, if charity were really made the principle of it, instead of faith." Sitting with the Hunts at home, he resumed the habit that they knew so well of reading and translating a passage from Plato aloud. Out in the dark he watched the fireflies in enchantment. " The last fragment he wrote, which was a welcome to me on my arrival from England, began with a simile taken from their dusk look and the fire underneath it, in which he found a likeness to his friend." And all this time Mrs. Hunt was enchanted too by Shelley's anticipation of every wish—" princely " manners—but she was struck by his saying that if he were to die to-morrow he would have lived longer than his grandfather ; he was really ninety years old. It was what he had said in a Note to " Queen Mab " but now it meant more to him.

Out of that first week of July, 1822, Leigh Hunt retained an impression of Shelley's great gift for finding contact with " ordinary people " ; and this was shown when their business led them to the docks. With captains and with common sailors he was equally at home, most unassuming, most responsive and intelligent. Going down to the cabin on Hunt's ship, Shelley reverted to his great subjects. Spreading out a sheet of paper, he " made a dot on it with his pen, and said, ' *That* is the experience of mankind.' ' The white then,' said I, ' is our inexperience —is time past or future, or what we don't know ? ' ' No,' returned he, ' if all the paper in the world were put together, the white would not be enough for the inexperience, and yet the dot would be the true representation of the other. *All space* is the white ; and the dot is all history.' " To this Hunt joins a word or two about that explorative thinker from Lord Byron : " He thinks gigantically. . . . If thought were light, and our planet visible by it, and space were time, the next ages would see us coming by a little ray, made up of such minds."

With what pleasure Mary Shelley would have been a listener there at Pisa ! Instead she was in extreme dejection at San Terenzo, and writing to Shelley that she feared something disastrous was overhanging them,—not a disaster to him but to their child. She stood alone on the terrace, watching the sunset and knowing that the scene was the most beautiful in the world but tormented by the thought that William had died and that Percy might not be fated to live longer than he. By Sunday night, July 7th, had she known it, Shelley was able to expect his early return to her. In the course of the day he had concluded that his mission to Byron had done all that he had intended, and calling on Mrs. Mason, who " saw him in better health and spirits than she had ever known him," he was glad to tell her that he had made the Hunts tolerably comfortable Under the circumstances Hunt could not make him any great return, but there was one thing : Shelley could not find his copy of Keats's last volume containing " Hyperion." Hunt had brought the book from home and insisted on Shelley's taking it and not returning it till he could do so with his own hands. The last word on the journal at that time to be called *Hesperides*, but later on published as *The Liberal*,—a title copied from a journal which had been appearing at Brussels,—was that Shelley should be an equal partner with Byron and Hunt and have a share in the profits ; but he had " a reserved intention " for the disposal of that share. Evening advanced and Shelley had to drive back to Leghorn, and before he said good-night Hunt made him promise, if the weather next day was violent, not to venture to sea.

Next morning, July 8th, there was plenty for Shelley and Williams to do. Byron had lent Shelley £50 and that meant a call at the bank for cash. Many supplies had to be bought for Mary and Jane, and a cask of wine for friendly Maglian at Lerici was not forgotten. Trelawny lent his assistance in these practical matters, and went to the harbour with the friends, meaning to accompany the *Don Juan* some way in the *Bolivar*. It was noon. The thunderstorm of the early hours had perhaps cleared the air, and the wind blew the way they wished ; but that shrewd and hearty man Roberts, with his spyglass under his arm, was suspicious. He smelt foul weather, and advised them to wait a day. Shelley wavered, the sailor-boy Vivian waited for orders, but Williams would not be put off ; they would be in Lerici by seven. When Trelawny was ready to set out with them the guard boat hailed him and held him up because he had not attended to his health papers, so he got no further ; the *Don Juan* sailed alone at about 7 knots. Roberts ran to the end of the mole to watch her ; and about three he did not like the wind and got leave to go up the tower, whence through his glass he could see the *Don Juan* ten miles or so out, off Via Reggio. Her crew were taking in the topsails. They vanished in the haze of the coming storm.

Into that haze innumerable people have attempted to stare more searchingly than Captain Roberts could do, and such facts and fictions as could be probably gathered by him, by Trelawny and others during the next days and weeks have been scrutinised by generations of writers. Roberts found some fishermen who said they had seen the *Don Juan* founder, in an instant, at four in the afternoon, and on boarding the fishing boat he recognised some spars belonging to the vanished yacht. Completing the task begun by Trelawny of raising the *Don Juan* up, Roberts first gave the opinion, since everything was found in her that he could possibly expect, that " she was not capsized. I think she must have been swamped by a heavy sea ; we found in her two trunks, that of Williams, containing money and clothes, and Shelley's filled with books and clothes." A little later he reported : " We found in the boat two memorandum-books of Shelley's, quite perfect, and another damaged, a journal of Williams's quite perfect, written up to the 4th of July. I washed the printed books. . . . On a close examination of Shelley's boat, we find many of the timbers on the starboard quarter broken, which makes me think for certain, that she must have been run down by some of the feluccas in the squall."

Deliberately or by accident ? And if deliberately, out of some impulse to have a cut at these mad English or in the hope of gain ? Thornton Hunt, who was a highly intelligent boy of twelve when his friend Shelley was wrecked, has preserved a story which went the rounds in Leghorn. In spite of the threatening weather when the *Don Juan* left port, an Italian boat immediately followed

her. " When Shelley's yacht was raised, a large hole was found
stove in the stern. Shelley had on board a sum of money in
dollars ; and the supposition is, that the men in the other boat
had tried to board Shelley's piratically, but had desisted because
the collison caused the English boat to sink ; and they abandoned
it because the men saved would have become their accusers."
This Leghorn story comes up in another form through Trelawny's
daughter and others who heard in Italy long afterwards of an
aged boatman's dying confession to a priest : " he was one of
five who, seeing the English boat in great danger, ran her down,
thinking milord Inglese was on board, and they should find
gold." Trelawny believed the tale.

The bodies of Shelley, Williams and Charles Vivian, which the
sea gave up and for which Trelawny searched the Italian shore
with such energy, were so long in the water that they revealed
very little of those last moments. That of Williams was found
first near the Tower of Migliarino at the mouth of the Serchio.
Trelawny noticed that Williams had taken off one of his boots
and had probably stripped in order to swim for life. Charles
Vivian's corpse lay at Massa in cotton jacket and blue and white
striped trousers. Shelley, whose body floated ashore near Via
Reggio, was still dressed in his double-breasted jacket of mixed
cloth, nankeen trousers " from Malta, and a pair of boots with
white silk socks underneath," as though he had not bothered to
copy Williams's example. The event appeared, he acknowledged
it instantly. In one of his pockets the sanitary guard, and
Trelawny, found a small edition of Sophocles, in another the
volume of Keats's poems so lately borrowed from Hunt—
" doubled back, as if the reader, in the act of reading, had hastily
thrust it away." A newspaper correspondent scribbled that this
book was a Bible, to the great anger of Lord Byron ; he said
nevertheless, " It would not have been strange, for he was a
great admirer of Scripture as a composition." As the regulations
required, these bodies were buried where they were found, and
quicklime thrown into the graves.

On July 8th, then, Shelley and Williams had perished ; and
on that day Mary and Jane thought it was too stormy for them
to have set out on their voyage, notwithstanding the arrival of
Williams's letter on his determination to end delays. Byron
dropped in on Hunt and was pleasant ; he was that day writing
to John Murray requiring him to transfer the manuscript of
" The Vision of Judgment " to John Hunt, and informing him
(as though on a separate subject) that Leigh Hunt was setting
up a new journal to which he would contribute. Shelley's week

of persuasion and remonstrance had not been in vain. As for Hunt he wrote to Elizabeth Kent of the pleasures of the preceding day—" I was at the cathedral service with Shelley on Sunday, and saw finer faces than in Genoa, and S. says these are surpassed by those in Rome "—and of the prospects of the journal : Byron was giving great help, "Shelley has some excellent MSS. also." On the night of July 8th Mrs. Mason, who had treasured Shelley's parting look as the happiest she remembered, had a dream that he came to her looking very pale and in dejection. A conversation ensued : " You look ill, you are tired, sit down and eat." " No, I shall never eat more ; I have not a *soldo* left in the world." " Nonsense, this is no inn—you need not pay." " Perhaps it is the worse for that."

Anxiety at Casa Magni deepened until on July 12th a letter to Shelley from Leigh Hunt was opened : Hunt asked his friend for a word to say that the home journey had been safe. Mary and Jane could no longer bear to stay in the house, and drove to Pisa after the minor comfort of hearing at Lerici that no accident had been rumoured. Byron and Countess Guiccioli could tell them nothing, and Mary (it was midnight) refrained from disturbing Hunt. At Leghorn they traced Captain Roberts at the Globe Inn, and he was too honest to conceal all that he had seen and surmised ; yet he did not reject the talk of the port, that the *Don Juan* might have been blown over to Corsica, and had been sighted far out at sea. Trelawny accompanied the ladies to Lerici, and on the way the news came that a small boat, very like that made by Shelley and Williams of the lightest materials for landing from their yacht, had been discovered near Via Reggio. On the evening of July 19th after a journey to Leghorn and numerous investigations Trelawny returned to Casa Magni, to end what faintest hopes remained. He offered Mary no consolatory phrases, but " launched forth into as it were an overflowing and eloquent praise of my divine Shelley—until I almost was happy that I was thus unhappy to be fed by the praise of him." Next day she and Jane left the house by the sea which she had always distrusted, and removed to Pisa.

There was one thing more for Trelawny to do before the episode off Via Reggio could be called complete. The wish of the mourners was that the remains of Shelley might be finally buried at Rome near his child's grave, and those of Williams in England. The quarantine laws appeared to make it impossible that the wish should be granted, and even when " the ancient custom of burning and reducing the body to ashes " was suggested the Italian authorities were strongly opposed to " such an un-

precedented proceeding." At this point Mr. Dawkins, the British
Minister at Florence, who had been a model of wisdom and
discretion in the disputations over the affair of the dragoon,
was ready to do his best again, and in a short time he informed
Trelawny : " An order was sent yesterday from hence to the
Governor of Via Reggio, to deliver up the remains of Mr. Shelley
to you, or any person empowered to receive them." Trelawny
proceeded with the quarantine officers and Byron and Hunt to
the sands near the mouth of the Serchio, and erected a furnace,
in which in the tremendous sunshine, with offerings of frankincense
and salt, wine and oil the poor remains of Edward Williams were
burned. And, human nature being unalterable in these matters,
" there was a considerable gathering of spectators from the neighbourhood, and many ladies richly dressed were amongst them."
At last the ashes were gathered into a small oak box, which now
rests with the coffin of Jane Williams in Kensal Green Cemetery.
This cremation occurred on August 15th, 1822.

On the following day Shelley's funeral pyre was built, and
before a similar concourse headed by Trelawny, Byron, Hunt,
Captain Shenley, Italian soldiers and officers, the same ceremonies
were observed in the same surpassing brilliance of nature. This
time however a new offering was made to the dead, and the copy
of Keats's last book—the only one procurable in Italy—made
part of the flame that rose from the pyre. The Englishmen all
agreed " that lovers of books and antiquity, like Shelley and his
companion, Shelley in particular with his Greek enthusiasm,
would not have been sorry to foresee this part of their fate." All
were taken with the extraordinary beauty of the flame, looking
" as though it contained the glassy essence of vitality," on the
yellow sands between the soft-shining Mediterranean and the
marble mountains ; but when Trelawny's description of the
whole occasion, not lacking in painful and mortal touches, was
given to the world in 1858, it was used as an argument against
cremation. Shelley would have well understood what undefined
thoughts made Byron turn away from the company and swim
out to the *Bolivar*—three miles there and back—in the sea which
could be so cruel and so kind. When all was consumed except the
heart, which Trelawny found a chance to rescue and gave to
Byron, and Byron to Hunt, and Hunt to Mary, Shelley's ashes
were conveyed to the *Bolivar* and after some vicissitudes were
buried in the Protestant Cemetery at Rome. As Leigh Hunt
had not forgotten his Latin, he was able to compose an epitaph
accordant with his lost friend's prejudice in favour of the dead
languages, though only the two words " Cor Cordium " were

eventually to appear on the gravestone; beneath which Trelawny's quotation,

> Nothing of him that doth fade,
> But doth suffer a sea-change
> Into something rich and strange,

most fittingly expresses not only the last hours of Shelley but the happy moments of his life in the south, towards its close, when he and all about him seemed to be living in the enchanted island of "The Tempest."

XXVI

THE UNDYING

ALL THIS, we say, happened long ago ; but, even if we deny the illusion that Shelley evades time and space in some mysterious way, it is not so long ago as we might think. In 1890 a photograph was taken of eight old people of Via Reggio who had been present at or interested in the cremation of Shelley. One had had the job of taking his father's dinner along on the occasion. Another had been rebuked by the quarantine men for boyishly getting too close to the pyre. Another had helped to beach Shelley's schooner and had not forgotten that there were several hampers full of bottled beer among other things aboard, and that his skipper tried on one of the suits of clothes in the trunk ; nor had he any doubt on the precise amount of the salvage money.

The same sense of approaching Shelley's time is wakened when we think that persons now living have seen and heard Trelawny, as well as Jane at her house which still stands in Maida Vale ; others remember or lately remembered Mrs. Bannister who did not think much of Shelley as a dance partner, after giving him a trial at J. F. Newton's London house. And probably one or two have enjoyed the conversation of cheerful Miss Christy Baxter who could recall quite clearly the girlhood of Mary Shelley, and had dined with Godwin, Shelley and Harriet and Eliza on November 11th, 1812—how brilliant a complexion, what lovely hair, what a charming purple satin dress Harriet had !

In this respect Shelley may be almost regarded as having survived in personal contact into the twentieth century, and it is curious to consider what would have been his experience if he had allowed Dan Roberts to have his way on July 8th, 1822, and kept Williams from taking the *Don Juan* out of Leghorn harbour. Trelawny long ago commented, " Shelley came of a long-lived race, and, barring accidents, there was no reason why he should not have emulated his forefathers in attaining a ripe age." Even if he had not stayed the course alongside Trelawny, who died in 1881, comparison with his father and grandfather makes it probable that he would have come within a few years of that date ; and we cannot help thinking that he would have found much to enjoy. In his life as it was we perceive the characteristics of one aware that immense changes, inventions, and revelations were just round the corner ; not aware with a technical exactness of any one of these new conquests, but animated with the recognition that they were due, or to use the term which Shelley humorously turned against his own serious harangues, with " a pure anticipated cognition."

For the advancement of knowledge he had spoken and written with impressive and confident phrase, although he did not overlook the dangers which accompany it, and his forecast of the future of man, included in the final movement of " Prometheus Unbound," can be translated into terms of present-day civilisation :

All things confess his strength. Through the cold mass
Of marble and of colour his dreams pass ;
Bright threads whence mothers weave the robes their children
    wear ;
Language is a perpetual Orphic song,
Which rules with Daedal harmony a throng
Of thoughts and forms, which else senseless and shapeless were.

The lightning is his slave ; heaven's utmost deep
Gives up her stars, and like a flock of sheep
They pass before his eye, are numbered, and roll on !
The tempest is his steed, he strides the air ;
And the abyss shouts from her depth laid bare,
Heaven, hast thou secrets ? Man unveils me ; I have none.

Within a few years of the drowning of Shelley the Stockton and Darlington railway was opened (1825) ; the electric telegraph was set up from Paddington to West Drayton on the Great Western Railway (1838) ; photography, which just missed the chance of settling some questions about Shelley's appearance, was making a great start ; while in 1831 Faraday hit on something which Shelley would have rejoiced to hear and contemplate. " It is difficult," Sir William H. Bragg has written, " to sketch in a few words the great edifices that have been built up on the discovery of electromagnetic induction." The telephone, car, plane, gramophone, and the rest became known rather later than we can suppose with Trelawny that Shelley might have stayed, but in all these things, in the progress of medical methods and equipment, in astronomical instruments and organisation, in television and in meteorology as it begins to be we may see Shelley's spirit delightedly sharing. The present controversy over the release of nuclear energy and its effects on civilisation would have found him ready. In life it was one of his characteristics to call on his listeners to consider not only discoveries along tracks that were already well known but the fact that new sciences as yet unapproached and unnamed would open out.

Reverting to " Prometheus Unbound," we have seen Shelley offering in his poetical form a number of visions connected with natural philosophy ; and one of them, the harmonious sphere which is as many thousand spheres, whence in its onward speed even intelligible words issue, and in whose central calm the spirit of the earth lies dreaming a child's dreams, is as yet of doubtful interpretation. If my conjecture be probable, that this marvellous complex emblem is assigned to the whole system of physics and whatever is ordinarily felt in the inclusive word " science," then again I would instance Sir William H. Bragg as having supplied the best prose comment on the passage. In his lecture " Craftsmanship and Science," he surveys the various parts of a modern ship with the purpose of illustrating how " the whole structure is linked by innumerable ties to the research work of the laboratories," and at the conclusion he adds what Shelley's multitudinous orb in its many-coloured progress seems to mean : " it is an important fact that science advances over a wide front, and the various branches of it move on together : not absolutely keeping step with each other, but preserving a general line."

In our daily lives now we see what Shelley was conscious of when he wrote, this time in prose : " The great writers of our own age are, we have reason to suppose, the companions and forerunners of some unimagined change in our social condition or the opinions which cement it. The cloud of mind is discharging its collected lightning, and the equilibrium between institutions and opinions is now restoring, or is about to be restored." Had he lived ten years longer he would have reckoned the Reform Act which did away with the chief corruptions of the English parliamentary institution as a limited but valuable fulfilment of his words. Whether he would ever have done what in his early years he was expecting to do, and become a member of parliament now that a fairer system of representation had arrived, it is impossible to say. At least it is unlikely that one so devoted to human kind would have been content to remain a wanderer in Italy, however glorious the climate and the works of art, however delightful his inland or his Mediterranean voyages.

Moreover there was a part of his genius which the small circle in which he moved in the south was not big enough in the end to circumscribe or even to exercise sufficiently. Mary Shelley says of his conversation, " He was eloquent when philosophy or politics or taste were the subjects " ; Trelawny puts the same thing in a more emphatic way. " It was not until he spoke that you could discern anything uncommon in him—but the first sentence he uttered, when excited by his subject, riveted your attention. The light from his very soul streamed from his eyes, and every mental emotion of which the human mind is susceptible, was expressed in his pliant and ever-changing features. He left the conviction on the minds of his audience, that however great he was as a Poet, he was greater as an Orator." It is admissible that Trelawny possessed no great insight into poetry, but he was the last man to be deceived or delayed by windy words ; and what he has written of Shelley's glory as an intellectual speaker agrees thoroughly with what we find even in Shelley's poetical works, since Shelley was more and more inclined as he grew older to prefix to them magnificent discourses, ranging beyond the actual needs of his book. In one form or another, as he passed into middle-age, this kind of oratory, challenge and dissertation would have been presented to the widest audiences that he could get.

Underlying his speeches and his essays, as indeed it underlies his principal poems, there was the incessant scholarship of the man. Shelley did not disrelish light reading, and was perfectly willing to throw away his cares for an hour in enjoying Tom Moore's " Fudge Family " or Hunt's *Indicator*, but he passed a great many hours of day and night in the strenuous examination of the most erudite and exacting authors of ancient or recent times. The tremendous list of books read by him has its pathetic side. His years were brief, and yet he gave up a large part of them to the pursuit of truth and information through volumes which, to say the least of them, should have been shorter. It was the gentlemanly habit of his day, but in him, like so much else, heightened into a passion, and there again Trelawny has the word to say : " His intellectual faculties completely mastered his material nature," in his sense of responsibility as an author and reformer as in other things. We may smile a little at Shelley's desire to figure in his turn among the composers of immense and unpopular treatises, to be another Sir William Drummond or a co-extensive though contradictory Paley ; he was likely to excel them, we know, but who reads even Godwin now ? He mentions his hope of living long enough to produce " a systematical history of what appear to be the genuine elements of human society," and although his model was to be Plato, the result would have been considerably nearer the explicatory method and vocabulary of the close of the eighteenth century.

Shelley's character as a thinker has been drawn by Leigh Hunt in a reply to the disdain or fancifulness of Hazlitt. The charge that he was a lover of paradox as such, or contradiction for its own sake, is not a strong one : he usually opposed what he viewed as "some great and tyrannical abuse" and what was "forced down his throat in defiance of the inquiries" suggested by his teachers. Hunt speaks of Shelley's prejudices, which are human and simple enough, and bring him into our midst. "Prejudices that he thought innocent, no man was more inclined to respect, or even to fall in with. He was prejudiced in favour of the dead languages ; he had almost an English dislike of the French and their literature, a philosopher or two excepted ; it cost him much to reconcile himself to manners that were not refined ; and even with regard to the prejudices of superstition, or the more poetical sides of popular faith, where they did not interfere with the daily and waking comforts of mankind, he was for admitting them with more than a spirit of toleration. It would be hazardous to affirm that he did not believe in spirits and genii." The opinions which Shelley held were not evidence of his rejection of the wisdom of the ages, for they were found in Plato and Epicurus, Montaigne, Bacon, Sir Thomas More. He did not undervalue them anywhere ; if Thomson or Akenside expressed them, he was open to receive them thence. Shelley acknowledged himself that he had " a tendency to imitate whatever he thought beautiful, in ancient or modern writers." This was true of idea and of expression, but all that he borrowed was in a deep sense his own already. The main reason for his seeming to be revolutionary in opinions was that he " was definite in his object : he thought it was time for society to come to particulars : to know what they would have."

With society, at least with English society, Shelley was of course anathema, and if paradox is not always amiss he may be said to have been quite popular in the part. Society has a place in its heart for the Villain, and somethings in Shelley's life, talked about in the regular way of gossip and credulity, made him resemble the kind of vagabond who was dear to the moralists of his age. Readers of Maria Edgeworth may remember the pattern given in " Rosamund," 1821, by the name of Folliott Brown. This young man, of distinguished abilities and spirit, was wanting in self-control, in moral and religious principles, but his father expected him to give up his wildness when he became a member of parliament ; instead he grew worse, lived in Paris and formed " a most disgraceful connection." Folliott Brown however did not crown his infamies by writing " Queen Mab " and other baneful works. He might yet become a Quarterly Reviewer. It was Leigh Hunt's impression that Shelley's holding

" with Sir Thomas More that a community of property was desirable " drew upon him more ill-will than his other opinions " in the class among which he was born." This heresy would not have been risked by a Folliott Brown, and Shelley could laugh in pretended self-pity when he remarked that but for his writings he would have been comfortably unknown.

To many of us now Shelley is known, apart from his poems of graceful idealism reappearing in collections of verse, by the constantly reproduced portrait from the brush of Amelia Curran. It has risen in the world from a discarded attempt, which Shelley's friends could not praise, to the rank of a classic of portraiture : and that is partly due to the absence of other authentic painted portraits, partly to its being a picture of the poet whom many imagine, a type apart, a frail flower. Mr. Peter Quennell sums up this figure as a " pantomime Ariel," and certainly its charm is rather of that kind than of Shelley's own appearance. One may call it beautiful and still wish that it had not obtained such a unique position. For it has contributed to the legend, which is in some ways more regrettable than the savage misstatements made against Shelley in his own day, that he was a kind of mimosa, unable to belong to the struggling world of men.

Unquestionably Shelley sometimes caused those who shared his life to feel that he had a spirit's volatile speed, if not something more ; a quality in his presence was not easy to explain in other than supernatural terms. The apparitions which he and his companions saw may prove that he had a psychic nature, and even after his death we find Marianne Hunt writing while she expected her own early extinction, " I have been particularly visited by Mr. Shelley to-day, he always seems to look placidly and steadfastly on me with an air of waiting.—I shall soon come, my dear friend." If Miss Curran's picture includes the spirit-gaze of Shelley, it yet casts a feminine softness and timidity over his memory ; and against such an association, upon the whole, a single plain description can stand. It is by Thornton Hunt, artist and author. " The outline of the features and face possessed firmness and *hardness* entirely inconsistent with a feminine character. The outline was sharp and firm ; the markings distinct, and indicating an energetic *physique*. The outline of the bone was distinctly perceptible at the temples, on the bridge of the nose, at the back portion of the cheeks, and in the jaw ; and the artist could trace the principal muscles of the face. . . . [The countenance] changed with every feeling It usually looked earnest,—when joyful, was singularly bright and animated, like that of a gay young girl,—when saddened, had an aspect of sorrow peculiarly touching, and sometimes it fell into a listless weariness still more mournful ; but for the most part there was a look of active movement, promptitude, vigour, and decision, which bespoke a manly and even a commanding character. The general tendency that all who approached Shelley displayed to yield to his dictates is a practical testimony to these qualities : for his earnestness was apt to take a tone of command so generous, so free, so simple as to be utterly devoid of offence, and yet to constitute him a sort of tyrant to all who came within his reach."

When this witness has spoken the voice of Trelawny is still to be heard, as he explains that people about to meet Shelley with their expectations formed by the journals of the day were prepared to find a monster more hideous than Caliban, and then the revulsion of feeling on seeing him was so extreme " that he seemed as gentle a spirit as Ariel. There never has been nor can be any true likeness of him. Desdemona says, ' I saw Othello's visage in his mind,' and Shelley's ' visage ' as well as his mind are to be seen in his works."

These reveal the author fully, and in his variety. They are not always considered in that spirit. Lovers of the beautiful, seizing on him (and it is very natural) as their darling, have ignored or deprecated his endeavours in realism, in satire, in humour and in combinations of the lovely and the unromantic. The ease and simplicity of his lyrical art have hidden some of his meanings, and he has been honoured for the surface rather than the depth of his poetry in consequence. His profusion of imaginary work, and the faults of his occasional hurry and exhaustion, have impaired his great parables in verse, and overcast the designs with a prodigal richness. At least, where he fails, he does not often fail for want of artistic passion. His manuscript books, such as have escaped destruction, show from what a throng of first ideas he gathered and formed his verse and prose ; the energies of genius glow in his broad studies. Sometimes he tested more than one way of treating his subject, and instead of variations of word and phrase we have the traces of a larger and more cogent process of the mind. Even so he was willing to revise and re-revise the least detail of his longest compositions, and with very little interval even at the crises of his personal life Shelley studied the art of writing and above all writing poetry with an absolute faithfulness and impersonal surrender.

Shelley was born with capacities which would have suited him for several careers, and with an inheritance which might have led to his fulfilling that which was within his grandfather's view if not his reach. From time to time some thought of these possibilities would wake in him, and yet no circumstances arrived to turn it into fact. He has left a note on this in a letter to Hogg of October 22nd, 1821. " I have some thoughts, if I could get a respectable appointment, of going to India, or anywhere where I might be compelled to active exertion and at the same time enter into an entirely new sphere of action. But this I dare say is a mere dream. I shall probably have no opportunity of making it a reality but finish as I have begun." The scientist, the philosopher, the theologian, the explorer, the statesman, the ambassador—all these characters haunt about the shape of Shelley, and are discerned as elements or colours in his writings ; but few have ever regretted that his presiding activity began and ended in a life devoted to an art, and in special to poetry. To refer that, except for the obstinacy of his belief in the art, and the relentlessness with which he governed his life for it, to any traditions and endowments observable in the lives of his ancestors is impossible. So far as they are concerned in his general character, they have been too little known and recorded ; but his selection of poetry as the triumph of his life, and his style and matter in it, belong to himself alone. In his work he has not disdained to imitate other artists, and he declares such imitation, which is not plagiarism or servile repetition, to be inevitable in a poet ; his experiences, the soil whence his poetry comes to flower, are not artificially trained so that his thoughts and feelings in reading others are shut out. The great and the final achievement is that he creates whatever he strives for with a personal originality, and none of our poets could say with greater truthfulness of his work, " This is my book." No other has this light, this music, this winding way through time, space and matter, harmonized in his longer and more deliberately prophetic poems or in his least and hastiest fragments scribbled down while (to take examples of late date)

> Faint with love the Lady of the South
> Lay in the paradise of Lebanon
> Under a heaven of cedar boughs,

or while

> I stood upon a heaven-cleaving turret
> Which overlooked a wide Metropolis—
> And in the temple of my heart my Spirit

> Lay prostrate, and with parted lips did kiss
> The dust of Desolation's altar
> And with a voice too faint to falter
> It shook that trembling fane with its weak prayer.

Even in translations the Shelley individuality takes charge, as when he takes some verses of Dante for his own purpose ; and addresses his own poem upon its probable enemies,

> I prithee comfort thy sweet self again,
> My last delight : tell them that they are dull,
> And bid them own that thou art beautiful.

The two Shelleys speak in this,—the follower of the immortal Hour, traversing regions of mind and spirit where few have risen, and the familiar creature whose conversation was the highest happiness found by his companions throughout human society.

It was Shelley's endowment to inspire others, and to enable them to know themselves ; but after a period in youth when he believed himself to be one sent among men with a modern salvation for them he became uncertain of his own capabilities. The chance that he was born a destined leader of a new day did not disappear from his musing mind altogether, or he could not have prayed the spirit called the West Wind to

> Drive my dead thoughts over the universe
> Like withered leaves to quicken a new birth ;
> And, by the incantation of this verse,
> Scatter, as from an unextinguished hearth
> Ashes and sparks, my words among mankind !

But what he observed of the workings of his own brain tended to convince him that the visionary power was as inconstant as the summer lightning, and that nothing done in the past by himself as creative writer assured anything in the future. It was from this point of view that he discussed his work and purposes with others, and treated them as quite as authoritative in the matter as himself. When he was writing the play " Hellas " he asked the amateur Williams what he should entitle it, and promptly accepted what Williams suggested. That serene friend was proud to be asked the question and to find that his answer pleased, but the circumstance like many others made him wish for a less modest Shelley: " his greatest fault is ignorance of his own worth." The criticism, even so, leaves Shelley with his own encompassing and sustaining outlook on the nature of the artist.

Had this man of genius in later years ever said of his poems, " These are mine," avowing that they were necessarily the testament and definition of a personality, and that such merit as they had was an individual thing, he would have speedily added, in order to disavow all higher claims in the property, what he wrote of his beloved Greek pastoral poems : " [We] may recognise them as episodes to that great poem, which all poets, like the co-operating thoughts of one great mind, have built up since the beginning of the world."

THE END

INDEX